ADVENTURE MOTORCYCLING HANDBOOK

CHRIS SCOTT

WITH CONTRIBUTIONS BY

**KYRIL DAMBULEFF, TOM GRENON,
NICKI McCORMICK, ALLEN NAILLE**

and

**SIMON McCARTHY, STEVE COLEMAN, SARAH CROFTS
SIMON FENNING, GREGORY FRAZIER, JON FINLAYSON
TRUI HANOULLE, IRIS HEIREMANS, RUPERT HUMPHREY
GRANT JOHNSON, GEOFF KINGSMILL, NOAH MALTZ
MAC McDIARMID, KEN McLEAN, ALEX MARR
CLEMENT SALVADORI, MICHAEL SLAUGHTER
COLETTE SMITH, TREVOR SPROAT
PETER THEUWISSEN, GARRY WHITTLE
PAUL WITHERIDGE and RICHARD WOLTERS**

ILLUSTRATIONS

PETER FLYNN
and additional drawings by
ALAN BRADSHAW

TRAILBLAZER PUBLICATIONS

Adventure Motorcycling Handbook
Fourth edition 2001; reprinted with amendments 2002

Publisher
Trailblazer Publications
The Old Manse, Tower Rd, Hindhead, Surrey, GU26 6SU, UK
Fax (+44) 01428-607571
info@trailblazer-guides.com
www.trailblazer-guides.com

British Library Cataloguing in Publication Data
A catalogue record for this book is available from the British Library

ISBN 1-873756-37-2

Editor: Emma Stanford
Series Editor: Patricia Major
Design and cartography: Bryn Thomas
Typesetting and layout: Chris Scott
Proof-reading: Anna Jacomb-Hood
Index: Patrick D Hummingbird

Travel by motorcycle is unpredictable and can be dangerous.
Every effort has been made by the author, contributors and the publisher to ensure that the
information contained herein is as accurate as possible. They are, however, unable to accept
responsibility for any inconvenience, loss or injury sustained by anyone as a result of the
advice and information given in this guide.

Printed by
Star Standard (☎ +65-861 3866), Singapore

ADVENTURE MOTORCYCLING HANDBOOK

CHRIS SCOTT

WITH CONTRIBUTIONS BY

**KYRIL DAMBULEFF, TOM GRENON,
NICKI McCORMICK, ALLEN NAILLE**

and

**SIMON McCARTHY, STEVE COLEMAN, SARAH CROFTS
SIMON FENNING, GREGORY FRAZIER, JON FINLAYSON
TRUI HANOULLE, IRIS HEIREMANS, RUPERT HUMPHREY
GRANT JOHNSON, GEOFF KINGSMILL, NOAH MALTZ
MAC McDIARMID, KEN McLEAN, ALEX MARR
CLEMENT SALVADORI, MICHAEL SLAUGHTER
COLETTE SMITH, TREVOR SPROAT
PETER THEUWISSEN, GARRY WHITTLE
PAUL WITHERIDGE and RICHARD WOLTERS**

ILLUSTRATIONS

PETER FLYNN
and additional drawings by
ALAN BRADSHAW

TRAILBLAZER PUBLICATIONS

Author

CHRIS SCOTT'S first motorcycle adventure got him halfway to Wales aboard a moped. Since then he's visited the Sahara and West Africa several times on two wheels, describing these eventful trips in *Desert Travels*. He also travels regularly in north and western Australia and has visited southern Africa and the US, but most frequently returns with bikes or cars to the Sahara where he occasionally runs tours.

His other books include *Sahara Overland* (also by Trailblazer) and the *Rough Guide to Australia*. He maintains two websites: the *Adventure Motorcycling Website* and *Sahara Travel Information*.

Acknowledgements

Contributions from riders all around the world help make the *AMH* what it is, a collective impression of adventure riding in five continents. Thanks are due to the two dozen-plus contributors listed on the title page as well as the credited photographers who kindly supplied material for free or for negligible fees. Some of their biogs appear on p.272.

Special thanks to Alex Marr, Dr Tom Warr, Tom Grenon and Mac McDiarmid for digging up cover images and Kevin Bannister for the puncture sequence.

A request

Every effort has been made by the author and the publisher to ensure that the information contained in this book is as up to date and accurate as possible. Nevertheless things change, even in the Sahara. If you notice any changes or omissions that should be included in the next edition of this book, please write to Chris Scott at Trailblazer (address on p.2).

Updated information and a whole lot more at:
www.adventure-motorcycling.com

Cover photo: Namibia © Anita Alden

CONTENTS

PART 1: PRACTICALITIES

PART 2: CONTINENTAL ROUTE OUTLINES

PART 3: TALES FROM THE SADDLE

APPENDIX

RIDERS' TRIP REPORTS

Adventure motorcycling

What exactly is adventure motorcycling? As far as this book is concerned adventure motorcycling involves a challenging journey into the wilderness or a significantly strange country. For most of us living in cities in developed countries, a visit to a wilderness involves leaving the security of the paved highways of Europe, Australia and North America and heading onto the dirt, while a strange country adds all sorts of Third World challenges that are all patiently waiting for you out there in Central and South America, Africa or Asia.

Mainstream touring is a fun way of getting to nice places or enjoying the thrill of a sharp-handling bike. But the *Adventure Motorcycling Handbook* sees motorcycles not as toys, but tools with which to escape from the mundane and predictable and explore the wild or exotic regions of our planet.

In Latin America, Asia and Africa, or in mountains and deserts closer to home, reaching out into the back country requires planning and confidence in your abilities, be they riding half a ton of bike through mud, or dealing with a shipping agent in a foreign port. In some situations the unfamiliarity adds an edge to your travels that you won't necessarily appreciate at the time. You'll be pitted against your patience, stamina and resourcefulness, and in all cases you'll find you have greater reserves of these qualities than you'd expect.

Sure you'll be glad to cruise restfully along the blacktop and stay in hotels once in a while. But ask any of the many contributors to this book and in most cases they'll vividly recall the places where the riding was most demanding, where every day was hard-won and threw up an unexpected challenge, a breathtaking view or a bizarre human encounter.

This book broadly spells out the practicalities of paperwork and cost, the choice of location and machine, as well as preparing your bike for the Long Ride. It's followed by an outline of routes around the world and ends with a dozen tales of two-wheeled adventure from all corners of the globe to give you a taste of what to expect.

Adventure motorcycling is not for everyone; besides the obvious dangers of 'a risky undertaking with an unknown outcome' (as the dictionary defines 'adventure'), the sheer tedium and expense of preparing for a journey into a remote or culturally unfamiliar area will demand a huge commitment.

There'll be times when you curse the very notion of leaving home. But make no mistake, it will be a lifetime's achievement that will remain with you forever.

THE HISTORY OF *ADVENTURE MOTORCYCLING HANDBOOK* (*AMH*)

In the summer of '91 I was dishwashing in a Mexican restaurant, recovering from a broken leg and another costly Saharan fiasco. The job was not too intellectually taxing so I decided to try and become a 'writer', having written about my travels for bike magazines in the eighties.

I decided to write a short report on the things I'd learned the hard way in a decade of motorbiking in the Sahara. Many riders, myself included, had trouble-strewn first trips on account of a complete lack of hard information on all aspects of adventurous motorbiking.

I bought myself an Amstrad, worked out how to turn it on and, following a lot of wasted paper, dropped off a 30-page report entitled *Desert Biking: A Guide to Independent Motorcycling in the Sahara* at the Royal Geographical Society in London. For all I know the original is still tucked away in their archives today.

Rather pleased with the end result, I figured the report might have some faint commercial value and proposed this idea to the

former Travellers Bookshop in London's Charing Cross Road. It was good timing as they were considering publishing niche travel guides and an expanded version of *DB* fitted the bill. I spent a couple of busy months in their Holland Park office padding out the RGS report into the 100-page first edition of *DB* which was eventual-

ly published in late 1993. It didn't exactly hit the bookshops: batches were Xeroxed in a copy shop in Notting Hill as demand trickled in, then stapled and sent out.

Following the moderate success of this handmade version, a revised and suitably expanded paperback edition was published in September 1995. The updated format included the addition of 'travellers' tales' in the back.

Seeing promise in this format, Compass Star Publications picked up the idea and took it a big step further with the publication of the snappily retitled *The Adventure Motorbiking Handbook* (*AMH*) in November 1997. It featured the practicalities and yarns of *DB* and also attempted to cover the globe with the aid of several adventure-biking contributors. At the same time I created the AM Website which features what-

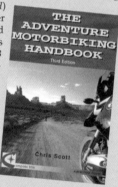

ever interests me at the time.

Which ten years down the line brings us to this fourth edition of the *AMH*, again refined and expanded, this time for Trailblazer. Enjoy the trip.

Planning and preparation

Prepare. That is the first word of the first chapter of this book. The motorbike adventure you are considering is going to be expensive, physically and mentally demanding, and maybe even dangerous.

Thorough preparation gives you confidence in a venture that is always going to be risky. By tying up every loose end you can think of before you go you can set off knowing that whatever happens your bike, documentation and knowledge of whatever lies ahead are as good as can be expected.

Certainly spontaneity is wonderful thing, but make no mistake, even if you're just heading off on a two-weeker to Morocco, up to Cape York, or down to the Baja, there'll be enough dramas to deal with to make your trip eventful without adding to them with inadequate preparation.

First steps

OK, so you've had your bathtime brainwave or your bar stool vision; you've seen the light and you're going for it. When? As a rule a first time, multi-national, trans-continental journey such as crossing Africa, the Americas or Asia needs at the very least **one year** of preparation. If you're heading right around the world (RTW) double that time; if you're just taking an exploratory nibble into the above three continents, **six months** will do. Preparing to explore a wilderness region of your own country may only require **a few weeks** which is a large part of the appeal.

You may not think so now but within a few pages you'll be getting an idea of the mushroom effect of Big Trip Planning. The more you learn the more there is to consider; for some people this burgeoning commitment will get too much and they give up or downsize the ambitious venture, usually because of financial or domestic commitments. Most of us are only too pleased to put our professional commitments in the freezer for a while but don't underestimate the cost of bike preparation, documentation, visas and shipping.

Time and money

Ask yourself realistically if you have the will and opportunity to put this money together in the time you've given yourself. To cross Africa budget on £4000/US$6000, plus the cost of your bike. Asia is much cheaper; you could probably ride to India and back for around £3000/$4500. To cross the length of the Americas costs as much as Africa and an RTW trip is going to cost you £10,000/$16,000, mostly in fuel and freighting your bike from one continent to the next. Many have achieved the above for less but these estimates account for at least some of the unplanned expenses which most trips encounter.

Your big trip is like a major civil engineering project; traditionally it will be **late and go over budget**. It's a rare first timer that leaves on their original departure date, so don't set this in stone and don't give yourself impossible goals. Although some biking trips add up to nothing more than doing something hard in a short space of time (often by younger, more virile riders) be aware that this puts you under extra stress in an already stressful situation.

Don't **over plan**, or if you're like me, expect to over plan. As I wrote in *Desert Biking*'s introduction 'Expect your itinerary – conceived on the living room floor with [a map] a couple of cans and all the chairs pushed back – to go to pieces once you're out there.' Once you find yourself riding out of an African port into the chaos of the city, or off the end of a highway into a remote area of dirt tracks, reality slaps you in the face like a ten pound trout. Sitting directly on the sharp end of your adventure, you want to be sure you have got everything right.

Travelling companions

Most people will instinctively know whether they want to ride off into the wilds alone, with their partner sitting snugly behind them, their mate in their mirror, or in a group. Nevertheless, below are some considerations to mull over when considering travelling alone or with others.

Alone

The perils and rewards of doing it alone are clear cut. On the debit side there's no one to help you in times of difficulty and no familiar face to share your experiences with. No one can help make decisions or guard the bikes while you nip into a store in a dodgy neighbourhood. All this will make your trip hard and inevitably introspective. This may be because you don't know anyone who's crazy enough to set off on a trip such as yours, or you're independent-minded and like the idea of doing it alone.

It sounds miserable until you consider the rewards of solitary travel. As a loner your social exposure is more acute and whether you like it or not, you're forced to commune with strangers who'll often make up the richest (as well as sometimes the most frustrating!) aspect of your trip; you have to look *out* at the world instead of being protected by the bubble of companionship. Anyway, unless you're going somewhere really outlandish, you're bound to meet up with others, quite probably on motorcycles too, and sometimes you'll be very glad to see them.

Tough overland stages like the Sahara, or intimidating countries like Iran or Sudan are where overlanders bind together, irrespective of their origins or mode of travel. You can choose to ride in the safety of a convoy for as long as you like and when you feel like going your own way, you can split with no strings attached. Overall, you'll get more of a raw experience alone. Be under no illusions that at times it will be utter misery and frustration, but loneliness lasts only as long as the next person, and even in the Sahara you'll meet plenty of fellow travellers on the main routes.

Two's company

The advantage of travelling with a friend is that psychologically and literally the huge load of your undertaking is halved. You also tend to be more brave; checking out a crowded market café or taking a chance on a remote short-cut become shared adventures instead of missed opportunities if you're alone.

There's no doubt about it, you can have a lot more fun if there are two of you and you get on.

One drawback to travelling in company is that you tend to remain rather exclusive to social interaction. There's no need to be outgoing because there's always someone to talk to, whine at or help you out. You can miss out on a lot that travel has to offer by reclining in the security of your **companionship,** because there's no need to meet others.

Another problem which won't surprise anybody is **getting on** with each other. Alone you can indulge your moods which will swing from one extreme to another as days go by. When in company, you have to put on a brave face when you might not feel like it; your partner thinks they're the problem, becomes resentful and the whole day becomes edgy as you wish the road would open up and swallow your chum.

Having a united goal doesn't seem to help, once the rot sets in your whole trip can be shrouded in tension and misery. If it gets bad, there is only one solution: **split up**. It may well be that they want to take the high road and you the low road, but whatever it is, it's far better to accommodate differing personal wishes, even if they mean temporarily terminating your fellowship. It's well known that these things happen on expeditions which is effectively what you're undertaking; try and anticipate how you might deal with these sorts of problems and don't feel that separation down the road turns the trip into a failure. Talk about the possibility of this eventuality during the planning stage and prepare yourself and your bike for independence.

Big groups

Big groups are much less common than solo or twinned overlanders, if for no other reason than forming a group of like-minded individuals is a tricky proposition. Numbers always fluctuate during the planning stage and even on the road the chances of a bunch of riders staying together for the whole trip are slim when what appeared to marginally enthusiastic members as a great adventure becomes a tiresome slog. As in any group, the dynamics evolve and harden as the trip moves on, although inevitably a leader will dominate from the start, alternately respected or despised by the others.

If you go in a group, expect never to want to talk to certain members of your merry gang by the time you return. With a large group there is usually a shared or even officially established goal which itself can cause pressures. It may help with sponsorship and the mutual support is enviable but, as you'll find on the road, most people are more comfortable alone or with one or two companions.

GETTING INFORMATION

However many of you are going, now your plan is underway there's work to be done. The countless things you need to know are all out there, but finding them is a lottery. Luckily, one of the best sources for your specific two-wheel undertaking is right in front of your nose, but *AMH* can't tell you everything and will always be getting out of date. You'll find updates to this book as they come in as well as plenty of inspiring links leading in all directions on **www.adventure-motorcycling.com**.

Embassies and tourist offices

An obvious place to start, but not very useful except in the most general terms concerning documentation, vehicle importation and possibly a free map or brochure. Some embassies and tourist boards have a habit of glossing over domestic upheaval or hard facts, and neither place will be likely to advise you about the condition of remote routes or what facilities you might find there. Sitting out cushy overseas postings, inevitably detached from what's really going on, consular officials are more interested in promoting mainstream tourism or international business and not hare-brained bike stunts.

Visa agencies

A better place to acquire the latest information about the ease and expense of visas applications for destinations worldwide are visa agencies. Usually located in your capital or nearest major city, they make their money by providing a speedy postal service while doing the queuing and applying for you. And though pricey, their couriers can make getting visas from consulates not represented in your country much easier, especially if you're busy working or live out in the sticks.

Indeed, because of the relationship they develop with their regular visits to certain consulates, a visa agency may have more luck getting your visa than you might have, stumbling about with your passport photos and heavily-tippexed form. If nothing else, a simple call asking 'how much, how long, what do I need for a visa for x, y and z' can give you a good idea about the application process and prices.

Government overseas departments

On par with the usefulness of an embassy is your country's foreign ministry. In the UK it's the **Foreign & Commonwealth Office Travel Advice Unit**; in the US it's the slightly superior **Department of Foreign Affairs** (both with usefully updated websites; see www.sahara-overland.com/links.html). Whatever they might claim, these civil service departments are primarily concerned with avoiding international incidents involving their nationals, if not urgently discouraging casual visits to countries with whom they are having some diplomatic tiff. Take everything they say with a liberal helping of salt and accept the inevitable taint of politics and convenience which colours their advice.

National motoring organisations

Again not a lot of help for the aspiring adventure biker but sometimes useful on documentation and essential when it comes to coughing up for a *Carnet de Passage* (see next chapter). In the UK this is all the RAC and AA do, although to be fair to both, adventure motorcycling is such a minority form of motoring, you can't expect them to take it seriously. Both are businesses making most of their money on providing roadside recovery and motor insurance.

Motorcycle owners' clubs

Again a bit too social to be reliably useful, owners' clubs (and especially their more active websites; see AMW links) can be a great source of information about available accessories, tips, and handy mods' for your chosen bike. You won't necessarily have to join the club, just writing a letter with a peculiar query is bound to get the enthusiasts sprouting forth with fertile solutions.

FOOLS RUSH IN...

Some trips were never meant to happen. Your months of preparation may have been marred by dispiriting bike problems, maybe you lost your job or didn't manage to save quite enough money to see the whole thing through properly? Perhaps you have begun to foster grave doubts about your travelling companion or you've had an unnerving crash or theft early in the trip. You might even have ridden for weeks to get to a key border crossing or route to find it implacably closed or dangerous? Because of the momentum that months of preparation and expectation have created, your pride is too great and you decide to just go through it, however bad or uncertain you feel.

Go back, give up, try another way or postpone your adventure. One thing this book can't prepare for you is your mind, so trust your instincts and resist the pressure to be seen as brave or a reluctant part of a team. The shame in returning to face your friends and family prematurely will be quickly replaced with relief.

You must be psychologically fit before you ride off to face the countless trials that adventure biking throws in your face daily. Without a confident attitude you'll be prone to further calamities and your trip will develop into a catalogue of miseries. My first trip started just like this: a half-baked XT500, banned from riding and so unable to earn, out of money at Marseille...

In a way it's amazing that I got as far as I did before the desert *djenouns* really turned on me, halfway across the Sahara. Turning back then was undoubtedly the right thing to do and a decision which probably prolonged my life. Returning after just five weeks but a lot older, it was not an enjoyable trip in any way, merely a depressing baptism of fire.

Your own trip is likely to be one of the major events of your life, give it your best chance and don't leave until you are as ready as you can ever expect to be. And if that inspiration or confidence never arrives then be wise and don't go.

Newspapers

Following news reports in the broadsheets is the best way of keeping up with the news in the region you're intending to visit. In the UK you still can't beat *The Times* for their detailed foreign coverage, but you've only got to live abroad to find out just how sketchy and polarised your home country's media can be, focusing on the more sensational conflicts in former colonies. Inevitably Australian media is strong on Asian affairs, North American is good on the south of that continent, and Europe good on Africa and west Asia.

Travel magazines and travel guides

Travel magazines are understandably geared towards producing glossy photo features alongside related advertising and if you regularly subscribe to such a magazine you'll know what to expect. From the adventure biker's point of view, travel magazines' best feature can be the latest visa or political information in the news pages, as well as readers' letters and all-important listings of clubs and other information. In the UK the best of a small bunch is the bi-monthly *Wanderlust*, while the US has the inspiring *Escape* monthly. The travel supplements of weekend papers tend to circulate the same stories over and over, although these can include 'trendy' motorcycling once in a while.

At least as good as the front pages and readers' letters of travel magazines are the free newsletters produced by travel guide publishers: **Lonely Planet**, **Rough Guides** and, to a lesser extent, **Footprint**. All contain travel information from readers and you can get on their mailing list for nothing. The established *Planet Talk* is currently the best, with latest hot spots and readers' tips as well as a customary advertorial from authors of forthcoming editions.

Useful motorcycle publications

When they cover travelling at all, rather than pegging the latest megabike, most mainstream bike magazines tend to feature sensational or badly written stories alongside scantily-researched 'how-to' text boxes, because outside Germany, adventure biking is of minority interest. The UK monthlies, *Bike* and *Motorcycle Sport & Leisure*, both regularly carry intrepid touring features and you'll find *Trail Bike Magazine* the best specialist publication for sourcing a used trail bike.

Indeed, overlanding-equipment-starved Brits might consider flicking through a couple of European biking magazines anyway. Try France's *Moto Verte*, mostly kids on high-powered mopeds doing somersaults, but with adverts for bikes shops should you be looking to buy a trail bike there (France has always been trail bike-mad with plenty of second-hand models and no import hassles into the UK); or Germany's leading bike monthly, *Motoradd*, a magazine that's bound to have some useful address and ideas for incipient two-wheeled overlanders. Another useful German publication is the bi-monthly *Tourenfahrer*, a great read (or flick through) to make you realise that your never-been-attempted-before expedition is regularly completed by flotillas of German bikers towing shopping trolleys.

If you live downunder, watch out for the bi-monthly *SideTrack* magazine, an inspiring publication focusing on the huge opportunities for adventure sport riding in Australia. In the US, *Rider*, *Cycle World* and *Motorcyclist* will all carry a travel feature once in a while.

The Internet

Far and away the most effective and wide ranging source of information is the Internet. Since 1997, the **Adventure Motorcycling Website** (www.adventure-motorcycling.com), which accompanies this book, has provided a forum and the all important **links** that stretch in all directions. Just one weekend of surfing out from the AMW will provide you with enough material not to leave home for months. There's nothing to be gained by writing any more about the Web, just double click and get surfing.

Oncoming travellers

Although too late to be of use in your pre-departure stage, don't underestimate the likelihood and usefulness of running into travellers coming from where you're going. You couldn't ask for fresher information unless you met the horse's mouth itself. They'll be able to fill you in on all your current anxieties about fuel prices, road conditions and the friendliness or otherwise of border officials, and likely as not, they'll be as keen to hear your news, too.

Documentation, money and information

Collecting the right documentation and sorting out your money arrangements before and during your trip is a tedious but vital part of your preparation. Many prospective adventure bikers worry about carrying half a year's cash on them, acquiring motor insurance, whether travel insurance is worthwhile or not, or if they can get by without a carnet. All these questions and more are discussed here. Without just one of the several documents listed below, your trip will eventually come to a standstill, and even with them there's no guarantee that some recalcitrant border official will not turn you away.

Travel documents

With all the documentation listed below it is essential to establish early on:
- what papers you already have
- what additional ones you must get before you leave
- what others you can get once underway

It's also important to know:
- how long it will take to get all this stuff
- and how much it will all cost

Do not leave things till the last minute (although with some visas starting from the date they're issued, this is easier said than done) and, as with any personal item, **keep all your papers with you at all times**. Some, like your passport or carnet, are extremely valuable and will be a headache to replace. With all these documents, **keeping photocopies** or at least a list of numbers, place of issue, expiry dates, etc, makes replacement much quicker. Obviously don't keep these details with the originals! – stash them somewhere secure where, failing a complete robbery or loss, you'll be able to retrieve them and start on the long road to replacement.

If you really want to be careful get four copies of your important details, keeping one on your person, one stashed on the bike, another with your travelling partner and another back home with someone who has access to a fax. Another good idea is to carry 'spares'; for example driving licences can be duplicated, either officially from your licencing authority or by simply 'losing' the original and claiming a new one.

Passport

If you don't yet own a passport, get on the case straight away; particularly during holiday periods, the issuing process slows right down. Don't waste days sitting in a queue watching the ticket counter click by; instead consider applying by post to a provincial issuing office. If you already own one, make sure it is valid for at least six months, if not a year **after** your anticipate journey's end as many countries won't issue visas for passports that have less than six months left to run. As ever, by ensuring that your passport has plenty of use left in it, you're one step ahead of some awkward official.

If you're heading around the world and expect to visit dozens of countries consider getting the 'diplomatic' versions with extra pages. Many countries have elaborate, full page visa stamps and anyone who's travelled before will know how police road blocks (in some African countries posted on either side of every town) or immigration officials love to slap their little stamp in the middle of a blank page. Still others will quibble about sharing a perfectly usable page with that aforementioned stamp.

Once you get your passport check all the details; discrepancies between it and your other vital documents, even just the misspelling of one word, can be all the excuse someone needs to bring your day grinding to a halt.

Although they don't exactly shout it from the rooftops, in Britain at least, it's possible to get a **second passport**. In applying the Passport Office will want to know what you are up to, and the easiest way to explain your need is that certain visa applications en route will take weeks when your passport will be unavailable or, most commonly in the case of Israel versus the Arab world, the fact that one country won't issue you a visa if there is evidence of a visit to another. If your reasons are sound then a second passport will be issued without a fuss.

Many foreign hotels insist you surrender your passport on arrival as security. Resist this unreasonable request and instead offer to pay up in advance, or hand over a spare expired passport. Never give your passport away to anyone other than a uniformed official, and even then be wary in suspicious situations. They know as well as you do that without this vital document you are trapped.

Visas

Visas are a temporary permit allowing you to visit another country and are a pain in the neck, being little more than an entry tax. Not all countries require them in advance – the stamp you get on entering a neighbouring country may be regarded as an 'instant visa' – but it's those that do which make up the bulk of your bureaucratic headaches. Brits will have few visa hassles riding though South America but across Africa might end up paying £400/$600 in visa charges. For all visitors, the arbitrary visa regulations in this continent provide part of the challenge of crossing it.

Applying for visas On a trans-continental trek applying for several visas will be a tricky game of timing and anticipated arrival dates; something that will hamper the spontaneity and mould the plans of an overland trip. Even if you're 'just' crossing Africa, don't expect to get all your visas nicely sorted out before you go. Instead, work out where you'll pass a consulate for your next country (besides that country's embassy in your own country, travel guides are a good source of addresses). This simple fact will have a crucial bearing on your overland itinerary and govern the duration of your stay in certain countries. You may find yourself racing across a country or taking a thousand-mile detour just to be sure you can cross into your next destination.

Allow plenty of time to obtain your visas and make it easy on yourself by using visas agencies in your home country. As mentioned earlier, some start from the moment of issue or insist on a date when you expect to arrive in the country concerned – something hard to pinpoint when there's 4000 miles of desert, jungle and swamp between you and that place. All you can do is give yourself plenty of time for problems; expect those problems to crop up and trust your ability to deal with them. Remember that countless others have succeeded in traversing the same route; they've all worked it out – by using your wits and being flexible, so can you. Avoid buying business visas where possible, they're more expensive and risk awkward questions on arrival. Stick to simple, innocuous tourist visas.

Before applying for any visa find out the answers to these questions:
- At what point does the visa start: from issue, a specific date, or arrival before a given date?
- What other documentation (besides your passport) must you present on application? Besides a handful of passport photos, this might also include bank statements or other evidence of funds, letters of introduction or onward travel tickets.
- How must you pay? Some countries are very specific.
- How long do you have before you need to use the visa (typically from one month to a year)?
- How long can you stay in that country?
- Is the visa renewable and for how long?
- Is it 'multiple-entry', enabling you to return to that country on the same visa?

In most countries visas are extendable, so that even though you may only be issued with a two-weeker for Iran, for example, renewing it is easily done at any police station. It must be remembered that having a visa will not guarantee you entry into that country; if they don't like you for whatever reason, or the rules have changed, you'll be turned back. And being turned back to a country which has just officially waved you goodbye can be tricky.

Then again on some borders where a visa is considered essential, just turning up may get you one issued on the border. Although what appears above seems like a rigid set of rules created to discourage international travel, these rules get a bit mushy once on the road: expired visas need not mean a firing squad at dawn. Take visas seriously but recognise that once on the road, the further you are off the beaten track anything goes. If you happen to stumble into a country via an unmanned back route, present yourself at the nearest police station unless you're leaving soon in the same manner. But a word of warning: most of the countries with which this book is concerned are paranoid about their security and have tense relationships with their neighbours. Accusations of 'spy' may be absurd to you, but will be taken very seriously, especially if you turn up in a country without the proper documentation.

Travel and medical insurance

Another possibly costly but recommended piece of documentation is travel insurance; something that everyone from your bank, post office or travel agent is keen to sell you should you dare to put just one foot on a deadly foreign shore. Ordinary travel insurance will probably not cover you for the hazardous activity that is motorcycling. Instead insurance companies who specialise in expeditionary cover will take on the job, and at not much greater cost. A recent quote from such a UK specialist, for a four month trans-African trip riding a £2000/$3200 bike came to £300/$450 or just under £2.50/$4 a day.

Whoever you end up insuring yourself with, make sure they're crystal clear about the nature of your intended trip. As well as covering you for all the mundane stuff like getting robbed, cancelling a ticket, losing your baggage, travel insurance also includes medical cover. For this, the worst-case scenario would be getting yourself evacuated by air from some remote spot and requiring intensive medical care.

On p.109 Trui Hanoulle describes a traumatic but fairly straightforward recovery from Pakistan. Anything involving repatriation to the US, even from neighbouring Mexico may run up to six figures. For this reason it's vital that your medical expenses easily cover the above figures: £500,000/$800,000 may sound like an astronomical sum but is just a starting point, £1m/$1.6m is better. Make sure that this figure covers everything to do with an accident, including medivac, ambulances, hospitalisation and surgery.

This is one good reason to go straight to a specialist; your credit card may give you 'package holiday' cover for nothing, but it's unlikely to cover a fraction of the cost of an evacuation from the middle of a Siberian swamp. If you're a European in somewhere like Africa, most medical emergencies involve repatriation, which is where the greater expense can lie. In Central or South America, the US might end up as your ultimate destination if you need urgent medical treatment, and no one needs reminding about the expense of medical care in that country.

Remember too, that to get a rescue underway you must first make that **all important phone call** to the country where the policy was issued. When you receive your policy, find this telephone number and write it clearly somewhere like the back of your passport or in your helmet; this way you can direct someone to ring the number if you can't do so yourself.

Vehicle documents

Just as you need a passport, visa and medical insurance, so does your motorcycle. Of these the carnet presents the biggest problems in financial terms, while getting third party insurance that's worth much more than the paper it's written on is simply an insoluble problem.

Driving licence and International Driving Permit

Like your passport, your driving licence must show correct (or, at least, consistent) information with other documentation and be valid long after your trip expires. If your licence does not show the bearer's photograph, then it should be supplemented with an International Driving Permit (IDP). These multi-lingual translations of your driving licence can be picked up over the counter by presenting your licence and a small fee plus a photo or two at your local motoring organisation's office.

Once on the road you may never have to show your IDP, but be on the safe side and get one anyway; with their official-looking stamps they can double-up as another document to present to a semi-literate official. Note that there are two IDPs which cover the whole world. If you're going for the Big Trip you'll probably need both.

Vehicle ownership papers

Other essential ID documents are your vehicle ownership papers. In the UK it's called a logbook or, officially, a vehicle registration document (VRD); in the States it's a pink slip. Most every border will want to see these papers and compare details with your passport, your carnet, your Blockbuster card and anything else they can think of. Perhaps more than your passport, it's crucial that the details on the ownership document, particularly the **chassis and engine numbers**, match those on your bike and carnet, if used.

The reason for these elaborate checks is to ensure you've not committed a cardinal sin against humanity by selling your vehicle, or part of it, in the country concerned. Even slightly damaged engine or chassis numerals (easily done) may be grounds for raising complications. Evasion of tax on imported vehicles is what the fuss is all about; in developing countries these can be many times the value of your machine. If your bike has had a replacement engine or other substantial mods, check those numbers or risk losing all to some nit-picking official down the track. Check these numbers now while you still have a chance to easily correct them.

Carnet

Just about every first timer's overland trip comes to a near standstill when they learn about the need for a *Carnet de Passage en Douane* and the need to indemnify the value of your bike, if not a whole lot more. It is this huge, if temporary drain on your funds that makes carnets such a pain, and can make you decide to do a trip on an old XT500 instead of that lovely 1150GS you promised yourself. If you're just riding around South America, they have their own system, the less expensive and less rigorously enforced *Libreta de Paso por Aduana*, known in some places as a *triptico*. There's more on *libretas* on p.168.

Written in French and English, a carnet is an internationally-recognised **temporary importation document** that allows you to bring your bike into a certain country without having to deposit huge duties with the customs. Issued by national motoring organisations recognised by the FIM, it lasts one year and, if necessary, can be renewed or extended from the motoring organisation in the country where it's about to expire. (Make sure this extension is noted on every page and not just the front cover).

The name of all motoring organisations licenced to extend your carnet are shown inside the front cover of all carnets. As you can imagine, making this country a Western, or at least an English-speaking one, is bound to be less hassle than contacting the Automobile Association of Tadzikistan. If you lose a carnet, you must apply to the original issuing authority. Sure, you can travel without a carnet as long as you don't mind depositing the value, plus duty, that they slap on your bike when you enter a country: this duty can be from two to four times the value of your bike.

Once you provide your local motoring organisation with details of your bike and every country you expect to visit, they estimate the value of your bike and the highest level of duty payable of all the countries you plan to visit. For a £3000/$4500 BMW heading overland from the UK to India, this bond might total £9000/$13,500, i.e. the bike's value plus the 200% duty which Iran charges. A recent figure for a well-worn five-year-old XT600 heading down Africa's east side was just £1750/$2600.

Ways of underwriting a carnet Coming up with this money is usually a problem for most overlanders and can be done in three ways:
- Pay an insurance premium to underwrite the cost of your carnet.
- Get your bank to cover the amount with your personal collateral (eg. stacks of money, property or shares).
- Leave the required bond deposited with a bank in a locked account.

Most people either borrow the money for the first option or pay up an insurance premium for the second. Your motoring organisation will put you in touch with approved insurance underwriters and what they charge depends on where you're going and the size of the bond required. Typically in the UK, they charge 3% of a bond under £10,000, so for the BMW example above, that works out at £270, plus a 'service charge' of around £60, plus refundable deposits of another £250. As you'll be gathering by now, it's all adding up to hundreds paid out or thousands locked in the bank, and that's just for a £3000 bike heading for India.

How a carnet is used Carnets come in a number of pages from five to twenty-five, each page is used for a country where this document is mandatory. A page is divided into three perforated sections, or vouchers: an **entry voucher** (*volet d'entrée*), an **exit voucher** (*volet de sortie*), and a **counterfoil** (*souche*).

When you enter a country that requires a carnet, the Customs will stamp your counterfoil and exit voucher and tear off and keep the entry voucher. When you leave that country, the counterfoil will be stamped again and then the exit voucher will be retained. When your travels are complete you return the carnet to the issuing organisation for discharging. What they'll want to see is a bunch of double-stamped counterfoils and possibly a few unused but intact pages.

Should you sell your bike on the side your carnet will not be discharged and you'll eventually be liable for the duty in that country – remember, they have your money. Should you sell your bike officially you'll need all the permanent export and customs documents to prove that you've done so legally and paid all duties. In South Africa, where bikes are often sold at the end of a trip, the rates are around 7.5% duty plus another 14% VAT for a 600cc bike. By comparison if you're hoping to sell your bike in the UK, you're looking at 10% duty plus 17.5% VAT.

Getting involved in **fake carnets** is not really necessary (or that great a saving for a pricey perfect copy) unless you plan selling your vehicle on the side; not something that most adventure motorcyclists get involved in.

Third party motor insurance

If you're boldly going where no one you know has gone before don't expect to be able to get third party motor insurance from your friendly local broker. Quite understandably, and despite the loss of some juicy revenue, your insurer won't touch an overlanding biker with the longest barge pole they could get their hands round. A UK company will cover you for Europe as far east as Turkey as well as Morocco and Tunisia, but even these latter two are becoming difficult. If someone does offer to insure you beyond this area, as in some cases I've heard, it's because they've not understood what they're getting themselves into or are just taking your money. It may be quite likely that you're not covered, even if you think you are.

What you do instead is buy it as you go. In an economic confederation of states like Francophone West Africa around £1/$1.60 a day will cover several countries, in Uzbekistan one rider paid £2-3 for 14 days cover. One rider even got his Triumph Trophy around the world without insurance. Indeed the only time he was asked to present evidence of insurance was on the Malay/Thai border where flashing his multi-stamped carnet was enough to be waved through. This is a good example of the '**library card effect**'; any official-looking piece of paper covered with rubber stamps plus a photo of yourself will please a bored border guard. Latin America is a place where even asking about getting motor insurance is likely to either take you days and cost heaps of money for something of dubious validity, or paying a bigger sum to some corrupt officer who'll stamp an empty packet of cigarettes and send you on your way. Basically it's the same as with carnets: if they don't ask don't offer.

The dubious validity of Third World insurance or the impossibility of getting it at all underlines the fact that should you cause an accident such as killing someone's child or worse still, a breadwinner, the complications into which you'll sink may take years and large amounts of money to resolve. India is a place which probably has the most demanding riding conditions in the world. In this desperately poor and overpopulated country, people are not averse to throwing Granny in front of a foreign rider and then nailing them to the floorboards for compensation.

Motor insurance is an unravellable quandary: rigorously enforced in your own country, out in the sticks it's mostly unattainable or of little value. The answer is to rest often, ride carefully and be alert.

Other travel and motoring documents
Additional motoring documents to those mentioned above include:
- Green Card for UK riders crossing Europe.
- An International Certificate for Motor Vehicles, a multilingual translation of your indigenous vehicle ownership papers issued by motoring organisations for use in countries which do not accept the original.
- Motoring Organisation Membership Card. Remember that some enlightened countries (such as Australia) offer reciprocal membership to their own motoring organisations for free. Your membership card will also be useful when renewing or extending a carnet and may also have value as a 'library card'.

Local permits
What's been covered above is only what you must try and arrange in your home country. Additional documentation will be gleefully issued for any number of reasons (mainly to get more money out of you, or 'fine' you for not having it). Typical examples include registering with the police within 24 hours of arrival, photography and filming permits (at the last count, only Cameroon and Sudan required these, although ciné can be a different kettle of fish), 'tourist registration cards', currency declaration forms (see below), or permits to cross remote areas such as Siberia or Egypt's Western Desert. As these are the sorts of places where police roadblocks are frequent, omitting to get one of the above permits when required may cost you more in the long run.

As much as following proper procedure (without which civilisation would clearly crumble), paperwork is a game of wits as well as an opportunity for corrupt officials to create difficulties which can only be solved with a bribe. By at least starting your journey with proper documentation you'll have a good chance to get well underway without unnecessary hassles until you learn the ropes and find out what can and cannot be got away with.

MONEY

Along with insurance, money and how to carry it is another thing that many adventure bikers worry about before they leave. The cost of any major trip is likely to be at least a couple of thousand pounds and riding with that sort of money through the insecure territories of Asia, Africa and Latin America is enough to make anyone nervous. For advice on changing money and dealing with the black market, see 'Life on the Road' starting on p.74.

Best currencies

Thanks in part to the far-reaching tentacles of the Coca-Cola culture, the desirability of the **US dollar** is well known in even the remotest corners of the world, places where other hard currencies might be stared at in incomprehension. Certainly, throughout South America and across most of Asia this would be the most readily-convertible hard foreign currency to carry. In Africa they're more used to European currency: the **French franc**, **German deutschmark** or **British pound**, some of which might have become the **Euro** by the time you read this. The pound sterling is also useful in the Indian subcontinent as the deutschmark is in Turkey. Avoid using British £50 or US$100 bills: they are rarely seen abroad and often thought to be counterfeit.

Security

How or where you carry your stash is up to you. You can hide it on the bike and risk getting it wet, burnt or stolen with the bike, or your can carry it on your person and risk losing it, the garment it's in, or just plain getting robbed. A good idea is to stash a portion on the bike (along with other small valuables like spare keys, document and copies and a credit card) and keep the rest with you. Wherever you put it on your bike (use your imagination to work that one out, but think laterally!) make sure you wrap it up securely against possible damage: use plastic bags and plenty of duct tape.

Another good idea is to secrete some more money on yourself: there are all sorts of devices sold in travel shops; above all go for something that's comfortable and convenient so you'll never be disinclined to wear it. Ordinary belts come with secret zipped interiors; money belts go around your waist, your neck or shoulder-holster style à la Dirty Harry. You can velcro your wad to the inside of your trousers or keep it in an elasticated bandage around your shin. The rest can be put in a secure inside pocket of your jacket.

Keep your 'day cash' separate from that large, tempting looking wodge; you don't want to be unpeeling a couple of dollars to buy a Coke in a crowded market. Another general point about pockets is get into the habit of using the same ones for the same things, and be forever checking that the zips are closed as you walk into a crowded area. Stick to this habit religiously: wallet and passport here; bike keys there; small change in that one. This way when something goes missing or you need something quickly, you know where it should be. It's one good reason for using a jacket with lots of secure pockets.

Credit cards

Credit cards are a very useful way of avoiding the need to carry large rolls of cash. While you are unlikely to see the familiar blue-white-and-gold bands of a Visa card halfway along the beach piste to Nouakchott, a compact credit card or two is definitely an item worth carrying on a long overland ride. Sometime, somewhere, you're going to bless that little plastic rectangle for getting you out of a fix, most probably in getting a painless cash advance from a foreign bank, or just paying for a restful night in a plush hotel when you're short on local currency. And across North America, Europe, Australasia and South Africa you need hardly ever use cash at all.

Contrary to the reasonable assumption that credit card companies hit you hard for overseas purchases, they actually offer the best rates of exchange for the day of your purchase and no service charges (at least with Visa). And there's always the faint hope that your overseas transaction may get mislaid in the electronic pipeline and never materialise on your statement. Then again, credit card fraud is common, so do check your statements carefully for any unsolicited purchases.

It goes without saying that you should keep tabs of how much you're spending on the card and, at the very least, get your minimum monthly payment sorted out (you can arrange this sort of direct debit with your bank before you go, assuming, of course, you have money in the bank to pay it off). Better still, get your credit card in credit before you leave.

A good travel guidebook should tell you which of the three main brands (Visa, American Express or MasterCard) are widely used in your destination, but with the negative connotation 'America' has in some countries or to some individuals, the anonymous Visa or less commonly seen MasterCard are more widely reliable.

Travellers' cheques and money transfers

A handy back up to hard cash are travellers' cheques, most useful in US dollar form: safer than cash but no more useful than credit cards. In the undeveloped countries don't rely on these troublesome forms of 'cash' – they're more commonly used on visits to the Western world and may prove unchangeable when you need them most. And despite what you're told, don't put your faith in speedy replacement of stolen items. First you have to declare them lost, and a working phone, let alone reimbursement, might be days away. Travellers cheques are merely a secure back-up which can be easily cashed (or in the States, used as cash) in Westernised countries. Furthermore, although issued in a rock solid currency like US dollars, you may find that cashing them in gets a handful of local currency at the official rate, not something you necessarily want. Some countries even levy a tax on imported travellers' cheques.

Money transfers or cabling, are generally more useful to students caught short while Interailing around Europe rather than adventure bikers pushing back the limits of human endurance. If you do end up using this service, such as the US Western Union, you must state a nominated local bank where the money will arrive. Again, in most cases a poorer country will want to give you their local currency rather than the dollars you may have been counting on. Also, be aware that no matter what may be promised, changing back a local soft currency into a hard currency is either impossible, heavily obstructed or achieved at such a bad rate that you'll be depressed for days. When buying local currency, get only as little as you need; it's easier to top it up with a little black market dealing as you start running out, rather than hope to sell your excess local currency to another traveller.

Choosing a motorcycle

Motorcyclists have been up the road and around the world on everything from scooters to one-and-a-half litre cruisers. All machines will do the job well to a lesser or greater degree, but ask yourself would you be pleased to chug up a mountain pass at walking pace or struggle across sandy tracks on an *autobahn-*tourer weighing nearly half a ton?

Important factors

If you need some guidance in choosing a bike here, in no particular order of importance, are some factors to consider:

- Lightness
- Economy
- Comfort
- Robustness
- Agility
- Reliability
- Mechanical simplicity

And here's another thing to remember: the bike you eventually choose is going to be loaded with up to 50kg (110lbs) of gear, more if you're riding two-up. This weight will reduce the machine's agility and braking performance as well as accelerate wear on all components, especially tyres and chains. So whatever bike you settle on, consider the worst case scenario: its utility when fully-loaded on a dirt road.

If you're not concerned about making an outlandish statement on two wheels then settle for a single or twin cylinder machine of around 600cc. A 40hp engine of this capacity produces enough power to carry you and your gear through the worst conditions while not over-stressing the motor. It'll also give reasonable performance and fuel economy of at least 50mpg (which equals 17.6kpl or 5.7l/100km). Multi-cylinder engines are unnecessary and, in case you hadn't yet guessed, **four strokes** are far superior to two strokes on a long trip, despite the latter's power-to-weight advantage (although see p.39).

Engine cooling and transmission options

Water-cooling is now the norm on modern, big-engined bikes, not because it's better, but because a water-cooled engine can be built with finer tolerances so producing higher performance and making it more impressive in influential road tests. Water-cooling also makes engines less noisy as manufacturers are compelled to make their machines more environmentally friendly.

However, power and acceleration are not among the seven factors mentioned earlier: mechanical simplicity is. As long as it's in good condition and well maintained, an **air-cooled** engine is no worse than a water-cooled equivalent. Water-cooling is just another thing to break and another dial to watch, and, on a motorcycle, radiators are difficult to position efficiently without being vulnerable in crashes. Despite the impression, a water-cooled engine will not necessarily run cooler in extreme heat.

Transmission by either **shaft or chain** is a less cut and dry issue. Shaft drive transmission tends to be fitted on non-sports machines, but due to its weight, rarely comes on true dual sport machines. Its weight and slight power-sapping effects are balanced by reliability and virtual freedom from maintenance.

Chains and sprockets on the other hand are a very efficient and cheap means of transmitting power from an engine to a back wheel. Although they're exposed to the elements, modern 'o'- or 'x'-ring chains can last for thousands of miles. So when it comes to transmission settle for shaft drive on a heavier machine or use a chain driven bike with **top quality chain and sprockets**. There's more on chains on p.44.

And if you happen to be wondering about a kickstart-only or **electric start** model: go for the button. One hot day, when your bowels are in freefall and you're stalled on a one-log bridge, you will bless that button.

Touring bikes – the comfortable compromise

Touring bikes have one huge advantage and one huge drawback when used for adventurous motorcycle travel. Even when loaded up, they can be supremely **comfortable and stable** over miles of highway, with fat tyres on small wheels and big torquey engines making this sort of riding a pleasure. When you're averaging a couple of thousand miles a week, comfort is an extremely important factor which doesn't just mean the size and thickness of the saddle. Comfort means multi-cylinder vibration-free engines and smooth power delivery, supple suspension, powerful brakes and protection from the wind. It allows you to **relax** while riding and so defers the inevitable fatigue; and when you're not tired you can cope better with the 101 daily challenges the long-distance riding throws at you. Comfort also means an **effective silencer**, the clothes you're wearing, and your state of mind: these latter two subjects are covered on p.64 and p.75.

It's when a big touring bike has to face the dirt that things turn pear-shaped. What ran as if on rails becomes an unwieldy dog that devours your energy and can jeopardise your entire trip. Even at less than walking pace, soft sand and especially mud are misery to ride on a road bike, as effectively bald tyres slither around to dump you again and again. Road bikes were not built for this sort of riding, and components will wear quickly or break, as will your own resolve to take spontaneous excursions or vital short cuts on dirt roads. Smaller road bikes of 600cc or less will be more manageable, but anything over the one-litre class will be unrideable in tough off-road conditions.

Still, of course you can have incredible global adventures on a road bike as long as you think about where you're going and the type of riding you expect there. If you're going to cross the US or even run down the Pan-American Highway, a road bike is fine, as it will be for most of the overland route from London to India. The main sites of South-East Asia are also accessible on tarmac and Australia can be ringed and bisected without leaving the blacktop (although you'll miss the best of the Outback this way). Only a true trans-Africa trip demands a dual-purpose machine to cope with the sands of the Sahara and the mud of the equatorial rain forests.

However, anywhere in the world a road can be cut by flooding or landslides and in this situation traffic either waits or finds another way through.

And anyone who's travelled extensively will know that the best adventures are waiting for you in the rarely visited places far from the beaten track and smooth sealed roads.

Dual sport or trail bikes

The best characteristic of trail or dual sport bikes can be summed up in one word: **versatility**. There's nowhere you can't go on your trailie that a flat-six Aspenlade can get to (albeit without a six-speaker airbag), but the whole thrilling realm of unsealed roads (or no roads at all) becomes open to you. Trail bikes have genuinely useful features, such as folding foot controls, 21" front wheels with steering geometry to match, long suspension travel and greater ground clearance. And, to a certain extent, they're designed to be dropped without suffering major damage.

Because they're trying to be the best of both worlds, some of the disadvantages of these bikes are what makes them trail bikes; they include:

- High seats make them intimidating for short riders
- Poor high-speed stability and cornering due to a combination of long travel suspension, high ground clearance, upright seating position, 21" front wheels, trail-pattern tyres and high 'wind-catching' front mud guards
- Narrow saddles give poor comfort, especially for passengers

Yet despite the above drawbacks, dual sport bikes will make your overland trip a whole lot more fun because you won't dread the thought of heading off the tarmac.

In the early 1980s the growing popularity of what was then the Paris Dakar Rally caught the imagination of the world's bike manufacturers and gave rise to a genre of 'rally replica' bikes whose large tanks, simple yet tractable engines, and plush suspension were ideal for adventurous off-road touring. Though long out of production, BMW's twin-valve GSs and air-cooled Yamaha Ténérés remain popular choices for adventure biking.

In later years these rally racers as well as their showroom replicas evolved into more complex machines, making them less suitable for long-range touring, although Kawasaki's KLR 650 has managed to remain in production much as it was a decade ago and so remains a firm favourite among North American adventure riders where that model is still available.

As the desert racer trend moved on, useful features like big tanks, quality wheel rims and other components were replaced by snazzy paint jobs and more weight: bikes like the Africa Twin, Cagiva Elefant and Super Ténéré. But since that time the rally-trend has turned full circle, and following the success of single cylinder KTM and BMW desert racers, road going replicas have again hit the showrooms. So 20 years on we can say that the choice of the long-range dirt touring machines for the new millennium are KTM's 640 Adventure-R or and possibly BMW's F650GS 'Dakar'.

Enduro racers

Four-stroke enduro racing bikes, such as KTM LCs, Honda XRs and Yamaha TTs and WRs are not simply lighter and more powerful versions of their dual-purpose cousins. While it's true that, unloaded, these bikes are much more fun to ride off-road than trail bikes, they differ in other respects too. The lack of body work and other road-oriented ancillaries may make them a good basis for a Spartan tourer, but the engines consume more fuel and require more attention due to their higher state of tune. Their no-frills nature also extends to the narrow seat, intended to enable standing up and easy shifting of body weight during off-road events instead of day-long support.

Something like a Yamaha WR400 or a Suzuki DRZ400 might sound great if you're serious about dirt: you get great suspension and a powerful engine. The truth is a machine like this would be all but wasted on a long touring trip. You must remember that by the time any bike is loaded up, all traces of nimbleness will be largely eradicated.

Survey of suitable motorcycles

Below is a review of recommended motorcycles, all of them dual sports suitable for adventure bike touring. This type of use is the specific basis for their evaluation, not all round motorcycling appeal – and clearly it's a personal choice based on my experience. The sort of riding that is covered in this book presents a tiny minority of global motorcycle activity which no manufacturer will ever respond to seriously. Therefore, most suitable machines will be compromises of leisure, sport or 'lifestyle' models, which by coincidence more than anything else happen to be good for adventure touring.

No attempt has been made to provide fuel consumption figures because baggage width, wind direction, terrain and riding style will affect this. However all these bikes ought to achieve at least 50 miles per UK gallon (17.6kpl or 5.7l/100km) if ridden with economy as a primary concern, while some mildly tuned singles can return half as much again.

On the AM Website you'll find **links** to homepages for many of the bikes described below, as well as the ever growing list of **AM Trip Reports** which include brief pros and cons on all the machines below, plus many more.

BMW

BMW F650

The original **F650 Funduro** came out in Europe in 1993, in North America a couple of years later, and became an all-round hit as a nice, inexpensive, mid-sized, middle-of-the-road machine with BMW's cachet and **build quality**. Despite the vaguely dual-purpose appearance (amounting to little more than wide 'bars) it never really caught on as a long-range dirt tourer, hampered by a weight not far short of a Transalp V-Twin, and a 19" front wheel which limited off-highway riding and tyre choice. The 17.5-litre tank was nearly useful – Acerbis offer a 27-litre unit that manages to look barely bigger while providing a useful 300-mile/480km range.

One of the F's biggest drawbacks was a **snatchy transmission** and a lack of torque at low speeds, although there was no doubt it was fast machine once the engine spun out. This juddering is of course common with many singles, but particularly bad on the relatively high-revving 650 where you're forever changing gear to find a smooth spot. In a tricky off road situation this makes the F hard work – especially in mud or deep sand.

On the plus side you have good comfort, economy and handling, so for a road-oriented trip an F with a big tank and an accessory high screen makes a good choice, but if you like the dirt, read my tale on p.225 first.

The new F650GS arrived in the UK in two versions: plain GS aimed at Funduro fans and an **F650GS Dakar** model featuring longer suspension, a 21" front wheel and a taller screen, all of which offer the promise of a great over-landing bike. Both models use electronic fuel injection and feature an **under-seat** 17.5-litre fuel tank. The seat on the road model is low and both remain adjustable for height which will again make the new GSs popular with women and shorter riders.

Just as this book was getting glued together I had a chance to ride a 'Dakar' for a couple of days in Wales at BMW's off-road school and compared to my previous Funduro the bike was a huge improvement. The EFI has smoothed out the low-rpm running: you could pull away from 1500 rpm without shaking the drive chain apart. It's still a revvy machine but a whole lot more enjoyable to ride.

EX-ARMY ARMSTRONG MT 500

The British army's Rotax-engined MT is an extremely robust and hard-wearing bike, which with some alterations would make a tough and inexpensive overlanding bike. However buy with care, the army is not the most careful of users and machines released as 'runners' can be anything but.

Auctions are the standard method of release by the British Ministry of Defence (MOD) and at first would seem to be the place to pick up a bargain. The trouble is you won't be allowed to start the bike, let alone ride it, and missing components, seized engines and sloppy internals are common problems that are impossible to evaluate before you pay up.

Private sales of roadworthy bikes are a better bet, saving a lot of messing about. Expect to pay £1000-1400 for a sound bike complete with pannier frames and toolbox. Chrome and red ex-Northern Ireland bikes go for more, but are extremely rare. Don't be fooled into paying more for Harley Davidson badged bikes – they're just MTs with new side panels.

If you've bought your bike from an auction the first thing to do is to strip it down and check the state of the engine. Some bikes have a preservative liquid instead of oil – run

the engine on this and things get expensive.

Old and dirty fuel leads to endless starting problems for newly-released bikes; the gauze filters in the tank and carb are often blocked with flakes of red paint from jerricans and settled water corrodes the passages in the float bowl and choke. While the carb is off, check the needle position – bikes used abroad have the needle setting changed and may have different or incorrect jet sizes. Change the spark plug too, because of the over-rich Amal, they can soon fail to give any spark whatsoever. And replace the crappy metal plug cap with a proper plastic one like an NGK.

Paul Witheridge

The Dakar sits two inches higher than the road model and I felt the comfort was superior to the old Funduro which I found a bit cramped. On the Dakar model the 'lip' in the seat is less pronounced and further back which gives the impression of a larger saddle. For a 440lb/200kg bike the Dakar felt agile, light and stable with the lowered centre of gravity thanks in part to the underseat tank. It will be interesting to see how Acerbis manage to make a bigger tank for this one!

F650 modified for desert use with a rear MT21 on the front wheel, Mich' Desert on the back and a 27-litre tank.

Electronics will be a concern but at least the Dakar does not have the rectifier mounted behind the bashplate as on the road model, and on that subject the bashplate on the new Fs adds up to little more than pressed tin. With some attention to protection (better hand guards), water hoses and a still higher screen, the Dakar could make a great dirt overlander. See the AM website for a fuller impression.

F650GS Dakar: better seat and suspension, smoother fuel-injected engine and a lowered centre of gravity with the fuel tank under the seat.

BMW GS series

From the beginning the most popular alternatives to ubiquitous Jap singles have been BMW's shaft-driven flat twins of 800, 1000, and lately 1150cc. So great is the world touring reputation of BMW that I've seen desperately cumbersome, road-oriented models struggling across the Sahara with a passenger on the back.

However, the older, dual-purpose 800 and 1000cc twin-valve **GS models** do make the bulk easier to handle with their 21″ front wheels, wider handlebars, altered gearing and weight saved where possible. BMW's old Boxer engines (as the twin valvers are known) have **unrivalled accessibility**, simplicity and strength, but they're heavier and use more fuel than singles; keeping under 60mph/100kph expect about 60m/UKg (21kpl or 4.7l/100km).

The weight and feel of a flat-twin BM gives a completely different ride to other bikes. Obviously less agile but much more comfortable, once loaded up and on the move the whole machine is reassuringly stable in a way big singles never are. Although BMWs are much heavier than singles of nearly similar capacity, the Boxer design puts most of that weight low down, creating a **low centre of gravity** and so good stability. This fact also makes them easy to pick up and, to a certain extent, the protruding barrels act as handy leg protectors if you crash.

The first R80G/S, with its then-radical single-sided swing arm, came out over twenty years ago and is now a rare relic. From an adventure touring perspective, this model's shortcomings lie in its hopelessly **soggy suspension**; a gentler riding style is the only solution, but riding off the highway on a big BM

R100GS – a great all-rounder.

demands this anyway. A token 'Paris–Dakar' version of the early G/S was briefly produced with a huge 32-litre tank plus a wider single seat with a rack immediately behind, but these models are very rare and the suspension remained unimproved.

In 1988 the series took a big step forward with the launch of the **R100GS** (along with an 800cc equivalent) with a 'Paralever' rear suspension linkage to counteract the shaft drive's inherent torque reaction under acceleration and deceleration (little more than a quirk of shaft drive bikes and something you just get used to). However, the Paralever bikes got **firmer suspension** and many other improved features, although the whole bike was made physically much bigger than the old 800, whose low seat height was most reassuring when you got out of shape.

The R100GS has a larger tank and an oil cooler vulnerably mounted on the cylinder protection bars, as well as a small windscreen – this is always a good idea. If you can afford to buy and prepare such a machine (let alone handle it when loaded-up off-road) it's a luxurious way to travel overland, despite the weight penalty. Rim-mounted spokes permit tubeless tyre fitment too.

Passengers will also have a more comfortable time on the back of a BMW GS than any other machine recommended here. A R100GS 'Paris–Dakar' variant is heavier than ever at 520lb/236kg, but has a 35 litre tank and a fairing wrapped in crash bars. Overall, however, the one-litre Paralever is the best of the GSs to take around the world. While production ended in 1996, there's still a chance you'll find a good one out there.

Points to consider when loading a GS for a long ride include the feeble **rear sub frame** which flexes noticeably without bracing and the dry, car-type air filter which can get choked in dusty conditions. Leaking seals in the 'dry' shaft housing can also cause problems but the Bing carb-balancing ritual is something every BM owner learns fast. As much as any bike featured here, Germany is one place you'll find heaps of overlanding GS know-how; check out the AM Website links.

An interesting variant popped up for a couple of years in 1996 as the Boxer

BMW Kalahari is a mix of old and not so old GS parts. The similar Basic model has a smaller tank and no screen.

GS series came to an end following more come-backs than Frank Sinatra. They were the 800cc **GS Basic** and its big-tanked South African counterpart, the **Kalahari**. You'll be lucky to find either on special at the corner shop, but what you do get adds up to a late-1980s GS with Paralever-quality suspension using Marzocchi forks and a White Power shock.

Stood alongside a titanic 1100GS (see p.31), a Basic looks tiny – positively inspiring for short riders. The moniker alludes to the no-frills collection of bits which got thrown together to made up these bikes, including a headlight nacelle as old as any G/S and brakes that Fred Flintstone would sneer at. But all this simplicity on good suspension is just fine for the Big Trip. The Basic's ex-ST tank holds 19.5 litres – you'll recognise one by the blue frame and white bodywork. The Kalahari featured a 35-litre tank, handguards and a small windscreen which to me seems just about all you could ask for.

Four valve twins

In 1993 the R1100GS was introduced, a radical design exercise featuring dive-less Telelever front suspension, fuel injection, ABS brakes, four-valve heads, a 19" front wheel, radial tyres, plus a Christmas Tree that pops out of the speedo every December 25th. You also get an extra 55lb/25kg over an RI00GS. This GS comes with a 25-litre tank from which you can squeeze 300 miles (60m/UKg, 21kpl or 4.7l/100km). The standard

1100GS – plenty of power and surprisingly capable off road until you get out of shape.

Metzeler radials aren't brilliant on the dirt where T66 Michelins are said to have the edge. Weak points which have surfaced on hard-pushed 1100s are **cracked gearbox mounts**, which support the rear subframe when bottomed out hard. The solution is to jack up the rear preload to the max and take it easy on very bad roads. Taller riders will find the screen too low and the seat is less comfortable than you'd expect; US-made Corbin custom seats are highly rated by long-distance BMW riders.

Plenty of riders who feel comfortable with big machines take 1100s (and the latest 1150 version) to improbable places. All that metal adds a feeling of 'get through anything' security; and German photographer Michael Martin used an 1100GS to tour all the African deserts for his picture book of that name. Where there's a will there's a way – though where there's soft sand or mud you could be praying for a crane!

Honda XL and XR

Honda's long-running XL series of trail bikes is almost as old as dual sporting itself. Of particularly interest to big trippers with small budgets is the short-lived **XL600LM**, from the mid-1980s, with its large tank and tubeless tyres but of course finding a good one will be a gamble after all these years. Early red, white and blue XLMs had unreliable electric starters and sometimes took a bit of starting with the kickstarter, but these old XLs tend to run some somewhat better than same-era Ténérés on low-octane fuel. No large capacity single is ever going to be as smooth as a multi-cylinder engine, but I've found XLMs to be comparatively lumpy at low revs, which can tire the rider and accelerate the wear of the transmission.

Honda XLs took a big step forward, with the street-scrambling **NX650 Dominator**, still considered one of the best big singles, featuring a great engine and handling to match. Now that you can get a 23-litre tank for this bike, what's stopping you? See Sarah Crofts' ripping yarn on p.230.

BUYING AND RUNNING AN ENFIELD BULLET

Today's Enfield India is a virtually unaltered thirty year-old British Royal Enfield pushrod single built in India using the original casts. Enfields bought abroad are superior to the ones you can buy in India, where Bullets are cheap but hopelessly unreliable. Buying new in India will give you more teething problems than a shark with gum disease, so go for reconditioned second-hand with the comforting thought that India roadside 'mechanics' know the inside of a Bullet like the back of their hands and you can get a new piston fitted for the price of an indicator lens for a Japanese bike.

If you can see yourself enjoying the enforced slow pace (50mph/80kph with archaic drum brakes) and the fact that they never actually fall to pieces, then a Bullet will give you a journey to remember and plenty of roadside encounters. Enfield India also produce a 500cc diesel, a rarity with the power of a moped but mind-boggling 400-miles per tank fuel economy! Across the developing world, diesel fuel keeps countries moving and costs a fraction of petrol.

Rule number one: go for the 350 Bullet, not the 500. On Indian roads the 500's extra power is wasted, they're less saleable and spares are scarce and expensive. If planning to ride to Europe, the export model 350 has been given the necessary EU modifications. Alternatively, if you come across a pre-'68 Royal Enfield, it doesn't need to be modified. The easiest place to find yourself a good, used Enfield is New Delhi in northern India.

New Enfields

Enfield specialists Madras Motors have branches in most major cities.

● 350 Bullet Standard: around Rs49,000 (£1000/$1600)

● 350 Export: around Rs55,000 (£1100)

● 500 Enfield: around Rs55,000 (£1100)

Second-hand Enfields

● **Private purchase**: Departing foreigners advertise in travellers' hotels, or at New Delhi Tourist Camp. Standard price for a 350, regardless of age, is around Rs20,000 (£400); you'll rarely pay more than Rs30,000 (£600).

● **Second-hand dealers**: The main Delhi bike market, Karol Bagh, has several dealers, the best known being Lali Singh and Madaan Motors. Both will sell you a bike with guaranteed repurchase (no time limit) at 30% less than you paid. Prices are around a third higher than buying privately, but depend on your bargaining skills. They also rent bikes. Beware of paying more for a rebuilt bike unless you're prepared to personally supervise the rebuilding.

The owner of Nanna Motors, near New Delhi Tourist Camp, is honest and a very good mechanic (highly recommended by owners of foreign machines) and can sometimes help with bike purchase (including new bikes). He also runs organised Enfield group tours.

● **Royal Enfields**: The original British bikes are normally priced midway between new bikes and good second-hand ones. They're

Perhaps the best single cylinder Honda currently available is the **XR650L**, a blend of Dominator engine and XR- frame that's finally given Honda a dual sport contender in the US again. Don't be confused by the sporty XR label, a trick Yamaha also use with XT/TT to make you think you're getting a wolf not a dual sport sheep. The XR-L is a heavy 150kg machine hampered by a high seat, but features a strengthened rear subframe capable of supporting the weight of your baggage which with a 22-litre Acerbis tank makes it a good overlander.

A Dommie in the highlands of Peru (see story page 230). © Sarah Crofts

Although true enduro bikes are not ideal for long range touring, the similarly

BUYING AND RUNNING AN ENFIELD BULLET (continued)

invariably full of crap Indian parts, but have more class!

● **Outside Delhi**: Dealers operate in tourist areas like Goa and Manali (north of Delhi), otherwise enquire locally.

Modifications

To modify the standard 350 to be EU legal, budget on around Rs6-8000 (£120–160) for the changes (bigger front brake from the 500, longer exhaust, 12v electrics).

Useful minor extras for Indian touring include: petrol filter, fuel tap lock, battery isolation switch, wider rear tyre, different handlebars and reshaped seat to improve handling and comfort, crash bars/leg guards, racks for luggage, super-loud horns. None of these additions costs more than a few hundred rupees.

Running an Enfield

● **Common problems:** How long have you got? It's an Enfield! You'll spend a lot of time nurturing your machine.

● **Maintenance**: Apart from regular carb cleaning, check nuts and bolts frequently – Enfields shake themselves to pieces on pot-holed Indian roads.

● **Spares**: Readily available in all but the smallest towns. Besides the usual spares carry cables, a chain link, rectifier and a coil. Always try to buy original Enfield spares: cheaper imitations inevitably have an even shorter life than the originals.

● **Repairs**: Be prepared for roadside fix-its everywhere, although most towns have a specialist Enfield 'metalbasher'. It's worth supervising all work to check it's actually being done and that no old parts are being substituted.

● **Common repair price guide**: Puncture repair Rs20; carburettor clean Rs10-20; oil change with new oil Rs100; rebore and new piston Rs700; new clutch plates, fitted Rs150. In India petrol prices average at around Rs20 a litre (40p/60 cents per l) and a 350 Enfield will return around 80mpg /25-35kpl.

Documents and regulations

● **Ownership papers**: Not strictly necessary to get these in your own name as long as the owner on the documents has signed the transfer. If planning to sell the bike in a state other than the one it is registered in, you must obtain a 'no objections' certificate. Most dealers will organise name transfer, for a fee although, being India, this can take up to a few weeks.

● **Third party insurance**: Mandatory, though worthless. Around Rs100-200 (£2-4) a year, obtainable at any insurance office.

● **Taking a Bullet out of the country**: You must produce currency exchange certificates to the value of the bike and a receipt showing purchase price and the bike documents in your name.

There's plenty of useful first hand information on Bullets on the Web. Start surfing the AM Website's Links page.

Nicki McCormick

---

venerable **XR series** has gained a reputation over the years and across the world as a reliable and robust do-it-all hack which can include taking it round the world's back roads. Naturally, comfort will be a pain as is lighting, economy and the lack of an ignition key, and XRs are not always road legal depending on where you live. If you can slap a plate on it, then obviously the 600s are the best bet although Alex Marr's XR400 managed to get to Cape Town via a short rest on an Ethiopian river bed (see p.214). Don't be tempted by the long awaited XR650R which came out in 2000. The substitution of 'L' for 'R' adds up to an alloy-framed desert racer that would be wasted under a pile of luggage.

Transalps and Africa Twins

The first of the so-called 'Adventure Sports' bikes was Honda's XLV600V Transalp. Designated 'Rally Touring' with a smooth V-twin engine, it was definitely more touring than rally. As its name suggests, a Transalp is suited to transporting you across smooth Alpine highways and is not up to an overland

Honda Africa Twin in Morocco.
© A Hanley

bashing; early models had plastic bashplates, flimsy chains, fast-wearing front discs (get a spare for India) and rear drum brakes which ovalised – go for the rear disc-braked model introduced in 1993 or the later twin front disced examples. And besides the twin radiators' vulnerability, that nice fairing soon breaks up after even mild 'fall overs'; try and anticipate damage to these components before you leave.

Now available as a 650, years earlier the dowdy Transalp spawned the much more exciting 650 and current 750 **Africa Twins** which, while having a great road presence, don't offer anything special for long range dirt touring and tend to use a lot of fuel doing it. Speed, comfort, Japanese reliability and looks are all plus points, but despite the rally racer looks, every rider that dares venture onto the dirt comes back with a lasting impression of the AT's weight. If you want a big road bike under you, go for a shaft-driven BM.

GLOBE RIDERS RATE KTM'S ADVENTURE-R

KTM Adventure 640: great bike, I would definitely use it again on a trip like this. I believe it's the only true long-range capable dirt bike available without spending a lot of time and cash modifying something else. I must admit though my personal taste is for a biggish single cylinder dirt bike, since I can see absolutely no fun in riding a German-style overladen BMW or the like along a rocky river bed... We've now come across three KTMs in Africa, so at least a few Europeans agree with us. The way I see it, the basic trade off with the KTM is:

● High initial cost.
● Slight discomfort.
● A little more fiddly than Jap bikes.

So, Latin America really doesn't need such a dirt capable bike, but for Africa it's #1.

Strong points
● Off-road performance – quite capable on tarmac up to 80-90mph/130-140 kph.
● Quality components and strong build (they've withstood some dramatic high speed wipe outs), great suspension, brakes.
● Fuel economy: the 28-litre tank will return up to 460 miles/700kms cruising at 50mph/80kph on tar).

Weak points
● Hellish seat: we had ours completely reshaped wider and flatter which is well

worthwhile for the added comfort factor.
● Electrics are iffy: be prepared for occasional earthing problems.
● They're a bit of a bitch if you're short, although the 1999 model's seat height was lower than the earlier ones.
● Replace the original tailpipe if buying the US spec – it's an absolute beast; the Euro spec is better.

A few mods we've done are apparently already on the 2000 model such as a side-stand. The Adventure-R is also not great if you're determined to carry heaps of luggage (although we came across a German with his hefty lady on the back plus large boxes, top box, tank bag etc).

For what it's worth, I am dead happy with my current system:
● Ortlieb soft bags (18 litre each side).
● Small lockable tool box on the bashplate.
● Small (about 40cm x 30cm x 15cm) lockable Pelican case mounted on rear rack for photo equipment.
● Two 5-litre plastic petrol containers for remote areas strapped to seat behind me and usually empty.

Noah Maltz

In 1999 Noah Maltz and Trevor Sproat set off to circumnavigate the world to raise money for the Save the Children charity. Follow their progress at www.globeride.com

KTM

As the last edition of this book came out KTM's big-tanked Adventure 620EGS hit Europe, reaching North America as the **640 Adventure-R,** and maybe renamed again by the time you read this.

Capitalising in the time-honoured tradition on the success of rally winning desert racers, these purposeful machines have caught on among riders who value competition-oriented off-highway utility.

The Adventure-R has caught on on both sides of the Atlantic as an off-the-shelf machine worthy of its name. This is the 'Rallye' version with a few extra bells and buzzers, including a 2-litre water container built into the bash plate.

As with the enduro bikes mentioned above (from which the Adventure originates) this single-mindedness comes at some cost to comfort as well as the reliability taken for granted with Japanese machines. **Weak points** seem to be electrical misfires or shorts, and high wear of alloy sprockets (steel is the answer), but you get a machine that is more race than replica and many owners have noted the Adventure's ability to withstand tumbles that would cripple a lesser machine. As Noah Maltz points out on the opposite page, there's a lot to be said for buying a machine that comes stock with quality components, even if it costs more.

There's talk of a big **V-twin KTM** coming out in early 2001. This evolution to a bigger and more complex machine seems to replicate the origins of the Africa Twins and Super Ténérés fifteen years earlier. Chances are, with KTM's background, the V-twin will be a lot more functional than its predecessors. As with the Adventure-R, you'll just have to wait for edition five of *AMH* for the full story in retrospect.

Kawasaki

The early Kawasaki water-cooled KLR600 singles were fast, light, revvy and hopelessly unreliable. Kawasaki has always gone for this high performance category, a smart marketing move but one which rules these bikes out for adventure biking. Avoid the kick-start 'A' model, no matter how cheap it is. Later, electric start models struggled to overcome

A feral KLR on the loose in Canada. © Tom Grenon

KLR 650

The KLR 650 has never been as popular in the UK and France as it has been in the US and Germany. Production began in 1987, superseding the rather fragile KLR 600. In Europe the KLR gave way to the Tengai which is similar, but with a larger and more brittle plastic fairing and an uprated twin pot floating caliper front brake. The KLR 650 is still a current model in the USA and Canada, while in Europe it has evolved through the showy motocross-styled KLX 650 and back to a budget green-laner, similar to the original KLR 650 but equipped with a small fuel tank and fairing.

In my view the **original KLR 650** as still sold in North America makes the best adventure tourer. The general construction and quality is good. The exhaust, for example, is all stainless steel so lasts the life of the bike. The fuel tank has a capacity of 23 litres (18 to reserve) allowing a range of up to 300 miles/450km. The fairing is small and flexible, and yet does a reasonably good job of keeping the wind off the rider. The frame, subframe and wheels are strong, so should not need alteration to cope with the hammering imposed on them by lengthy rides over rough terrain.

The KLR does have **weak points** though. Like most dual purpose mounts, the seat is painfully uncomfortable. To increase comfort fit a Corbin seat that is wider and firmer. The motor is basically tremendously strong, but it is let down by the balancer mechanism. I'd recommend replacing the balancer chain at a

belt 'n' braces 30,000 miles/ 50,000km, and to check the balancer sprockets very carefully at the same time. To get an idea of the condition of the balancer sprockets, take a look at the mesh oil strainer behind the right-hand engine cover: if it's full of bits of rubber, you're better off replacing the balancer chain sprockets and guides. Valve-stem oil seals fail fairly quickly, so replace them before setting off on a big trip and while you're there get the valves shimmed; they should last 20-25,000 miles/30 to 40,000 km without needing attention. The gearbox output shaft can suffer on early models, so check to make sure the splines are in good condition. If they are damaged, they'll get worse quickly so, it'll be necessary to replace the output shaft – only about $120 in the US but of course requiring the whole engine to be stripped.

The KLR also has **design faults.** The sidestand cut-out switch is bound to fail sooner or later, so bypass it by bridging the two wires to the switch on the loom side. The clutch safety switch prevents the motor being started while in gear, so disconnect this too, as it'll prove to be a handicap when you stall in soft sand.

If you're planning to cover vast distances on metalled roads, it makes sense to fit a larger 140mm **radial tyre** that'll last, so eliminating the need to carry a spare. I like the **Bridgestone 140/80 R1769H TW152**.

Some are put off by the **water cooling**, but the fact that the KLR is water-cooled has not increased its weight compared with

their predecessors' bad reputation. In the UK the short-lived **KLR650** was available from 1987–90 and can still be bought in North America, 14 years later and largely unchanged.

Featuring a 23-litre tank, the 650 is a sound machine with light steering and a spacious feel. The long production run in North America has led to the bike becoming a firm dual sport touring favourite as the Yamaha Ténéré was in Europe. This adds up to lots of expertise, opinions and know-how. There are Travellers' Tales featuring KLR650s in all sorts of thrilling situations starting on p.209 and p.263.

The current KLR/KLX650 models are snazzy street bikes: light, fast and small tanked, they're not suited for an overland biker's needs.

Suzuki

Less common for overland use are Suzuki DR four-stroke singles. Since the original SP/DR400 of the early 1980s, capacities have gone up and down from

KLR 650 (continued)

similar machines. The KLR weighs 180kg wet, while an XT 600E weighs 175kg, but the KLR's carrying more fuel. In the event of a tumble, the loss of coolant would be a problem if water was scarce. However there are advantages. Because the KLR's operating temperature is more precisely controlled, tolerances are finer, which leads to a more efficient motor. There's a fan to help reduce coolant temperature when necessary. I don't think the cooling system needs modification, but a larger radiator could be fitted, as could an oil cooler.

All components of the electrical system have proven to be remarkably reliable. On the earliest model, the KLR 650 A1, the lower mounting point of the fairing subframe was solid, rather than rubber mounted as on later models. This caused the headlight bulb to fail regularly. To overcome this, cut a gasket from an old inner tube and install it onto the bulb so that the retaining spring is isolated. It's not easy to modify the subframe.

The rear shock will overheat and die if worked too hard. Wind it up to maximum and it'll last. The front forks are not performance items, but are capable enough. The simplest improvement to cope with extra weight is to add a 25-35 mm spacer between the top of the spring and the fork cap, and use a 15 W fork oil.

Carb removal is a horrible job, but if you replace the float-bowl retaining screws with Allen bolts it's then possible to remove the float-bowl without removing the carb.

Avoid abused or high mileage despatched examples. Age is not such an important factor, as most are old anyway. Be careful if you're buying second hand in Germany as they got the very gutless 27hp version as well at the usual 48hp version that was sold in rest of Europe.

The standard gearing using a 15-tooth front and 43-tooth rear sprocket is a good compromise that provides an indicated top speed of over 100mph/160kph with the ability to plough through soft sand and mud.

Other tips

Because of the shape of the fuel tank, the last few centilitres of petrol are unable to find their way into the carb. So by lying the bike over on its left-hand side, you'll be able recover the last few drops to ride a few extra kilometres before having to push.

It can be quite difficult to fit the standard foam air filter correctly so that no abrasive dust can find its way into the motor. Because of this I like to use a K&N air filter.

EBC pads work well in my experience and a stainless steel braided front brake line is a worthwhile improvement.

It's possible to relocate the fuse holder behind the left-hand side panel, so that it's accessible without having to remove both sidepanels and the seat.

I've found that WD 40 is very good for drive chains. It prevents the links seizing, and being a light lubricant it attracts less grit.

Rupert Humphrey

600cc rally clones to the odd and overweight DR750/800S and, at present, the excellent little DR-Z400S and DR650SE. Engines and components are basically similar to their contemporaries, that is: four-valve overhead cams and progressive rate single-shock rear suspension.

However, Suzukis do have a relatively poor record for reliability and more significantly, suffer from Suzuki's **inferior build quality**, which is why they've never caught on for adventuring. Anything after the DR650SE from 1996 is a safe bet though.

It may not have a useful fuel tank, but the suspension is very good. One notable point about 650 DRs is that like F650 BMs, they feature an **adjustable seat height**. Forty millimetres isn't much, but it's 40mm more than most other manufacturers provide. Despite their temptingly large tanks, DR750s and 800s are nearly as heavy as some twin cylinder machines, but undoubtedly not as smooth; if you plan on riding a Suzuki, stick with the more popular 600-650 models.

Y2K TÉNÉRÉS

Adventure bikers are now beginning to realise the true value of the simple, but strong air-cooled Ténérés for overlanding. Yamaha still produce the air-cooled engine in the form of the XT600E, a no frills trail bike produced alongside the flashier but stagnating 660 Ténéré.

With the difficulty sourcing a decent old Ténéré (France is a good place to start), people are now 'Ténérérising' a 600E which can be up to 25% cheaper than an equal-aged Ténéré, or maybe even new. These are the items you'll need to transform your XT into a Ténérésque overlander:

- Bigger tank
- Alloy wheels
- Oil cooler
- A bash plate
- Braided steel brake lines

You can add as many other mods as you like to improve your bike but the above five items will get the plain XT6 off to a good start. The next thing to consider would be better suspension and somewhere to go.

In the UK, David Lambeth Engineering knows XTs better than most and even **hires out ready-equipped overlanders** for up to two years (see his advert in the back).

XT5: they don't make 'em like they used to (thank goodness).

Ténéré with Metzeler 'Sahara' tyres – not much good in the Sahara.

Twin-lamp Ténérés are the ones to go for.

For those preferring a smaller and lighter machine, the **DR350** – in either the basic 'E' for enduro format or the 'S' for street mode (with bigger lights, indicators and an electric start), is a much better off-road tourer than Yamaha's lame XT350, although it has the same limitations of less torque at low revs and a light build.

Yamaha

Once Yamaha XTs were the most popular range of bikes used by European overlanders, particularly across Africa, specifically the 600cc **Ténéré** version (pronounced 'Tenner-ray', if you're wondering). North America never got the Ténéré, but they still have a similar-era KLR650.

The original early-1980s kick-start Ténérés were everything that home modified XT500's tried to be. **XT500**s are still much loved today, and even preferred by some riders who possess a certain amount of retro chic to overlook puny six volt electrics, suspension and brakes. Standard equipment on Ténérés included a 29 litre fuel tank, 'o'-ring chain, powerful brakes and lights, an oil cooler and motocross-derived suspension, all wrapped around a simple air-cooled, four stroke single cylinder engine based on the exceptionally economical XT550.

Subsequent models gradually moved away from this ideal, despite some detail

THE ROAD LESS TRAVELLED...

A quick trip around the bike shops in Nairobi, lets you know that Africa is a continent apart from Europe. In Africa, functional and affordable machines score high above fashion and technology. So while XT600s and even XR400s can be found, most showrooms display bikes based on 20-year-old Japanese designs. Remember the good old DT175, XL185 and TS185? Well, they're all still on sale in Africa.

A couple of years ago while forcing my XR600 through sand, I was passed by a Moroccan chappy on his moped, coping very easily with the soft, sandy conditions. So when I returned to Africa with my girlfriend for three glorious months touring, I took the opportunity to see if a small two-stroke could take the pace and weight of touring.

Two new Suzuki **TF125s** were bought for $3150 each, and over the following months we travelled 9000km, most along dirt roads, tracks, footpaths, mountain passes, or just plain following the sun. From sea level to 3000m (nearly 10,000') and temperatures up to 35 degrees, we'd give the little bikes a test ride they'd never forget.

The TFs are farm bikes with no concessions to style. Throwbacks from the 1970s, they're good, hard-wearing workhorses with a list of standard features that puts the average dual sporter to shame. Headlamp guard and rack, lever guards to protect your fingers, a large rack behind the single seat, mudflaps front and rear, bashplate complete with extended tubing to protect gear and brake levers, parking brake and even two side-stands, the list goes on...

The standard knobbly tyres were still usable after 9000km, and this is the first bike I've ever ridden where the front and rear wheels wear at the same rate. Neither the endless DID o-ring chain, nor either of the steel sprockets showed any signs of wear, which is probably thanks in part to the bike's diminutive 11bhp. While the air-cooled, reed-valve engine feels nippy in town or on winding tracks with enjoyable mid-range power, out on the open road it's just plain slow. With a cruising speed of about 75kph (45mph) it's better to sit back and enjoy the scenery as it rolls by at a leisurely pace, and providing there aren't any hills to tackle, the TF will cruise all day at that speed.

A 13-litre petrol tank and 1.2-litre oil tank allows approximately 300km (200 miles) between fuel stops, and twice that before the oil is in danger of running out. About every 1500km (1000 miles) the plug needs cleaning, while the gearbox oil will last 6000km. A CDI takes care of the ignition so apart from occasional checks of the air filter, there really isn't much to be done to keep it running. The head mechanic at Suzuki in Kenya recommends fitting new piston rings at 40,000km/25,000 miles! Try that on your KTM.

Riding the bike all day is no problem, as the wide single seat is comfortable for hours on end, and well positioned in relation to the footpegs and bars – even for a six-footer like me. With 10kg of luggage and the preload set at maximum, the suspension copes fine, but you can rest assured that long travel suspension and linkages were not developed because they look good. This bike feels like it's from a distant age (which it is) and the almost complete lack of rebound damping can launch the rear end on occasions. Sooner or later the suspension cries enough – so just slow down a little and take things at the African pace. Despite rudimentary suspension, the bikes got us through the deep sand of central Tanzania, the high mountain passes of Uganda, and the more deserted regions of Kenya, not to mention forcing our way through the deep mud of Rwanda.

Okay it isn't a bike to pretend you're a Dakar winner on, nor to race across the continent because you have an urgent rendezvous in Cape Town. But it's a machine that'll take you to all of those strange, out of the way places away from the main tourist routes. And if something does go wrong, there's a mechanic in every town with spares on the shelf. As the African equivalent of an Enfield Bullet, it's both easy to repair, simple to maintain but a whole lot more reliable.

Andy Gray

Originally published in *Trail Bike Magazine*.

improvements (notably in the positioning of the oil tank and cooler, and bigger air boxes). Electric starts, rear disc brakes and fairings had all been paid for by retrograde cost-cutting features elsewhere – a common story with all manufacturers. These later models appear to be less durable and less economical than the original but still make great machines. The ZE model comes with a 23-litre tank and twin headlamp fairing, and is these days the most popular of the surviving Ténérés for adventure biking.

Currently the 660cc version of the Ténéré introduced in 1990 with a five-valve water-cooled engine is still available. Yamaha's usual high attention to detail is still apparent in the vulnerable water pump protected by an extension of the bashplate and the reasonably well-protected radiator. The XT660 is, however, some 66lb/30kg heavier than the first XT600Z and even the man from UK Yamaha importers, Mitsui, advised one enquiring biker to stick with pre-'89 Ténérés for an overland trip. Meanwhile, the plain, air-cooled, small tanked XT600E is still available, though definitely getting long in the tooth, and coming last in comparison tests, while XLs and even Suzuki DRs continued to improve. Other bikes in the Yamaha range, notably the XT350 or 750 Super Ténéré twin are for various reasons inferior to an XT 600 or other alternatives from Suzuki or BMW for our kind of touring.

Bike preparation and maintenance

Thorough preparation of your machine is just about the best assurance you can give yourself of having a mechanically trouble-free trip. And because long range adventure tours will require modifications, the more time you spend riding your altered machine before you leave the better. Better still, if you're heading overseas with a new set up like metal boxes and racks, try to fit in a short **test run** beforehand to see how the bike handles and if everything works. The fewer surprises you encounter in the sometimes nerve-racking early days of the actual trip the better. In somewhere like Africa, Asia or Latin America, you'll have enough on your plate without finding that the suspension bottoms out on what sometimes pass for roads out there.

For a trip to any of the three continents listed above, you want to start getting your machine together at least a year before departure, double that if you're working full time or are planning to go RTW. Try and do as much of the work yourself, or under close guidance so that when something gives trouble, you have a clue how to fix it. Complex things like engine rebuilds or welding can be (or have to be) left to competent mechanics, but elementary repairs like changing tyres and oil, or cleaning an air filter are things you must be able to do before you go.

As a general rule, if you doubt whether any component will last the entire length of your planned trip, renew it and finish off the partially worn item on your return. This applies especially to things like tyres, chains and sprockets which wear faster on fully-laden bikes ridden off-road. Alternatively, on longer trans-continental trips, these are the sorts of spares to be taken along, or arrange to have sent ahead when they're unavailable.

If you're buying a bike especially for your trip, get it well in advance of your departure so that any teething problems can be sorted out. Lastly, bear in mind that modifications other than those recommended here may be necessary or useful on the machine of your choice.

ENGINE

It goes without saying that your engine should be in top condition before departure. If new or re-bored it should be run-in, recently serviced, oil-, air-, fuel-, and water-tight, with ignition tuning spot on and cylinder compression to within 15% of the manufacturer's recommended figure. Excessive oil consumption in older engines should be dealt with before departure unless your XT500 has been doing so happily for years. Even then, consider the extra strain on the motor when fully loaded on a hot day in soft sand.

If you do rebuild the engine, treating with a teflon or PTFE additives reputedly reaps huge benefits, and reduces wear when starting from cold.

Fuel quality

Most modern, single-cylinder engines have a relatively high compression ratio and can run terribly on the low octane fuel you'll often be forced to use in outback Africa or Central Asia. Air-cooled engines in particular should always run on the highest octane fuel available. Only if you're off on a very long trip of six months or more is it worth **lowering the compression** (most easily, by fitting an extra base gasket), with the consequent alteration in ignition timing (something easier said than done on bikes with electronic ignition). This will reduce the power produced, but enable your engine to run better on low octane fuel. BMW produce an alternative ignition rotor for their R1100GS (and possibly the newer 1150 too) which enables the electronically fuel-injected motor to run on low-grade fuel.

An alternative to messing about with compression is **octane booster**; a potent fuel additive used in racing. A litre of this stuff (available to off-road competition shops) is enough to last up to 1000 miles/660km on low grade fuel, assuming you put in 10cc per litre and do 50m/UKg (17kpl). Signs of an engine straining on poor fuel (known as detonation or 'pinking') are a light tapping from the cylinder head even under gentle throttle loads. What's happening is that the fuel charge is igniting before the piston has reached the top of its stroke. Low power, overheating and feeling that your engine is about to destroy itself are also evident, and this may well happen if you push a motor using bad fuel in power-sapping conditions.

Engine temperature

An **oil cooler** is not an essential addition to your air-cooled motor unless, broadly speaking, you expect to be riding through the summers within 30° north or south of the equator. If you do decide to fit a cooler, dry sump engines, that is those with separate oil tanks, lend themselves more easily to this modification, as any of the external oil lines can be cut and a cooler spliced in with extra hosing.

Fitting an oil cooler reduces the pressure and increases the capacity a little. However, having an oil cooler does not mean that important things like oil level, ignition timing, valve clearances and carburation can be neglected if the bike is to run well in hot and demanding conditions. Water-cooled engines don't need an oil cooler; if they're overheating then there's something wrong with the cooling system or you're revving the engine hard at low ground speeds with a tail wind. In this case stop and park into the wind to let the running motor cool down. Although most water temperature gauges are pessimistic you shouldn't get into the habit of running close to the red zone unless you can face having to change a blown cylinder head gasket with a smile.

Mount an oil cooler up high and in front of the engine; under the head lamp or cut into your fairing is an ideal place. Accessory manufacturers may make kits to fit your bike, but a good-sized unit from an old car like a Citroen 2CV can be picked up from a breaker's and made to fit; otherwise any cooler from a crashed street bike will do. Mounting on the front of the bike may mean chaffing hoses around the headstock. If you're not using expensive braided hose with proper fittings, tough 5mm-wall rubber hose with jubilee clips will do. Wind wire around the chaffable sections and then cover in duct tape.

If you move into a colder climatic zone wrap up the oil cooler with tape or bypass it altogether – something easier done on home made jobs. An over-cooled engine wears quickly and runs inefficiently.

Some German bike accessory outlets produce oil temperature gauges which screw in place of the cap/dipstick in the frame of air-cooled XTs and the like. Although not really essential, these gadgets are a handy way of gauging the *relative* temperature of your engine.

If using thicker 20-50 motor oil in your engine, as recommended for air-cooled bikes in hotter climates, take care to warm your engine up properly on freezing mornings, which you may experience at higher altitudes. In desert areas it's common to experience a 30°C temperature variation between dawn and mid-afternoon.

Then again, when coming to a stop on a very hot day, keep your air- or water-cooled engine running for a while, or do not turn it off at all if it's just a quick stop. When the bike stops moving, the lack of airflow over the motor or through the radiator causes the temperature to rise dramatically. Turning the engine off at this point causes the temperature to rise even more. By keeping the engine running during brief stops on hot days the oil is kept pumping around, cooling the engine.

At 35°C+ fuel evaporated in the filter and the engine died. A cardboard heatshield duct taped between the fuel line and the barrel fixed the problem (see p.226).

Fuel filters

Whatever time of year you expect to be riding, it's a good idea to fit an in-line fuel filter into the fuel line(s) of your bike. The inexpensive translucent, crinkled-paper element type (right) work better than fine gauze items, which most bikes have inside the tank as part of the fuel tap assembly. Make sure you fit it in the right direction of flow – there should be an arrow moulded into the filter body. These filters can be easily cleaned by simply flushing in a reverse direction with fuel from the tank. In desert areas, dust is always present in the air and even in the fuel, and in Iran or Pakistan it's common for roadside fuel to be dished out from a drum using an old tin. The fact that they pour it through an old rag draped over the funnel is little compensation.

A gallon of fresh goat's cream keeps this XT500 running smoothly. © Trui Hanoulle

Clutch

If your bike has more than 20,000 hard miles (32,000km) on the clock or is heading off on a long trip, consider replacing the clutch plates before departure. In soft sand or mud on a hot day, it will be working hard and if it overheats and begins slipping, it may never recover. It is possible to squeeze a little more life out of a slipping wet clutch (as found on most singles but not on BMWs) by boiling the plates in detergent or pre-loading the springs with washers, but neither of these bodges can be expected to last long in the heat of a desert.

Most air filters prefer to stay at home on days like this. © Trui Hanoulle

Air filter

Air filters will require possibly daily cleaning during high winds, sandstorms or if travelling in a dusty convoy. The **reusable multi-layered oiled-foam types** such as those by Twin-Air, Multi Air or Uni Filter are best. Carry a ready oiled spare in a plastic bag that can be slipped in as necessary while the other gets cleaned when you get a chance. Make sure that the airbox lid seals correctly and that the rubber hoses on either side of the carburettor are in good condition and done up tightly. **Greasing** all surfaces inside the airbox is messy but catches more airborne particles and keeps the air filter cleaner for longer; a stocking over the filter is another way of keeping it clean. If you're *pushing* your bike through deep water put a plastic bag around the filter and refit it to keep water out of the engine.

A freshly-oiled XR foam filter. Some bikes' air boxes work better than others.

This exposed paper air filter element on a BMW may be easy to get to but is not such a hot set up for a long tour.

On a recent desert tour I found the two KTMs and a CCM had wide open-air intakes that totally caked the filters in sand in one day. The less racy Yamaha Belgarda had no such problems (and returned 50% better middle fuel economy). At the cost of some power, it may be worth closing up or pre-filtering the air intake on bikes like these, as well as resisting roosting in deep sand.

To wash a re-usable foam filter rinse it out in petrol a few times until the fuel drains away cleanly, let it dry on the handlebar and then soak it with engine oil. A good way of doing this if you don't have latex surgical gloves and don't want to oil your hands, is to put the cleaned filter in a plastic bag, pour in some oil and squidge it around. Then squeeze out the excess, let the filter oil dry if you're using it (see below), and reinstall.

Note that some foam filters swell up on contact with petrol (diesel will do) and that engine oil is not the ideal air filter solution as it tends to seep to the bottom of a filter leaving parts unprotected. Proper **foam filter oil** available in tins or aerosols is designed to semi dry into a tacky, dust-catching compound that does not seep. It's far more effective in the long run and so adds up to less maintenance, but is another thing to carry.

CHAIN AND SPROCKETS

Enclosed from the elements, **shaft drives** are virtually maintenance free. In this respect they're ideal for overland bikes, though they're usually fitted to heavier machines which can bring about their own problems on rough terrain.

However, most trail bikes are fitted with more efficient (when correctly oiled and tensioned) roller chains and sprockets. Such an exposed system is obviously vulnerable, and lubricating an ordinary chain would immediately attract grit and accelerate the wear of the chain and sprockets. Automatic chain oilers (like the well known Scott unit) are only suitable for long road rides; in sand they'll merely guarantee an encrusted chain and although **enclosed chain cases** are a better idea, as far as I know only MZ ever managed to make a sufficiently robust item. After market versions are only up to road riding; on dirt roads they eventually fall apart and make wheel changes horribly messy.

Avoid all standard or so-called 'self lubricating' chains – the latter are not to be confused with sealed 'o'-ring versions described below.

Sealed chains

By far the best solution to chain and sprocket wear is to fit a **top quality sealed 'o'-ring chain**, such as those manufactured by DID, Izumi or Regina. These types of chains have a quantity of grease between the rollers and pins, sealed in with tiny rubber rings between the rollers and side plates. If you can't visualise what on earth this means, don't worry; just recognise that good sealed chains are worth their weight in gold. Only when those rubber seals finally begin to wear out after many thousands of miles (even in desert conditions) will the chain begin to wear out like an ordinary chain, stretching and hooking the sprockets as it goes. Oiling with a little engine oil, when appropriate, is only necessary on the sprocket-to-roller surface and not between the plates as on standard chains. Chain aerosol sprays are not needed. A DID chain fitted to a trans-Saharan Ténéré lasted me over 10,000miles/16,000km, with only half a-dozen small adjustments in all that time. Indeed DID's 'x'-ring chain (an 'x'-ring is effectively two 'o'-rings side by side) is guaranteed for 12,000 miles, providing it's matched with good quality sprockets.

Sprockets

Good quality, hardened steel sprockets last much longer than lighter alloy versions which are popular on flashy motocross bikes. Beware of buying cheaper brand 'chain and sprocket kits' from some mail order suppliers who sell obscure makes of chains and inferior steel sprockets. Original equipment (OE) sprockets, i.e., those made by Honda, Yamaha, etc, are as good as any, especially when matched with a heavy duty sealed chain. Both items are worth the

An Acme 'o'-ring chain ruined this sprocket in just 4000 desert miles – stick to the well-known brands.

extra expense for a longer service life. High sprocket wear and loosening sprocket retaining bolts have cropped up with some recent KTMs.

Chain tension

Your chain should be adjusted to provide **40mm of slack**, measured midway along the chain, *fully loaded and with your weight on the bike*. On most trail bikes with long travel suspension, this will give an impression of an overly slack chain when the machine is unloaded and at rest, but this slack will be taken up once the suspension is compressed to the correct level when the bike is fully laden and on the move.

FUEL TANKS

One of the best features of 'rally replica' bikes like KTM Adventure-Rs are their large fuel tanks. On a economical machine like a Yamaha Ténéré, a 30-litre tank is enough to comfortably cover 400 miles/650km. Most bikes will, however, require a bigger tank or at least 10 litres to be carried in reserve. For remote stages across the Sahara for example, all bikes will require either a double-sized fuel tank or a bulky 20-litre jerrican, and in some cases even this will barely be enough.

Big plastic tanks

Although a major expense, an enlarged tank holding up to 40 litres is preferable to taking up valuable space with jerricans. A big tank places the heavy weight of fuel in front of and below the rider, close to the machine's centre of gravity. In this position it has a less pronounced effect on the balance of the bike, though you'll certainly feel the difference when you first try and ride off with a full tank of fuel.

Acerbis makes a number of large plastic tanks to fit many of today's popular dual sporters, with IMS and Clarke taking up the slack in the US and Australia. Most come in moderate capacities of around 20 to 25 litres, but a couple of examples are much bigger; the 45-litre tank for GS BMWs costs an incredible £500 in the UK, but can be made to fit some other bikes. Where there's a will...

Despite their expense for certain models, plastic tanks combine the best in **strength, lightness and durability**, as well as providing resistance to vibration damage and, if necessary, they can also be easily repaired with glue.

Building your own tank

A well-constructed and sturdily-supported tank with internal baffles can be built to hold up to 45 litres, giving a range of up to 500 miles/800km. When tanks get this big, strong and well-thought out **mounting points** are vital.

Aluminium is popular in custom tank manufacture only because it's soft and easy to fabricate into complex shapes that make the most of a bike's capacity needs. Its drawback is that it copes badly with vibration, from both the engine and the terrain, and the great weight of a full tank doesn't help here. Fractures can be repaired with glue or braised with blowtorch alloy welding rods; alloy tank users should carry these as a matter of course as high-temperature alloy welding facilities are rare in the bush. If you end up using an alloy tank, be sure that it's well supported underneath with heavy-duty mounting plates locating it securely in place and foam pipe lagging around the frame's top tube for additional support.

An inexpensive alternative to increasing your fuel capacity is to cram on a big steel tank from any old bike and bashing it in the right places. A fiddlier option is to **enlarge the standard steel item** by welding on additional sections, or even welding another tank on top of the cut down original. This latter method sounds like a real bodge but has the advantage of keeping the original mounting points, although **extra or strengthened mounts** should be considered and any welding will, of course, have to be fuel tight or sealed with resin.

A less permanent alternative that still keeps the extra weight in the right place is to mount a pair of 10-litre **jerricans** on frame-mounted racks, one each side of the tank, making sure there's enough clearance for your knees and the arc of the handlebars. This method may not do much for the bike's streamlining, but does have the useful advantage of protecting your lower legs in the event of a crash and when not needed the cans can be sold and streamlining restored.

Jerricans are tougher than you think, but the tank rack you build for them should be strong enough to withstand occasional spills and be easily repairable. There's more on jerricans on p.64.

A 40-plus litre tank on a KLR.

Wheels

Modern dual sport machines are built with lightly-spoked alloy wheels to reduce unsprung weight and improve road performance. Some rims are not up to the heavy beating they'll encounter over potholed tarmac and corrugated tracks. Back wheels will be carrying maximum loads and are especially prone to damage.

Unless you're competent at rebuilding wheels and tensioning spokes correctly, you can save yourself a lot of bother by fitting **heavy duty spokes** or, better still, uprate your wheels altogether with quality rims (Akront, Excel or DID are as good as they get), and getting the work done by an accredited wheel builder. This is also a consideration which applies to **cast wheels** on heavy road tourers which will eventually dent and crack unless you keep to

A FEW MORE TIPS

● **Trail bike seats** are not only narrow, they're often made of foam that feels nice and cushy in the showroom but is agony to sit on after a hundred miles. Older bikes too, will have sagged-out foam. Without getting the whole thing re-upholstered, here's an easy way of firming them up. Remove the vinyl cover carefully (it's usually stapled on to the plastic seat base), disclosing the bit where you sit. Then cut out as big a block of foam as you can without severing the original foam. Get an offcut of firmer foam from an upholsterer and fit it into the hole. You might also want to cut down the seat height while you're at it. Then re-staple the vinyl cover and enjoy your new 'full-day' saddle.

Or, as is popular in Australia and Germany, cover your seat in a soft **sheepskin**: either properly fitted, or slung over like a rug. If you're heading for Tunisia you can pick up a nice fluffy one for 15 dinars.

● **Weld a wider foot** onto the end of your side stand. A three-inch square piece of steel will support your bike on soft ground.

● If you're not using **hand and lever protectors** on your handlebars – still oddly unpopular on overland bikes – keep your lever mounts a little loose on the bars. This way they turn rather than snap the lever when you fall off.

● A **small perspex screen** of just a few inches in height bolted to your bike's plastic headlight cowling weighs virtually nothing, keeps the wind off you and, unlike a fairing, doesn't get in the way of visibility on the dirt.

First make a template from cardboard or bendy plastic, tape it in place and take the bike for a blast. Resist the temptation to cut yourself a big screen which has a greater chance of cracking and remember that your 3–5mm thick perspex version should have a lip on its upper edge to hopefully throw the air up and over your head.

Experiment with different shapes and heights now so your final version works. Once you've got it right, jig saw your perspex to match, incorporating plenty of overlap on the lower edge to give the new screen rigidity. Now comes the tricky part: softening the perspex over a naked flame to give it the smooth curves which provide rigidity and limit turbulence. Take your time, do it slowly and wear gloves. Once you've got the right vertical curvature, add that gentle top lip which has the effect of adding several inches to the screen's height. Next smooth off the sawn edges with a file and offer the screen up to the cowling, making any last-minute bends before carefully drilling two crack-free mounting holes.

● A good way of keeping an eye on your **throttle's position**, and thereby your general fuel consumption, is to draw a mark on the throttle housing along with an adjacent mark on the grip. Make one with the throttle closed and another when fully open.

Especially on smaller-engined bikes, riding into a head wind or up a long incline, you'll find yourself inadvertently winding the throttle right open in an attempt to keep moving. It doesn't make you go any faster but it sure wastes fuel. Keeping an eye on the throttle markers will remind you to use minimal settings which can be vital on the longer stages of your trip.

Some big singles have two carbs, a slide unit for low throttle openings and a CV version which cuts in at bigger throttle openings. Again by marking the grip at the point where the second carb cuts in – you can just feel it if you open the throttle slowly – you can keep the bike running on just one carb.

On an early Yamaha Ténéré using this system I was able to get as much as 80mpg or an amazing 480 miles/700km from a single tank and a helpful tail wind.

the smooth roads they were built for. The benefit of having this work done is the difference between possibly having to check and tension your standard wheels every evening, or ignoring the strengthened items for the entire trip. As with sealed chains, this is one modification worth carrying out if you have some tough off-roading lined up. To a certain extent, high tyre pressure and chunky off-road tyres protect rims from damage, so always ride with the highest pressure for the terrain concerned. They only really need letting down in mud and sand, but when you do it makes a huge difference.

In case you're wondering, it's not worth changing a trail bike's standard 21" front wheel for a 19- or 18-inch item for the sake of tube interchangeability, unless you're planning a long trip. What you get is heavy steering and mixed-up steering geometry which are detrimental to off-road riding control. Exempting bikes with gearbox-driven speedos, the crucial odometer reading will also become inaccurate.

TYRES

Tyre choice can be difficult for a long journey which may include thousands of miles on all sorts of surfaces. Basically, it boils down to **long wear but poor dirt grip** from street or dual purpose/trail tyres, or **faster wear but better grip** in the dirt from competition-oriented knobbly tyres. And it's as well to remember the Golden Rule: whatever works for someone in one situation, that's the *best* tyre, even if *you* can't get to the end of the street on it without falling over or the tyre wearing out. In the end, it depends on your route, your riding style, your bike's power and weight, and your priorities.

Dual sport or knobbly tyres may look more rugged but if you envisage doing a long road trip, or a route where picking up replacements may be difficult, you may as well run **street tyres** which will last longest, give much better grip on wet tarmac as well as a smoother ride.

Tyre choice is subjective but below are some general outlines to steer you in the right direction. Whichever tyre you choose, make sure it has at least **four plies**; anything less is designed for light unsprung weight and will not be resistant to punctures.

Trail or dual purpose tyres

These can be neither here nor there in terms of grip, giving off road looks with compromised wet street performance, but an important consideration is that they will still last much longer than a full-on knobbly. Michelin T66, Avon Gripsters, Bridgestone Trail Wings and Dunlop Trailmax have all been commended for their high mileages, if not foot-out grip on the dirt.

It's when you do put some dirt into the equation, be it dirt tracks, mud or sand, that things change. Certainly on dry gravel tracks, a street or conventional trail tyre will manage OK with a bit of slithering about and a careful throttle, but if grip and off-road control are important considerations then **Pirelli's MT21** works and lasts well on both surfaces due to a combination of rounded profile, low knobs and hard rubber.

A rear 19" MT21 transformed the front-end handling of this F650 on the dirt – at the cost of a 'riding-on-marbles' feel on the tarmac.

Similar tyres include Michelin Bajas and T63s, Metzeler Karoos or Dunlop 905/903s, but none of these will handle the power of machines like Triumph Tigers, Africa Twins or BMW twins, where something like Michelin T66s or (better still) **Continental's Twinduro TKC80**s will give you the edge.

Knobbly tyres

Off-road competition tyres are made for a wide variety of track types. Knobbly or dirt-biased dual sport tyres like MT21s will make a huge difference to the control and enjoyment of your machine on the dirt. Instead of nearly falling off every few metres, you'll ride the ranges with security and a smile on your face. All you have to remember is to take it easy on the tarmac, brake and corner moderately and ride *very* gently in the wet.

Choose a tyre designated for hard ground and rocks, not sand or mud. Models with a deeper tread and soft compound will soon disintegrate when loaded up for overland conditions.

Knobbly tyres are designed to take a hammering off-road (admittedly on lighter motocross bikes) and are generally sturdier than trail tyres. A front knobbly wears much less quickly than a rear, and so it's possible to get away with a front knobbly and benefit from the better steering and braking off-road – but worse on tarmac. A rear trail tyre may slide around a bit but at least the front will stay put. If your trip is short, say under 2000 miles/3000km, and mostly on dirt, hard-wearing knobbly tyres like Metzeler Multicross, Michelin H12 or Pirelli MT81 will be great off-road as long as you take it easy on wet tarmac.

Michelin 'Desert' tyres

Names like 'Sahara' and 'Enduro' are merely marketing tags, but Michelin's 'Desert' tyre is the real thing, designed for rim-bashing desert use and once used by most of the two-wheel contingent of the Dakar Rally. Riding on Michelin Deserts with heavy-duty inner tubes (again, 'Desert' tubes are available) and strong wheels is one of the best modifications you can make to your bike if you intend covering a high off-road mileage heavily loaded.

These tyres were originally designed for heavy and powerful desert racers which, fuelled-up, weigh more and travel faster than your overlander. Despite their notorious stiffness they can be fitted easily, provided you use good tyre levers, some lubricant and the right technique (see following pages). This may be the last time you will have to use your levers until the tyre wears out thousands of miles later; punctures with Michelin Desert tyres are rare.

Robust and hard wearing Michelin Deserts are now widely available and relatively well priced.

Deserts can (and sometimes have to) be run **virtually empty of air** to allow the spreading necessary for optimum traction in soft sand, mud and snow. I found on my lightly loaded F650 that I couldn't get enough spreading from the rear Desert to give me satisfactory traction in very soft sand. The revvy engine certainly didn't help, but I found myself struggling where a less rigid tyre would have spread out to create a larger surface area and so better traction.

RTW TYRES ~ AN EXPERT SPEAKS OUT

Having gone RTW, I've settled on Metzeler ME88 on the rear of my R80G/S, and usually BS Trail Wing 101 on the front. The pair usually wear equally. We managed Africa on one set, and South America on another. True DS/Enduro tyres in my opinion aren't all that necessary on a fully loaded tourer, especially an R80G/S two-up!

It's rare to need more traction, given our weight and low-down power, and the need NOT to crash in the middle of nowhere makes you considerably more careful. We never had a problem with traction, and appreciated the long life of the tyres.

Furthermore, a heavy payload can put a DS tyre over its load limit, even at max pressure. With the Metzeler, I've something like a 900 lb/410kg load limit at 49psi (3.4 bar). I find that running at 49psi, even at high speeds at 50°C keeps my max pressure under 60 psi (4.1 bar), an acceptable cold/hot pressure range. Running at around 38-40 psi bumps the hot pressure sky high due to the added flex of the tyre body. Note that the 'perfect' cold/hot range is around 7psi/0.5 bar.

I've been asked many times about where and how to stash/buy new tyres in the middle of Africa or Thailand or South America – and it's always a problem, usually the local tyres are too small or of poor quality, and shipping and organising pickup can be an expensive hassle.

I think the best plan is to use tyres that will get you from Civilised Point A to Civilised Point B, with fresh tyres fitted at each point.

As for the tubeless tyre debate, I have also had a number of flats in my 35 years riding, all on tube type. After the last one – two-up, fully loaded, 70mph, 8000 feet in the Andes, exiting a turn with a 2000 foot drop about 10 feet to the outside of my lane, and no guard rail – I'm going full tubeless! A three inch screw instantly deflated the tyre, sending us into a not-to-be repeated series of lock to lock gyrations ending with the tyre completely peeled off the rim and the screw going right through the tyre and out again via the sidewall.

Just as soon as I stop shaking I'm installing an R100GS swingarm and wheel, mostly so I can have a tubeless tyre.

Grant Johnson

Grant runs ⌨ www.HorizonsUnlimited.com *'The Motorcycle Travellers Website'*

On any tyre when running at **extreme low pressures** (0.5 bar or 7psi), speeds should be kept down to avoid overheating which will accelerate wear and may induce punctures. See also 'Tyre Creep' opposite.

Tubeless tyres

The trend for tubeless tyres on dual trail bikes started with Honda XLMs in the mid-eighties and continues with big bore trail bikes. The advantage of tubeless tyres is that they run cooler and so last much longer. Furthermore, they don't blow out suddenly like a tubed tyre can do, but deflate relatively slowly so giving you more chance to control the machine and bring it to a standstill.

Problems can arise when **making your own roadside repairs**. Assuming the tyre has not come off the rim, the normal method (outlawed in some countries) is to plug and glue the hole from the outside with a ramming tool fitted with a rubber bung covered in rubber solution; unbelievably easy compared to messing around with tubes and levers, and reliable even off-road.

The problem with tubeless tyres is they sit behind a lip on the rim, and if the tyre comes out of this groove or is destroyed you'll need some extreme leverage to get them off the rim and plenty of technique to fit them again. In other words it's not something you can do by the roadside without practice.

Tubeless tyres coming off the rim is rare but this will always be in the back of your mind if you have a puncture: can you repair the tyre by the side of the road, even with an inner tube fitted as a short term measure?

Because rims designed for tubeless tyres make them so hard to remove by hand, fitting inner tubes makes things worse as you *must* remove the tyre to repair it – avoid tubes on tubeless rims and stick to the external plug kits if you expect to have to make your own roadside repairs. If you do decide to run tubes on a rim designed for tubeless tyres, you'll need to grind away the rounded lip which keeps the bead of the tyre on the rim, to enable conventional roadside repairs with tyre levers.

Tyre creep

Besides causing a tyre to overheat, riding at the very low pressures necessary for traction in deep sand can cause the 'underpressurised' tyre to get pulled around the rim, especially on the rear wheel of torquey engines. It's not a problem with tubeless tyres of course (which is one reason why they're catching on with 4WDs in the Sahara) but the inner tube will be dragged along with the tyre turning while the valve stays where it is and may eventually get ripped out, destroying the tube.

Keep an eye on your valves. If they begin to 'tilt over' it means your security bolt isn't doing what it should.

Therefore, for low-pressure use, it's essential to have **security bolts** (also known as rim locks) fitted to both rims, but definitely the rear, to limit excessive tyre creep. Security bolts clamp the bead of the tyre to the rim and, if not already fitted, require a hole to be drilled into the rim: an easy job. A slightly larger than necessary hole makes tyre fitting easier.

Keep an eye on your valves. If they begin to 'tilt over' it means that your security bolt may need tightening or your tyre repositioning, as creep can occur even with rim locks. Always keep the nut at the base of your valve loose, or do not

Self tapping screws drilled through the rim and just biting on the tyre bead are an alternative to security bolts.

use it at all. They're only useful as an aid to refitting tyres.

An alternative to security bolts which don't always work are **self tapping screws** drilled into the rim so they just bite into the tyre bead and limit slippage. Two each side of the rim set at 90° intervals should keep the tyre in place.

Punctures

Punctures are the most common breakdown you'll experience on your trip and something you must be confident you can fix yourself before you leave. The advent of 'lifestyle motorcyclists' has led to many riders taking their wheels to the shop to get them changed or fixed, but in my day we all knew how to do this tedious repair ourselves (to a greater or lesser extent).

Practice at home, so that when the inevitable event occurs you can be sure that the operation will be accomplished smoothly. Any emergency repair

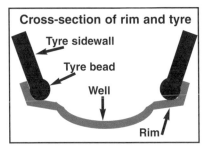

Cross-section of rim and tyre

Tyre sidewall

Tyre bead

Well

Rim

By getting one half of the tyre bead in the well, you gain the necessary slack to lever the opposite side of the tyre over the rim.

undertaken in a remote location can be a little unnerving; the better prepared you are to deal with these surprises the less likely you are to make absent-minded mistakes, like forgetting to tighten a wheel nut or leaving your tools by the roadside.

Puncture repair outfit

Assemble most of the items pictured below and fit what will fit into a small lunch box. As for spare tubes, depending on your tyres' sturdiness and the terrain, carry **up to two spare inner tubes per wheel** – especially if you intend riding through areas like the sub-Saharan Sahel where thorn punctures are common.

Compressed CO_2 cartridges save pumping but eventually you're going to run out so if you're averse to pumping (generally ten strokes from a big mountain bike pump equals one psi) consider the type of **mini electric compressor** you buy in car accessory shops. They're designed to plug into the car's cigarette lighter socket; fit one of these (they're also useful for running a GPS as well as other gadgets) or cut off the plug and fit a pair of crocodile clips to attach to your battery terminals.

From the top left: 12-volt compressor (this one's a bit too bulky for a bike), talc in a film canister, tyre levers, roller/grating tool, valve removing tool, glue, valve cores and caps, patches, compressed CO_2 cartridge, digital pressure gauge, spare pressure gauge, tubeless tyre plugs and valve, tubeless plugging tool and glue.

Tyre levers

Like all tools, using a well-designed and quality item makes the job at hand easier. Taking into account the variables of personal preference, in my experience a good tyre lever is a blade just 20mm wide, up to 7mm thick, and 300mm long. The crude wide, flat-ended types or bars with flattened spoon ends are too wide and make lifting the bead harder which can lead to pinching a tube – one of the most depressing experiences in motorcycledom.

The ideal blade has a slender curved lip at each end which readily hooks under the bead of a tyre to lift it, but without pushing in too far and pressing against the tube. Although I've never seen them, Kawasaki levers are said to be good, and I still use a great little BMW lever from a long gone R100. In the UK, *Bike Mart* in Bristol can get hold of the gold anodised Italian levers used in the photos over the page. In Germany, *Heyco's* Chrome-Vanadium levers listed in the Därrs catalogue (#021 503) cost only £5/$8 each, and also look to be ideally formed for easy tyre mounting. Whatever lever you use, take care in the last stages of tyre mounting (photo 18): avoid brute force and practise the right technique before you go.

Tools needed
• Wheel nut and security bolt spanner
• Two good tyre levers
• Jacking prop if no centre stand

Basic puncture kit
• Patches – go for the German *REMA Tip-Top* brand
• Tube of rubber solution (plus a spare as they often split)
• Sandpaper or grater
• Talc
• Spare valve caps, valve cores
• Valve core removing tool
• Tyre pressure gauge
• Liquid soap bottle
• Mountain bike pump

Tyre pressures

Depending on the load capacity of the tyre and weight carried, **15psi/1 bar** is the optimum all round pressure for a trail bike off-road, 10psi for soft sand, 20 psi or more on rocks. On a heavier tourer it's best to leave them as they are and just take it easy. Avoid labour saving aerosols which are messy, unreliable and usually explode in your panniers anyway. Although I've never used one, some **puncture-sealing fluids** such as *Slime* are said to do an amazing job of plugging thorn pricks. But the best way to repair a puncture is to fit a new tube without pinching it, though with some tyre and rim combinations this is easier said than done. Protect your pump from dust and loss; it could be vital.

If, for whatever reason, you can't repair a puncture, try stuffing the tyre with clothes or anything else that comes to hand to vaguely regain its profile. If you do a good job, you can carry on almost without noticing, but if the tyre is damaged or starts to disintegrate you're better off dumping it and carrying on on the rim.

1. First of all find a flat place to work away from the road. If you have no centre stand, jack up bike with a jerrican or U-lock, or lay it on its side (taking the usual precautions with fluids).

2. Loosen the wheel nut (noting chain cam position), and push it forward. Unhook chain and take out axle retaining pins if present. Withdraw the wheel allowing brake to drop away. Collect all loose parts carefully.

3. Remove the valve cap and valve base nut and loosen the security bolt or rim screws if present. Unscrew the valve core, releasing any remaining air and push the valve and security bolt into the tyre as far as they'll go.

4. Lay the wheel down and stand on tyre, jumping up and down if necessary to push the bead of the tyre off the rim. Check again that security bolt is pushed into the tyre so it's not getting in the way.

5. Kick the bead over security bolt into rim with the front of your heel. Then, standing on the tyre to keep the bead off the rim, push in the first lever to hook under the tyre's bead.

6. Getting the second lever in is hard until you release the first lever a little, hook the second lever under the bead, and then pull them both up in close succession.

7. Keep working round the tyre, checking that the bead is in the well until one half of the tyre is outside the rim. Now stand the tyre up, push the valve into the tyre, stick your other hand in and drag the tube out.

8. Lay the tube to one side and examine the outer tyre. If you can't find the cause of the puncture, pass your fingers over the inner surface to feel for any thorns or whatever. Taking the tyre right off may be necessary.

9. Refit the valve and inflate the tube to find the hole. If you can't hear the hiss of escaping air, pass the tube over wet lips or eyes where the pinprick will be felt as a cold jet of air. Or, if available, submerge the tube into a basin of water or a pool and look for bubbles.

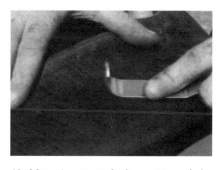

10. Memorise or mark the position of the hole(s), release the air again and place the tube on a firm surface to roughen the area around the hole with sandpaper or a grater. The roughened rubber should have an scratched, matt appearance.

11. Wipe away the rubber dust with a petrol rag and apply a thin film of rubber solution over a broad area. Wait a minute until it's dry to the touch (test away from the contact area).

12. Choose an appropriately-sized patch. On most patches it is the **foil** side that is stuck to the tube. Press the patch down firmly, using a knife handle or roller to bond the surfaces together and eliminate air bubbles.

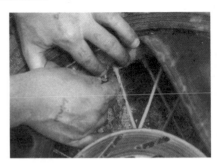

13. Sprinkle some talc over any exposed glue (ash will do) and if the tyre was wet, put some inside the tyre to reduce the chance of the tube snagging or twisting.

14. Stand the wheel up and push the tube into the tyre starting by pushing the valve through the hole in the rim. This can be tricky with stiff tyres – lever up the other side of the tyre to make room for your fingers to align the valve.

15. Now loosely attach the valve nut so it doesn't slip out during remounting. Make sure the valve is perpendicular to the rim by tugging the tube around. Refit the valve core and *partially* inflate the tube; too much will risk pinching the tube.

16. Standing on the tyre, position two levers at 10 and 2 o'clock and start levering them towards 12 o'clock. At 6 o'clock check the bead is in the well and as you move each lever on, stand on the tyre to stop it working its way out.

18. Check again that the valve is at right angles, if not try and drag the tube and tyre around the rim to line it up. Now re-inflate and watch the bead remount the rim. If it doesn't, keep inflating and deflating while pouring in soap and levering if necessary...

19. ... but don't worry if it doesn't remount the rim. Once ridden on it'll work its way on. Check the pressure and that it's not going down. If it is go back to #5. Otherwise, tighten the security bolt and fit the valve cap.

17. Wetting this last part of the rim with watery soap can help. Take great care on the last moves not to push the lever in too deep and possibly pinch the tube. Gently lever the last 6-8" over with a satisfying 'pop'.

21. Reverse steps 1 and 2. Make sure the chain is correctly tensioned, the axle retaining pins are back in and the axle is tight. Re-store tools, wash hands (soap with sand works) and re-attach baggage. Check the tyre pressure one more time and off you go.

Load carrying

The noted soul historian, James Brown, pointed out several years ago that: '*Man made the car, to take him onto the road. Man made the traaaaaiiinnn, to carry the heavy load*'. What he never got a chance to add was that man made the motorcycle to have fun on. There's a guy pictured on p.76 of the *Rider Wearhouse* catalogue and I'm still not sure if it's a joke. Compare it with the two KTMs (© Noah Maltz) above. Not making your bike look like a war refugee's handcart requires discipline and might be summed up as The Psychology of Overloading. The more stuff you have the safer and more independent you'll be, right? That's what you may think, but the more you travel the less you find you need. You can either take my word for it now or learn from experience.

BAGGAGE SYSTEMS
Usually it's a choice between **soft fabric panniers** or **hard metal containers** along with some kind of rack. Convenience of access, ease of removal, robustness and security are important considerations. Ideally, no item wants to be buried so as to discourage its use, nor a bag criss-crossed with fiddly straps when one or two thoughtfully arranged attachments will do the job. For example, if your treasured copy of the *AMH* is at the bottom of your aluminium box, you may not bother checking out some vital information, resulting in subsequent gnashing of teeth. Everything should be close at hand, and this is where large aluminium boxes with top lids lose out. Also remember that all baggage should offer enough room or be easily demountable so as not to impede wheel changes. One good thing about metal boxes, and probably the reason why many people fit them, is their security.

SOFT LUGGAGE – PROS AND CONS

Pro	Con
● Light	● Can tear, burn, stretch, melt or fall off
● Cheap to buy or make	● Not theft-, dust- or waterproof
● Can be used without a rack	
● Immune to vibration damage	

HARD LUGGAGE – PROS AND CONS

Pro	Con
● Capacious	● Heavy and expensive
● Secure	● Needs a strong rack
● Strong	● Can get in the way and be dangerous in crashes
● Neat	● Awkward access

The baggage on this KLR is neither low nor central. It's hard to imagine a worse set-up.

When it comes to strapping things on the outside of your containers or on to your bike, don't rely solely on elasticated bungees – back them up with **adjustable straps** (available in various lengths from outdoor shops) to help secure the gear on your bike. And make sure you carry lots of spares; they're easily lost, damaged or pilfered and are always useful.

Whichever way you decide to carry your gear, it's important to distribute heavy weights **low and as centrally as possible**. Doing this will result in real benefits in the balance and control of your machine, especially off road. Light things like clothes, sleeping bags or empty containers can go on the back of the seat or in front of the head lamp. If you're carrying extra fuel in jerricans, top up the tank regularly to keep the weight in that ideal location.

And don't worry about getting all this right on the day you leave. While a test run will iron out a lot of possible problems, a couple of weeks on the road will have your baggage and its contents ideally arranged for convenience and security.

Hard or soft luggage?

The Theory of Relative Space states that no matter how large your luggage, it will be filled. Keep it small and you'll take little; use big containers and you'll fill them will unnecessary stuff and overload your bike. For a short trip (less than four weeks) or one where you don't expect to encounter bad weather or spend much time in cities (where most thefts occur), soft luggage will be adequate. On a longer trip or simply if you prefer it, hard luggage answers most needs while adding weight to the bike as well as time and expense to fit.

Hard luggage

At first thought hard luggage might sound like a good idea, being secure, strong and neat, but this system needs time to work out properly and must have a **strong rack** to support it. Most racks bought over the counter don't fall into this category but in Germany, Därrs, Bernd Tesch and Touratech all sell aluminium boxes from 32- to Tesch's own massive 51-litre-capacity boxes weighing up to 3kg each at a gauge of 1.5mm. The Därrs boxes (right) are cheaper but items like hinges, handles and locks are extra.

Därrs 'Bike Boxes' come in capacities from 31 to 40 litres and cost 150-170 DM. Quick release brackets are available but for the dirt a solid fixture to the rack will be better.

In the USA, Al Jesse makes a tough metal box system, available from *Rider Wearhouse*, but it costs nearly $1000! The good thing about the best of these models is that they avoid the nasty sharp corners of homemade or simply manufactured items. Curves add to the cost but you'll welcome those round corners when you're sliding down a hill with your bike cartwheeling behind you.

A heavily-loaded Ténéré on the Fadnoun plateau in Algeria.

Touratech have sort of got round big box accessibility limitations by producing neat, **box-shaped holdalls** which slip inside their 35- and 41-litre boxes. It's an idea worth imitating if you're fabricating your own alloy cases, as it encourages you to make a strong, permanent fixing to the rack while being able to take the gear held inside where you please.

Do not underestimate the stress on a loaded alloy box off-road. If your rack doesn't have a tray supporting the weight from underneath (as with Touratech's versions where the box 'hangs' on the rack via channel mountings bolted to its back) be sure that

The KTM on the left has soft bags; on the right a medium-sized alloy box.
© Noah Maltz

these mountings are up to carrying the full weight.

Plastic Givi- or Krauser-type cases, as on the Honda on page 32, look neat and are easy to use, but are not up to the strain of off-roading unless you substantially modify the mounting arrangements. One Africa Twin rider summed up his Givis as 'panniers brilliant, racks dreadful', although Happy Trails in Idaho fabricate a proper rack to carry Givi's Monokey luggage system.

A small top box, in plastic or thick fibreglass can be useful (see the KTM on p.59) if you like the idea of at least one lockable compartment, maybe for your expedition's film gear. Situated on a back rack or even behind your seat (better for handling but awkward when getting on and off), it doesn't need heavy rack support. Again, you can buy chunky and **rounded** aluminium top boxes up to 40 litres that won't stab you in the ribs when you crash.

One good place to have a small metal box (such as an ex-army ammo box) is bolted to the front of the bashplate. It's a good place to carry heavy items like tools while offering ideal access, robustness and reasonable security.

Soft luggage

Soft luggage usually means some kind of throwover panniers or saddlebags slung over the back of the seat with a rucksack or kit bag across the back and other bags strapped on where they'll fit. This system has its drawbacks as listed earlier but is light, cheap and versatile.

Panniers or saddlebags

Throwover panniers come in Cordura, a tough woven nylon, canvas, PVC or can be made in leather. With Cordura, go for items made in at least 1000-weight (Dernier) material which will be tough enough. The good thing with throwovers or saddlebags is that they **require no rack** as they just sling over the bike. They need fixing down of course and can stretch, burn, melt, fall off, tear, disintegrate or simply get stolen. I've experienced all but the last of these saddlebag woes in one eventful day! Some of these drawbacks can be overcome with careful thought and planning but you should keep these limitations in mind. One problem particular to trail bikes is their high silencers. Even with heat shields, it's still possible for panniers to get pressed onto the pipe at high speed or when bouncing over rough ground. Nylon and plastic tends to melt while canvas actually burns – another soft luggage scenario I've enjoyed. The best solution is to hook the front edge of your panniers securely onto the frame or rear footrests to stop them sliding back and to fabricate a **proper guard around the silencer** so that there's no way they can come into contact. This is one reason why racks are a good idea with soft luggage.

In the UK, the Oxford 'Sovereign' series of throwover luggage (pictured on the 1100GS, and the Funduro on p.29 and p.31) are toughly sewn, have useful pockets and zips that on my set are still hanging in there. Plus they expand up to a very useful 56 litres by simply undoing another zip. Gearsack, and in the US, Chase Harper are other well regarded brands of smart and well designed soft luggage. Oxford 'throwovers' are actually individually removable with clips which aren't up to the strain when packed to the limit on a corrugated track. With any fully-loaded bag swinging about – bought or homemade – something's bound to break, rip or get caught in the wheel. Avoid this by supporting heavy bags with a light rack (see below).

Nets are best used for catching fish, not wrapping up a pile of luggage.

Other materials

Relatively new to touring are PVC bags like the Vaude items pictured on the KTM on p.59 or the Ortlieb Dry Bag and QL2 Side Bags which clip onto a rail. The Dry Bag is a standard tube-shaped kit bag of 60-litre capacity, but with a full length opening that rolls over and closes with a rainproof seal. Less expensive and developed for canoeing are similar shaped tubes like Cascade's SeaLine range. However, the opening at the end, makes access a little less easy. PVC also suffers from limited resistance to abrasion, melting as you slide down the road, and it must be kept well clear of exhaust pipes.

Ex-army **canvas panniers** (see the KTM, p.59) or rucksacks are cheaper still, allowing you to trim your needs exactly and are at least as hardwearing as PVC. They don't always come in the size needed for long-distance touring and closures usually make do with studs or straps rather than zips; unsophisticated maybe, but ultra-reliable. The trouble is canvas burns rather than melts so again you must be sure they're clear of the pipe or seated on a light rack.

RACKS

If you happen to possess unusual self-restraint and travel light, you might just get away with using soft luggage without a rack. But even with, say, a 10-litre jerrican on the back seat, the rear subframe can flex, possibly inducing a weave at speeds over 50mph/80kph on loose surfaces, especially if you're running road or trail tyres. And if your baggage is much heavier or the ground rough, sub frames can sag, bend or crack.

Most overland bikers accept that a baggage rack is a good idea because of the relative flimsiness of single shock subframes. The German outfits mentioned above supply racks for GSs, Africa Twins and the main singles. Touratech's racks resemble Krauser pannier racks and rely on strong fittings bolted to the back plate of the box which hang on the horizontal tubes of the rack. It's a neat idea which avoids the shin-cracking trays of the home-made example pictured on p.63, but with the huge carrying capacity of a 41-litre metal box, Touratech racks are more suited to big, tarmac-cruising trailies.

In the USA, Happy Trails in Boise make round-tubed racks in various designs to fit the big singles available there. But even with these few outfits making racks, if you have an aptitude for engineering (or know someone who has) you can make something better and stronger yourself as pictured on p.62 – a good alternative to the tray-rack described below.

Building a rack

In the UK at least, it's still normal for biking overlanders to get their racks hand-built rather than sending off to Germany or the US, as no one there produces suitably tough items off the shelf. Here are some things to consider when fabricating your own rack or getting one built:
- Build in easily re-weldable mild steel, not aluminium
- Think about how the maximum weight will affect the rack and where the stress might lie
- Weight for weight, tubes are stronger than a same-sized square section; avoid curved sections in either
- Bolt the rack to your bike in four to six places. Don't weld it on

Rear frames have a hard time when loaded up. A rack must add to the frame's strength, not stress it. This poor old XT was carrying huge Därrs boxes.
It's a good idea to disconnect the battery when welding directly on a bike. Something could get fried. © Trui Hanoulle

A neat and chunky home made trayless box rack. Note the lower lip which helps support the box and three mounting points per side as well as the all-important support brace behind the number plate (this one appears not to be fixed) The drum brake arm is reversed to keep it clear of rocks.

This well-designed rack made of rounded tubes spreads the load over three sections per side without adding the excess weight of square section.

- Make sure there's enough room for wheel removal, chain adjustment, suspension compression and the swing of a kick-start
- A strut across the back is essential to stop inward flexing

Unless you have your own ideas, the basis of a bike rack is a beam from around the rider's footrests to the region of the rear indicators. It can be a tray rack as in the diagram opposite, or a trayless rectangle as on the Yamaha on the left. Based on this arrangement supporting the bike's subframe, further attachment points can be fitted to other frame lugs in this area, spreading the load over several mounts. Try to use the same sized bolts for all mounts and carry spares in case they sheer.

A tray rack (as shown opposite) can hold a holdall snuggly and securely, but think carefully about the location of these trays. Are they far enough forward to provide enough leg room to 'paddle' the bike through sand, etc, as well as swing a kickstarter?

There's no real advantage to sitting heavy metal boxes in a heavy tray rack. A trayless rectangle design is sufficient, using the strength of the box as a stressed part of the structure, or at least supporting itself. You can bolt a box straight on, providing the material of the back plate is tough enough, or weld on a couple of chunky long 'U'-sections which when fixed upside-down (see below) will 'hang' the box on the rack's horizontal beams Padding along the beam will help spread the weight. This done, it's easy to think up a quickly-

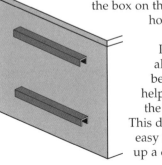

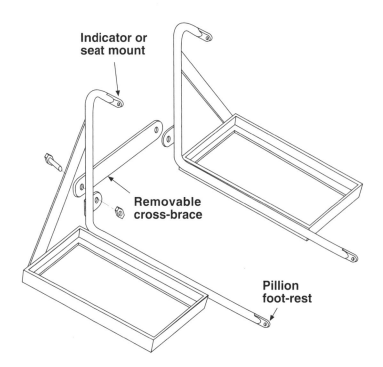

Indicator or seat mount

Removable cross-brace

Pillion foot-rest

detachable way of locating the box securely to the rack so that it doesn't rattle or jump off.

Finally, it's crucial to brace both sides of the rack against inward flexing by fitting a supporting strut across the back, beneath the number plate (see above). This strut must be far enough back so as not to interfere with the tyre on full compression of the shock, and it must be easily detachable to enable rear wheel removal.

Testing your system

Once you've established how you're going to carry all your gear, it's essential to take the fully-loaded bike – with all tanks and cans filled – for a test ride to see how it holds together and if custom-made components make contact with the swingarm or tyre during suspension movement. Sitting a friend on the back and getting them to jump up and down a bit is not the same thing!

Riding your bike in this state for the first time will be alarming and you'll wonder how on earth you're going to ride it from Anchorage to Ushuaia as you wobble down the street. This may be your last chance to seriously re-assess your personal requirements and consider cutting down on the weight. Many riders end up sending stuff home in the early days.

While loaded up, lay the bike over on its side and try and pick it up; if you can't then it's too heavy and unless you're certain there'll always be someone around to help you, you must consider reducing, or re-arranging the weight.

JERRICANS

Despite their awkward bulk, jerricans are the simplest and cheapest method of safely increasing your fuel capacity. Original and serviceable WWII items can still be picked up in Europe for £5, although you should inspect the interior of any used jerrican for rust. (Don't use a naked flame unless you're tired of having eyebrows.) The Far Eastern pattern copies commonly available these days are quite safe and reliable.

The standard jerrican (originally copied from a wartime German design, hence the name) holds 20 litres or 4.45 Imperial gallons when filled up in the upright position. Filling up a level can leaves an **air gap** just under the handles which should not be filled by tipping the can backwards unless you're really

This XL600R will certainly need extra fuel capacity after mounting a jerry like this.

desperate. The air pocket, as well as the X-shaped indentations on the sides, allow the can to bulge as the fuel expands, so relieving pressure on the rubber seal and resisting leaks. Because of petrol's effervescent nature, a jerrican that's been shaken and warmed up on the back of your bike should be opened with great care; the clamp design of the lid makes this easy. Suddenly opening an agitated jerrican full of petrol will result in a massive spurt of precious fuel.

The clamp-on spout (with an integral gauze filter and breather for smoother pouring) is easier to use than a funnel and less wasteful than trying to pour the petrol straight in. You should also earth the container (drag it on the ground) before filling up your tank, especially if it 's been carried on another vehicle, so as to disperse any static electricity that may have built up. Static is common in dry desert conditions.

Besides holding fluids, jerricans make useful seats, pillows, small tables or bike props for wheel repairs. They're also a valuable and exchangeable commodity in remote areas, often fetching higher prices than at home. Jerricans can be knocked about and dented for years while still remaining useful, but once rust or flaking paint begins to come out with the fuel a fine filter should be used or the thing discarded.

(Opposite) Top: A shady spot in the Libyan Sahara (see p.118), but watch out for thorns.
Bottom: Two heavily loaded XT Yamahas moving across the Fadnoun plateau in Algeria.

Clothing for the long ride

As much as any advice given in this book, clothing is a matter of personal taste but, whatever image you decide to cultivate, you'll need to protect yourself from wind, sun, heat, cold, dust, rain, stones and falling off. Comfort, lightness, utility and quality of construction are all important features to consider as you'll probably end up wearing the same kit most of the time.

In fact, forget about taking spare clothing at all and instead just wash what you wear every few days until it wears out. Save space by opting for multifunctional items that are light and quick-drying and resist the temptation to pack a spare pair of shoes, jeans or a jumper 'just in case'. In the unlikely event of an invitation to an embassy soirée, you'll create much more of a stir in your weather-beaten leathers than crammed into a crumpled shirt and tie.

Blending in

A word about looking flash. Being an adrenaline sport to some, apparel manufacturers produce a lurid range of riding gear. Plodding round the world at 50 miles per hour is a different game; just about every country you visit will be poorer than your own, and people's attitude towards you will be governed by your appearance. Although it's obvious you're hundreds of times richer than the locals, a low-key dress sense and muted-looking bike at least avoids underlining this fact. Furthermore, the poorer (i.e. more normal) you look, the less chance there is of getting ripped-off as a rich tourist or turned over by an unscrupulous border guard. Painting your bike a plain matt colour may be more than most want to do, but it does make your machine less conspicuous. Don't worry about getting lost in the crowd; give it a few weeks and the attention you attract will be enough to make you wish you were invisible.

JACKETS

Any jacket should seal up snugly around your neck, wrists, waist and hem for cold days while being adjustable with zips and air vents as days or climates warm up. The waist draw-cord feature is particularly useful as it seals off your torso, so keeping the core of your body warm on a cool morning, while being easy to release.

A good jacket needs to have all the qualities mentioned earlier and should also have enough pockets to carry valuables. Overland biking being what it is, keeping these items on your person is the only way of ensuring their security, so look for **big zipped pockets**, at least one of which is internal. Make sure the ones on your chest are not so high up that you can't get your hand in without taking it off.

Probably the best jacket to fill all the above criteria most of the time is a **Cordura touring jacket**. Cordura is a tough woven nylon that is light, looks good, abrades well, is easy to clean and forms a tough shell for a Gore-Tex liner. In the UK, Hein Gericke, Frank Thomas and Belstaff all make jackets

(Opposite) Coming through the Todra gorge in the Moroccan Atlas. © Matt Ball.

EQUIPMENT CHECKLIST

These are the basics you'll need on a long overland trip. It's unlikely that you'll take just these items, but consider it a useful checklist to give you ideas on essentials you may have overlooked.

Documentation
- Passport
- Travel tickets
- Travel insurance
- Green Card and/or Third Party Insurance
- Carnet
- Vehicle ownership document
- Driver's licence (including international)
- Cash, credit cards, travellers' cheques
- Photocopies of all essential documents
- Passport photos
- Address book or personal organiser

Camping and sleeping
- Sleeping mat or air bed
- Sleeping bag with stuff sac
- Tent or treated mosquito net
- Alarm clock or watch
- Collapsible stool
- Ear plugs

Cooking
- Stove and fuel (if not petrol)
- Spares for stove
- Tea towel and pan scrubber
- Lighter and matches
- Spoon and fork
- Cooking pot(s) and pot gripper
- Swiss Army penknife
- Washing-up liquid
- Mug
- Water container plus water bag/bottle
- Water filter or water sterilisation tablets

Toiletries
- Soap, flannel and towel
- Razors
- Detergent
- Toothbrush and toothpaste
- Toilet paper
- Sun screen and skin moisturiser
- Insect repellent
- Universal basin plug

Navigation
- Maps and GPS
- Compass
- Mini binoculars

Clothing
- Motocross boots and spare shoes
- Socks and underpants
- Thermal underwear
- T-shirts or shirt
- Fleece jacket
- Gore-tex riding jacket

- Gloves
- Thermal gloves
- Leather trousers or MX pants
- Shorts
- Balaclava or sun hat
- Crash helmet and goggles
- Spare dark lenses or sunglasses
- Kidney belt
- Needle and thread

Bike spares and tools
- Spare keys (including ignition)
- Front and rear inner tubes
- Extra tyre(s)
- Puncture repair kit (see p.53)
- Connecting link(s) for chain
- CDI unit or points and condenser
- Ignition coil
- Control levers and cables.
- Oil and air filter(s)
- Speedo cable
- Wire and duct tape
- Spare nuts and bolts for rack fittings
- Instant gasket
- Epoxy glue
- Diaphragm for CV carbs
- Jubilee clips
- Small tub of grease
- Electrical wire, connectors and bulbs
- Small G-clamp
- Radiator sealant
- Spark plug(s)
- Petrol pipe
- Spare bungees and straps
- Spanners, sockets and wrench
- Adjustable spanner or mole grips
- Allen keys
- Cross-and flat-bladed screwdrivers
- Pliers with wire cutters
- Feeler gauges
- Spoke key
- Junior hacksaw with spare blades
- Top-up oil and rag

Miscellaneous
- Mini- or headtorch
- Camera and film
- Pen and notebook and envelopes
- Books (guide, phrase, plus *AMH*!)
- Spare batteries for electrical gadgets
- Solar calculator
- Pack of cards or other compact games
- Waterproof bags
- String or rope
- Postcards from your country (as gifts)

GORE-TEX

The efficacy of wonder-membrane Gore-Tex is much discussed when applied to motorcycling – and some think it is over-rated. The micro-pore membrane that you'll never see is sandwiched in the layers of your jacket and releases water vapour – condensation formed by sweat – while miraculously resisting the ingress of water (aka, rain).

The thing is, for Gore-Tex and its many imitators to work, a certain amount of 'pressure' and heat must build up inside the jacket for the vapour to reach 'escape velocity'. This heat energy will be easily generated jogging up Kanchenjunga with a 60kg pack, but not when clinging to the 'bars of a motorbike at 70mph.

So Gore-Tex may not always work, some condensation may be present, and leaks do occur if the construction is not so good or the membrane has been damaged.

One thing's for sure: it's important to keep Gore-Tex clothing **clean** and **treat the outer shell** with a water-repellent coating like ScotchGuard or Nik-Wax for it to be effective. This stops water soaking into the outer shell and so 'blocking' the evaporative action through the membrane.

On balance, even if it only works partially, compared to oilskins or PVC rainwear, do-it-all Gore-Tex or similar clothing is a real benefit to the adventure tourer, even at the price you have to pay.

from light but strong synthetic materials that are thankfully a long way from the crappy nylon products of a decade ago. For something around £250/$400 you get a lot for your money.

The German-designed Hein Gericke, in particular, offers a huge range of good quality gear that has helped drag British manufacturers out of the medieval waxed-cotton era. You could happily spend hours drooling through the HG or even Italian Dainese catalogues without buying anything. Finnish firm Rukka have also hopped on the Cordura bandwagon. Fifteen years ago just about every London despatch rider, myself included, wore Rukka's durable and compact PVC rain gear and their current range of AFT Cordura bike jackets are just as smart looking as well as functional.

All these jackets feature a some kind of **protective padding** along the shoulders and elbows as well as Kevlar patches on high-wear areas, and some include vents so you can keep cool while still being protected.

In the USA, one brand has become a firm favourite with long-range touring riders: Aerostich's two-piece **Darien outfit** or one-piece **Roadcrafter** suit are rated across the continent. They're not cheap but are considered an investment with a long line of satisfied customers. Quality construction and attention to detail is where most of your money goes, as well as an after-sales alterations and repair service. An Aerostich suit will last you many years.

Leather jackets have good wear properties and age nicely, but can be uncomfortably heavy when the going gets physical. They also have awkwardly small pockets. If you're into leather, consider a longer coat like Roadgear's **Oregon Trail** jacket rather than the usual waist-length bomber-style jackets.

Trousers; alternatives to jeans

With trousers the accent is on comfort and protection, pockets are not important. Here a good pair of leather trousers is an advantage: they're hard-wearing and still look good when caked in filth. Avoid cheap thin leather; look for soft supple cowhide and one piece legs (no seam across the knees) which jacks the price up. Bare in mind that leather trousers will sag and stretch over the months and because they're heavy, you'll need a belt or, better still, strong braces to avoid the crotch eventually splitting in the countless times you swing your leg over the machine.

Leather trousers are unsuitable on a hot trip, especially in humid, jungle areas with plenty of river crossings. Wearing nylon in these conditions is not ideal, but a pair of **motocross pants** is still a good all-round choice, offering proper dirt biking protection, padding and durability, while being light and quick to dry. Fit plastic **knee protectors** which slip into inside pockets on most brands. Even if you don't crash in them, it makes kneeling on the ground and working on the bike a whole lot more comfortable.

Your choice of sober colour schemes will be limited of course, you'll need to flick through a few catalogues to find something that won't frighten the horses. Get a quality pair of pants fit for riding into the ground. Alpine Star's Global Pants come in a looser fit than close-fitting MX versions while still having the same construction and provision for padding, as do MSR's Gold Line pants.

Boots and gloves

Invest in a tough pair of boots that will last the trip and protect your feet and lower legs in the frequent low-speed tumbles. The better you're prepared for these small accidents, the more you'll be able to enjoy your riding without fear of injury. **Full-on motocross boots** are as valuable as a good helmet and gloves; made to take a beating while protecting your legs. At some point on your trip you'll be glad you were wearing them. The trouble is they're not exactly light footwear when it comes to walking; ex-army or high-shinned work boots will cost a fraction while still giving your feet and ankles some

---

COLD WEATHER GEAR

All year-round bikers are familiar with the agony of riding through cold weather in inadequate gear. Little wonder most adventure bikers, especially Europeans, head south and east towards the sun. But some perverse individuals will still choose to head in the opposite direction, and round-the-worlders may eventually run into a cold season or high altitude. Cold weather clothing adds a lot of bulk to your gear, but when correctly chosen will give you the insulation you need to face freezing temperatures with enthusiasm rather than dread.

If you're heading for the high mountains, the winter or the poles, the best specialist item you could wear other than a silk balaclava is a one piece under-garment, made from silk (the lightest and least bulky), synthetic thermals such as those made by Damart, or a one-piece fibre pile/fleece as used by cave divers and mountaineers. They work by eliminating the gap or waistbands in the kidney region where much body heat can be lost on a bike and they really make a difference. Fibre pile is bulkiest but would only be needed when riding close to freezing point. The advantage is they require only a good jacket and overtrousers to keep you comfortably warm. The drawbacks of one-piece under-clothing comes in the palaver needed to get it off, either when things warm up or when nature calls.

Other than that, do all you can to keep the blast of the wind off your body. Remember, it's the **trapped, still air** heated by your body that keeps you warm, not bulky materials, the best of which create capacious air cavities. Nothing can beat a quality down jacket worn under a breathable outer. Weighing next to nothing, it's effective at keeping you warm and comfortable without giving you that 'stuffed dummy' feeling when wearing heaps of layers.

Heated clothing as well as handlebar grips are another way of conserving body heat: with a warmed trunk blood can reach out to warm the frigid extremities too. Various versions of Aerostich's **Unobtanium Electric Vest** are recommended by all-season riders in North America.

And if you just get caught out in a cold area, stuffing newspapers or cardboard into your clothes, especially around your torso, will help keep the cold out, while giving you something to read or burn once you've dug your snow hole.

protection. KLR-riding racoon trapper Tom Grenon has had a hand (or foot) in designing the Canadian Viberg boots advertised in the back of this book.

Wearing a pair of padded palm motocross gloves is the most comfortable way to protect your hands on the dirt while giving good feel at the bars. At other times you may find Damart inner gloves or overmitts useful. Fingerless cycling gloves are also cool and comfortable to wear when the weather and pace really warm up, but however hot it gets, always wear some kind of gloves. To a certain extent **handguards** keep the blast of the wind and rain off your hands allowing you to wear a lighter and more comfortable pair of gloves.

Helmets
For riding on the dirt a full-face motocross helmet and a pair of motocross goggles is most convenient; light and comfortable MX goggles will seal-off your sensitive eyes from dust, wind and glare better than a full-face road helmet's visor, whether tinted or used with sunglasses.

Bell and Arai are well known for their quality MX helmets and Arai make the particularly useful Dual Sport model which can be used either with goggles or with a visor for highway or town riding when a quick flip up of the visor is handy. These better-quality helmets come in plain colours and with removable and washable linings. While costing a packet, they'll offer a level of comfort you'll appreciate.

Take your helmet off when talking to people, especially officials. While not as quiet as a full face lid, many long-haul riders settle with **combination helmets** like those from BMW or Nolan. The front hinges up to reveal your face, and if that doesn't go down well you can just open the visor in conventional full face mode.

Many developing countries don't have helmet laws but, while being very agreeable, riding without a helmet invites sun stroke within a couple of hours or spilled brains in the event of an accident. In the last edition of the *AMH*, RTW-er Robbie Marshall's told how his Shoei deflected an Ecuadorian gunman's bullet!

OIL HEATED CLOTHING

Electric vests are all very well but they drain your battery, set you on fire when you least need it, or even electrocute you if you inadvertently plug them directly to the HT lead.

Years ago, having to face another freezing mid-winter transit of France on the way down south to the Sahara, I came up with a cunning alternative.

My Yamaha Ténéré at the time had been modified with an oil cooler from a scrapped Haulpak R380 ore transporter fixed over the headlamp. What a waste of lovely engine heat I thought – how can I harness it?

The answer was simple: craft a cowling/scoop device out of cardboard and duct tape to collect the heat coming off the cooler and have a pair of hoses running out of the heat collector and up my sleeves!

Zip ties round the cuffs sealed the tubes off nicely, the only problem was attaching the armpit-warming umbilicals up each sleeve before setting off – and then dealing with things like reaching the reserve tap without falling off.

Did it work? Well even if it was 15 years ago, the fact that I don't have warm glowing recollections of cruising across the bleak fogbound plains of northern France, means that probably no, it didn't. I think the bike never really got hot enough, and when it did, I was in the desert and pretty hot myself.

A year later I discovered an even better system to heat my clothing: an SNCF sleeper train that transported me from Paris to Marseille quicker than I could ride. Vorsprung Durch Technik.

Shipping overseas

(Based on original material by Simon Fenning)

For UK-based riders heading across Asia or Africa, shipping a bike is not essential, though avoiding trouble spots or linking up with South-east Asia, Australasia and the Americas will require transportation by sea or air. World-lapping North Americans, and in particular Australian and New Zealand riders, all have to face the need and expense of getting their bikes to adjacent continents, which is why many fly to Europe and begin their travels there.

Air or sea?

Sea freight is primarily geared towards cheap transportation of bulk commodities; agents would rather shift 250,000 tons of iron ore than fiddly things like motorbikes. Shipping agents do of course deal in personal effects of individuals not in a hurry to recover their belongings but, as is described below, the secure packing and complex documentation required with vehicle importation can become a container-sized headache.

The sole drawback to shipping by air is the higher cost, but in all other respects it's preferable. It's much quicker, being measured in days door-to-door, rather than weeks, and being geared to small, high-value shipments the quality of handling and storage is generally better. Prices vary wildly around the world but you may well save money when you consider the time involved in waiting for your bike to leave one port, cross an ocean, get to another, get lost and found, tampered with and finally released.

Even to this day the geographically contiguous Americas remain divided by the all-but impregnable jungles and streams of the Darien Gap in southern Panama. Unless you plan replicating Helge Pedersens's feat and winching your bike through the creeks for a week, you'll have to fly or use the smuggling boats which run from Colón to quiet beaches near Cartageña in Colombia (see the story on p.209). The Crucero ferry stopped running in 1997.

In some instances, such as the Baring Straits separating Russia from Alaska, air freighting is the only option short of riding across the frozen sea in mid-winter. Some guys paid the same to fly their DR350s across this twenty-mile-wide channel as they did to cross the 3000 miles of the Southern Atlantic from Buenos Aires to Cape Town. Then again, with an enviable trade connection, another guy paid just £125/US$200 to fly himself and his Triumph from London to New York, but a hefty £1100/US$1800 to ship the bike from Chile to Sydney, including £300/US$480 for crating and transportation to Santiago docks. Shipping by sea or air freight is a lottery. Sometimes you win, but especially in South America, you pay a lot for bad service and headaches. Just put it down to experience if there's no other way through short of building a raft.

Shipping from home: finding an agent

No commercially-minded shipper will turn away business, even a one-off relatively low cost shipment such as a bike. Unless specifically recommended by a third party, the best way to judge whether a shipping agent really can be trusted is probably by the amount of information and attention provided prior to offering them your business. If they're at all offhand, try someone else.

Once actually on the road, the tight set of requirements listed below become a little fuzzy. Ask around, be flexible, but be wary. Save money by crating yourself (simply strapping the covered bike down onto a pallet can do the trick) and expect problems and surcharges out of the blue. Above all, save space (volume) when crating properly and, on a plane, save weight where possible by taking your luggage with you.

A checklist for using shipping agents should include the following:
● Your shipper must have an office at the destination point of entry or at the very least a local agent that they deal with on a regular basis. In either instance you want the full names, telephone and fax numbers of the employees at both departure and arrival points. Before you consign your bike to the shipper make contact with the individual at the destination end and ask them what is involved in temporarily importing a used motorcycle into that country. Naturally, if they're at all negative do not use that shipper. On the other hand don't abandon your plans just because they say it can't be done, because they may be wrong.
● Your shipper must be able to supply a written list of compliance formalities for the country of destination. This may include proof of ownership, proof of locally recognised road risk insurance, manufacturer's vehicle specification, bonds, carnets or other transit documents. See 'Documentation' below.
● Your shipper must be able to tell you exactly how the bike should be packaged. See below for further guidance.
● Your shipper must be able to provide a fully itemised pro-forma invoice. To do this they will need the dry weight and physical dimensions of the bike which you will have to provide. They will also need the exact destination address. This will be the place at which the agent's responsibility ends, so be sure that it's a suitable point for uncrating and spannering.
● Your shipper should be professionally accredited. For air this will be with IATA; and for surface or 'ocean' they should be a member of BIFA in the UK or the national equivalent.

Documentation
For seriously unusual destinations it may be that no shipper will be fully familiar with the documentary requirements. The internationally published bible is *Croners Book For Exporters* which contains the shipping requirements for most of the world's routes – you'll find it in larger libraries. Alternatively, when such information is unavailable, it will list the phone number and address of the trade desk of the relevant embassy. If you're proposing to contact the immigration desk of the embassy, it's a good idea to seek advice about importing bikes at the same time. Who knows, they may even reply.

Having established what is required, copy all the documentation, take several copies with you and leave a further copy of everything in a file with a friend at home. Remember also that your shipping agent should keep copies on file until the job is finished.

If you are packing other items with the bike don't forget to inform the shipper and check that they are itemised on the manifest (see Richard Wolters' report on p.147). This is to satisfy both insurance and customs requirements.

Surface in shared container

This is commonly used on routes on which personal effects are regularly being shipped in both directions, such as UK-Australia, and there are companies that specialise in shared containers. Your goods are wedged into a space within a 40-foot container and wooden shuttering is nailed around them. It's cheap and efficient, and the shippers are used to dealing with private individuals. Deliver the bike to the shipper, remembering to remove all projecting and vulnerable parts like mirrors or wide, trail bike handlebars, bubble-wrap these and stash them alongside the bike.

Surface loose

When a shared container is not an option, or you want to virtually eliminate the chances of damage, then the bike needs to be put on a pallet and commercially shrink-wrapped or cardboard-boxed. If you have a choice, the best pallets around are Harley ones; most dealers will be happy to give you one. Try and avoid the Electra Glide ones, as they're much stronger and heavier than you'll need – unless of course you happen to be shipping a Glide.

The advantage of shrink-wrapping over building a box on the pallet is that a box has an easily calculated volume the weight of which may be over-estimated, so adding to your costs, although this is more relevant to the higher rates of air freight.

If you're determined to protect your bike fully within a box then remove the front wheel and lower the handlebars to reduce the overall height and thereby the volume. As mentioned above, on a single cylinder dual sport bike without excessively wide panniers, removing the wide bars will save still more space.

FLYING OVER THE DARIEN

In 1998 I flew my BMW G/S with Gurag Air Freight from Panama City to Bogota for $250. I needed no crate or pallet, just rode it to the air cargo terminal at the airport (at the other end of the runway from the passenger terminal), drained the gas, disconnected the battery, took off the mirrors and windshield, and left it.

Next day it was in Bogota. I did not use a freight forwarder in Panama City, but rode directly to the Air Cargo terminal and worked out the deal with the airline itself. Some other travellers paid three times as much to fly their bikes over the Darien, had to have them crated, and used a forwarder. Their bikes went on the regular passenger airlines, a lot more expensive. It cost $75 and a day to get the bike cleared in Bogota.

Others spent longer in Bogota with lots of running around and paperwork (I used a handler who got the $75). My flight from Panama City to Bogota was $160 one way.

The problem I expected (no exit stamp in my passport from Panama for the motorcycle) never came up as I was not asked for it at the passenger exit. I did try to get Customs to stamp the bike out but no one wanted to do it. I probably could have got the stamp for a little cash but, for once, no one asked.

I talked with several bikers who took boats from Colón to Colombia. All had bad experiences and most paid about the same. Some took as long as four days to get across and were dumped on the beach in Colombia.

Dr Gregory Frazier
Author of *Riding South*

DIY packing

Doing your own packing will be far cheaper than having the shipper do it, but they'll not be responsible if the packing fails in any way. That said, it's practically impossible to claim against a third party for damage or theft to goods in transit without proof of exactly when and where the problem occurred. Use tie-downs straps (available from motocross shops) to fix the bike to the pallet by compressing the suspension. One across the back seat and another pair pulling down from each side of the handlebars should do the trick; centre and side stands have to be raised.

Don't forget to label the package but avoid describing the contents as this only attracts attention. You may be required to nominate a recipient other than the shipping agent. If you haven't got a friend to nominate ask your bank if they have local connections. Failing that, get the name of a local lawyer, but expect to pay.

On a long trip you're bound to end up getting your bike crated in a country you're not familiar with; the golden rule here is to check the crate yourself and make sure that your machine is in there, and not something else. Only contemplate shipping a bike loose on its wheels if you attach no great value to it and are don't mind finding unscrewable items missing on arrival.

Air

Airlines are naturally much more particular about what they carry than shipping lines and anyway, in most cases, only lighter bikes will be economically viable using this method. The shipping agent is responsible for ensuring that the goods are packed properly, but they'll effectively indemnify themselves from being liable for damage arising from the nature of the goods themselves, such as leaking battery acid, by preparing a 'hazardous goods certificate' and asking you to sign it. Note that if there is a possibility that your bike may be transported in an unpressurised hold, you'll have to remove the air and valves from the tyres. Expect some pumping at the other end.

Shrink-wrapping the pallet works out cheaper than cardboard or wooden boxes; the shipper should have a supplier for both.

Cost breakdown

Expect to see the following items appearing on your invoice:
● Collection of goods, unless you actually ride the bike to the shipper
● Packing
● Export documentation and administration (usually a flat fee)
● Other documentation charges, such as preparation of the hazardous goods certificate
● Airline or terminal (ocean) handling
● Freight costs, per kg by air; per cubic metre or kilogram by ocean. Many shippers only quote this part of the total cost in advance, not to mislead clients (although this is often the result), but because this is the most negotiable item on the invoice
● Destination charges, customs clearance, handling and portage
● Temporary import charges, bond payment or evidence of a carnet (see p.19) in countries to which this applies
● Transit insurance. This option will cover all risks from door to door and

should be charged at a flat percentage of the agreed value of the bike. The shipper will insist on packing and unpacking your bike to inspect it prior to shipping. This will increase the overall cost but has the great advantage of not requiring proof of negligence in the event of a claim. Without this sort of cover your bike is effectively uninsured.

Very few of these costs can be avoided and, unless you have a lot of spare time, it rarely pays to cut corners. You may baulk at the idea of paying a shipper to present documents at say, the Qatari Embassy, until you discover that an appointment has to be made twenty-one days in advance, and that's just to collect the blank forms! At the end of the day it comes down to the price you are prepared to pay for peace of mind.

Life on the road

The Big Day is approaching and the nation's media or just your friends and family are gathered to see you off. Then again, maybe you're slipping off quietly into the dawn. One thing will be certain: you'll be chewing your lip and your throbbing hangover won't help.

If you've managed to prepare thoroughly then pat yourself on the back; you've done well. But if you're like most people, you're bound to have forgotten something crucial. This is normal and you'll deal with the customary moment-of-departure crises, large or small.

SETTING OFF
You start the engine, heave the bike off the stand (don't forget to flick it up!), click it into first and wobble off down the road, appalled at the weight of the machine. Once out on the open road you wind it up and allow some faint optimism to creep in to your manifold anxieties as passing motorists stare at you with what you hope is envy. I recall the snowy night I first set off for the Sahara. A little black kid stared at my ludicrous XT500 and asked:

'Where yew goin?'

'Africa my lad,' I replied nonchalantly.

'Nah ya not!' he sneered. In a way he was right.

Finally on the move after months, if not years of preparation, the urge is to keep moving, especially if you're heading out across a cold continent. Try to resist covering excessive mileages in your early days even though movement will probably be the best tonic for your nerves. Don't make any crazy deadlines to quit work and catch a ferry the same night.

If you've got a long way to ride, even to get to your port city, aim to spend the night there before the ferry departs. The **early days** of a big trip, especially in unfamiliar countries with perplexing road signs and wrong-side driving are when most **accidents** happen. If an estimated 75% of all overlanders achieve hospitalisation due to *accidents* rather than commonly-dreaded diseases (as I heard recently), you can imagine what that figure is for bikers…

Take a test run

All this strangeness rushing at you from all directions can be soothed by taking yourself on a **test run** a few weeks before lift off. If the run takes you to Mexico or Morocco then so much the better. You can use this trip as a 'systems shakedown' to acclimatise yourself with your bike's handling and foreign drivers' habits without the added nerves of the Big Day's departure. Maybe the new tank bag keeps sliding off, or you can't reach the reserve tap easily on the new tank. Perhaps your home-made rack hits the swingarm on full compression or the sidestand plate grounds easily because the shock is overloaded. All these things are better discovered in advance, so when the day comes you're pretty sure how the bike is going to run, if not so sure of what exactly lies ahead.

KEEPING IN TOUCH

When you're on the road, getting news from home is a morale booster that the sender can never imagine. Standing in a queue at a foreign post office and walking away with a batch of letters can be the highlight of your week. The **poste restante** or mail collection system enables you to pick up mail at any post office in the world, provided they keep it for you and can find your letter. In some countries a small charge is sometimes payable.

Always get the sender to write your surname first and underline it, followed by your first name and the address, as this is how it will be filed. Remember though that the chances of your birthday card turning up in some

---

STRESS

One aspect of travel health that is rarely talked about is stress, usually what you come on holiday to get away from. It will come as no surprise that you're likely to find overland motorbiking, especially alone, **just about the most stressful thing you've done in a long time**. The obvious but often underestimated effects of culture shock, as well as fears of being robbed, murdered, getting lost or becoming ill are all the more acute when you're on your own with everything you possess for the next few months amassed within arm's reach.

The need for constant vigilance can lead to all the common symptoms of stress: headaches, irritability, paranoia and, more commonly, absent-mindedness and susceptibility to minor ailments like colds. This kind of tension isn't made any easier by riding along remote tracks for days at a time.

A common way to deal with these perceived threats is to keep moving and to end your dangerous heroic escapade as soon as possible. I have experienced this nervous restlessness in myself and in others, and have recognised it for what it is: an inability to relax or trust anybody for fear that something bad is going to happen. (This is different from the 'running for your life' panic when your long-cherished adventure is falling to pieces about you: in this situation getting home fast makes sense.) It's not uncommon for overlanders who have taken long, hazardous but ultimately successful trans-continental journeys to have nightmares once they get back home, as the subconscious turns in on recent memories and ponders 'what if that truck hadn't...' etc.

Fortunately, this understandable paranoia slowly abates, especially when you've had a chance to get used to your surroundings and meet local people (other than the officials), who'll offer you a generosity and hospitality that you rarely encounter elsewhere. Sadly, by the time you get to this level of psychological equilibrium you may be out of money and on your way home.

It's mentioned here in the hope that you won't waste the trip for which you've planned so long in useless paranoia – try and get as much out of the people you meet as out of the roads you ride.

countries is slimmer than others: Mali, Peru, and Nepal spring to mind. An exclusive alternative for American Express card holders is their unlimited mail collection service at Amex offices anywhere in the world.

Sending mail home is a hit and miss affair in places where underpaid postal employees snip off the unfranked stamps for reuse. In one instance a tourist found a snap of herself sent in a letter that very morning for sale in a postcard rack! Take letters to the counter and watch them being franked.

Telephones and e-mail

Three-quarters of the world may never make a telephone call in their lives, but the will to communicate and the hopelessness of many countries' internal telecommunication systems has seen entrepreneurs open up international telephone centres in many towns. You'll have probably seen them in your own High Street; you walk in, select a booth, get connected and pay for the call, often with a credit card. These days you no longer need wait for hours in a post office for a line, or paying through both nostrils at the local Novotel. International telephone centres will often have fax sending and receiving facilities too; an ideal alternative to snail mail.

Anyone who owns a **mobile phone** will be aware of their variable utility and certainly beyond your home country just about all will be out of range and cost a fortune, but **international phone cards** are another way of keeping in touch inexpensively, as long as you can get through to the code number from wherever you happen to be.

E-mail is of course the way to go: it's the cheapest way of communicating speedily, but again requires the necessary hardware or an Internet café. The latter are becoming common in touristy places all over the world while to e-mail from hotel rooms **Psion personal organisers** have become the preferred telecom gadget, although keying in a long e-mail will require some dexterity.

There are plenty of **free web-based e-mail accounts** now like Hotmail and Yahoo, while Bigfoot.com will forward all your e-mails to one place for free as long as you get people to reply to it.

ATTITUDES TO SECURITY

Now that you're travelling deeper into the unknown, you'll be getting worried about your security. Four-wheel overlanders have it easy, but on a bike all your gear is out there for the taking and it's understandable to feel vulnerable, exposed and obsessed about security. This section could be filled with any number of canny tricks about secret pockets and booby traps, but the only knack you need to develop is common sense and vigilance backed up by comprehensive travel insurance.

Accept that you're going to lose something or even everything, either through carelessness or theft. Much has been said earlier about the need to keep your valuables safe, but in the end it's all just stuff that can be replaced, albeit at a price and great inconvenience. This is just a simple fact of travelling: riding bikes through distant lands is risky.

Fear of the unknown is an understandable self-protection mechanism and since man has travelled, others have preyed on him. The perils of travel are probably no greater than they were five hundred or two thousand years ago, and the need for vigilance has always been the same.

On a boat or in a town, only let things out of your sight that you can afford to lose – and don't think that Europe is any less risky than Africa or Asia; petty pilfering in the developing world is as likely as outright theft in the West.

Cities anywhere are the lairs of thieves who prey on rubberneck tourists and are one good reason to avoid them. In these crowded places keep any evidence of your wealth or your confusion under wraps. Wallets should always be zipped into an inside pocket and cameras not dangling temptingly around your neck. Markets, ports or crowded travel termini are favourite haunts for pickpockets. As you wander into these places check everything is zipped up and be alert. One good tip I read in Gregory Frazier's *Riding South* (see p.169) is having a **dummy wallet** with your day cash plus some expired credit cards and even an old passport. If you get mugged they'll be happy with this and the more expired crap and other junk the better.

Avoid looking at maps on street corners; in heavy city centres plan your route corner by corner before you walk out of your hotel room and when you do walk, imitate the advice given to women walking alone at night: march with a single-minded motivation that emits the signal 'Don't fuck with me!' in a Sylvester Stallone accent. Beware of pats to the shoulder and other distractions which are well known snatch-and-grab set-ups.

Coping with robbery

During the months preceding your departure, it's likely at least one person – an individual who watches a lot of television and doesn't travel much – will have expressed alarm at your adventurous itinerary. 'Libya/Iran/Colombia [take your pick], are you crazy?' You might knock back some bluff reply, but underneath you can't help thinking they might have a point.

While theft is usually an urban problem, robbery, or what's quaintly know as banditry, usually occurs in remote regions, and is as likely in the US or outback Australia as anywhere else. Again be wary of set-ups like broken down cars needing help.

If you ride straight into an ambush or are set upon by armed bandits in the middle of the night, the common advice is let them take what they want and live to tell the tale. If you're smart then you'll have a stash of cash on the bike which itself is rarely a commodity worth the hassle of stealing.

CROSSING BORDERS

The vagaries of border crossings are perennial worries to adventurous travellers. Even as I write this, I hear that the Mexican border with Arizona is nearing crisis level with an epidemic of robberies and travellers passing through in convoy. The truth is, this situation is unusual and anyway, after half a dozen countries, you'll have got the hang of crossing frontiers without delay, or at least be inured to the inevitable hanging about. Nevertheless, adopt this Platonic strategy at all border crossings:

- Remain calm and polite
- Be patient and smile a lot
- Never grumble or show unnecessary irritation
- Obey all the petty instructions for searches and papers
- Accept delays and sudden 'lunch breaks'
- Never argue: bite your lip in the face of provocation

If you're being given a hard time, stoicism and good humour may diffuse a tense situation. Try to remember that the glamorous benefits of a uniform and a machine gun soon pale when you're living in a tin shed far from your family and haven't been paid for six months, as is often the case in Africa. Read the situation. If there's a request to make some untoward payment or 'tourist tax', stick up for yourself, ask for a receipt, negotiate, but in the end pay up. Remember that they're not just picking on you.

Bribes aren't daylight robbery, but a way of life in many developing countries. You may resent this custom – and many travellers boast that they've never paid a penny – but that's just what it is, a custom. A couple of pounds can save hours. You'll know when you're expected to pay – accept it as part of travelling, but don't think you have to pay your way through every border or tricky situation. In all my travels in Africa, I've only succumbed to an open bribe once; coughing up a packet of biscuits and a map of the Ivory Coast. Both parties went away satisfied.

Finally, although it is rare for motorcyclists to be asked for lifts across borders, decline all such requests unless you want to be involved with the hassles of an unwanted immigrant.

CHANGING MONEY

Some borders have currency changing facilities, others out in the bush don't. Try and anticipate this eventuality or possibly an approaching weekend by buying a little currency in the preceding country. Use credit cards where possible and remember that changing a weak local currency back into US dollars or whatever, is either impossible or comes at such a bad rate that it's hardly worth it. Changing money can take hours in some banks, but get used to it: it's the same for everyone. Currency dealer booths in large town centres are not as dodgy as they look, can save hours and might even offer a better rate.

'Sorry, no change' is something you're bound to hear when paying for a local service with a high denomination note; it's one of the first things taxi drivers learn to mouth after they're born. When you've got nothing else there's no way round it, but learn to hoard low denomination notes, they're useful for tips and small bribes.

Currency declaration forms

Some countries try and undermine their black markets by insisting you complete a Currency Declaration Form (CDF). On it you fill out all the foreign currency you are bringing into a country and possibly other valuables too. Any further exchange transactions you make in that country must be matched by receipts or entries on the CDF, so that when you leave, the cash you brought in equals what you're taking out, less the money you officially exchanged. Half the time these forms aren't even checked when you leave, but don't count on it. Any money you don't declare on the form (i.e. smuggle in) must also not be discovered on departure.

Black market

The use of the black market to change foreign currency into local at an advantageous rate is an accepted part of travel in countries with weak or 'soft' currencies. It's also a popular set-up for naïve travellers and by its very nature illegal, leaving you liable to fines, confiscation of funds and even imprison-ment. To many locals your hard currency is a valuable ticket out of their coun-try or access to desirable foreign goods which their feeble currency cannot buy.

Libya had a thriving black market, of sorts. As you approached the border from Tunisia, roadside boys would wave you down with huge wodges of Libyan dinars offering a rate four times better than the artificially high official rate at the Ras Ajdir border. Here various paperwork must be paid for at the bad rate but the border officials turn a blind eye to your stash of dinars. Lately some banks are now offering tourists the black market rate, but as finding, let alone recognising, a bank in Libya is hard work, you may as well save time by buying in Tunisia and selling back your excess, if you return via Tunisia.

Making deals

Use the black market by all means (sometimes there is no choice and some banks even encourage it to save queuing), but keep your eyes open and your wits about you.

If you're a beginner here are some guidelines:

● Establish exactly how many dinars you're being offered for a dollar (for example). Repeat to them 'So you are offering me 300 dinars for one dollar?' and if they agree then spell out the total amount you want to exchange, i.e. 'So you will give me 4500 dinars for fifteen dollars?'
● Ask to see the currency offered and check that the notes have the right number of zeros. It is also helpful to learn to read the nine cardinal Arabic numerals if heading that way.
● If there's room for negotiation, go ahead. A wily black marketeer is going to offer as little local currency as he can for your valuable dollars
● Deal one-to-one and don't get drawn into any shady corners or deals

Watch out for sleight of hand. I'm sure I was diddled with the Romanian Hand Trick in Tunisia once. There is some ploy in which they count out the money offered, give it to you to count, which you do, and find everything in order. At this point your guard is down and they *take it back* to check, and even though you are staring at their hands something happens and you get back less than you thought. If this 'handback' scenario happens, be on guard, try and resist it or count it all again. Obviously the black market rate will represent a major boost to your funds, but don't stick your neck out to gain a measly ten per cent. While you should never take them for granted, you'll soon get the hang of making these useful if illegal street deals. And if you're ever unsure, trust your instincts and walk away.

Coping with begging and rewarding favours

Like the custom of bribery, riding through the world's poorer countries will expose the widespread practice of begging, particularly by children. It's com-mon to feel guilt at the thought of your indulgent adventure in the face of the extreme poverty you encounter. The daunting disparity between the wealth of the First World and the Third hits you square in the face as you're confronted with millions of needy people and only one of you.

Over the years sponsored overlanders and rally teams have got into the habit of throwing out branded commodities as they tear past, be they pens (the

PERSONAL CONDUCT IN MOSLEM COUNTRIES

The following guidelines all boil down to respecting local laws, customs and sensibilities. Many of them derive from the mores of Islam which, like other oriental religions, is much more a 'way of life' than Christianity is in the West. Islam has great respect for Christianity, with which it shares many of its early myths; Jesus Christ himself is mentioned as a prophet in the Koran, Islam's Holy Book. However, devote Moslems will be contemptuous of anyone who denies the existence of a God. Therefore, if, you're the fortunate recipient of Moslem hospitality, it's best to swallow any atheistic principles you may hold dear and call yourself a Christian, or whatever, when the topic turns towards religion.

There is a certain fear about transgressing social etiquette when dealing with Moslems and Arabs. This can make an extended stay among traditional Arabs of a high status a nerve-racking experience. The 'left hand' rule (a favourite of sniggering book reviewers) is commonly known. Moslems find our use of toilet paper as disgusting as we find their use of the left hand for the same purpose. However, there is no need to become paranoid about such things. By observing and mimicking the behaviour of your host or those around you, you are unlikely to cause intentional offence. Contrary to impressions, people do not struggle to perform daily tasks one-handed; like many taboos, this one has its roots in a common sense of hygiene.

Another anticipated ceremony is the preparation and drinking of sweet, mint tea in tiny glasses. Nomadic lore suggests that the offer of a third glass is a signal to make your farewells and move on, failure of which would cause gross offence (or, more likely, inconvenience). The truth is, you can drink as much or as little of the brew as you wish. Any offers of further hospitality will be made clear without recourse to obscure rituals.

Many of the guidelines listed below are a matter of common sense, with many of the most strict taboos only observed in the devout regions of the more fundamentalist countries. Life is hard enough and, especially amongst desert nomads, the interpretation of Islamic law tends to be pragmatic rather than dogmatic.

● For even the most perfunctory exchange, always introduce yourself to strangers with a greeting and a handshake.

● Men should not talk to, touch or even look at women unless they approach you.

● Avoid touching other people, passing things or eating with your left hand.

● During Ramadan (a month of daytime abstinence similar to Christian Lent) do not eat drink, smoke or otherwise enjoy yourself in public during daylight hours. Ramadan depends on the moon and in 2001 begins on November 17th. See 🖳 www.moonsighting.com/calendar/html.

● Although hashish may be widely used in some Moslem countries, being caught in possession of hash or harder drugs will carry stiff, even terminal, sentences.

● The Moslem 'weekend' begins on Thursday, with Friday being the day of prayer. Shops and other services close at midday on Thursday and reopen on Saturday morning.

● You may dress as you wish of course, but whatever the weather, dress conservatively in towns. To Moslems the sight of a bare body is either offensive or unequivocally provocative.

● Anywhere in the world, always make a point of asking people first if you may take their photograph or film them. This is a typical area of tourist insensitivity. Disregarding the belief that photography steals the subject's soul, consider the rudeness of being photographed as an 'exotic local' while walking down your own High Street.

origins of the incessant plea 'Donnez moi un Bic!' heard all over West Africa), lighters, stickers or T-shirts (some guide books even provide lists of nifty hand-outs you might consider packing). Their interaction with the communities was limited to a trail of dust and a glow of goodwill watching scores of kids scrabbling in their dust for their presents.

Ask yourself why you're giving someone money (motorcyclists are unlikely to be carrying a surplus of commodities to give away) – is it to make yourself feel less bad or to improve their lives? Begging is endemic in Moslem countries where the giving of alms to the poor is one of the tenets of Islam, and in India the heartbreaking mutilation of children to improve their professional begging opportunities is well known.

While your trip may well change your attitude or at least open your eyes to the hard lives of three-quarters of the planet, accept that you can't help them all. A simple policy to adopt is to give tips or gifts in return for help: be it directing you to the right road or hotel, looking after your bike or taking you to a mechanic. You may have even have been put up as a guest.

One of the ironies you'll soon discover in Africa or Asia is that extraordinary generosity and hospitality are inversely proportional to wealth. Poor people will ask for nothing but to have the honour of helping you. A small gift of cash or food may not be asked for, but will be heartily appreciated.

Women and adventure motorcycling

Nicki McCormick

Half a day's drive west of nowhere, three rusty oil drums by the roadside revealed themselves to be a petrol station. As fuel was being filtered through a scrap of cloth, the inevitable crowd gathered. Faces pressed closer and the questions began:

'You lady? You man?'

'Lady.'

'LADY?! Alone? No husband?'

'Uh huh.'

'But madam', my interrogators demanded, 'Who drives the motorcycle?'

This was Pakistan: an unaccompanied young woman riding from Delhi was so far removed from people's concept of 'female' as to be impossible. My gender established, I was shown to the only hotel in town which was way outside my meagre budget, so I said I'd camp instead. The manager suddenly became animated.

'No, madam, you can't possibly camp round here! It's far too dangerous!' I silently agreed with him, and was relieved to see the price tumble as I half-heartedly insisted I'd be fine in my tent.

The only guest, I spent the evening on the veranda listening to tales from the days of the Raj. Charming and well-educated, the manager was the perfect host, until he casually slipped into the conversation, 'Do you need your own room tonight, or would you prefer to share mine?' I acted suitably horrified and haughty, demanded my own room and barricaded the door, just in case. But the manager had already forgotten the incident.

Next day I entered the notoriously dangerous state of Baluchistan with trepidation, but luckily instead of baddies I found only friendly restaurateurs who invited me to meet their families and insisted I devour extra chapattis (for strength).

Climbing into the mountains, storm clouds threatened, dusk was approaching, and the road dwindled to a muddy track. I felt alarmingly insignificant and alone, and I wasn't quite sure how far the next town was. Then, just as I thought I was getting the hang of riding in mud, I suddenly found myself pinned under the bike in a pool of slippery ooze. A group of camel drivers, looking every inch the ferocious tribesmen I'd been warned about, ambled round a corner. Masking my fear with a forced grin and a nervously friendly wave, I appealed for help. Realising I was female, they rushed to my aid as I righted the bike. 'Very strong. Very brave,' they gestured but, concerned for my safety, they commanded a passing motorcyclist to stay with me till Ziarat, where I arrived at dusk.

'Come and meet my family' someone insisted. In a courtyard sat 60-odd women in their Friday finery. I was flabbergasted. So were they, and the whole crowd froze as this mud-encrusted foreigner was led into their midst. Then questions came flying from every direction.

'Where are you from? Where is your husband? How did you come here?' Like a visiting celebrity, women and girls fought to shake my hand, others looking on shyly from the back. Meanwhile, my host had arranged for me to camp for free in the hotel grounds. All too soon they had to leave, and a matriarch tried to press a leaving present of cash into my hands. Instead, I accepted her phone number in Quetta and promised to come for dinner in a few days. The manager of the hotel clucked sympathetically at the state of the bike, boasted approvingly of my adventures to everyone within earshot, arranged for several buckets of hot water and then rustled me up the best biryani on earth.

And that was the end of another good day in Pakistan. In fact, most of them were good days. The ones that weren't were more to do with bikes and bureaucracy than being a woman alone. It was a pleasant surprise as I'd been apprehensive about the idea of a long motorcycle journey alone and possessed only basic mechanical knowledge.

Choosing a bike

There are things women planning a trip have to think about more carefully than men, one of these is the bike. Most recommended overland bikes tend to be tall and heavy for the average woman, but there are other options. I used a low and slow Enfield 350; while Anne-France Dautheville rode around the world on a Kawasaki 125 in the mid-Seventies. There's no point taking a big bike travelling if you can't drag it out of a ditch, though having said that, adrenaline can improve muscle power and mechanical skills in an emergency.

Personal safety

A more important consideration is personal safety. Many of the events of that one day in Pakistan could have become problems. The ideal solution is a tricky balance between maintaining a strong, brave, capable woman image which projects the respect you need to avoid hassles, while at the same time being feminine enough to allow a bit of chivalry and protectiveness. If you know yourself fairly well and are prepared, many of the potential disadvantages and risks of travelling as a woman can be eliminated, or even turned into advantages. It is possible to have the best of both worlds.

To stay safe, you must be respected. The bike is your biggest asset here – the concept of a woman travelling on a 'male' form of transport is often so incomprehensible that you are treated as an honorary man. A woman with a motorbike does not come across as vulnerable but fearless, slightly crazy and intrepid, someone not to be messed with. People are shocked, but you are far more likely to encounter admiration than hostility as a result.

When I walked through the bazaar of one town, even fully robed, I was stared at, catcalled by giggly young men and felt a little vulnerable, a shameless foreign women unaccompanied in male territory. The next day I rode to the same market. No giggles. No lewdness. Previously disapproving old men decided I was worthy of a nod. Young men approached to make intelligent conversation and ask about the bike. Suddenly I became a person, I had respect again. A bike takes the focus off you and your marital status, opens doors and is a great conversation starter.

The most common stress-inducer for women travelling alone (even in Europe) is sexual harassment. Mostly it's low-level stuff – propositioning or the odd furtive grope. If you act cautiously, more serious harassment is very rare and paradoxically, the further you are from touristy areas, the safer you're likely to be.

Incessant 'romantic' offers can be more irritating than threatening. It's usually more a case of 'well, we've heard what these Westerners are like – you never know if you don't ask'. Reacting angrily can often provoke laughter and more teasing, especially among young men. Ignoring the comment entirely works well, and it can help to act shocked and disappointed that someone so friendly, in such a hospitable country, could think such shameful thoughts. Declaring yourself to be the daughter or sister of the potential suitor usually stops all offers before they start by putting the guy into a protector role. A calm appeal to another, preferably older, man nearby can often shame someone into desisting.

In general, the safest accommodation is a room with a lock (preferably your own) in a full-ish hotel, or with a family. Camping near people is normally OK if you ask someone senior-looking for permission first, thus making them your 'protector'. Free-camping is only really safe if it's somewhere totally isolated, where inquisitive passers-by aren't likely to spot you and pay a nocturnal visit.

Male companions

Travelling with a male companion doesn't necessarily reduce harassment, but if you are travelling with a man, make sure he knows he's expected to defend your honour aggressively! And call you wife. Women travelling with male partners can expect to be ignored in conversations and treated as invisible, especially in Moslem countries. It can sometimes be hard to keep your cool, but it's worth bearing in mind that in many places low-level lasciviousness is par for the course, and the creeps aren't worth ruining your trip over. It's not all roses travelling with a man, of course: in sticky situations there's no holding them back and they love to take charge – for better or for worse – as you can read on p.258.

In many countries, contact between the sexes is strictly limited, and men's media-fuelled image of Western women is that they are all promiscuous and available. But riding a bike doesn't fit too well with the perceived bimbo scenario. Mentioning your father as often as possible also helps, as does a stash of family photos to prove that you too, are someone's daughter or sister and not just a foreigner. A chaste, high status profession, such as teacher, gives credibility and respectability. If you are a topless dancer, it's good to lie! Some women find it useful to invent a husband. This can, of course, pose the question 'Well, where is he, then?' ('dead...?', 'arriving any minute now...?'). A well-received reply to the innumerable questions was to tell people jokingly that I was married to my motorcycle. 'It's just as much trouble as a husband, but I can sell it if it gets tiresome!' Humour can defuse most situations.

Dressing and acting discreetly

In Moslem countries especially, clothes showing the shape of the body or expanses of flesh are seen as shameful or provocative. It can be difficult to conform to local dress norms while keeping protected for riding, but a long, baggy shirt is usually enough to cover any curves.

Actions that seem natural at home, like shaking hands or walking alone with a strange man, can often be seen as a huge come-on. Instead of shaking hands, salaaming with the right hand on the heart and a slight nod of the head is acceptable. Giving lifts to men is risky, as it is anywhere, and if accepting a guide, it's wise to let someone (a hotel manager, for example) know who you're with, and to subtly make sure your companion knows they know. Sometimes this might not be possible, but the most important thing in any potentially risky situation is to act calmly and confidently, and never show fear. Trust your instincts, without being paranoid.

The distressed damsel ploy

Not speaking to anyone because they might harm you takes away the enjoyment of the trip, but it pays to be wary. If and when you need help, the most common reaction to a maiden in distress is chivalry – you're far more likely to be treated sympathetically than a man might be. Both men and women feel the need to look after a lone woman. This can mean cars stopping to offer assistance when you're stranded by the roadside, a mechanic giving your bike extra special attention because he wouldn't want to feel responsible for you breaking down somewhere, or priority at border crossings. Rooms may be found for you in full hotels, and in many countries, as a woman you'll be welcomed into a side of family life that male travellers never see.

Distressed? Who are you calling distressed?
© Nicki McCormick

Throwing feminist principles to the wind and playing the helpless girlie when necessary can work miracles in getting your way. (Freya Stark once said that the biggest advantage of being a woman is that you can always pretend to be more stupid than you are and no one will be surprised). Women have a greater chance of successfully pleading ignorance and charming their way out of difficult situations, flattery gets you everywhere, and it's often a lot simpler than wounding a vulnerable male ego and creating an enemy.

And finally
Your perception of yourself affects other people's perception of you. If you manage to act as if it's the most natural thing in the world for you to be trundling your bike across Asia or wherever, chances are the people you meet will accept and respect you for it. The reaction from home may often be along the lines of 'Oh, you're so brave! We're so worried about you'. Things can go nastily wrong for a woman alone on a bike in Central Nowhere. But they can also go wonderfully right.

Off-highway riding

It's possible to traverse South America and Asia and rarely leave the tarmac, but if you're heading across Africa, gravel roads, sandy pistes and muddy jungle tracks are an unavoidable fact of life. A deviation along a dirt road, be it smooth gravel, mud, sand or snow requires much more interaction with your bike and the track and wherever you go in the world, mastering the techniques of riding your heavy bike off the highway will be one of the major elements of your adventure. When there's a trail of dust billowing off your back wheel you can't help thinking you really are abroad, far away from civilisation and heading into the unknown. Sealed highways are handy for shopping or getting to work but the dirt is where it's at!

On the dirt traction is unpredictable and constant reading of the terrain ahead is vital. It is this keyed-up involvement that makes off-roading so rewarding. Ever since Kenny Roberts rewrote the book on GP racing, it's common knowledge that today's top racers developed their rear-wheel steering and sharp reactions from sliding around on dirt bikes. And besides the improvements to your road-riding skills, off-roading provides the exhilaration of road racing at a fraction of the speed. By the end of the day you'll be parked up in some scenic and remote location, shagged-out, filthy, but satisfied. It's what adventure biking is all about.

Gently does it
Riding off-road is fun, but until you get the hang of handling your loaded bike on various surfaces, you should take it easy. As a general rule you'll find **50mph/80kph** is an optimum cruising speed on any dirt surface. At speeds greater than this it's not possible to react quickly enough to the ever-changing terrain and riding on dirt is never predictable.

Off-roading can improve your riding skills – or eat your bike. © Karim Hussein

Overland biking is not about smoking kneepads (but if you do, choose the filtered brands); it's about long-term survival, so never take risks, resist the impulse to show off and always ride within the limitations of:

- your vision
- the terrain
- your experience
- your bike's handling abilities

and be aware of the consequences of:
- an accident
- getting lost
- running out of fuel or water

Ready for a beating

Don't be in any doubt about the hammering your bike is going to get on dirt roads, or the just as frequent crumbling tarmac roads that you'll find beyond your home country. Much of the advice on bike preparation given in earlier chapters is concerned with limiting damage when riding over rough terrain. Lightly-framed trail bikes with heavy loads or cast-wheeled road tourers were not built for a beating on corrugated tracks and frame, rack or tank fractures are the second most common problem after punctures. Besides offering agility in the dirt, a lightly-loaded bike will put less stress on the already hard working wheels, suspension and transmission. Make sure they're up to it.

DIRT ROADS

Most of your off-roading will be on dirt roads of varying quality. At their best they're straight and flat, with a smooth and consistent surface requiring little need for reduced speeds. But dirt being what it is, this won't last for long and most tracks will have been rutted by heavy traffic, washed-out by rains, blown over with sand, littered with rocks and, likely as not, corrugated.

Corrugations and berms

Corrugations are another name for the washboard surface which an unconsolidated track develops as a result of regular, heavy traffic. The accepted explanations for these infuriatingly regular ripples of dirt are braking and acceleration forces of passing traffic or the 'tramping' shock absorbers of heavy trucks with antediluvian suspension.

The 500-mile/700km Gibb River Road in Australia's north-west is a notoriously corrugated dirt road pounded by triple-trailer road trains and recreational 4WDs. Especially in its eastern half, the rattle of your bike can put severe tests on your equanimity, wheels, tyres and rear subframe.

In a car you grit your teeth and pray that the shock absorbers won't explode; the best solution is to accelerate up to about 50mph/80kph and skim across the top of each ripple, reducing vibration dramatically. On a bike, the same practice gives a smoother ride too, but at this speed your wheels are barely touching the ground and your traction is negligible. In a straight line this is not too dangerous, but on a bend it's possible to skid right off the track.

Wealthier countries grade their corrugated dirt roads once in a while – Australia's Northern Territory is notable for smoothing off its many dirt highways – but the honeymoon only lasts a few weeks. In the developing world, the passing of a grader is most likely an annual event.

Corrugations: nature's answer to suspension warranties and overloaded racks.

The good thing is that on a bike you only have a few tyre-inches of width to worry about and you'll often find corrugations shallowest or non-existent on either edge of the track, though rarely for more than a few metres at a time. You'll find yourself forever weaving around trying to find the smoothest path. On a desert plain it might be easier to avoid a corrugated track altogether and ride in far greater comfort and freedom alongside the track, but realistically this option is rare.

Corrugations do have one small saving grace. A very easy place to get lost anywhere in the world is near a settlement, be it a capital city or African village. Near a small settlement there may be many minor tracks leading to places connected with the village and the main route might go right through or bypass it altogether. Generally, the most corrugated track is the one most frequently used by vehicles passing through and probably the one you want to follow. There may even be times out in the desert when, a little lost, the sight and feel of corrugations will be an immense relief, signifying that you've relocated a major track from which you may have inadvertently strayed.

But, overall, corrugations are just a miserable fact of dirt-roading and a good place to have knobbly tyres with slightly reduced pressures, a well-supported subframe, a comfy seat and a firmly wrapped kidney belt. Even on the Gibb River, or the equally spine-powdering accent to Assekrem in Algeria's Hoggar mountains, the worst, denture-loosening patches last only for 20 minutes or so. Who knows why corrugations periodically flatten out, but its a chance to rest before gritting your teeth for the next lot.

When the going gets rough, stand up

Standing up on the footrests over rough ground is probably the most important technique off-road riding neophytes should master because when you're standing up:

- suspension shocks are taken through your legs not your back
- your bike is much easier to control
- being higher up, your forward vision is improved

Contrary to the impression that standing up raises your centre of gravity and makes you less stable it, in fact, has the opposite effect. It transfers your weight low, through the footrests, rather than through the saddle when you're seated. This is why trials riders and motocrossers always tackle tricky sections standing up on the pegs.

When standing up, grip the tank lightly between your knees to give your body added support and to prevent the bike from bouncing around between your legs. Padding on the inside of your knees or on the tank helps here.

As you get the hang of things, standing, just like sticking your leg out on a slithery bend, will soon become instinctive. You'll find it's not always necessary to stand right up; sometimes just leaning forward and pulling on the bars while taking the weight off your backside will be enough to lessen the jolt. In a nutshell: **sit down when you can, stand up when you must**.

DESERT BIKING

If there's one environment in the world where you can guarantee a high quality off-road experience it's the desert, be it the Sahara or Australia's less-demanding outback. Deserts being what they are, exploring rather than simply crossing them represents one of the extremes of adventure biking: something that either appeals to you or fills you with dread. Unsupported motorbikes are not the ideal vehicles for this sort of travel and, more than ever, thorough planning and preparation are vital.

The biggest problems will be **navigation** and carrying enough **fuel and water**. GPS allied with reliable maps has made the former more reliable, but riding a fully-loaded bike on remote, sandy tracks will be very demanding and something that's best left to experienced riders. Plan well within your range and limit your tour to the cool winter months. Using wells or waterholes can extend your time in the desert, if not your range.

Never consider biking independently in deserts during the summer months (May–September anywhere in the Sahara, December–February in the remote corners of central Australia). With temperatures above 40°C, you'll need to drink every half hour and daily water consumption will easily be ten litres. Then again an unladen bike accompanying a 4WD or two makes an ideal reconnaissance vehicle in the desert, skimming over soft sand where the heavy cars can get bogged for hours.

It's not uncommon for bikers to lose their heads a bit in the desert and belt off across the sands as if it were a beach at low tide. Initially, riding this way will be a very exhilarating experience until you come across a rock, a soft patch or a shallow depression, indistinguishable in the midday glare. This 'lack of shadows' is a striking characteristic which I wrote of in *Desert Travels*:

'There's a subtle but significant difficulty when riding northwards on a piste in the northern hemisphere when the sun is generally behind you; it's hard to explain but here goes. Imagine you're crossing a road with the sun in your face casting a black band of shadow underneath the kerb ahead. Even if everything around you is the same hue, you'd still spot the shadowy lip of the kerb and adjust your step accordingly as you approach it. Try this in the opposite direction with the sun behind you, and you'll find the glare much greater, with no helpful shadows highlighting the relief of the ground or the step of the kerb ahead of you. Before you know it you trip over and go sprawling with your shopping. So it is when heading south in the Sahara; the sun is generally high and in your face, highlighting a host of tiny but informative shadows and shades of the terrain ahead, most especially defining the lips of sharp-edged ridges which you can then steer round.

Heading north I couldn't work out why everything was so bright and why it was so hard to ride smoothly after yesterday's valuable lesson. Are some days brighter than others in the Sahara, I wondered? After a few near misses I hit the unseen foot-high creek bank and went over the 'bars. Fortunately everything breakable on the bike was already broken so damage was negligible, but the harmless spill unnerved me. Checking the repaired tank for further leaks, I forced myself to slow down, watch where I was riding and take it easy.'

As you hit a rock or soft patch too fast, the front wheel gets deflected or digs in and you fly over the bars, closely followed by your cart-wheeling machine. In this type of accident it's the bike that usually causes the injury to the rider and on many desert trips I've come across, or heard about, riders who have come to grief in this way.

In the desert it's not so much the riding as the relentless concentration demanded by riding and navigating safely that will wear you out, and although you'll often be riding through spectacular scenery, the only chance you will have to fully appreciate this splendour is to stop.

You'll find more information on motorbiking in the Sahara in *Sahara Overland* (also published by Trailblazer).

Berm bashing

As any enthusiastic dirt rider knows, 'berms' – the built-up bank on the side of the track – can be used to ride around bends much faster and more safely than can be done on the flat part of a track. In effect, by riding the bank you reduce the amount of lean required for a given speed – a milder version of a gravity-defying 'Wall of Death' scenario – so berms can be ridden round at alarmingly high speeds safely. This isn't the advanced motocross

Get up, stand up, stand up for rights (as well as machine control and visibility).

technique it may seem, as angles of lean are moderate. Rather, it's a way of riding out bends without having to resort to tiring (for yourself) and inefficient (for your bike) braking and acceleration. And when you get it just right, berm bashing is also a whole lot of fun!

Riding in sand

Sand can be great to ride over if it's consistently firm, but in somewhere like the Sahara riding on sand requires a high degree of concentration – at it's most demanding when riding through very soft fine sand or when forced along a track rutted by cars. Riding along rather than just across a sandy creek presents the most difficult condition that a desert biker regularly encounters. Here, fine waterborne sand is washed down by occasional rains, and you can find yourself riding standing up in one- or two foot-wide ruts for miles at a time. Extremely tiring!

The keys to riding soft sand are:

Low tyre pressures

By dropping the air pressure to as little as 5psi, a tyre flattens out and its 'footprint' on the sand lengthens significantly (rather than widens, although it does that a bit, too). Doing this changes your normally round tyre into more of a caterpillar track, increasing your contact patch and improving your traction dramatically, even with a trail or a road tyre. It can mean the difference between riding confidently across a sandy section or slithering around barely in control, footing constantly, losing momentum and finally getting stuck or falling over – every few minutes.

The trouble is that in this severely under-inflated state a tyre gets much hotter, due to the internal friction created by the flexing carcass. Being soft and hot the tyre becomes much more prone to punctures. Keep your speed down on very soft tyres and be sure your security bolts or similar devices are done up tight as it's in just these low-pressure/high-traction situations that the dreaded tyre creep occurs.

Momentum and acceleration

These are often the only things that will get you through a particularly soft stretch of sand, so don't be afraid to stand up and accelerate hard at the right time. A quick snap of the throttle in a middle gear gives you the drive and sta-

Blast over cross ruts in sand as close to right angles as possible while standing up. © Yves Larboulette

bility to blast assuredly across a short, sandy creek as the front wheel skims over the surface. No matter how much your bike weaves and bucks around, keep the power on and your backside off the seat for as long as it takes. So long as the front wheel remains on course you're in control. Keep off the brakes, especially the front. If you need to slow down use the engine to decelerate and be ready for the bike to become unstable.

Riding like this is very tiring, but in most cases even trying to slow down and stop will mean falling over or getting bogged. For those keen to ride to Timbuktu, note that the track from Bourem in the east requires riding like this for 200 miles/300km! Sand riding can be hair-raising stuff and you'll often come close to falling off, but the above techniques are the only way to get through soft sand short of paddling along at 1mph.

Braking, turning and keeping going

Braking and turning will demand great care in soft sand. On very soft terrain it's best to avoid braking altogether and simply roll to a halt, otherwise the trench you dig might keep you there when you try to pull away. If this happens, hop off your bike and run alongside until it's moving freely without wheelspin, and then jump on.

As anyone who's ridden on a beach knows, turning hard on smooth sand creates its own little berm, enabling radical foot-out cornering, but out on a desert plain wide gradual turns under firm acceleration are best made using your body weight rather than turning the handlebars and leaning.

No matter how far the tread extends around the edge of your tyres, the best traction and the greatest stability is achieved with your bike upright.

It's said that 'weighting' the outside footrest improves your bike's carving qualities in sandy turns, but this technique has little effect on a lardy overlander and unless you're an experienced off-roader you want to avoid sliding around. There'll be plenty of occasions when you get crossed up involuntarily without trying to do so for fun.

Sandy ruts

About 25mph/40kph in third is the best speed/gear combination to maintain when riding along sandy ruts, the low gear and high revs giving quick throttle response to further difficulties you may encounter. Slow down through the gears not the brakes and don't be reluctant to rev your engine hard if necessary. It's in this situation where unreliable or ill-tuned engines begin to play up or overheat.

If you are in a deep rut, stay in it and don't try to cross ruts or ride out unless absolutely necessary. If you must change ruts urgently, hurl your bike and your weight in the preferred direction of travel while standing up and gassing it… but don't expect to get away with these kind of moves on a tanked-up Africa Twin with a passenger on the back.

Getting stuck in sand

Luckily, getting an overlanding bike stuck in the sand is nowhere near as big a problem as getting stuck in a car and a solo rider is usually able to get moving again without assistance. You may have hit an unexpected soft patch in the wrong gear or at too slow a speed, and gradually your bike gets dragged to a halt as you drop frantically through the gears.

In this situation do all you can to keep moving. As you slow down to walking pace, pull in the clutch to avoid futile wheelspin and, with the engine still running, hop off the bike. Now push the lightened bike with the help of the engine, jumping back on once you're moving on firmer ground. This sort of activity is tiring and not something you want to do more than a few times a day, but keeping moving is the only answer short of even more laborious digging, pushing and shoving.

Nevertheless sometimes you get caught. When the wheels are buried up to the hub and the bottom of the engine is resting on the sand, stall the machine and turn off the engine. The bike will be standing up by itself at this point, so turn off the fuel taps and lay the bike on its side. The rear wheel should now be hanging over the hole it excavated. Kick the sand back into the hole and pick the bike up again; the bottom of the engine should now be off the sand.

Lower the tyre pressures if you haven't already done so, turn on the fuel and start the engine. It's at moments like these you'll be pleased you chose an electric-start model. With your engine running and your front wheel pointing straight ahead, let the clutch out slowly and push the bike forward. If the rear wheel begins spinning again, as may happen on an upward incline, stop immediately. Try and flatten the ground in front of the wheels so that they have no lip to roll over, and consider letting still more air out of the rear tyre, even if it means you have to reinflate it again once you're free.

DUNE RIDING: A WARNING

When passing an alluring range of dunes the temptation to dump your baggage and have a quick blast can be hard to resist. The exhilarating freedom from other traffic, white lines and linear routes can appear like off-road heaven, but accidents in dunes with overland and especially recreational off-road vehicles are very common. On a recent tour in Libya we came across two riders with broken limbs and heard about another who had broken his neck in the Ubari Sand Sea, a popular venue for dune driving out there.

On a bike the sand may appear cushion-soft, but a cart-wheeling bike certainly is not. Desert dunes are a maze of varying but like-coloured slopes which can be hard to distinguish, especially at noon where shadows are non-existent. Even recognising the very presence of slopes can be impossible. Most accidents happen when the speed you're compelled to maintain on soft sand sends you over an unexpected drop. If you're lucky it's just a harmless tumble, if not it's the end of your trip and the beginning of a stressful evacuation.

Limit your dune bashing to mornings or evenings when the low sun highlights the definition of the slopes; let your tyres right down, wear protective gear and don't lose your head.

Left: Well and truly buried. **Right:** The easiest solution is to lean the bike over (removing the baggage if necessary), fill in the hole, pick the bike up and push it out with the engine running in first gear.

Also consider dragging your bike around so that it faces down the incline, from where it will get moving much more easily. This may require removing your luggage. As a last resort, use your jacket under the back wheel as a sand mat to give that initial bit of traction you need to shift onto firmer ground. All this energetic activity and shredding of your prize jacket assumes that there's no one else around to give you a helpful push.

Getting bogged down in sand is usually the result of limited experience, or of not reading the terrain correctly, also of having too high tyre pressures or of spinning your wheel when you should have got off and pushed. As you become more experienced on the dirt these events should occur less and less often, if at all.

In conclusion, never let your concentration drop while riding in sand, even if it appears easy. Attack soft sections standing up on the footrests and with the power on. Maintain momentum at all costs, even if it means slithering around and riding in totally the wrong direction, or jumping off and running alongside.

ROCKY MOUNTAIN TRACKS
On a rocky plateau or in the mountains, dirt tracks provide the type of terrain where a well set-up bike is at its best, being faster, easier and more enjoyable to ride than any other form of transport.

However, the danger here lies not only in damaging your wheels and getting punctures, but also in colliding with an oncoming truck or riding off a precipice. Some rocky mountain sections demand reduced speed for no other reason than you cannot be sure what is around the next bend or over the brow of the hill. Bus drivers along the Karakoram Highway or the Andes are well known for leaving their brains on the roof rack and you must always be ready for them to come hurtling round a bend straight towards you. 'Your' and 'my' side of the road are all academic on a blind bend where the biggest truck with the most useless brakes owns both sides of the road. Look on the bright side – you could be a white-knuckled backpacker stuck in that bus…

Keep your hands over the levers and be ready for anything from grazing stock to tracks buried under a landslide (in the Karakoram earth tremors are a daily event) or tracks missing altogether following heavy rain. At some stage you're bound to come upon a lorry groaning uphill at walking pace or another broken down altogether. Despatch riders will adapt well to the alert and anticipatory riding style required here.

Again, in the mountains as much as anywhere, you must ride within the limits of your visibility and the terrain. Read the ground constantly. A steep descent may end at a

Rocky mountain tracks: sensational views but not much chance to look around. © Karim Hussein

sandy creek or a washout, while a steep ascent rarely continues down the other side in the same direction. After just a few hours of this you'll find your judgement and reflexes improving noticeably.

Ride light

First-timers on the dirt tend to tense up, gripping the bars with stiff arms as the bike does its own thing and they absorb all the bumps like a plank. Be aware of this and consciously try to relax your body which, when rigid, has a detrimental effect on handling. Over rough terrain resist clenching the bars, instead hold them gently, guiding the front end while allowing it to deflect over the bumps.

By being relaxed and responding fluidly to the knocks, you'll preserve both yourself and your bike from sudden and ultimately tiring shocks. Riding light includes weighting the footrests over any cross ridges or V-shaped dips. During the course of a long day on the dirt you'll find this kind of responsive riding saves both physical and mental energy.

RIDING THROUGH MUD

Even on a 120kg competition bike with fresh knobblies, mud and especially bogs or swamps can present the dual challenge of negligible traction and treacherous suction. Coping with this sort of terrain on an overland porker is plain exhausting, and while sand riding responds to certain acquired techniques, the occluded consistency of water-logged terrain has no cut and dried rules, but if you can, then:

- avoid big mires if at all possible
- ride in one muddy rut and stick to it, either attacking it standing up or, if you don't feel confident, paddling through at walking pace
- approach deep water-logged sections with caution; ride through slowly to avoid drowning the engine or coming off on submerged obstacles. For more on deep water see p.94-97.

The tracks cut through the central African jungles are a notorious challenge for overlanders. Hundred-meter-long puddles stretch before you with queues

Without the right tyres you're better off paddling through muddy ruts at a snail's pace. © Matt Ball

of vehicles lining up behind a bogged down lorry.

On a bike, tyres are critical, with aggressive treads at low pressures making all the difference. Blasting into a huge puddle on a Zairian track is a recipe for a muddy face plant. If you can't find a way around the side, recognise that it's going to be a slow and tiring paddle, and be ready to stop if the trough deepens. You're usually forced to ride through the trenches dug by the last truck's spinning wheels, but depending on the period since the rains ended these pits can drown an entire car. If you're not sure, wade through first.

Trying to ride through wet muddy ruts might be hard, but worse still is when they harden into concrete-hard trenches. In mountains areas, where you can't necessarily ride around these, manoeuvring a big bike or one with ordinary tyres will be sub-walking-pace torture. You'll have to drop into the ruts and paddle along, being careful that the sides don't deflect the wheel and dump you on the hard surface. It's the only way forward except for those skilled riders who can style through on the footrests with a light front end and one hand on their hips.

Bogs and swamps

Large expanses of water-logged ground found in temperate zones can be harder still to deal with, and no one in their right mind would push a track through this sort of terrain. Perhaps the best known example is the high route across Siberia, only feasibly crossable in summer at which time the tundra melts into a quagmire.

This is not a place to ride alone: in the desert you can extricate a bike from sand with a little digging and along the flooded channels of central Africa there are usually enough other travellers or villagers around to help out. Riding your bike up to its bars into a Russian bog may be the last time you ride it. Learn to recognise what sort of vegetation, be it reeds or moss, inhabit water-logged ground; keeping to high ground is not always the answer. Even with help, in terrain like this your mileages may drop to as little as ten miles per day while your ability to deal with this exhausting pace can be numbered in hours. Take on challenging new routes by all means, but be under no illusion as to how hard this task will be.

RIVER CROSSINGS

Mud and bogs can be a drag but who can resist the thrill of cutting a V-shaped shower of spray as you blast across a shallow river? The other end of this photogenic scenario is a bent crankshaft in an engine ruined by hydraulic lock: the consequences of a piston sucking in and trying to compress uncompressable water.

The first thing to do when you come to a substantial and unfamiliar water crossing is to stop and have a good look. Just because tracks lead down one bank and up the other doesn't mean the crossing is safe. In tropical or arid regions distant storms can raise an unfordable creek miles from the downpour

If there's a bridge, use it. © Tom Grenon

in a matter of hours. And in a few more hours that river might be just a series of trickling pools. Furthermore, in recreational or farming areas 4WDs can churn up the river bed, creating mud or ruts which may tip you over.

Walk first

If in doubt about the river crossing walk across first: a wet pair of boots is less inconvenient than a drowned engine. Walking across establishes the strength of the current, the nature of the river bed and, of course, the maximum depth. Australian riders will be aware of the one exception to this rule: man-eating crocodiles inhabit northern coastal creeks between Derby and Cairns. There's more on this route on p.183.

If you feel the combination of current, river bed and depth make riding possible – generally, if you can walk it, you can ride it – then ride the bike through slowly, following the exact route of your foot reconnaissance. Still waters are usually deepest, so pick a spot just above some rapids; the water may be moving fast, but it's shallow. Keep the revs high in first or second gear. This runs through any electrical spluttering, avoids stalling and keeps a good pressure of exhaust blowing out of the silencer. Resist splashing which sprays electrics and kills the engine. Generally the 'plimsoll line' on most bikes is halfway up the barrel, below the carb, but wet electrics can snuff out an engine when blasting through a two-inch puddle.

Waterproofing your bike's electrics should have been part of your pre-departure preparation, but before you take the dive, spray in and around the plug cap and other vital ignition components with a water dispersing agent like WD40. Some engines, particularly Yamahas, cut out when the carb breather, usually down near the right footrest, goes underwater and other bikes may suck water in this way. A T-piece spliced into the breather with an extension leading up under the tank will solve this.

Remember that the consequences of falling over are as bad as riding in too deep; keep your finger over the kill switch and use it the moment you lose control. Once on the far side expect your brakes not to work and a bit of spluttering as the engine steams itself dry.

If you're confident or have walked it first, ride through, otherwise play it safe and push. © Craig Hightower

Pushing across

If riding is too risky walk your bike across with yourself on the upstream side so there's no chance of getting trapped under the bike should you get washed off your feet. If your baggage looks like getting soaked, you may prefer to unpack it and bring it over on your shoulders. It may be a good idea anyway, lightening the bike if you have to push it across the river with the engine off.

Whether you walk the bike across with the engine running or not depends on the risk of the water rising about the air intake. If you go for a running engine keep your thumb on the kill switch and cut the engine at the first sign of spluttering.

Truly, madly, deeply

Very rarely you might come to a river crossing which is way too deep to ride through but which, for whatever reason, you simply must cross, most likely because you're too low on fuel to backtrack. With careful preparation it's possible to totally submerge a bike providing the fuel, induction and exhaust systems are completely sealed off.

Doing this is no small job and you risk losing or ruining your bike, so make sure there's no alternative. Naturally the maximum depth you can walk through is limited by your height, but realistically don't attempt anything deeper than the height of the bars and don't try this radical procedure alone. Before you go ahead, establish the answers to these questions first:

- Is there a bridge or a ferry in the vicinity?
- Is there a shallower place to cross?
- Can you get the bike in a boat or on the roof of a 4WD?
- Can you leave the bike and swim across instead?
- Are there enough of you to carry lightened bikes across (on your shoulders or on sticks)? This will take at least three people per bike.
- Do you have the means to waterproof the bike and can get across without putting yourself in danger?

If the answer to all these is 'no' then this is what to do:

- Remove as much weight from the bike as possible, including the tank
- Kick over the engine so that it's on compression with both sets of valves closed

(Opposite) Top: Sometimes a flooded track is just what you want (Botswana). © Alex Marr.
Bottom: A jungle road through the Pygmy region of Cameroon. © Peter Kik.
(Following pages) With a jerrican and a set of Michelin Deserts, the Sahara is yours.

DROWNED ENGINE: WHAT TO DO

The worst has happened and your bike has taken a lung-full while running, or has fallen over and filled up. It's not the end of the world; this is what to do:

- Stand the bike on its end and drain the exhaust
- Drain the petrol tank
- Take out the spark plug and kick or tip out the water
- Drain the carb and dry the filter
- Remove the stator cover (on the left side of most singles), drain and dry it
- If the engine oil has a milky colour, it's contaminated with water and needs changing
- Once everything has dried out, test for a spark first and, if the bike runs, give it a full re-lube at the earliest opportunity

- Plug the exhaust securely
- Disconnect the battery
- Take out the air filter, wrap it in a plastic bag and reinstall it
- Fold over all oil tank, battery, engine and carb breather hoses so they're sealed and tape them up
- If you have some rope, set up a line from bank to bank, or to the bike so someone can help pull it through from the far bank

Once you're certain the engine is watertight and you're all sure you can manage the feat, then push it in, at least one pushing from behind and one steering on the upstream side of the bike and another pulling the bike on a rope. Now the bike's totally submerged there is no rush, take it easy; don't be distracted by bubbles rising from the bike; whatever's leaking it's too late to do anything about it now.

On the far bank let the bike drip dry – do not attempt to start the bike until you're sure it's fully drained. Pull out the exhaust bung and stand the bike on its back wheel to drain any water which may have leaked in. Release the breather hoses, take off the carb and drain it, making sure there's no water in the inlet manifold. Take out the air filter, drain the airbox and reinstall the filter. Drain other items like lights, switch housings and speedometers. Remove the spark plug and kick over the engine, hoping that no water spurts out of the plug hole, if it does check your engine oil over the next few miles of riding. If it's turned milky it has become contaminated with water and you should change it or continue slowly until you can.

Once all these procedures have been completed check for a spark and if all's well, fire the bike up and hope there's not another deep river a few miles further down the road!

ROAD RIDING

Much as riding on the dirt is fun, road riding is likely to make up the majority of your overlanding tour unless you're a committed dirt biker. While it may be easier on your back, riding the roads of over-populated developing countries will be stressful in the extreme, nowhere more so than India where a collection of animal, vegetable and mineral hazards combine to give your brakes plenty of exercise.

(Opposite) KTM Adventuring through the Black Mountains of Montana. © Tom Warr.

Basically, with all the many hazards listed below and probably some more that haven't been considered, be ready for anything. Sudden stops without brake lights, cutting in, drunken drivers, things thrown out of windows, dead animals, holes in the road, a barbed wire road block, the list goes on and on. Anything goes on the highways of most of the world – just make sure those things don't get you.

Other traffic

You may complain about inconsiderate car drivers in your own country but you've seen nothing until you ridden in Ecuador, Ethiopia, or India. Every year of motorbiking experience will stand you in good stead as you try and anticipate the hare-brained driving of most commercial drivers. Short of staying at home, alert, assertive riding and frequent use of your horn is the only way to deal with hazards posed by your fellow road users.

In poor countries ancient vehicles are kept running on the proverbial wing and a prayer. Expect not a shred of courtesy, instead be prepared for downright homicidal hostility. Don't count on insurance either, by and large other drivers won't have any and neither will you. All you can do is keep your speed down, your eyes open and ride to survive.

Pedestrians, carts and animals

What is it about animals and some villagers that makes them run out as you approach? They certainly wouldn't try it in front of a fume-spewing truck. As if dangerously driven cars and trucks weren't enough, most roads in developing countries are thoroughfares for anybody or anything on the move. Again, all you can do is give them a wide berth at slow speed with the brake levers covered.

Children and wild animals, like camels or kangaroos, have a habit of running startled across your path at the last second so always exercise extreme caution when nearing villages or herds of grazing beasts.

Potholes

Potholes are contagious. Once one appears, you can be sure that there'll be more ahead. You have to concentrate hard in these sections, as the mindless routine you have been used to on the smooth, empty highway is soon disrupted by hard braking, swerving and re-acceleration. A pothole's sharp edges can easily put a dent in a wheel rim so be prepared to manoeuvre to avoid this.

Luckily, on a bike you can squeeze through tyre-wide sections of solid tarmac where two holes are about to meet and generally you'll have an easier time of it than cars. In the end, if the road gets really bad, you may have the option of riding alongside, which may be no quicker but will prove more consistent than a badly damaged road.

Encroaching sand

Another hazard on a tarmac highway in a desert area is dunes encroaching with tongues of sand across the road. Two ruts are formed on the sand by passing traffic and to ride through successfully you must balance speed with caution. Although it's momentum that gets you through, riding into these sandy ruts at highway speeds will almost certainly knock you off. The sudden build-up of sand in front of the front wheel will dramatically alter the castor effect

---

NIGHT RIDING? – ONLY IN A DIRE EMERGENCY

Don't make the mistake of thinking sealed roads are safer to ride at night than dirt roads. Being more used by traffic, with or without lights, the contrary is true. If you want to give your trip a good chance of success don't ride on unfamiliar roads at night, no matter how powerful your headlight. Unless it's a dire emergency, it's not worth the risk. One tip if you do get dazzled by oncoming lights: force yourself to look away from the lights and steer by staring resolutely at the near side of the road or track.

---

of the steering and flip the wheel sideways, sending you over the bars.

Suddenly having to ride on soft sand after cruising quietly along the highway takes more adjustment than most can manage in the few seconds they have to think about it and accidents here are common. If you don't want to paddle over the dune – not a bad idea if you're riding on trail tyres at road pressures – slow right down to about 25–30mph/40–50kph, drop a couple of gears and then accelerate hard, allowing the back wheel to weave around while you concentrate on keeping the front wheel in the middle of that rut.

Navigation and survival

RIDING IN REMOTE AREAS

When riding in remote areas, three things will virtually ensure that you reach your next destination safely:

- A reliable and well-equipped bike
- Ample provisions for the route
- Common sense

The fact that you're in a potentially perilous situation does not need underlining. Your decisions and the way you conduct yourself will be fundamental to your survival.

Riding and navigating in a wilderness require a clear thinking mind aware of its own fallibility. It is very rare that you will become completely lost. More likely you'll be, in the words of the time-worn adage, 'temporarily unaware of your whereabouts'. You must use your logic and common sense to work out where you went wrong, and correct your mistake sooner rather than later.

NAVIGATION

Navigation anywhere requires knowledge of where you are as much as where you are going. Even on the tarmac highway where distances between settlements are vast, you should always take the trouble to know your position as accurately as possible. When on the dirt, landmarks such as major river crossings, distinctive mountains or steep passes should be anticipated with regular reference to your map, odometer and guidebook or route notes.

Anticipating landmarks becomes all the more important when riding in remote areas – generally deserts or mountains – when confirmation of your position adds much needed confidence. For example, stopping at a fork in the road, your map indicates a distinct turn to the south about 70km ahead where your route enters a narrow valley. Add 70 to your current odometer reading and memorise or write down the total figure 'turn south, valley, xkm'. As the 'xkm' reading rolls up on your trip you should expect to turn south, allowing a bit of slack for your rough estimate.

Maps

A good map and knowing how to use it is of course essential to this sort of riding. As a rule, a detailed map with a **medium scale** of 1:1 million (where 1cm = 10km or 6.2 miles) is adequate for riding across regions with tracks but no signposts. A scale of 1:500,000 is better if you're looking to pick your way around sand seas or over indistinct passes. If you're trying to pin point some unmarked historical or archaeological site, for example, a **large scale map** of 1:200,000 (where each centimetre represents 2km or 1.2 miles) or less will help you distinguish every valley, mountain and river. At this level of navigation a GPS unit (see below) becomes very useful.

Don't count on getting large scale maps in the African or Asian countries you're planning to visit. They're usually hoarded by the military and may require complicated applications to buy while being more easily available in your home country. Note that in barren wilderness areas, the age of the map may not be so critical as in urban areas; things don't change much in the Sahara or the Hindu Kush. The French IGN maps of West Africa produced over thirty years ago at the scales mentioned above are as good, if not better, for riding off the main routes than the commonly used **small scale** 1:4,000,000 Michelin 953 which gets updated every other year.

Trip meter and orientation

On a long route of a few days it's a good idea to note down the details of the complete itinerary such as distances, landmarks, forks in the trail, lakes and rivers, and stick them to your handlebars or tank bag for easy reference. Estimate your total fuel range conservatively and work out the mileage reading at which you expect to run out. Ensure that your destination is a maximum of 75% of your range allowing 25% leeway.

Reset your trip odometer at the beginning of a stage when all your reserves have been replenished, and only reset it at your next safe destination or when you totally refuel your tank. For this sort of riding the resettable trip is a far more useful instrument than your speedometer needle, and is why a spare speedo cable should be carried amongst your essential spares. It tells you how far you've travelled, and so acts as a guide to your position and, crucially, your remaining reserves of fuel.

For quick checks on your orientation (south-east, west-north-west, etc) it's easier to use the sun rather than referring to your compass, which requires stopping to get away from the bike's magnetic influence – at least ten metres. The fine degrees of accuracy a compass can offer are not usually necessary for ordinary navigation.

In the northern hemisphere, the sun always travels left to right throughout the day. Always keep half an eye out for the sun and get to know the directions of the shadows at various times of the day. After a while, a quick glance at your shadow and your watch will instantly tell you whether you are riding in the right direction.

Not getting lost

All these precautions are designed to mitigate the apprehensiveness of riding into a wilderness. Blindly following tracks without giving a thought to landmarks, orientation or maps is the most common way of getting lost. Sometimes a track can inexplicably begin to turn the wrong way or

'According to the map the three cups of tea should be very close'. © Yves Larboulette

peter out altogether. If you're tired, low on fuel or your bike is running badly, these moments of uncertainty can lead to careless decisions, such as trying to take a short-cut back to your last known position. Correcting these sorts of mistakes in your navigation is where a bike's barely adequate fuel reserves are often used up. Off a track and in mixed terrain, getting totally disorientated is as easy as falling off your bike; and if you're pinned down by your bike just a mile off a track, but out of sight, you may never be found.

If you're ever in doubt, don't hesitate to stop and think – never carry on regardless hoping that things will work themselves out. Look around you and consult your map, compass and odometer carefully. Look out for stone cairns, traces of corrugated track or any other clues as to where you might be. If you're lucky enough to have a major landmark such as a distinctive peak which is marked on your map take a bearing to help narrow down your position. It's a rare luxury to have two such landmarks in view but if they are sufficiently far apart you can accurately triangulate your position on a map and you're no longer lost. If this is not possible and you haven't a clue, you must turn back.

Riding together

Getting completely lost is rare, but losing sight of your riding companions is very common. Before you set out on an unknown section, establish some clear rules and signals. When travelling in a convoy with cars the pace is usually slower and a bike generally has no difficulty keeping up.

Out on the plains, bikes can ride side by side, but if riding in line on narrow tracks, one rider should take the lead and keep it, glancing back regularly for his companions. If the group is of mixed riding ability then it's best for the slowest rider to lead, even if it becomes frustrating for the hotshots who have to eat his dust. The simplest signal should be flashing headlights: 'I am slowing down or stopping' – on seeing this the leader should stop and wait or turn back if necessary. For this reason it's worth retaining at least one of your rear view mirrors.

RIDING CROSS-COUNTRY

Unless you know exactly what you're letting yourself in for, navigation far from all tracks is beyond the capabilities of unsupported motorbikes, with their limited capacity for provisions and narrow safety margins.

You might look at a map and think it would be interesting to cross to a parallel road 200 miles/300km to the west, or explore a remote range of mountains. While this might seem like an adventurous idea, in reality it's extremely risky for all but the most well-equipped and experienced riders.

If you're into this type of extreme adventuring, you're much better off doing it as part of an expedition which includes 4WDs to carry the essential reserves of fuel and water. Bear in mind also the wisdom and safety of riding into unvisited terrain, especially near sensitive border areas (which includes just about all border areas in Africa and Asia). Bored army patrols or trigger happy smugglers might be delighted to see you – but not for reasons you'd care to remember.

A common way to lose each other is when the leader stops to wait for the follower to catch up. After a while of waiting and wondering, the leader retraces his route to look for the other rider. In the meantime the following rider, having seen the leader rider struggle through some mud (for example), has taken another route around a rise and races ahead to catch the leader, who by now is inexplicably out of sight. It is the responsibility of all riders to look out for each other – this should stop any arguments about whose fault it was. The leader should slow down or stop if he gets too far ahead of the rest of the group, who in turn should never stray from the route.

If you do lose sight of each other, ride to some high ground, turn off your engines, look around and listen for the others. In this position, you're also more likely to be seen by the others. Failing this, an agreed procedure should be adhered to. For example, after a certain time out of contact, you should all return to the point where you last stopped or spoke together. If fuel is critical you should stop ahead at a clear landmark, such as a village or junction.

The whole point of riding together is to give each other much-needed support during a risky endeavour, so resist any individualistic tendencies and stick together while traversing remote tracks.

GPS

GPS (Global Positioning System) receivers are **navigational aids** which use

A selection of GPSs at 0° longitude, Greenwich, London. None was right but all were very close.

satellite signals to pinpoint your position anywhere on earth within minutes and now with an accuracy of just a few metres. The size of a mobile phone, they are now available in the US from just $100 so any outdoor enthusiast or gadgetarian can easily afford one.

GPS is owned and operated by the US Defence Department who originally developed it for military reasons. Although it's been around since the 1970s, GPS only became fully operational in 1995, when the complete constellation of 24 satellites was attained. Just three or more satellites are required to get a '3D' fix (longitude, latitude and height), ideally under an open sky with one satellite overhead and the other two close to the horizon. GPS signals are weak so cliffs, buildings and even light tree cover will all hamper acquisition, although the external antenna fitted to some models gets round this limitation. Heavy cloud should not impede signals.

How they work

On turning on your receiver, the position and signal strengths of available satellites are clearly displayed on an LCD screen followed in a couple of minutes by your co-ordinates. These are displayed in traditional longitude and latitude or localised versions such as the British Ordnance Survey grid which corresponds to OS maps or European UTM coordinates. If you've just bought the unit, changed the batteries or moved more than a few hundred miles since your last fix, you can greatly speed up satellite acquisition by entering your estimated position – a straightforward procedure called 'initialising' which recollects satellite data.

With the commonly-used handheld GPS units you'll be pushed to read the small screen on the move.

For most people the above function is sufficient, but receivers can also store information and compute calculations such as 'waypoints' along your route, average speed, estimated duration and arrival time to a given point, as well as a bearing towards a given point. They can do all this and more as you move along, though this will reduce battery life (commonly 4 AA units) down to around 10 hours from a possible 18 hours. To run your GPS continuously, get a car socket adaptor and fit a plug to your bike's 12-volt supply.

Do you need one?

GPS receivers are undoubtedly wonderful things, but are they necessary or even useful for adventure bikers? GPS comes into its own for navigation and position fixing at sea where no visual landmarks exist. In recreational land use, GPS is merely a navigational aid, albeit a phenomenally accurate one. Only navigating a trackless wilderness like a desert will render a GPS unit an indispensable supplement to a map, compass and common sense. The map data included in some GPSs is only useful in the US where CD-ROMs supply waypoints to use with large scale maps like the Delorme series. For anywhere in Africa, Asia or Latin America, the map supplied will be utterly basic and of little use to navigation.

Contrary to popular belief GPS does not replace the need for fastidious map reading and orientation. Furthermore, any co-ordinate is only as accurate as your map. Knowing exactly where you are is academic if you've just run out of fuel or have broken a leg. GPS receivers won't get you out of trouble when lost, but they can quickly stop you amplifying navigational errors in the first place by confirming that you're off course.

SURVIVAL

Compared to cars, motorbikes are fairly reliable by virtue of their simplicity. The most likely cause of immobility other than a puncture or an accident is running out of fuel. If this happens there's obviously nothing you can do until someone offers you some fuel or a lift to get some. Usually you won't have to wait for more than a few hours. If you're alone and someone offers you a lift in a remote region, leave a timed message on your bike explaining your actions and don't leave anything you want to see again.

A more serious situation might occur when you find yourself trapped by an immobile or irretrievable bike, or an unrideable situation, such as flooding, a sand storm or an accident. Once you're certain that riding your machine out is not an option, your next priority is to rescue yourself. Act in accordance with the '3 Ps' of outdoor survival.

Protection (shelter)

Arranging shelter from the elements, primarily heat, cold wind or precipitation, will greatly extend your ability to survive, now that you're solely dependant on your body for mobility. In the case of an injured partner, shelter will be essential while you go to get help.

Depending on where you are this means erecting shade or windbreak, if you're not carrying a tent. Get in the habit of wearing some kind of head covering to minimalise heat loss or sunstroke, a crash helmet or a scarf will do if you've no hat. With protection secured you can now turn your attention to either recovering your bike, rescuing your partner, or preparing to walk out.

Position

If you've been regularly referring to your map, odometer and available landmarks, then your position should not be hard to pinpoint. It may be just a short walk back to the last village, where someone can help you drag your bike out of a ravine, or it may be sixty miles to a minor highway. If you're sure no one will come this way then you must be prepared to walk back to the last known sign of human presence.

Look on the map to see if there may be some place you could get help which you'd overlooked. Think about the easiest way of getting there avoiding steep gradients. Consider torching you bike, or just a smoky component like a tyre or a seat, but only when you can see someone who can't see you and there's a chance the smoke might be seen.

Provisions

Establish all your provisions, how much food and water you have and how many days it will last, including any emergency rations you may have stashed. Water is by far the most critical aid to survival. Wherever you are you can survive a lot longer without food which you should consume frugally anyway, as digestion uses up water.

Staying where you are obviously uses less energy but might not be an option offering much hope. Think about what provisions you might find along the way. If there's a river, stick close to it, settlements or human activity usually accompany them.

EMERGENCY EQUIPMENT

- Lighter or matches
- Aluminium space blanket or sleeping bag – for daytime shade and night time warmth
- High energy compact rations
- Rescue flares: hand held smoke or rocket. Use your rocket flares only

when you are certain they will be seen by potential rescuers
- Compass and map
- Torch
- Binoculars. Useful when looking for lost companions or distant landmarks
- All the water you can carry

Walking out

It's often said that staying with your vehicle is the key to survival but this usually refers to cars, which are more conspicuous. Certainly if you've checked out along a certain route, there's a chance that someone will come looking for you – but don't count on this in most Saharan countries where the locals have long since wearied of organising expensive searches.

Use the comfort and facilities of your makeshift camp to prepare carefully for the walk out. You should carry as little as possible, wear light and comfortable clothing and, most importantly, cover your head against the sun during the day and the cold at night.

As soon as you begin walking, your water consumption will increase. Even on firm ground you're unlikely to average more than two miles per hour. If you've more than a few miles to walk in a desert, wait till evening or early morning when lower temperatures make distance walking less tiring.

The first four items listed in Emergency Equipment above are best wrapped up in duct tape and stored in a secure place before you leave on your trip. Now they will be needed. To carry water efficiently, a harness should be made up to support this heavy weight on your back – your rucksack may now be useful. Check out the water consumption figures in the following chapter. Avoid carrying heavy items in your hands. Follow your tracks religiously and avoid short cuts and/or steep ascents unless you are certain they are worthwhile. Conserve energy and, therefore, water at all costs.

Walking out should not be considered lightly, it's a last resort to save yourself when all else has failed. Attempt it only if you're certain your emergency situation could not be solved less drastically by staying put.

Rules of survival

The following rules will help ensure your well being in remote areas; they are not in any strict order of importance.
- **NEVER TAKE CHANCES** Keep on the track, carry adequate reserves of fuel and water, and ride within your limitations.
- **DON'T WASTE WATER** Get in the habit of being miserly with your washing and cleaning needs, but drink as much as you need.
- **INSPECT YOUR BIKE DAILY** Oil level, wheels and home-made components may need regular attention.
- **CARRY ENOUGH FUEL AND WATER FOR YOUR ENTIRE PLANNED ROUTE** Recognise that difficult terrain and maximum loading may increase consumption of these vital fluids.

● **CARRY ESSENTIAL SPARES AND TOOLS** And know how to use them. You should at least be familiar with tyre removal and repair (see p.55), oil and air filter changes and fault diagnosis.

● **NEVER CARRY ON WHEN LOST** Stop before you go too far, accept that you have made a mistake, and retrace your steps if necessary.

● **IF YOU CHECK OUT ON DEPARTURE, CHECK IN ON ARRIVAL** An essential courtesy that may prevent wasted searches.

● **KEEP YOUR COMPANIONS IN SIGHT AT ALL TIMES** Or tell them what you're doing and where you're going.

● **NEVER DRIVE AT NIGHT** Even on tarmac roads there is a danger of unlit vehicles, stray animals and potholes.

Health and water

While common sense precautions should never be disregarded, the dangers of ill health when travelling abroad are much exaggerated. Look at the dozen or so trip questionnaires spread around this book and you'll find only one group caught an inordinately plentiful collection of exotic ailments.

This chapter is only a brief introduction to the complex and ever-changing subject of travellers' health. It outlines practical precautions and the most common ailments. For more detailed knowledge check out the books recommended on p.271 and consult your doctor well before departure. If you do get ill abroad don't be squeamish about using overseas hospitals or clinics; in just about all cases you will find dedicated, knowledgeable and enthusiastic staff held back only by possibly inadequate resources.

FIRST-AID KIT

Organising an effective and compact emergency first-aid kit is an important step in your pre-departure preparation. A plastic lunch box makes an ideal container, which at the very least should include the following:

- Paracetamol
- Malaria pills (see below)
- Anti-diarrhoea medication
- Laxative
- Thermometer
- Antiseptic cream or spray
- Insect repellent
- Multivitamins
- Various dressings, plasters, bandages, safety pins, tape and cotton wool
- Steristrips for closing wounds
- Oil of cloves for toothaches
- Sterile syringe set
- Rehydration powders (see also p.110)

If you are able to get some antibiotics and proper painkillers from a sympathetic doctor then so much the better.

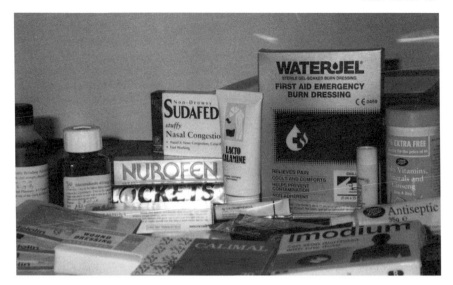

IMMUNISATION

The sometimes painful series of inoculations known as 'getting your jabs' is a traditional part of setting off abroad and if you've had a heavy session of jabs expect not to feel 100% for a few hours afterwards.

Depending on where you're going, these are the ten most common diseases for which you'll require immunisation (malaria is discussed below):

- Hepatitis A
- Hepatitis B
- Tetanus
- Typhoid
- Polio
- Rabies
- Yellow Fever
- Diphtheria
- Japanese B Encephalitis
- Meningitis

None of these jabs will guarantee that you do not come down with the disease, but in all cases they will inhibit its development giving you more time to seek proper medical attention – the most important step if you think you're becoming ill abroad.

The cholera vaccination is absent from the above list as it has long been known to be ineffective. In 1989, the World Health Organisation stopped publishing cholera vaccination certificates and no longer recommends immunisation for travellers. The trouble is, not every border guard at a far flung outpost knows this, and so a token stamp on your immunisation certificate along with a small injection may be useful for a long trip – many inoculation centres co-operate in this practice.

TRAVEL HEALTH TIPS

Follow these steps before, during and after your travels to ensure you stay in good health:
- **Get immunised** against commonly-known diseases
- **Avoid getting bitten** by insects, snakes, mammals and, of course, larger predators
- **Take malaria pills**, but better still use a mosquito net and repellent
- **Take a first-aid kit** containing at least the items listed on p.106
- **Drink frequently** and if necessary rehydrate with a teaspoon of salt and eight teaspoons of sugar per litre of clean water
- **Water purification** – be sure that your water source is clean
- **Eat nutritious** freshly cooked food and avoid re-warmed meals
- **Ride sensibly** and recognise that motorcycling abroad is especially dangerous. Be alert, rest often, avoid congested cities if possible, and regard other road users as a threat
- **Travel insurance** is useful but in the end medical cover is more important than property insurance
- **Back home**, if you don't feel well (re-adjustment often produces some ailments), consult your doctor and tell them where you've been

AILMENTS

On the road, common ailments include:

- Colds and headaches
- Diarrhoea or constipation
- Dried and cracked lips, runny nose, sore eyes and throat
- Burns and cuts to hands
- Sunburn
- Stress and fatigue

Taking it easy when ill, along with a first-aid kit, will help you deal with most of the above. Less common are some more serious ailments:

● **Scorpion and snake bites** These are very rare and rarely fatal. Avoid rocky camp-sites and shake out footwear in the mornings. Snakes are very shy but migrate towards sources of warmth at night.

● **Dysentery** A serious illness which feels like a severe form of diarrhoea, it can be either amoebic or bacillic. Both need to be treated under medical supervision, as tests are required to diagnose the exact nature of the illness. Fluid levels must be maintained during these types of illness as extreme fluid loss can lead to dehydration and death.

● **Malaria** The most common cause of death in the world. The best way to avoid malaria is not to get bitten by mosquitoes. They are active between dusk and dawn in malarial zones and tend to hunt at ankle level so cover this area and all exposed skin with mosquito repellent. Use an inner tent or mosquito net treated with permethrin: the 'four-point' wedge nets are most versatile.

Always avoid camp-sites near stagnant water. Lastly take malarial prophylactics before you go. Mefloquine (sold as Lariam) tablets are taken once a week; Paludrine is taken daily. The latter tastes vile, but the former's nasty side effects are now well known, including depression, anxiety, nightmares and, most commonly, dizziness. All of these are better than malaria. Follow the prescribed course to the letter, which may include taking the drug weeks after you've left a malarial area.

WHEN THINGS GO WRONG

One morning, in an attempt to avoid the scorching heat on the Indus plain, we set off from Dera Gazi Khan. As we had grown used to long rides, and the temperatures stayed on the bearable side, we both enjoyed the ride very much.

Early in the afternoon, the unthinkable happened: a man jumped out from the bushes and I hit him square on. The XT slid across the road with my right leg trapped underneath. The result was an open fracture of the two bones and cracks all around.

The horror of a scenario like this is hard to put into words: one person is in terrible pain and you have no idea for how long; the other, if there is one, has to take care of everything else. Having an accident in the West is bad enough; crashing in Pakistan makes the ground give way beneath your feet.

There's no telephone, no one speaks English, no ambulance. A hospital? How will you get there, how close is it, how unprofessional and unequipped? Police? – all too willing to earn an extra dollar and a hundred witnesses ready to vouch you rode too fast. Your embassy? Probably shrugging their shoulders at a reckless adventure. Though ours had a happy ending, I still shudder when going through the details of the event. It's something you would never want to happen to anyone, ever.

After the accident, we were both taken care of extremely well. The doctors, local police, and Belgian embassy, which we thought would all be nightmares to deal with, all proved to be efficient, friendly and professional.

I was brought to Khushab by private car and a few hours later we were taken by ambulance to Islamabad, to a hospital recommended by the embassy. By then the pain had been numbed by morphine, and to some extent I could even enjoy the full moon rising over the Salt Range.

The surgeon in Islamabad proved to be one of the finest and most competent doctors we have ever met, explaining at length every single detail. Eventually the bones should heal completely, hopefully to a point of regaining the Incredible Kickstart Leg which my XT500 needs!

Of course our journey was over. It took a while to sink in, but thanks to all the heartwarming care, our morale quickly recovered.

At the hospital we stayed in a private room too and a woman from the Embassy delivered three meals a day, brought Belgian newspapers and solved lots of issues, such as the recovery of our bikes and shipping them home. We ourselves flew back home two weeks later.

Of course we're still sad and confused and incredulous this really happened to us, but on the whole we're fine, and neither Iris nor I want to forget the wonderful journey we had. But we also learned a few things the hard way: mount crash bars and take a First-aid course before setting off on a venture like this.

Trui Hanoulle

WATER

Water is vital to the human organism and in hot climates you'll be amazed how much water you'll need to keep it together. Drinking 10 litres a day is not uncommon in the Saharan summer and just sitting still at 38°C you're losing a litre an hour. At this rate it takes just five hours for you to become seriously dehydrated and without shade you'll be close to death in less than two days.

In the very end, when everything else has broken down, run out or fallen off, it will be your water that keeps you alive. In arid or remote areas be sure to attach your water containers securely to your bike and check regularly that they're still there, particularly over rough ground or following a fall.

Water and the human body

The average male, weighing 155lb/70kg, is made up of 88pts/50 litres (110lb/50kg) of water. If even just a small percentage of this volume is lost through sweating, urination or vomiting, the individual will soon begin to experience some of the following symptoms of dehydration:

Water lost	up to	Symptoms
5%	4.4pts/2.5 litres	Thirst, lack of appetite, nausea, headache, irritability and drowsiness
10%	8.8pts/5 litres	Dizziness, difficulty in breathing, slurring, clumsiness, lack of saliva
20%	18pts/10 litres	Delirium, swollen tongue and throat, dim vision and deafness, numb and shrivelled skin

Thirst is, of course, the first sign of the need for water and this impulse should never be suppressed. Rationing your drinking habits is the last thing you should do; if water is scarce and you can't get more, save on washing and be frugal with your cooking needs instead.

Dehydration is not always immediately obvious in hot, arid climates where sweat evaporates instantly. For this reason (as well as avoiding sunburn) you should imitate the locals by **covering exposed skin** and your head as well as always seeking shade. On a bike, where ambient temperatures exceed body temperature (37°C) you should actually *wrap up* to keep the hot air off you – or expect vastly increased water consumption. With furnace-like heat blowing at you, sealing all your clothing apertures creates a mildly humid and cooler sub-climate around your body and greatly limits water loss. You'll feel hot but you'll slow down dehydration.

Extreme and **fast dehydration** can be felt as a progressive drying up of the gullet, something I've encountered myself while riding through hot winds in Algeria. The dryness inches down your moist throat, which becomes parched from breathing very hot air, and gradually dries you out from the inside. With ambient temperatures at around 45°C you realise just how quickly you'd die without water and shade, and such temperatures are normal on most summer days in desert areas.

As a rule you should **urinate** as often as is normal, about four to five times a day. The colour of your urine should also remain the same as normal. A darker shade of yellow means your urine is more concentrated because you're not drinking enough or are losing more through sweating. Drink more water.

DIARRHOEA – WHAT TO DO

Just as your bike is bound to suffer the nuisance of punctures, so will you too experience the inconvenience of diarrhoea as your body adjusts to an exotic set of bacteria.

In most cases it will last a few days but if symptoms persist despite the actions outlined below seek medical help: it could be something worse.

● If at all possible stop riding and rest in a cool dark place until you're fit enough to carry on

● Eat nothing or very little. Rice or soup are good. You will be weak with hunger, another good reason to stop and rest

● Take oral rehydration powders, or make some up: eight spoons of sugar to one of salt per litre

● Drink plenty of sterilised water

● Take 'stoppers' like Lomotil only if you must keep moving – your body is urgently trying to flush out the bug, stoppers delay this action and so delay full recovery

Salt and the body: isotonic drinks

When drinking very large quantities of water, attention must also be paid to **minerals** lost in sweat. The correct combination and concentration of salts is vital to the body's electrolytic balance. This governs the transmission of nervous signals to the brain and explains why your senses become impaired as you become seriously dehydrated. A slight salt deficiency is manifested by headaches, lethargy and muscular cramps, though it can take a day or two for salt levels to run down enough for these symptoms to become noticeable.

If you feel groggy, taking some **salt in solution** may make you feel better. In fact, after any exertion, such as helping recover a car from a deep bogging in the Sahara, a cup of slightly salty water or, better still, an isotonic drink instantly replenishes the minerals and water you have lost through strenuous activity. If you don't want to contaminate your water bottle with salty water and don't have a cup handy, lick the back of your hand, sprinkle on some salt, lick it off and swig it down with some water. However, **too much salt** in one go (easily done with salt tablets: avoid them) will make you nauseous and may induce vomiting, which means that you lose fluid and so return to square one. Remember salt must be taken with a substantial volume of water. As you become severely dehydrated your body's salt levels actually increase – taking too much salt at this stage would be catastrophic.

Commercial sachets of rehydration solution are designed to replenish lost minerals including salt and sugar and are a useful addition to any expedition first-aid kit. So-called **isotonic sports drinks** like Gatorade (available in flavoured powdered form from sports shops and easily packed) are a more economical way of doing the same thing. If you don't have a supply of such drinks and get severely dehydrated, **make your own rehydration** solution (see box on p.110).

Taking regular but moderate doses of salt in hot climates is the best way to prevent feelings of lethargy and possible illness, and it's a good idea to get into the habit of liberally salting your evening meals. I've also found that a lunchtime mug of Japanese instant miso soup was a great way of keeping our salt levels stable. On one arduous trip, a German guy I travelled with proclaimed miso to be the most refreshing drink he'd ever tasted! – although it has to be said we were all pretty thirsty by this stage.

Hydrators like this 3-litre Platypus unit, are a good way of making sure you drink enough while you're riding. You can either buy the complete backpack or just the clear plastic bladder and tube to put in your own daypack.

WATER PURIFICATION

Water is lost through sweating, urination and vomiting and in hot climates must be drunk constantly. Unfortunately most of the diseases listed on p.110 are transmitted in water or caught from food prepared in unclean water.

Polluted water is most commonly found around settlements and is caused by poor sanitary conditions and unhygenic practices. Luckily, **bottled water** is now commonly available throughout the world. Use it but check the cap seals as refilling empties is a well known scam in poorer countries.

A well in the Libyan Sahara. If you plan to use wells, carry a long rope and bucket as they're not always present in remote areas.

Eliminating bugs from water can be done in three ways:

- by boiling for four minutes
- by sterilising with chemicals like chlorine, iodine or silver
- by filtration

Boiling uses up fuel and, along with tablets, does not clean impurities from dirty water. Also, water boils at lower temperatures at altitude, so add a minute to your boil for every 1000 feet/300m above sea level.

Sterilising tablets (or liquids) are a less fiddly way of getting pure drinking water. Cheap and effective, their drawbacks include giving the water an unpleasant taste (especially in the case of chlorine-based tablets), the need to wait for ten minutes to two hours for the tables to take effect, and the fact that they don't clean the impurities from dirty water. Iodine can be poisonous if overdosed and silver takes a couple of hours to be effective. For visibly dirty water it's a very good idea to sieve it through a filter; this removes cysts in which some bugs (notably giardia or amoebic dysentery) lie dormant to survive in cold water.

Manually operated **filter pumps**, like the well-known Katadyns, or the MSR pictured below are a quick way of safely cleaning even the dirtiest of

water. Purifying and sterilising at up to half a litre a minute (depending on the state of the water) they can be easily cleaned and last for months. More basic filters include UK manufacturer Pre-Mac's range of filter pumps such as the inexpensive, disposable but slow SWP/Pocket model which is the size of a cigar and cleans up to 88pts/50 litres at five minutes per litre. Alternatively, there's the slightly larger MWP/Trekker which filters four times the amount at twice the speed and has replaceable cartridges.

These filters are recommended for travellers on long trips or those travelling for long periods away from reliable water sources, or in the case of the compact Pre-Macs, as an emergency back up. In most cases, however, tablets added to water pre-cleaned with a filter bag will do where no fresh or bottled water is available.

Pump-action filters like this MSR work fast to provide drinking water. (First Ascent)

PART 2: CONTINENTAL ROUTE OUTLINES

Africa

For many riders, Africa represents the ultimate adventure overlanding destination. The combination of desert, jungle, unstable politics and crumbling infrastructure, along with the diversity and vitality of its peoples, make a visit to Africa unforgettable if not always for the right reasons.

This vitality, when faced with many of the world's poorest and most misgoverned nations is something that will make you wonder about the value of wealth. Add to that the stamina required to cross the *pistes* of the Sahara, or the flooded trenches of the Congo basin, and you'll have an experience that'll swing your moods from euphoria to despair every few days.

Regional explorations

Even if you could, you don't have to cross the whole continent to get an authentic impression of Africa, and a bag full of adventures. Indeed, such localised regional explorations can be more rewarding if somewhat less sensational than claiming a trans-continental trek.

North of the Sahara, **Morocco** is easily accessible from Europe and offers a perfect introduction to Africa plus, in the south, a great experience in its own right. **West Africa** offers a fabulous chance to experience the continent too, but needs greater commitment. If you don't want to **cross the Sahara**, it's shippably close to Europe or even east-coast USA. At twice the size of Texas, Mali is a favourite, and you could easily spend three months exploring this region's dusty back roads and mud hut villages.

At the other end of the continent, **South Africa** makes an easier if unrepresentative introduction to the countries which lie to the north, notably the eastern states of **Tanzania**, **Kenya** and **Uganda** offering timeless images of African plains and celebrated wildlife parks. Many South African riders are now able to explore the continent again without undertaking the full slog.

THE WEATHER IN AFRICA

Crossing Africa from the north, two climatic factors govern your departure date: **summer** in the Sahara, and the **equatorial monsoon**. The former (May to October) adds greatly to a motorcyclist's perils on account of the vast amounts of drinking water which must be carried. Don't even think about it – see how I got on in *early April* in Libya on p.225.

In central Africa the rains and their saturated aftermath bring all but river traffic to a standstill from June to September, and to a lesser extent from February to April. Along the equator the big rains fall from June to September. South of here the network of sealed roads make the heavy rains in southern Africa from November to April less of an issue.

Therefore if you're heading across the continent from Europe and want an easy time of it set off around **October or November**, riding into the Saharan winter and the central African dry season.

MAIN TRANS-CONTINENTAL ROUTES

Reading African travelogues of forty years ago gives the impression of a Golden Age of African travel. European adventurers were saluted by border guards as they trundled across the French-controlled Sahara to British controlled East Africa. The political instabilities which now push African nations ever closer to the brink had yet to develop.

These days travelling across Africa is a game of snakes and ladders and it's not uncommon to change your itinerary on the eve of departure as another danger zone emerges. As a rule, political instability is **quick to develop and slow to subside**, while lawlessness at the remote frontiers of an ostensibly stable country can also be a hazard to overlanders. Once in a while some brave or unhinged individual always manages to cross a country thought to be deadly without any difficulties, the word spreads and the ladders shift. The unpredictable nature and logistical contortions of merely getting across Africa from one end to the other are what make this trip such a challenge.

The two traditional trans-African routes

Access permitting, the main way to experience Africa in the full has been to ride down from the Mediterranean to South Africa: traditionally ending at the continental toe of the Cape of Good Hope. Typically this is an 8–10,000 mile/12–16,000km journey of at least two months.

Riders departing Europe are immediately faced with their first obstacle: the political and geographical challenge of the Sahara; a desert the size of the continental US or Australia. As this is written both Libya and Algeria have exits to their southern neighbours, offering an alternative to the Atlantic route from Morocco via Mauritania to West Africa which became established in the 1990s.

CURRENT HOT SPOTS

Three-quarters of the countries listed on the British Foreign & Commonwealth Office's 'do not go' list are in Africa. Nevertheless, at the time of writing a genuine overland trans-African trip from north to south is possible if you can get from Chad across Sudan to Ethiopia, although, due to visa problems, few have managed this route so far.

Along with the instability in some West African nations, the unrest in former Zaire (now known as the Democratic Republic of Congo, not to be confused with plain 'Congo' to the west) has cut-off the Congo Basin for all but the very brave or foolhardy.

By all means investigate the possibility of an unconventional itinerary and be aware that in certain instances your nationality may eliminate certain visa hurdles. Furthermore it is not uncommon for some countries to gain a bad reputation where little real evidence exists – Libya, Uganda and southern Algeria being good examples.

Also note that certain countries through which overland traffic regularly passes have no-go areas – be they dangerous like northern Chad, northern Algeria and Ethiopia's borders, or merely requiring permits like southern Tunisia or south-western Egypt.

This list is a rough guide only and liable to grow or shrink within the lifetime of this edition of the *AMH*. Keep up to date by consulting the information office of your government's foreign ministry; Internet addresses appear on the AM website.

● Angola
● Congo
● Central African Republic
● Liberia
● Sierra Leone
● Southern Sudan
● Somalia
● Democratic Republic of Congo
● Rwanda

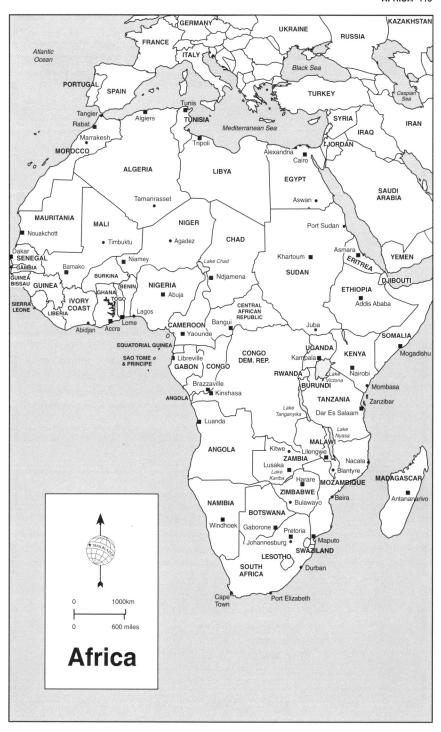

Africa

MOROCCAN ATLAS ~ YAMAHA TÉNÉRÉ

Name	Craig Exley
Year of birth	1959
Occupation	Data communications
Nationality	British
Previous travels	Plenty, but none in North Africa
Bike travels	Most of mainland Europe

This trip	Morocco
Trip duration	2 weeks
Departure date	March 1999
Number in group	Solo
Distance covered	4000 miles (6000km)
Sponsorship	None

Best day	Off the Atlas and into the Sahara
Worst day	Lost off piste south-east of Zagora
Favourite place	Anywhere in the desert or Atlas
Biggest headache	Losing most of my water whilst lost
Biggest mistake	Using bungies to strap water!
Pleasant surprise	Atlas mountains and Berber people
Any illness	Yes, after eating camel with nomads
Cost of trip	Under £1000
Other trips planned	Wife won't let me!

Bike model	Yamaha XT600Z Ténéré
Age, mileage	1987, 20,000 miles
Modifications	640 gas-flowed, H/D spokes & rims
Wish you'd done...	Nothing
Tyres used	Metzeler Enduro I & II
Punctures	Despite best efforts, none!
Type of baggage	Throwovers and tank bag

Bike's weak point	None, if you don't overload it
Strong point	Comfort, all-round ability
Bike problems	Rear brake calliper seized
Accidents	None
Same bike again	Yes
Any advice	Read ground-to-map, not vice-versa

THE ATLANTIC ROUTE TO WEST AFRICA

A full and regularly updated account of the entire Atlantic Route from Tan Tan in Morocco to southern Mauritania is at: www. sahara-overland.com/routes/atlantic.html. It includes GPS points for the 530km Beach Route from Nouadhibou to Nouakchott.

From West Africa the direct route of fewest borders is east though Niger and Chad and then across the jungles of northern former Zaire (DRC) and into east Africa where the true difficulties end for the Cape-bound rider. Lately though, because of instability in the Congo area, those travellers who don't give up and ship from West Africa to southern Africa are getting through to Ethiopia via Chad and Sudan and then heading down the east side

The other main route runs from Cairo to the Cape also via Sudan and Ethiopia into Kenya, so basically the two main overland routes meet these days in Sudan.

NORTH AFRICA AND THE SAHARA

Easily accessible from Europe, north Africa provides a taste of Moslem Africa quite distinct from the Africa south of the Sahara. With the Algerian trans-Saharan routes avoided through most of the 1990s, traffic funnelled along the Atlantic coast of Morocco and Mauritania.

Although you obviously cross the desert, Saharan purists consider the Atlantic route a bleak and unsatisfactory slog down the tarmac into Mauritania. This route lacks the distances and scenic drama of Algeria's Tassili and Hoggar route, but it's currently the most popular way to ride across the Sahara.

As you all know I'm not one to blow my own trumpet, but my 550-page *Sahara Overland* book (also published by Trailblazer) and the associated website (see box above) add up to the best English-language sources of information on travel and detailed routes in the Sahara. There is plenty of stuff in there that it would be dumb to repeat here so if you're interested in exploring the Sahara rather than just crossing it at speed, get yourself a copy.

Morocco

Morocco is the best destination for an eye-opening experience of North Africa without committing yourself to a desert crossing. In this country you'll find ancient Moorish cities on a par with their counterparts in Asia Minor as well as a range of tracks (*pistes*) rising over the High Atlas Mountains to the fringes of the Sahara beyond. At many points on the southern edge of the Atlas ranges, the drop from the scrubby high mountain pastures down to the oases on the desert floor will be a dramatic highlight of your visit.

Ferries leave southern Spanish ports for Morocco every few hours and cross in as little as 20 minutes . There is no need for a carnet or, in some cases, a visa, making entry and paperwork relatively undemanding.

Dangers and annoyances include the **relentless hustlers** in towns like Tangiers and Marrakesh. I've met people fleeing Morocco after just a couple of days, so bad was their experience. And that's not including the hashish hard sell in the dope-growing area around Ketama. If you're tempted by a smoke, don't try and score here; set-ups are common.

Visits to Morocco are best in the **intermediate seasons** when it's neither baking at 40°C+ or freezing in the High Atlas, where snow commonly blocks the higher passes and lowland rain makes riding miserable. At any time of year in the mountains you can expect sudden **downpours** which quickly erode the Atlas's steep slopes and unmade roads. You'll find fuel prices in the north about the same as Europe (excluding rip-off UK), but otherwise the cost of living is less, with food and lodging about half that of continental Europe.

The Grand Traverse of the Moroccan Sahara

While beach life around Agadir might be tempting (as well as being a place where southbound overlanders congregate), a good crack for the adventurous rider is the 600 mile/1000km trail of pistes which stretch from the Atlantic coast of the Western Sahara inland to more or less the dunes of Erg Chebbi, following the southern edge of the Atlas all the way. You can't ask for a more satisfying, relatively easy and mostly dirt track adventure. Range need be no more than 150 miles/250kms so massive tanks or jerricans are not needed, and even wells are fairly common. Routes M1, M3 and M6 in my *Sahara Overland* book cover most of the traverse and you'll also get the full story on Moroccan immigration and other excursions around fabulous southern Morocco. With a sense of adventure and the one-million-scale IGN *Maroc* map, there's no end to the routes you could explore along the passes of the High Atlas itself. Check out Simon McCarthy's tale about the highs and lows of riding in the Atlas on p.254.

Tunisia, Libya and Algeria

While the expensive 24-hour ferry from Marseille or Genoa doesn't put off central Europeans, for Brits at least Tunisia is a long way to go for not much. It has similar stability, lack of bureaucracy plus a well-developed tourist infrastructure as Morocco but with much less hassle. The thing is, once you've got to Tunisia, you might as well carry on and have a real adventure in Libya or Algeria, or even the rest of Africa.

But southern Tunisia has plenty of something Morocco lacks – sand. The eastern fringes of Algeria's **Grand Erg Oriental** flow over Tunisia's southern borders, creating the dunescapes which many associate with the Sahara. There are no great pistes here and access without permits into the deep south is limited, but once south of the Chott El Djerid you'll find enough sand to give yourself and your GPS a workout. Just make sure you know what you're letting yourself in for.

Libya

While sealed roads lead all the way south to Ghat and – up to a point – Kufra in the far south-east, riding the tracks of the Libyan Sahara is the real thing for which you must be prepared. Forget outdated fears about Libya, it has now become the favoured Saharan destination with mainland Europeans, with the spectacular **Fezzan** of the south-west by far, and deservedly, the most popular

Libyan Sahara ~ KTM Adventure

Name	Walter Arossa
Year of birth	1950
Occupation	Doctor
Nationality	Italian
Previous travels	Tanz', Niger, Ethiopia, Mali, Mauri'
Bike travels	Above; Tunisia, Algeria & Senegal

This trip	Libya
Trip duration	3 weeks
Departure date	October 1999
Number in group	3
Distance covered	6000km (4000 miles)
Sponsorship	None

Best day	Crossing Erg Awbari (dunes)
Worst day	400km of hamada before the Erg
Favourite place	Salt lake in the middle of the Erg
Biggest headache	Libyan Customs
Biggest mistake	None
Pleasant surprise	Kindness of Libyan people
Any illness	None
Cost of trip	US$1300
Other trips planned	Al Koufra – Libyan Tibesti

Bike model	KTM640 Adventure
Age, mileage	1998, 4500km
Modifications	Bigger tank and open silencers
Wish you'd done...	None
Tyres used	Michelin Desert, heavy duty tubes
Punctures	1
Type of baggage	Soft

Bike's weak point	None
Strong point	Engine, frame and suspension
Bike problems	None
Accidents	None
Same bike again	Yes
Any advice	Ride at 60% of your skill

MAURITANIA ~ CLOSE TO THE EDGE

Name	Karim Hussain
Year of birth	1968
Occupation	Chemical Engineer
Nationality	British
Previous travels	Asia and Australia with backpack
Bike travels	London to Cairo, 1992

This trip	UK to Cape Town (failed)
Trip duration	4 months
Departure date	October 1997
Number in group	Solo
Distance covered	6000 miles (9000km)
Sponsorship	No

Best day	Flying through dunes north of Atar
Worst day	36 hours lost without water
Favourite place	Dunes between Tidjikja and Tichit
Biggest headache	Chinguetti to Tidjikja (7 days!!)
Biggest mistake	Going alone in some areas
Pleasant surprise	Rescued by nomads when dying
Any illness	Dehydration
Cost of trip	£4000
Other trips planned	Mauri to Cape Town; UK to Beijing

Bike model	1991 XT600ZE Ténéré
Age, mileage	New
Modifications	Homemade tank, Micron pipe
Wish you'd done...	45-litre *plastic* tank
Tyres used	Michelin T63s (very good)
Punctures	About 15
Type of baggage	38L alloy boxes, tank bag, kit bag

Bike's weak point	Heavy in soft sand
Strong point	Reliability, styling, simplicity
Bike problems	Vapour lock in fuel pump
Accidents	Hundreds off-road, none on the road
Same bike again	No. KTM Rally or XR600 maybe
Any advice	Don't fight the sand, ride with it

region. Again, my Sahara book offers 1500 miles/2500km of GPS-ed tracks in Libya, though not all are short enough for unsupported bikes. All roadsigns are in Arabic and checkpoints are common in the north, but fuel is just 3p/5 cents a litre: as cheap as anywhere in the world.

If you want to leave Libya from the south, you can now do so from Ghat to Djanet in Algeria and, at a push, across the Djado plateau and Ténéré to Dirkou and Agadez in Niger – although for this one you'll need the support of a four-wheeler to carry extra fuel. The Tibesti of Chad is still a bit risky and mine-ridden at the moment, although exiting into Egypt on the coast is no problem, apart from hours of messing about photocopying forms.

Algeria

The new millennium is seeing tourists' interest slowly open up again to the Algerian Sahara. While news of appalling massacres continues in the populated north, there's no doubt that the amazing south-east of this country has long been safe and tours (including my own) are once again returning here.

It's not all rosy though. The Tanezrouft area in the far west still remains dangerous with smuggler gangs

Exploring the backroads in Algeria's Hoggar mountains.

taking it out on the odd foolish traveller, but by the time you read this the Hoggar route from Tamanrasset to Agadez in Niger could well be flowing again, seeing a welcome return to the classic trans-Sahara route.

Even then, a visit just to Algeria itself provides what many consider to be the best country for an off-road Saharan adventure. Distances can be a bit of a stretch for a bike, but there are more established routes here than in Libya. If you've used a copy of my original *Desert Biking*, you'll know that you're in for a treat. DB is now well out of date but in the winter of 2000-1, I was back in Algeria, GPS-ing routes that will by now be available on 💻 www.sahara-over land.com and feature in the second English edition of *Sahara Overland.*

WEST AFRICA

West Africa includes the sub-Saharan region from Senegal to Cameroon in the east. Much of it was once a French colony and today French, and to a lesser extent English (in the Gambia, Sierra Leone, Liberia, Ghana and Nigeria) will be the languages you'll use the most.

If coming across the desert from Mauritania to Dakar in Senegal, buy a **laissez-passer** (the local alternative to a carnet which is valid across Francophone West Africa) for around 2500CFA (£5/$8). If you're heading south to Dakar (to get a Malian visa, perhaps), the road is sealed all the way.

Otherwise you may be meeting your bike at the ports of Dakar or Banjul in the Gambia. Senegal and Gambia are not especially interesting countries when compared to their more intriguing neighbours of Guinea and Mali. Note that both Guinea and Guinea Bissau have consulates in Banjul which issue visas without a fuss.

WESTERN EGYPT ~ BMW 80GS

Name	Shai Battersby
Year of birth	1950
Occupation	Art Director
Nationality	Israeli
Previous travels	Europe, US, Kenya, South Africa
Bike travels	Many

This trip	Western Desert of Egypt
Trip duration	14 days
Departure date	September 1999
Number in group	Solo
Distance covered	5600km (3500 miles)
Sponsorship	None

Best day	Siwa and Farafra hot springs
Worst day	Stuck in sand 400km from anything
Favourite place	White Desert near Farafra
Biggest headache	Eight hours at the Egyptian border
Biggest mistake	Not asking a friend to join me
Pleasant surprise	Egypt more than pyramids. People
Any illness	None
Cost of trip	US$480
Other trips planned	Lots: Turkey, Africa, South America

Bike model	94 BMW 80GS
Age, mileage	2 years, 30,000km
Modifications	Big Fiamm horns
Wish you'd done...	Bigger gas tank
Tyres used	Metzeler Sahara 3
Punctures	None
Type of baggage	BMW panniers, CamelBack

Bike's weak point	Did not find one
Strong point	Comfort (and won't answer back)
Bike problems	New alternator when I got home
Accidents	None
Same bike again	Yes
Any advice	Do not ride at night in Egypt!!

On to Mali or Guinea

To get to Bamako directly from Nouakchott take the 700-mile/1100km sealed Route D'Espoir to Néma, then head south on dirt via Nara, or leave the Espoir halfway at Kiffa and head south to Kayes.

If you're coming from Senegal, the northern route along the Senegal River from Rosso to Tambacounda is all but sealed and increasingly scenic. At Tamba' a notoriously rough track leads to Kidira where you cross the river and head through the light jungle to Kayes. Otherwise you can load your bike on the train at Kayes (or even Dakar or Tamba), but expect the usual planet-sized complications in getting this done.

Kayes gives you plenty of options. A fun two-day jungle track leads to Bamako via Kita, now running south along the railway line, or you can reach Bamako via Nioro du Sahel. Both are rough but rideable outside the rainy season. There's also a mass of tracks further south of the Kita piste, a lure to anyone seeking some adventure in this remote area of gold mines and smuggling. Remember there are some big rivers here and very isolated towns who never see tourists. It's a good precursor to the even wilder tracks of Guinea's Fouta Djallon highlands to the south. Steer well clear of the rainy season; in Guinea it pours from June to September, especially on the coast.

Eastwards to Central Africa

Like a lot of West African capitals, Bamako can be an intimidating city for the unprepared, and don't expect to get so much as an inner tube for your bike in the way of spares. If you're determined to cover the thousand-odd kilometres to Timbuktu, north-west of Bamako, your best bet is to get above the Niger river's inland delta at Segou from where roads are good gravel as far as Niafounke. From here deep sand sets in for the last fifty kms to the legendary oasis.

If soft sand ruts are your idea of fun, you couldn't ask for more than the exhausting piste just north of the river to Bourem and Gao, 200 miles/320km to the east. Gao can be reached much more easily along the sealed highway from Bamako, so avoiding Burkina Faso and the need for another visa. A ferry crosses the river to Gao on the far bank from where a sometimes very sandy track gets easier over the border into Niger and its capital, Niamey.

From Niamey roads are sealed all the way south to Ghana or Togo and east to northern Nigeria or Zinder. Here you decide which route to take around Lake Chad: the easier way is from Zinder in Niger to Kano and then east to Maiduguri and into Cameroon at Mora. Nigeria has the advantage of having some of the cheapest petrol in Africa, though beware of watered-down border scams.

The route around the top of Lake Chad is a sandy rutted track with delays, heavy searches and paranoid officials. Route 'C1' in *Sahara Overland* is an account by Alex Marr on an XR400. He managed it without a guide in a few days of tiring riding.

I've not yet heard any reports of riders succeeding in getting across Chad through Abéché to El Fasher in Sudan, but at the moment that's the only safe way to go if you're trying to reach east Africa without putting your bike on a plane. Visas for Sudan are the stumbling block for some nationalities.

Trans Africa & Back ~ XT600

Name	Geoff Hardwick
Year of birth	1969
Occupation	IT Trainer
Nationality	British
Previous travels	Europe, Asia, N Africa, Cameroon
Bike travels	Various trips in Cameroon

This trip	Cameroon-Congo-Cape-London
Trip duration	1 year
Departure date	August 97
Number in group	5
Distance covered	40,000 km (25,000 miles)
Sponsorship	Mitsubishi Cameroon

Best day	Crossing the Namib desert
Worst day	7 punctures on Christmas Eve
Favourite place	Ethiopian highlands
Biggest headache	Punctures, police, no carnet
Biggest mistake	Letting someone fix a puncture
Pleasant surprise	Met my (now) wife in Ethiopia
Any illness	Some minor stomach problems
Cost of trip	£5000
Other trips planned	South America

Bike model	XT 600 Ténéré
Age, mileage	12 years, about 60,000km
Modifications	Back and front racks
Wish you'd done...	White Power suspension
Tyres used	Michelin Bajas
Punctures	37! I am now an expert!
Type of baggage	Bags strapped on

Bike's weak point	A bit temperamental
Strong point	Large fuel tank. Very strong
Bike problems	Alternator (vibration broke wires)
Accidents	2
Same bike again	Probably
Any advice	Cows are not as soft as they look

EGYPT AND THE HORN OF AFRICA

While anything more than excursions off-highway in Egypt are more hassle than they're worth, a ride down the east side of Africa to Cape Town is why most adventure bikers come here. Currently the southern border of Egypt with Sudan is open again to overlanders and the north of Sudan is now accessible (the exact opposite of the situation reported in the last edition of *AMH* – and it could change again).

Crossing into Sudan from Egypt requires traversing most of the length of Lake Nasser and disembarking at the Sudanese frontier post of Wadi Halfa. As long as this ferry keeps running, exit from southern Egypt, officially at least, remains possible. The southern marshlands of Sudan leading to Uganda or Kenya have been inaccessible for nearly twenty years.

Another turn around from the last edition sees the Eritreans and Ethiopians at war again, but this does not seem to disrupt access into Ethiopia from Sudan. As Alex Marr describes on p.214, Ethiopia has some of the most spectacular riding in Africa, along the northern reaches of the Rift Valley. This north–south axis through Ethiopia is relatively stable but the lateral borders of that country are still the haunt of bandits or rebel forces from the strife in neighbouring Somali and Sudan. Anyone who's read Wilfred Thesiger's books will know what agonising fate befalls those who venture uninvited into the lands of the Danakil.

In addition, Ethiopia, or more particularly Addis, is no stranger to suffocating bureaucracy. Keep on the road south to Moyale and northern Kenya and you shouldn't encounter any untoward danger, although you can join convoys once in Kenya to get travellers though the bandit lands of the northern provinces.

CENTRAL AND EAST AFRICA

In Central Africa your route options narrow significantly. The likely-looking western route via Congo or Gabon across Congo Republic's neck and over into Angola has long been a marginal option due to expensive visas, Angola's continuing instability and the sheer difficulty of riding through one of the world's wettest regions. Jonny Bealby managed it in 1991 (read *Running with the Moon*) proving that, with a will, the adventurous biker can take unconventional overland routes. On the other hand, overlanders have been shot (and/or robbed) in Congo (1997) and Angola (1992) and even northern Namibia (1999). Bealby himself seems to get through again and again by the skin of his teeth.

When they can, most take the less hard option from Bangui in the C.A.R over to Kisingani in the northern Republic of Congo. 'Less hard' reflects the ride across the waterlogged tracks of former Zaire, at their worst between Kisingani and the Ugandan border. You'll find the riding more physically demanding than the sands of the Sahara, but without the route-finding complications. In a car it's not unusual to take a day to cover a couple of miles. Currently, due to civil disorder, this route appears as doubtful as ever.

From Kinsingani you ride via Epulu and up into the Eastern Highlands around Bunia. Crossing the border you have the odd experience of riding on the left side of the road. From here the truly exhausting mud slides end as you head south-east towards Kampala and the Rift Valley.

SOUTHERN AFRICA ~ AFRICA TWIN

Name	Alex Munro
Year of birth	1975
Occupation	Actuary
Nationality	South African
Previous travels	Zimbabwe, South Africa
Bike travels	Local weekend trips

This trip	RSA-Nam-Zam-Malawi-Mozam-Zim
Trip duration	2 weeks
Departure date	September 1997
Number in group	1
Distance covered	8000km (5000 miles)
Sponsorship	No

Best day	Amazing sunset arriving in Malawi
Worst day	Sore butt the next day
Favourite place	Lake Malawi (Cape Maclear)
Biggest headache	Nearly broke in Zambia
Biggest mistake	Only taking R800 ($120)
Pleasant surprise	Namibian dollars work in Malawi
Any illness	Some bilharzia and other parasites
Cost of trip	R2000
Other trips planned	Plenty! Not sure when though

Bike model	1997 Africa Twin
Age, mileage	New
Modifications	None – extra clutch cable
Wish you'd done...	Hard luggage would be better
Tyres used	Michelin Desert on the back
Punctures	1 front puncture
Type of baggage	Rucksack on the seat behind me

Bike's weak point	Really heavy in the sand
Strong point	Speed, comfort, reliability, looks
Bike problems	Expensive damage after small falls
Accidents	1
Same bike again	Yes, or a cheaper lighter bike
Any advice	No reason why you can't do it

On a bike your river crossing or cruising options are much more flexible than those available to cars. You can balance the bike in a dug-out as Jonny Bealby did or you can take the river-boats from Brazzaville in Congo up river to Kinshasa and Kisingani (DRC).

The cool highlands of East Africa. ©Andy Gray

KENYA & THE ROAD SOUTH

Having crossed either Ethiopia, or both the Sahara and the steaming Congo basin, trans-African overlanders customarily take a breather in Kenya, sub-Saharan Africa's most visited and touristy country after South Africa. Mombasa and its adjacent Indian Ocean resorts are the preferred hangouts, where vehicles and bodies are serviced and repaired.

South of Kenya you can follow sealed highways all the way to the Cape, with road- and official hassles decreasing with every southward mile. From Tanzania, whose game parks and natural spectacles equal those of better known Kenya, the route continues via **Zambia** or **Malawi** and **Mozambique**, although travel in this latter country is still plagued by mines.

After the drama and difficulties of the north, southern Africa can be either an anticlimax or a blessed relief depending on how you coped with it all. Both Botswana and Zimbabwe can be crossed in a day or two, while, to the west, **Namibia** is well worth a diversion if you have a few miles left in you. Other than that, southbound riders find little to distract them across the smooth bitumen roads of South Africa.

Asia

For the overland biker Asia offers fully sealed road links from London's Piccadilly Circus all the way to Kathmandu at the foot of the Himalayas, or to the southern tip of India. What makes Asia so attractive is the **low cost of living** (much less than Africa, for example) and fabulous architecture. You could easily fill months of travel in Asia. Access to both the mine-ravaged countries of Indochina as well as the 'stans of Central Asia and Siberian Russia have all returned to the adventure biker's map, with China the only major destination still maintaining a frustrating and expensive series of hurdles to all but the most determined visitor with their own wheels.

So, coming from Europe, the overland route ends in India or Nepal, where China and Burma block access to South-east Asia. Once you've transported

---

COUNTRIES TO AVOID OR DIFFICULT TO VISIT

Afghanistan, Bhutan, China, Indonesia, Iraq, Myanmar (Burma), North Korea, Saudi Arabia, Tajikstan, Yemen.

Things will change, of course, so check the travel advice from your country's foreign ministry and the latest travel websites.

THE WEATHER IN ASIA

For trouble-free bike travel across Asia there are two things you want to avoid: the tropical monsoon on western coasts from June to October, and winter anywhere north of the Himalayas.

For Asia-bound riders departing from Europe, if you're heading south-east towards

India, ride into the autumn. If Central Asia or even just eastern Turkey is your destination, plan to arrive in the spring or early autumn – winters and Central Asian summers can be extreme. Further north, Siberia will only be tolerable or even passable in the summer (see p.153).

---

your bike to South-east Asia (see box p.150) and completed your mainland travels, it's easier to freight on to Australia direct rather than trying to get your bike into Indonesia. It's something that requires a fair bit of bribery and negotiating a reputed ban on bikes over 450cc. Most overland bikers don't bother.

Where to go

The re-opening of Iran in recent years has led to the resurgence of Indian-bound overland traffic from Europe while the break up of the Soviet Union has led to the possibility of travel through Central Asia and right across Siberia.

Like Africa though, Asia has its fair measure of headaches and there are certain countries it would not be safe to visit, while others make it very difficult to get so much as a wheel over the border (see box above).

OVERLAND TO INDIA

Based on original material by Nicki McCormick

Since the 1960s the overland trail from Europe to the exotic Orient via Turkey has always been a firm favourite and the good news is that this route can be re-traced with ease today.

Traditionally Asia begins once you cross the Bosphorus Strait from Istanbul into Asia Minor. Turkey itself offers few difficulties and plenty of amazing sights so don't rush through. The east and north-east regularly feature as highlights in a trans-Asian journey and in the Kurdish areas many riders have a positively good time even though some current guidebooks write this region off altogether. Eastern Turkey does appear on the 'travel with caution' lists of official government agencies although the Kurdish PKK movement experienced a reversal of fortunes with the capture of its leader in 1999.

Border crossings excepted, travel in Iran seems to be lightening up and even the Baluchi badlands of western Pakistan are on the way to getting sealed with tarmac. Still, this is just the main route: excursions off the trunk roads leading to the subcontinent could fill another book.

(Opposite) **Top:** Two well-dressed young ladies at the Iranian border (see p.132). © Trui Hanoulle. **Bottom:** The end of the road, South Africa. © Peter Kik.
(Following pages): Enfield Bullets at 4800m on the Manali-Leh road in Ladakh, northern India. © Rob Callander/Himalayan Roadrunners.

HAND SIGNALS

From Brasov, I went down to the Black Sea and into Bulgaria. Bulgaria was beautiful, but as I'd spent nearly a month in Romania, I only stayed for five days. I had quite an eventful time though. I stayed for a couple of nights in Sozopol, which is a family beach resort. I met some people from a circus there and ended up staying with them. None of them could speak English but we, sort of, communicated OK.

They spoke to me in a mixture of Bulgarian and German with the odd French word thrown in, none of which I speak at all. Their body language was also quite tricky to understand.

To say 'yes' they'd shake their head and to say 'no' they'd nod. But sometimes they'd use European conventions and I was never quite sure which applied.

Another gesture that took some getting used to was when they pointed towards me and did a downward hand motion. This usually happened when they got up to go somewhere. I thought this meant I should stay where I was. But when I stayed where I was then they would look at me and keep repeating the motion. It took me ages to understand that they wanted me to follow them. It was bizarre.

John Finlayson

Turkey

Eastern Turkey has been dogged by Kurdish unrest and many embassies advise against travel in this area. As with Western Sahara, however, they are way out of date and hundreds of travellers cross through to Iran every week. The majority of Kurds are overwhelmingly hospitable even if the military do their best to ensure contact is limited and are likely to usher you back to the main road should you be caught taking tea in a Kurdish village.

In south-east Turkey, tanks, gun emplacements and watchtowers are everywhere, and there are police checkpoints every few kilometres, manned by friendly, bored, military service boys counting the days till their posting is over. Avoid driving or wandering off the road at night in these areas as you might be mistaken by the military for a smuggler or a PKK activist – or the other way round. Whoever it is might not bother to ask for ID before shooting. Sheepdogs in eastern Turkey and western Iran are notoriously savage, and rabies is not uncommon. These dogs don't bark and chase you for fun – they're out for blood, if they can catch you. A touching custom you'll encounter is rural children throwing stones at passing vehicles.

Riding and running a bike

Petrol is readily available at around a dollar a litre and you can pay with credit cards in most places. Cities in Turkey usually have mechanics who can fathom modern bikes and western Turkey even has unleaded petrol. Main routes are generally reasonable tarmac, while minor roads in the east offer great off-roading potential through some stunning mountain areas as described by Kyril Dambuleff on p.219.

Borders

A carnet is unnecessary, though if you show one, they'll stamp it. The main crossing to Iran is near **Dogubeyazit**, continuing to Tabriz. The north-eastern

---

(**Opposite**) Top: Uraling across the steppes of Central Asia (see p.156 & 258). © Nicki McCormick.
Bottom: Shopping for spares at the flea market in Tashkent, Uzbekistan. © Nicki McCormick.

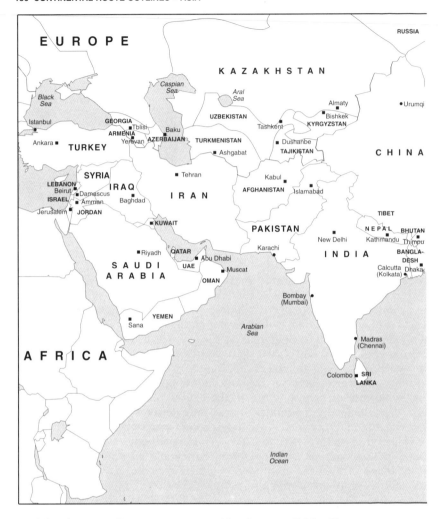

land border into Georgia is open with visas available. If you get across
Azerbaijan there's a twelve-hour ferry crossing from the port of Baku across
the Caspian Sea to Turkmenbashi (formerly Krasnovodsk) in Turkmenistan.
Again, Kyril gives the lowdown later in the book. There are several crossings to Syria if you're trying to do a Mediterranean loop or cross the Red Sea
to Eritrea.

Iran

In Iran, Farsi rather than Arabic is the national language. Older Iranians
might speak English, German or even French, but don't count on it. Iran
is very inexpensive and you can live well on £6.50/$10 a day. The cur-
rency is the rial. Iranians commonly quote prices in toman: one toman
equals ten rials. The black-market rate fluctuates around $1 for 8100 rials,
but be careful: it's better to pay someone else to do it for you. Otherwise

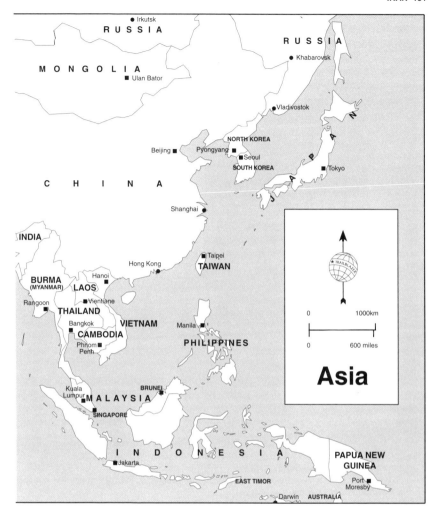

bazaar jewellers are the best bet. Bank rates are about 3500 rials for a dollar, and banks don't accept travellers' cheques or Visa, except in Tehran, where bureaucracy is rife.

Visas

At the time of writing five- to seven-day transit visas are issued to overlanders with vehicles which makes for a dawn-to-dusk rush across the country. And getting a visa itself takes ages, with the need for a 'Letter of Recommendation' from your embassy or passport office and a wait of anything from around three weeks up to three months. It's better, however, to leave with a visa as even if it's already expired getting a re-issue is much quicker than waiting in Turkey or Pakistan for an average of six weeks with no result.

Luckily, whatever they say at the embassy, transit visas are **easily extendable** in most cities once inside Iran. This takes a few hours, plus several

VEILS ON WHEELS

On the last day of April we cross into Iran, nicely dressed Moslem girls expecting a full day at the border. To our great surprise the paperwork is cleared within two hours and we ride into the country, ill at ease all the same.

We decide to skip the north and Teheran as distances here are far greater than in Turkey and the scenery far more dull. Only in towns do we need triple vigilance against that global menace: the taxi. Whatever is behind a taxi is immaterial, only what's in front of them matters. We soon learn that big trucks are banned from town centres, so whenever you spot the 'trucks and buses prohibited' sign you know that's the way in.

Dressed as flying nuns we look the part in this country! As everyone knows, the dress code in Iran is controlled by the hejab law and, especially for women, it's rather far-reaching: bodily profiles must be disguised; hair, neck, legs and feet must all be covered.

To dress acceptably while not catching the rear wheel is tricky, but we succeed and even manage to look impressive! Iris's disguise is so convincing she often gets addressed in Farsi (the language of Iran). On the other hand, I'm taken for her mother rather too often!

Moving east the heat becomes intolerable. Repeatedly we get soaked in sweat and then cooled at 100 kph, so we throw away the black coats and buy long thin cotton *manteaus*. Many Iranians, both woman and men, still find us slightly overdressed, but we've found that riding a bike in Iran causes enough commotion, whatever we look like.

Kurdish, Zoroastrian, Armenian and other women of non-Persian origin wear more colourful dresses or pants, coats and scarves, adapted to the Iranian dress code.

Tourists generally look like rich Iranian women, but the French... they beat everyone! Pants or leggings, shirts with décolletes, and a tiny loose scarf is the furthest they will bow to the hejab. Seeing a flock of them wandering about is shocking even to us, and by the looks on Iranian faces, they've gone too far.

One afternoon we notice an exhaust has vibrated loose. I dig up some tools and set to work. What is at first a curiosity soon grows into a full scale commotion. A woman riding a motorbike is inconceivable; a woman *repairing* it transcends reality. Soon the police arrive and Iris inquires in fluent sign language if there's a problem, but they're just there to control the traffic jam we've caused. When we're ready to go, Iris addresses the crowd in Dutch: 'Dear audience, thank you very much for your kind attention. The performance is now over. Adieu!!'

During our preparations, we met up with the only woman we knew who'd ridden this country by herself on a motorbike, Nicki McCormick. She was the only one with first-hand information on Iran from a woman's point of view. She assured us that Iranians had always been very hospitable and enthusiastic to her riding her Enfield through the country, and said our egos would be like Zeppelins by the time we left.

One morning, ready to take a short ride in Kashan, a group of rich Teherani women, academics of a university, surrounded us, chatting and laughing away in total surprise at seeing us on our bikes. They video us and take pictures, pulling back our head scarves and picking out bits of hair. We invite them to sit on a bike and they go completely out of their minds. We're left perplexed, both covered in kisses and hugs.

The following day, another group of women introduce themselves. As their English is again very good, they turn us inside out with questions. When I point to the WIMA-sticker on my pannier, telling about the Women's International Motorcycle Association, they actually begin to applaud; jumping up and down in sheer delight. In the end, one woman says they're all 'very, very proud of us, that we, as women, are riding motorbikes and accomplishing this kind of journey'.

Some days later, we have a long talk with four male high school teachers, one of whom speaks French fluently. They call us 'lion-femmes' and so we conclude that Nicki's tales are obviously not unique: our egos strain against our chadors. Starting a WIMA-Iran division is probably a bit premature, but they were certainly extremely heart-warming encounters!

One morning in Esfahan, as we were about to enter the main mosque, Iris turns around and stares in disbelief at a Western woman close by.

'NICKI!?'. Nicki stands two metres away from us, guiding an American group around Iran!

Trui Hanoulle

TURKEY AND IRAN ~ KLR600

Name	Mito Garan
Year of birth	1964
Occupation	Sales
Nationality	Turkish
Previous travels	Iran, Europe, South Africa
Bike travels	Local

This trip	Turkey and Iran
Trip duration	August 1997
Departure date	3 months
Number in group	1
Distance covered	7000km (4375 miles)
Sponsorship	None

Best day	Morning in Chalus, Caspian Sea
Worst day	Rain in the desert
Favourite place	Chalus
Biggest headache	Getting in and out of Iran
Biggest mistake	Small tank
Pleasant surprise	One in three speaks Turkish in Iran
Any illness	None
Cost of trip	US$2500
Other trips planned	Trans-Africa

Bike model	KLR 600
Age, mileage	3 years, 9000 km
Modifications	None
Wish you'd done...	Bigger tank, kick start
Tyres used	Michelin Deserts
Punctures	Around 25, I suppose
Type of baggage	Tank bag, waistbag and saddlebag

Bike's weak point	Small tank
Strong point	Everything else
Bike problems	None
Accidents	None
Same bike again	Yes but with a bigger tank
Any advice	Go

photos and fills up a passport page. You can usually get at least two extensions, more if you're persuasive, although the length depends on where you go. Esfahan is a good choice for trouble-free extensions. Coming from Turkey, the Foreigner's Registration Office in Tabriz was giving automatic one-month extensions on the spot and Kerman, the first stop coming from Pakistan, gives ten days.

Borders

A carnet is necessary, though it is possible to enter without one with a bit of baksheesh and a healthy dose of luck. Currency exchange forms are now obsolete. The main crossing for Turkey is at **Bazargan** where there are reports of incoming vehicles being charged 'road tax' of up to $100. The Farsi on the form allegedly instructs the bank to divide the cash between the accounts of various officials! It can be difficult to avoid and border bureaucracy can be intimidating and certainly longwinded, but be patient and you'll get through.

Access to Azerbaijan is said to be by train only from Tabriz, but there's no reason you couldn't put the bike on the train and see what happens. Most recent information on Turkmenistan is that the land border is still closed, though there are strong rumours of it opening up as rail and trade links are consolidated.

Hassles

Regular police checkpoints. Usually they just want to shake hands and meet you to alleviate the boredom. Though sometimes officious, they are never threatening. Revolutionary guards and hassles by religious police are thankfully a thing of the past. Corruption towards foreigners is rare but if you get arrested, you might not have too many rights. There are no restrictions on travel, though border areas can be sensitive. Foreigners' movements within the country are not checked, though Iranian friends might be checked up on. Beware of putting local people in compromising situations.

Riding and running a bike

Main (and most not-so-main) routes are pristine and empty tarmac highways. Asphalt is spreading rapidly across the country, but there are many desert routes. In the western and northern mountains there are networks of dirt roads through the hills of Iranian Azerbaijan.

At about two pence or three cents a litre, petrol must be around the cheapest on the planet. A crappy ten-litre jerrican costs twice as much as the contents. Multigrade oil is now easy to find, 10-40W more so than 20-50W. Petrol stations are few and far between – each city has only a handful and road houses are virtually unknown so fill up when you can, after all, it won't cost you much!

Pakistan

The national language is Urdu, which has many similarities with Hindi, though English is widely spoken except in the remotest parts. The exchange rate is around £1/$1.60 for 50 Pakistani rupees with travellers' cheques and Visa cards accepted in larger towns. Be aware that most places on the Karakoram Highway (KKH) except Gilgit and Sust don't have banks.

UK TO BOMBAY ~ APRILIA PEGASO

Name	John Finlayson
Year of birth	1962
Occupation	Economist
Nationality	New Zealand
Previous travels	Brazil, America, Australia, Europe
Bike travels	None

This trip	London to Bombay
Trip duration	7 months
Departure date	June 1998
Number in group	1
Distance covered	18,000 miles (29,000km)
Sponsorship	No

Best day	Baluchi Desert and KKH
Worst day	Camera stolen by cop after a crash
Favourite place	India and northern Pakistan
Biggest headache	Indian and Pakistani driving
Biggest mistake	Riding with a blown rear shock
Pleasant surprise	Friendly Pakistani checkpoints
Any illness	Diarrhoea a few times
Cost of trip	£4000
Other trips planned	Australia, lots

Bike model	1995 Aprilia Pegaso 2 (650cc)
Age, mileage	2 years, 10,000 miles
Modifications	None
Wish you'd done...	Bigger petrol tank
Tyres used	Michelin Macadam 50
Punctures	2
Type of baggage	Soft

Bike's weak point	Layout for maintenance is poor
Strong point	Good engine, comfortable to ride
Bike problems	Blown suspension, leaking radiator
Accidents	1
Same bike again	Probably not, maybe a Jap bike
Any advice	Go slow

Visas
Costs vary according to nationality (£40 for Brits, £5 for New Zealanders for example). If arriving without a visa, you're usually given a minimum of 72 hours at the border. Extensions are obtainable in Islamabad, but can take up to a week to sort out. One-month and three-month visas cost the same so get the longer one just to avoid the hassle of extending. If applying for a Pakistani visa in India, you need a Letter of Recommendation from your embassy.

Borders, hassles and risky areas
Pakistani frontier officials are friendly, straightforward, seemingly not corrupt and lightning fast by Asian standards. A carnet is necessary for Pakistan, though vehicles have been allowed through without them in the past. There is one border crossing to Iran, at Taftan, and one to India, at Lahore.

At the top of the Karakoram Highway is the Pakistani border post at Sust leading to Tashkurgan in China. People have been known to get permission to ride into China, but don't count on it. See 'China' in the box below.

Men can expect homosexual overtures: a chance to find out what it's like for women travellers! Travellers are often warned of bandits in Baluchistan and especially in Sind Province, and to avoid travelling at night or in remote

---

EXPLORING THE KARAKORAM HIGHWAY

The Karakoram Highway (KKH) runs from Islamabad to the Chinese border, a rise of nearly 13,000ft (4000m) over 625 miles (1000km). It's considered one of the engineering wonders of the world, carved out of the cliffs along the Indus and Hunza rivers. The road is sealed all the way, but landslides and rock falls are frequent, especially in late spring or as a result of the frequent earthquakes. The KKH and its branches are also one of the Five Wonders of the Adventure Biking World and to ride a bike to Pakistan and not come up here would lead to a lifetime of regret.

To the Chinese Border
The stupendous Hunza Valley is the highlight of the KKH. Most hotels are in Karimabad, but just down the track, the Kisar Inn at Altit is friendly and cheap with a vine-shaded veranda. Further north around Passau, a walk incorporates two 300m rope bridges which will get certainly your adrenaline flowing!

The border post with China is 80km below the **Khunjerab Pass** at Sust. To ride up to the Pass, you'll have to leave your passport at Sust to stop you dashing off into China (if only the Chinese would just sit back and give you the chance!).

The Pass is officially open from 1st May to early November, though there can still be a lot of snow near the top early in the year.

The scenery is stunning, fuel is not a problem but your carburation may get rough with the altitude. (Consider a smaller main jet to run with the reduced oxygen).

China
It's not currently possible to enter and tour China independently with your own vehicle. The only way you can ride your bike in China is to import and register your bike as a Chinese vehicle with special plates – this involves a combination of mountainous paperwork, pots of money and friends in high places. You must reputedly pre-book all accommodation and give officials a planned itinerary. Your bike and documents will be checked by police in every town. Altogether it doesn't sound like much fun.

If attempting to transit across Xinjiang (north-west China) between Pakistan and Kyrghizstan, arrange to put your bike on a truck, though you'll probably need permission to do this too. It takes months of negotiations, culminating in a fee of at least $1000 for permits plus a guide to lead you along a previously approved route.

Ignore regulations at your peril – Chinese officials have no qualms about confiscating bikes and fining or imprisoning miscreants. On the bright side, regulations are steadily being relaxed year by year giving you a chance to explore this fascinating country on your own terms.

areas. Access to some sensitive border areas is forbidden by the police. The tribal areas bordering Afghanistan are still under the control of tribal chiefs – the Pakistani government cannot guarantee the safety of foreigners there and will refuse permission to travel, notably for the direct road along the Afghan border between Quetta and Peshawar.

The route down the west side of the Indus from Peshawar via Dera Ishmail Khan to Quetta is also officially closed but is commonly travelled. At worst you'll be turned back by the police as your safety is dependent on the caprices of local tribespeople.

Riding and running a bike
You can cross Pakistan entirely on sealed roads between Iran and India. Fuel is widely available as is multigrade motor oil, but as always it's advisable to fill up when you can in the more remote areas. Petrol costs 18R a litre or about half that near the Iranian border.

Iranian border to Quetta (650km/400 miles)
When leaving Iran (overnight in Zahaden), fill up every last container about 40km before the main border checkpoint at Taftan. Once border formalities on

---

KARAKORAM HIGHWAY (continued)

Skardu and Beyond
There's a good road branching off the KKH to Skardu which clings to the mountainsides above the Indus. Beyond Skardu, the route to Askole is constantly being rebuilt and repaired by local jeep drivers who use it to take climbers and trekkers to the Baltoro glacier. It has some very rough sections and can be quite daunting with extremely tight hairpins high above the river. The road from Skardu to Hushe, via Khaplu and Kande, again presents some rough riding but astonishing scenery. There is a small guest-house in Hushe or you can camp.

Chitral via the Lowari Pass from Peshawar or Islamabad
The pass is just under 13,000ft/4000m and is amazing, a tightly winding, steep but beautiful route. In spring when the streams are flowing strongly expect plenty of fording! Once over the pass and on flatter ground the road into Chitral is straightforward. On the south side of the pass in the town of Dir the Abshar Hotel has a great setting by the river.

A must in this area are the **Kalash valleys** as described in Eric Newby's *A Short Walk in the Hindu Kush*. The Kalash practise their own pagan religion and the women are unveiled, wearing brightly coloured orange and yellow beads and cowrie shells. Sadly, the area is becoming overrun by Moslem influences. Rumbur and Bumburet are the two motorable valleys with the former being more picturesque and culturally more interesting. The road in is quite rough, though spectacular, following a narrow track beside fast-flowing rapids.

Chitral to Gilgit via Shandur Pass
This is the highlight of any Pakistani off-roading with utterly awesome scenery. The road goes from Chitral to Mastuj, where fuel and lodgings are available. Coming from this side, the pass is not too difficult. The best part is the top of the pass; a plateau surrounded by snow-capped peaks. There's a lake nearby where you can camp. Coming down the far side of the steep pass is not for the faint-hearted. From this point to Gupis there are many very steep and tight sections and the occasional river crossing. From Gupis to Gilgit is fine.

Babusar Pass
Another great, if rough route, cutting off a large corner of the KKH and only navigable (as with all these routes above except for the main KKH) in the summer. Further south another rough but fantastic route runs from Dera Ismail Khan to Zhob via Daraban and Mughal Kot. Many river crossings and very rough in sections, though a lot of the stretch from Mughal Khot to Zhob is newly paved.
Colette Smith and **Steve Coleman**

TRANS-BALUCHISTAN

Some sections of our trip had bothered us long before leaving. The notorious run from Taftan in Iran east to Quetta in Pakistan was one. It runs along the Afghan border, across the Baluchistani desert, and has a reputation for banditry and shootings. While staying in Bam, we read that a Dutch couple on bicycles had been shot at only months before, when camping out.

Our host came up with good advice: leave Bam at dawn and clear the border the very same day, so it's possible to make the 650km to Quetta in one very long haul, avoiding tricky stop-overs.

Following a windswept ride to the border, the crossing was painless. Not only do we slice through red tape in just three hours, but also get hosed down in tea. Pakistan has clearly made an effort on the road, which used to be unpaved all the way. Now only the last 150-200km remain badly potholed, including a few really rough sections.

Riding in the vast, arid desertscape is absolutely splendid. Only once do we nearly miss the steel wire, hung across the road at one of the checkpoints. After our longest day on the road, we enter Quetta, exhausted but very satisfied. Yet another obstacle tackled without so much as a hiccup!

After Iran we feel relieved to be able to wear normal clothes, read signs and escape censored television – but we also missed the clean towns and tap water, women in the streets, virtually free petrol, smooth roads with foreseeable distances and schedules. We hadn't prepared for sudden changes like this.

Iris Heiremans and **Trui Hanoulle**

both sides have been completed, the first 90 miles/140km as far as Nokundi are on a reasonably paved road. Remember to switch back to riding on the left.

Strong winds blow sand onto the road and get worse as the day progresses. The new sealed highway is complete in many areas with stretches of tarmac for as much as 30km at a time. Unfortunately these sections are interspersed with sand and rock. The rubble lies just 100m away is the old road, pot holed and badly corrugated – you take your pick.

Depending on how quickly you get through the border formalities, you could ride to Quetta in one very long day, but two days is considered normal and gives you a chance to enjoy the great Baluchi hospitality. There's a rest house in Dalbandin which makes a good halfway stop. It's a hard, hot and dusty ride. At border checkpoints throughout Pakistan watch out for steel ropes hung across the road: they're especially difficult to see at sunrise or sunset.

India and the Enfield experience
Bruce Clarke

Thanks to the heart-tugging appeals from various charity groups, when most Westerners think of India they conjure up images of a squalid Third World country swarming with masses of starving children. Certainly there are slums in the larger cities that fit this unfortunate stereotype, but I found most of my riding through rural India to be a fascinating visit to a beautiful land. The villages are crowded, colourful, and perhaps not as hygienic as in the West, but then there are no fast-food restaurants, chain hotels, or billboards. India is bristling with life and excitement. In fact, in many ways I think the Indian countryside is ideal for touring by motorcycle if done in the right way.

In January 1999, I joined a three-week tour around southern India on a Enfield Bullet 500. We travelled from the former Portuguese colony of Goa to the tea hills of Ooty, north to the temple ruins of Mysore, and back to Goa.

INDIA PRACTICALITIES

You'll find English is widely spoken, even in the smallest village. Amex travellers' cheques are accepted in most banks and Visa cards in at least some banks in major cities and £1 equals about 50 Indian rupees ($1 is about 30 rupees). The black market is not significantly better, but is much less tedious. Bureaucracy for anything from buying a train ticket to extending a visa is truly mind-boggling.

With your own vehicle the best guide is the Footprint *India Handbook*: concise and with information on sights between major tourist destinations and routes. The Rough Guide and ubiquitous Lonely Planet equivalents are more suited to travellers using public transport.

Visas and borders

In Pakistan, visas are available in Islamabad in three days. You need a Letter of Recommendation from your embassy (the British embassy charges £20). Three-month visas are valid from the date of entry, but are non-extendable, so get a **six-month visa**, even though it's usually valid as soon as it's issued.

There's only one open land border to Pakistan, at Atari, 25 miles/40km from Amritsar. It's straightforward if lengthy as long as all your papers are in order. The border's open from 10am–4pm, but arrive early and bring some lunch. Vehicles are often stripped in the search for drugs. You must have a **carnet** to bring a vehicle into India.

There are several crossings into Nepal, where you don't need a carnet if you're riding an Indian bike. Sometimes there's a per-day charge if you stay more than two weeks; it depends on the border officials.

Riding and running a bike

Road surfaces vary from acceptable to horrendous remnants of tarmac, with many minor roads unsealed. It's said elsewhere, and I won't disagree, that highways are dangerous torrents of homicidal truck- and bus-drivers who give way to nobody. Give way to everything, drive with your horn, and expect the unexpected at every turn. For your information, the road with the highest accident rate in the world runs between Bombay and Ahmadabad.

Riding at night is also a risky endeavour as the road quality is erratic and drivers rarely use their lights. Non-automotive hazards include bike-chasing dogs and holy cows who wander at will. If you have any sort of accident, the general advice is to disappear as quickly as possible.

For very long trips **putting your bike on the train** is straightforward along main routes and costs a fraction more than the sleeper fare for one person.

For more information on buying and running an Enfield Bullet in India, see the box on p.32.

Nicki McCormick

Currently there are dozens of motorcycle models available on the Indian market but they're generally in the 100- to 150cc range. The average Indian's income is about $1500 per year, so even a $1000 scooter is a major purchase. The motorcycle of most interest to a visiting foreigner is the ubiquitous Indian-built version of the old British Enfield Bullet.

Back in the mid-1950s the Indian army needed some simple hardy motorcycles for patrolling the northern borders. A few Enfield Bullet 350s were imported and they were so well liked by the Indians that a factory was set up in the city of Madras (now Chennai). Despite the fact that the original factory in England closed in 1970, the Indians just kept churning out the same old bike year after year.

Today the Chennai factory still builds about 20,000 Bullets a year. The bikes are a plain-looking air-cooled four-stroke single and have a very classic British bike look. Some updates have been carried out in recent years: the Bullet now has 12-volt electrics, some modern electrical components, and the engine is available in a 500cc version. A new Enfield costs approximately

INDIA TO UK ~ 350 BULLET

Name	Dave and Helen Kelly
Year of birth	1968/1964
Occupation	Teachers
Nationality	British
Previous travels	Europe
Bike travels	Europe lots of times

This trip	India to UK
Trip duration	9 months
Departure date	September 1996
Number in group	2
Distance covered	20,000 km (12,500 miles)
Sponsorship	Nope

Best day	With an R100 near Kumbulgah
Worst day	Early monsoon, Shimla
Favourite place	Multan, Pakistan
Biggest headache	Rear brake: all noise no action
Biggest mistake	Coming home
Pleasant surprise	Greek Enfield agent posting parts
Any illness	Burnt valves, bronchitis, Delhi belly
Cost of trip	£10,000 (inc 4 months in Africa)
Other trips planned	In Egypt now: spoilt for choice

Bike model	Enfield Bullet 350 Deluxe
Age, mileage	New
Modifications	Racks, tool box, vintage seat
Wish you'd done...	None
Tyres used	OE Nylons
Punctures	3
Type of baggage	Rucksacks and daysacks

Bike's weak point	Performance up hill and into wind
Strong point	Simplicity
Bike problems	Brakes, valves, condenser
Accidents	Just made the toilet in Jaisalmer...
Same bike again	Yes, or maybe a Ural
Any advice	Wear a helmet

INDIA ~ 350 BULLET

Name	Charley Snow
Year of birth	1963
Occupation	Engineer
Nationality	British
Previous travels	Lots
Bike travels	UK, Europe, Oz

This trip	India
Trip duration	14 Months
Departure date	1994
Number in group	1
Distance covered	No idea, speedo didn't work enough
Sponsorship	Only in my dreams

Best day	Pondicherry to Madras
Worst day	Madras to Pondicherry
Favourite place	The mountains
Biggest headache	Bureaucracy
Biggest mistake	Don't think I made a real big one
Pleasant surprise	Travelling by train can be fun too
Any illness	Of course. I was in India!!
Cost of trip	Not as much as I thought
Other trips planned	Yes

Bike model	Indian Enfield 350 Bullet
Age, mileage	New
Modifications	Every optional extra available
Wish you'd done...	Lots. Wider handlebars
Tyres used	Indian
Punctures	None
Type of baggage	Stainless steel panniers. Rack

Bike's weak point	Bad off road, heavy, unreliable
Strong point	Easy to fix, breaks ice with locals
Bike problems	Want a list or just a few ideas?
Accidents	Only a few bumps but I saw plenty
Same bike again	Surprisingly, yes
Any advice	Don't hit cows

55,000 to 60,000 rupees, or about £1000/$1500. To a typical Indian this is a lot of coin: owning an Enfield in India is equivalent to a Westerner owning a high-end Harley or BMW.

Visiting India involves more red tape than a May Day parade in Beijing. Most foreigners require a visa and an International Driving Permit is mandatory. Doctors recommend you get shots for tetanus, diphtheria, typhoid, polio and hepatitis A. I also tried to wire an advance payment of $500 to the company I rented my Enfield from, but my bank couldn't get the money through the Indian bureaucracy. I later found out this is a common problem, but most motorcycle rental vendors will be more than happy if you just pay the full amount in cash when you arrive.

Helmets aren't required in India. I have to recommend an open face, as even a well-ventilated full face would be extremely warm. Good boots and gloves are a must, as is a decent jacket for the cool mountain roads.

When you first step out of the plane you'll almost certainly be struck by how much of a hellhole the airport is – any airport! Take the most dilapidated run-down bus terminal you've ever seen, surround it with planes instead of buses, and you'll have a good picture. Don't let it bother you; just realise that once you get out of the major cities India becomes a lot more pleasant.

Like I said, be ready for the Indian bureaucracy; it'll take over an hour just to get stamped through Customs, collect your bags, and get in a bus or taxi. I recommend booking a hotel room ready for your first night so in all the confusion you know where you're going and can rest up from jet lag.

The Motorcycle Bazaar

Buying an bike is actually quite easy for a foreigner. I visited several motorcycle shops and all the dealers claimed that it would cost about 30,000 rupees (around £470/$750) for a good used 100cc bike like a Honda CD100, Yamaha RX100, Kawasaki KB100 or a Suzuki Samurai. I also found that the paperwork or registration for a foreigner only takes about three days to complete (provided small amounts of silver cross several palms). That's about as long as it took Richard Wolters to import his bike at Madras port (see p.147)!

I won't be surprising anybody by confessing that I found the Enfield Bullet to be unreliable; most of the dealers I met recognised that the Japanese bikes are better and that the Yamaha RX100 has probably the best reputation for reliability on the Indian continent.

CONQUISTADORS OF THE OBVIOUS

There are dozens of different castes in India and top of them all are the Brahmins. They have the same aloof attitude as the Brahman cattle. A classic encounter happens when we stop to check the map. Fifty people surround us before the stands are down, a Brahmin pushes through and asks if we need help. We reply 'No – we're just checking the map.' So he asks 'Where are you going?' and we might say for example 'We are going along here to the next town. I can see from the map that we must go across the bridge, turn left and then turn right'.

'No, no, let me explain it to you. You continue to follow this road, when you reach a bridge you cross it and quickly make a left turn, followed by a turn to the right and then you are on the right road.'

Thank you sir!

Richard Wolters

ASIA OVERLAND ~ YAMAHA TÉNÉRÉ

Name	Paddy Gibbins
Year of birth	1969
Occupation	Sales
Nationality	British
Previous travels	America, Europe, Asia, Africa
Bike travels	Two week 'Euro-Tours'

This trip	London to Sydney
Trip duration	9 months
Departure date	September 1998
Number in group	1
Distance covered	27,000km (17,000 miles)
Sponsorship	Hein Gericke

Best day	SE Turkey, Northern Iran, KKH
Worst day	RFDS, Outback NT, Australia...
Favourite place	Pakistan
Biggest headache	Getting spare parts sent to India
Biggest mistake	Should have taken a newer bike
Pleasant surprise	I can fix motorbikes!
Any illness	Not really
Cost of trip	£7000
Other trips planned	London to Cape Town

Bike model	XT600 Ténéré
Age, mileage	1986, 45,000km
Modifications	Fuel filters, tyres
Wish you'd done...	Bigger tank, box, 'water' bash plate
Tyres used	MT21s
Punctures	2
Type of baggage	Därrs box, homemade rack: Crap!

Bike's weak point	Head gasket. Blew three times
Strong point	It's solid and takes the knocks
Bike problems	Carb, wiring, clutch, do I carry on?
Accidents	One only. But it was a good one
Same bike again	Considering an F650 for Africa
Any advice	Get your luggage right

INDIAN TRAFFIC HAZARDS

Bovids

General Purpose House Cow (GPHC) Varying in colour from brown to black and white, they wander aimlessly through traffic. Dangerously limited ability to reason.

Buffalo Black with laid back horns – used for working the fields, pulling carts and obstructing traffic. Walks slowly and once moving keeps going in that direction no matter what. Make sure you're not coming the other way.

Brahmans or Sacred Mobile Roundabouts (SMR). Grey to white, smaller in the south, up to 1.8m tall in the north. Cocky, will not budge under any pressure. Creates its own roundabout with other Brahmans. Has eyes with 180-degree vision. Objectionable 'Holier than a GPHC' attitude. Immune to all intimidation; scoff at warp-factor air horns.

Goats

Commonplace and also contemptuous of traffic. Whole families cohabit in permanent squalor on median strips. The young ones are dangerous as they make sudden moves and lack respect.

Pigs

Have the tendency to cross the road in gangs and change course midway. Often seen stranded across median strips where they are able to disrupt *both* directions of travel. Highly intelligent, verging on conspiratorial.

Dogs

Most run away at the sight of big bikes. Less intelligent than a GPHC with learning difficulties. Minor hazard.

Monkeys

Very dangerous and unpredictable – jump out of the bush screaming and race along the road baring their teeth. Avoid braking hard on any Fresh Flat Monkey Formations (FFMFs), which otherwise have passed their most dangerous phase and are on the path to reincarnation.

Old men on pushbikes

There are two varieties: the 'I can't afford a hearing aid' type. Prone to making sudden right turns with perfectly bad timing.

The second variety usually wears sawn-down coke bottles polished with coarse sandpaper and held on by copper wire. These guys steer straight towards you with an 'I can't believe my eyes' attitude and change course just prior to impact (you hope).

Truck/bus drivers

The biggest threat to motorcyclists on a daily basis. Drip-fed on amphetamines and have adapted the Nietzchean axiom 'That which does not kill me and is not an SMR can be run at/run over/run off the road.'

Government vehicles and army jeeps

Attitude: 'We own the road so we drive in the middle – what are you going to do about it? I am too important/have a big gun'.

Yield or face the consequences, including several forms requiring stamping and countersigning by a Permanently Unobtainable Person (PUP).

Grain crops in need of thrashing

Can appear on the road in all arable areas up to one foot deep. Apply same caution as with FFMFs. Dry stalks can wedge against your exhaust and set you ablaze.

Everything else I forgot to mention

Whatever it is, it's out there on the road and heading for your spokes!

Richard Wolters

Once you find yourself a machine and get out of the city, you'll find the land of India ranges from hilly curvy roads in lush jungle to dry dusty deserts and rocky, awesome mountains. In my short three weeks of riding in India I don't think there was a single type of terrain I didn't encounter.

For the most part, motorcycling in India reminded me of riding in Central America: there are many buses, trucks and two-stroke scooters dodging around. The only real traffic rules are 'give way to the bigger vehicle' and 'honk instead of signal'. You'll notice that most bikes are not Enfields but Indian-built versions of small Japanese two-strokes. If you've never ridden a kick-start bike, count on spending a good ten minutes learning how to start an

Enfield. I found the hand controls are not difficult, but the steering a bit ponderous. And the Bullet doesn't have much turning radius.

For someone used to modern motorcycles, the biggest problem is stopping. Following the old British-style, the Enfield's rear brake is on the left side. This drum brake is actually pretty strong but grabs very easily. Until you get used to it the front brake will seem little more than a wrist exerciser. Most modern motorcycles will stop with just a gentle two-finger squeeze on the front brake – trying this on the Enfield has no effect but if you squeeze hard with all four fingers you may experience some decelerative effect.

Another problem is gearing 'down' as you brake. Since the Enfield has a British right-side shift, first gear is actually 'up' and two-three-four are all down. Watch out that you don't shift into a higher gear as you slow.

Traffic can be awful in urban areas! Anarchy is the name of the game. Be ready to do some weaving between buses, trucks, ox carts, dogs, pedestrians, bicycles, pigs: you'll find every imaginable obstacle on the roadway at some point (see the box opposite). And don't expect other vehicles to offer you much courtesy; I had a couple of very close calls because of bus drivers not giving a damn who else was on the road.

It's a good thing the folks are so friendly and helpful (at least when not behind the steering wheel of a bus or a truck!), as outside urban areas English road signs are almost non-existent. You will find, though, that many Indians will speak at least a few words of English and are willing to try and get you pointed in the right direction to your next destination.

Luckily it's not all crazy urban traffic: there are plenty of small peaceful villages, tranquil rivers, fields of rice and palm trees. If you avoid the monsoon (starts in the south-west in late May and rain everywhere by July) you'll find the sky is always blue and the temperature warm and pleasant.

Be ready to ride more slowly than you might at home (about 30mph/50kph in the villages and 50mph/80kph in the countryside). It's not because of the

THE WORLD'S MOST PANORAMIC COMFORT STATION

Travel is strange stuff. You can plan for months to visit exotic places, to travel roads and see sights granted to only a fortunate few. Yet when you finally get there, the odds are that for part of the trip at least, you'll be preoccupied not by the magic of the Orient, or wherever you happen to be, but by something far more mundane. I'm talking bowels, friends. Bowels.

Mine awoke me with a sharp, strident pain at 3am in the utter blackness of the Snow Leopard Guest House, Tingri, Tibet. It was probably lucky that the electricity came on for only two brief hours each evening, otherwise I might have been tempted to try for the switch, a mess of cracked insulation dangling from bare wires near the door.

Instead, the panic was blind and the need desperately urgent. Find cigarette lighter, tripping over boots and baggage, to find torch, to find the crapper without falling through the hole in the floor into the vile pit of god-knows-what beneath. I'll spare you the details but it was close, very close. The relief was exquisite.

By my fifth trip I could find the way in the dark – just as well since my torch batteries had long since given up. Then the sun rose over the hills to the east and I noticed two very memorable things. One, the stinking void below, whilst far from intrinsically lovely, was bathed in the most brilliant yellow light. And secondly, this must be the only bog in the world with a view of Everest. When your guts are in this shape, you'll take your pleasures in any way you can.

Mac McDiarmid

LONDON TO SYDNEY ~ BMW F650ST

Name	Lance Wiggs
Year of birth	1967
Occupation	Management consultant
Nationality	New Zealand
Previous travels	USA
Bike travels	Europe on K75RT

This trip	London to Sydney
Trip duration	3 months, fast
Departure date	August 1998
Number in group	1
Distance covered	20,000 miles (32,000km)
Sponsorship	Nope

Best day	Zaheden to Quetta
Worst day	None yet...
Favourite place	Cappadocia and KKH
Biggest headache	Speedo broke on Quetta leg
Biggest mistake	Running low on food while off-road
Pleasant surprise	People in Iran
Any illness	Nothing serious
Cost of trip	Too much
Other trips planned	Always, but pay this back first

Bike model	F650ST
Age, mileage	1 year, 7000 miles
Modifications	Acerbis tank, racks, boxes
Wish you'd done...	Stronger racks
Tyres used	Metz' Enduro 3s
Punctures	2, one in a camp-site!
Type of baggage	Därrs boxes, Givi top box

Bike's weak point	No history, 19" front, clearance
Strong point	Light, agile, reliable
Bike problems	Speedo
Accidents	Dropped in river; stuck in mud only
Same bike again	Yes
Any advice	Lightness is everything

slow bike or the physical condition of the pavement but rather the amount of traffic can be so bad that you probably won't feel comfortable going any faster. I found that even at these very low speeds there was always a dog or a GPHC stumbling out onto the lane every few hundred metres without warning.

I tried to like the Enfield but I had countless mechanical problems so I'd never rent one again. Be prepared for flat tyres, snapped cables, fouled plugs and loose bolts. I suppose it's all part of the charm of a classic-style bike, but I've promised myself that the next time I visit India I'll go Japanese.

Don't plan to cover long distances quickly while touring India; I honestly think that even at say 125 miles/200km a day you'll zoom past many interesting towns and sites. You never ride more than a kilometre without seeing some sort of activity: oxen ploughing rice fields, schoolchildren cheering as you ride by, smiling Indian women carrying huge bundles on their heads, ancient temples, or other motorbike riders zipping their 100cc steeds between buses.

I loved India and its incredible, raw scenery. It is an absolutely beautiful country.

'India: you're standing in it'
The perils of importing by air. By Richard Wolters

After months of preparation, Charlie, Peter and I are strapping the bikes onto an aluminium aircraft pallet, just large enough to hold three BMWs. The bikes flew from Brisbane with Malaysian Airlines (cheaper than shipping) and arrived in what was then Madras (now Chennai) a day later.

The hotel was chosen from the Lonely Planet *India* guidebook and this turned out to be a wise decision as in India chaos rules for approximately 24 hours every day.

We have no Indian rupees but, as usual, one does not have to look for the black market as the black market soon finds you. The official exchange rate is 27 rupees to an Australian dollar but we are offered around 30 which is better and saves queueing in a bank. Memo: don't open up a bank account in India. On the way back we passed a busy intersection and watched the traffic for about ten minutes, utterly horrified – soon we would be part of all this! I didn't want to think about it for the time being.

It was at this stage that I first noted Peter's excellent navigational skills. He must have spent a lot of time with pigeons as a young boy. I had no idea where we were, but he lead us straight back to the hotel via a few backstreets. Peter displayed this skill many times on our trip and we were glad to have him along.

The hotel taxi took us back to the airport area as we had to check in at the Air India office. Months before, friends of friends had warned me of what was likely to happen when attempting to clear Indian Customs – so we were ready for several days of paperwork hassles.

As soon as the Air India office opened we were greeted by an Air India mamma, wrapped in a red sari and running an all-woman office. After a few minutes she announced that everything was in order.

'Please proceed across the road and get a gate permit.'

We looked at each other and thought 'Stone the crows, that was easy!', as she handed the papers back. She continued in her pleasant Indian accent, 'By

NEPAL

Border formalities were surprisingly easy as Indians and Nepalis are able to cross unchecked. Our arrival created some variety for the Customs Officers and we crossed into Nepal at around 2pm. The first thing that caught our eye was two donkeys on top of each other – right in the middle of the road! We tried not to stare and embarrass them.

We thought that we'd make the 170km to Pokhara that night. Such optimists! Two hours later we'd only covered 30 kms. The first 20 or so were still on the flat plane, but the road suddenly rises at an astounding rate. It's no more than a track and after 50km we gave it away, totally exhausted. The next day we covered the remaining 120km in six hours. The scenery is breathtaking. I have to pinch myself – I am riding in the Himalayas!

Road workers push their hands together and smile as we ride by. 'Namaste' I hear them say, 'Welcome!'. The men gaze at the bikes and the kids give us a wave and smile.

I am lucky to be here, I think, as my front wheel disappears into yet another pot hole. We ride on to Tansen and check in for the night. We can't take the risk of being caught in the dark again – certainly not with these road conditions.   **Richard Wolters**

the way, who is your agent?' 'Agent?' we said, 'No madam that's OK, we'll do the clearance ourselves.'

As if rehearsed for days beforehand, several of the nearby women looked up and the mamma raised an eyebrow and gave us a very special smile as if to say: 'You fools don't know what you are in for.'

Ten minutes later we entered a dark building with offices straight out of *Barton Fink*. Brown, grey and dark green were the predominant colours and few filing cabinets were to be seen. Instead, walls were made of pigeon holes crammed with files held together with bits of string, flapping in the gentle breeze caused by the creaking overhead fans. Computers were clearly a future fantasy.

'Please explain your business, sir – what is your good name?' Pleasantries over, we were sold some forms and filled in another form in quadruplicate. It was now 11am. We went upstairs.

'What is your business? Your name? Three motorcycles? Please go downstairs and fill in one more form, then come back.'

Noon, we go back upstairs. 'Excuse me Sir, we have lunch break, please wait one hour.' Later a guy examines our papers. 'You have to pay import duty, what is the value?' We explain we have carnets.

'You have to go to the Harbour Customs House – better you go now!'

What followed was the first of several 45-minute dodgem slaloms across town in a three-wheeled taxi. The back seat was made for slender Indians and not for bonzer-shearing champs like us. However, we managed to squeeze in without blowing the rickshaw apart and tried not to watch. Traffic clearance was measured with a feeler gauge.

Arriving at the Customs office we proceeded to another office called 'Preventive'. 'Preventive what?' we wondered.

'You need special document sir – here is one, please go to other floor to Xerox it.' We filled in the forms, showed carnets, make special hand signals and explained everything for the tenth time. Two hours later... 'Please come back at 10am so we can do it quickly. But first you must go back to the airport to get the xyz document and bring that with you in the morning.'

When we left the office I cast my eyes on the sign in hallway, 'Preventive' it said. 'Preventive of us from getting our bikes!' came to mind.

Another 45-minute white-knuckle ride in the taxi contraption and we were back at the airport for more documentation. We were kept waiting and although hungry and very thirsty refused the tea offered – organising a kettle would only slow things down. I was now dog-tired and a few hours later, back at the hotel, collapsed on the bed after just two bottles of beer.

Next day. 'Please explain why your documents show one consignment of three packages and ours shows seven packages?' We explain that the pallet was a small one and we had removed the bags. They were placed on the floor individually.

'You might have to pay import duty on them.'

We say 'No sir, they are part of the bikes.' New accessory forms are filled out. No wonder the Indonesian rain forests are in jeopardy!

'Please explain your CB Radios plus value, you might have to pay duty!'

We say 'No sir, they are on the carnet.'

'I see! I will send you to another officer who will check the details. Your good names, why you are in India...'

It's 11.30am 'Lunch time, please come back at 2pm.'

We went outside and walked the streets for a couple of hours after which time we returned to the office as requested – but no officer. He arrives at 2.30pm and must wait for his assistant.

'Please follow me. Passports please. Please go upstairs and Xerox pages one and two of your passports.' We go upstairs to the designated office and ask about the photocopy machine.

'Ah sir, you mean Xerox.'

'Yes, I suppose I do!'

He looks at our papers and starts a conversation about our bikes, Australia, and Pauline Hansen. After ten minutes he comes out with the following statement spoken in a heavy Indian accent.

'Gentillmens, I am only too pleased to Xerox your passports for you but our Xerox machine has broken down!'

Shit! We look at each other in amazement.

'Sorry' he says, 'Also, I would like to inform you that there no other Xerox machines in this building.'

We go outside and find a machine in another building.

At 3 pm: 'I will dictate you a letter as follows. Name and address, details of carnet, 'Dear Sir, I have come to India for the purpose of... etc. I will not sell the above motorcycle as described in detail on carnet form. I will be in India for etc etc... I will not sell accessories, radios, etc...'

We offer him a bribe but he refuses. What are we doing wrong? We were hoping to have our bikes by the weekend.

Although the bribe didn't work something else did and the officer went into a different gear. Maybe he thought that we judged him as being incompetent. Lord knows how he got this idea but things started to move.

'Please wait while I get this stamped.' We now have to go back to the airport to complete documentation where there are more security checks, Customs checks, genetic fingerprinting and two more forms. We decide to employ an agent.

EAST FROM INDIA – BY SEA OR AIR

As Richard Wolters' story (pp.147-152) shows, shipping a vehicle either to or from India is likely to stretch your tolerance levels to their limits. We met one rider who managed to get his bike on a ship from Kenya to Bombay and got as far as riding along the docks, but could not get a release for two weeks, and only then when he'd lined a few pockets. And a British couple who flew their bikes into Delhi spent a solid week of twelve-hour days chasing officials and exploring the corridors of Indian bureaucracy. Few people realise that Franz Kafka actually wrote *The Trial* after trying to import a CZ250 ISDE Replica into Trivandrum.

We shipped from Madras (now Chennai) to Singapore, in theory the most direct and cheapest link to South-east Asia. In fact it turned out to be the most stressful part of our whole two-year journey. The voyage should take five days, but plan at least a week of organising in Madras and two days in Singapore to get out of the port.

Singapore is fast and efficient and a pass from Customs will allow you into the port warehouse where you'll be given a hammer and left to get on with it. Don't forget to get your carnet stamped by Customs.

In India insist on accompanying agents to the Customs Office with your carnet and passport (in India the bike is entered into your passport and must be stamped out before you can leave the country). Supervise the crating of your bike, making sure luggage is locked. Fully enclosed crates are more expensive, a basic skeleton crate will suffice.

Strikes in Indian ports mean a constant backlog of containers waiting to be shipped. Don't leave the country until you know the bike is aboard. Our container sat on the docks for a month before finally leaving India. The Customs Office runs on backhanders, best leave this to your agent to negotiate as it's included in your charges. Cubic metre rates are fixed, but haggle over costs for administration, crating and transportation to docks. After our experience we'd advise you to give shipping agents Binny Ltd in Madras a wide berth.

In addition to the actual shipping fee, extra costs include a basic skeleton crate: £30/$50, shipping agents' handling fees in India: £45/$75, and in Singapore: £60/$95.

Flying from Kathmandu

Thai Air operate regular flights between Kathmandu and Bangkok, a popular and painless way to cross from the subcontinent to South-east Asia. Nepalese airline and Customs officials are reasonably efficient, as are the Thais when you get to the other end. Depending on available freight space your bike can often end up on the same flight and be picked up the next day.

Air freighting costs around £350/$550 but is so much quicker than shipping it's worth the extra. You must crate your bike (relatively expensive compared to India due to dwindling wood supplies) emptied of fuel and have the battery disconnected and secured. The above cost includes crating, possibly transportation of the crated bike to the airport, handling and documentation at both ends, plus the actual freight price.

Colette Smith and **Steve Coleman**

(See also the box on p.160 for air freighting from Singapore to India)

It's now 7.30pm, dark and the mozzies are out, probisci oiled for a night on the town. We go to the military guard and sit under the fan in his hut. A cow walks through the gate without documentation. Is this a good omen?

Charlie is back and a new officer goes through everything. 'Please explain why you have seven packages and I can only see three motorcycles? I see, OK. I will fill out some clearance forms for you to sign. Problem Sir, we only have one computer, the program for clearance can only handle six digits, your names have seven digits. I will have to get the forms and do it manually.' We are stunned but say nothing.

We have been at it for twelve hours solid. The compound is now almost deserted and we must now pay overtime for all remaining personnel. Calculations are

DUBAI TO UK ~ BMW R1100GS

Name	Mark Powell
Year of birth	1960
Occupation	Regional manager
Nationality	British
Previous travels	40+ countries
Bike travels	Europe, RSA, Namibia, UAE

This trip	Dubai to England
Trip duration	2 weeks
Departure date	July 1999
Number in group	1
Distance covered	9126 km (5703 miles)
Sponsorship	Wife and two kids

Best day	All of them!
Worst day	Each day was a buzz, warts 'n all
Favourite place	Snow-capped Mt Ararat after Iran
Biggest headache	Clearing the bike in Bandar Abbas
Biggest mistake	Not taking time to stop and explore
Pleasant surprise	Parking inside the Ishak Pasa Hotel
Any illness	None – apart from mozzie bites...
Cost of trip	£690
Other trips planned	KKH and maybe Mongolia

Bike model	1998 BMW R1100GS
Age, mileage	New
Modifications	Touratech gearbox/frame kit
Wish you'd done...	More comfy seat
Tyres used	OEM – Michelin T66
Punctures	One – the mother of all holes
Type of baggage	Touratech ally boxes

Bike's weak point	Haven't found it yet
Strong point	Unstoppable
Bike problems	None
Accidents	None
Same bike again	Definitely
Any advice	Mind and wallet: the only barriers

made and after paying 3200 rupees we finally proceed to the bikes and quickly connect the batteries and mount the windscreens. We keep smiling and answer all the questions about the tank capacity, speed, etc but keep working quickly

'Is this a double engine – is it a diesel – how fast?'

'Yes, yes, yes' we answer.

'Before you go, we must drink tea together' says the Customs officer.

We start the engines, the steel gates open and WE ARE OUT!

What did we learn from this? Use an agent and make sure if the cargo documents state three items there are three items. Unless you're a cow, that is.

THE CAUCASUS AND CENTRAL ASIA
Kyril Dambuleff

The overland route to Kathmandu may well be a classic, but I chose to take the high road across Asia and had no regrets. After Turkey, I encountered no other travellers with their own vehicles and most of the time was pleased to have the place to myself. Suffering the vestiges of Soviet colonisation to varying degrees, the Central Asian '-stans' can be bureaucratically demanding at times and the food a bit bland compared to the wonders of India, but those wide-open desert highways are a dream to ride.

Visas
Visas are required for all Westerners, for sure for US citizens. Visas are difficult to obtain and can be expensive. In most cases, an invitation from an organisation or a private party is required. The best thing to do is to pay a visa agency to deal with the visa issues. Even transit visas are tough to get – I had to call the Turkmenistani consul at least a dozen times before he agreed to issue a transit visa. The biggest headache about visas is that you have to state on your application when you intend to enter the country. The visa starts on that day and runs for its duration which makes planning rather difficult.

Money
US dollars seem to be the currency of choice. Bring new, latest edition bills, nothing more that three or four years old. Exchange kiosks are everywhere but you'll get much better rates on the black market. There is no need to look for it, it will find you. One country's currency is no good in another so exchange only what you need and spend it all before crossing the border.

The 'three-day' rule
There is a rule which is supposed to be valid for all CIS countries that states that a holder of a valid visa for any of the CIS countries can spend up to 72 hours in any other CIS country without a visa for that country. The trick here is knowing which of the former Soviet countries are CIS members. It appears Turkmenistan, Georgia and Azerbaijan aren't. There is a five-day agreement between Georgia and Azerbaijan meaning that you can spend five days in one with a valid visa for the other. For example I crossed from Turkey into Georgia without a Georgian visa but had a 30-day tourist visa for Azerbaijan.

'Halt, papers!'
Borders are slow but relatively painless. A valid visa is all you need and a **carnet is not necessary**. Everybody wants you to complete a currency/valuables

declaration form but I don't remember anybody wanting to see it on the way out or wanting to see my money. **Insurance** does not appear to be required either. I had the so-called 'green card' insurance but no one asked to see it.

Bringing a motorcycle into any of these countries doesn't appear to be a problem of any kind, and, better still, doesn't cost anything. The only exception is Turkmenistan where you'll have to pay something like $50 gasoline tax (the government's way of compensating itself for the low price of fuel).

As far as other paperwork goes, the only exception was that on crossing from Turkmenistan into Uzbekistan I had to show my **immunisation certificate**. A lot of people will want to sit on your bike and wear your helmet. As any other traveller I too was at their mercy and always allowed them to do it hoping that this would speed up the process. The bastards dropped my bike three times but at least I did not catch lice.

Roads
Open, rarely travelled and affording a magnificent view of open desert and big skies, the roads in Central Asia give you the I-am-the-king-of-the-road feeling and make the region a paradise for adventure bikers. Most roads are hard top, and all in some state of disrepair or another. None have seen much, if any, maintenance in the last ten years. Potholes vary from the size of a K100 on the M27 in Georgia to almost none on the M37 from Turkmenbashi to Ashgabat in Turkmenistan. Some have sections of dirt road which can last up to 100 miles/160km.

Fuel
There is no shortage of it, although it very rarely comes in the 96-octane variety. The most commonly available grades are 73 and 76 octane. Stations can be as much as 400 miles/640km apart although there'll always be a helpful local who will magically produce a 20-litre can of fuel. Petrol is very inexpensive, running about from around 1–30 cents per litre in all of Central Asia.

TRANS-SIBERIA

Despite the greater opportunity for independent travel since the break-up of the Soviet Union, crossing the width of this huge region is still a feat of physical endurance.

Importing a vehicle is no longer an insurmountable hassle, but the absence of reliable long-distance roads in the eastern half of Russia still makes for a challenge that is hard on both rider and machine. Summer is of course the only time to consider a crossing, with the real difficulties beginning once you get past the Central Asian republics to Novosibirsk. From this point aeroplanes, railways or to a lesser extent rivers are the normal ways of continuing east, while bloodthirsty horseflies and mosquitoes pester you night and day. This main route may appear disappointingly southern, but the entire bulk of Siberia north of the 60th parallel is barely populated and densely forested *taiga*, cut with huge rivers and brief summers.

East of Novosibirsk expect mud, shallow river crossings and the occasional juddering ride over the sleepers of rail bridges. The hardest part is the so-called **Zilov Gap**, a barely motorable 500-mile/800km section of flooded logging tracks between Svilengrad and Yakutsk. Allow at least a week to cross it. Once through that, you're riding for 940 miles/1500km on the 'Road of Bones' to Magadan, built by Stalin's political prisoners.

If not heading down into Mongolia or China, most eastbound overlanders head south for the port of Vladivostok from where it's a relatively short hop over to Japan. The weekly flights from Magadan to Anchorage were suspended a few years ago.

GERMANY-LONDON (VIA TASHKENT) ~ BMW

Name	Kyril Dambuleff
Year of birth	1958
Occupation	Scientist/biochemist
Nationality	USA
Previous travels	Europe, North America
Bike travels	Down the PCH

This trip	Germany–Kazakhstan–England
Trip duration	3 months
Departure date	March 1998
Number in group	Solo
Distance covered	10,000 miles (16,000km)
Sponsorship	No

Best day	The day the trip began
Worst day	The day the trip ended
Favourite place	Turkey
Biggest headache	Borders, Caspian ferry
Biggest mistake	Hoping the Chinese will let me in
Pleasant surprise	Moslem hospitality
Any illness	None
Cost of trip	About $10,000
Other trips planned	Lisbon to Istanbul via North Africa?

Bike model	BMW K100RS
Age, mileage	6 years, 12,000 miles
Modifications	None
Wish you'd done...	Better saddlebags
Tyres used	Michelin
Punctures	None
Type of baggage	BMW saddlebags, tank bag

Bike's weak point	Front suspension hates potholes
Strong point	Riding is easy and enjoyable
Bike problems	Gearbox problem; fixed in an hour
Accidents	None and thank God for ABS!
Same bike again	Most of Europe/Asia yes; Sahara no
Any advice	Travel light. Very light!

Food and drink

There is plenty of it and variety too (depending on the season) contrary to propaganda press reports. Food stands are abundant along major highways and every major town has a huge bazaar where you can find just about anything you need for survival. No need to worry about water – nobody drinks it anyway. Tea (*chai*) is what everyone drinks. Coca-Cola has a bottling plant in the region and all of Coke's products can be found everywhere.

Accommodation

Unless you want to pay £45/$70 a night for a drab hotel with no hot water and cardboard sheets in an ugly town, bring a tent. In the vastness of the land, it seems that you can camp anywhere in the countryside and nobody will bat an eyelid. If the locals see you, they'll come and drag you out of your tent to their homes where they'll offer you everything they have.

Everything you've heard about Moslem hospitality is true and then some. Chances are you'll be invited to stay at somebody's house at least three times a day. I always took them up on their offer. If there is a teahouse (*chaihana*) alongside the road, spend the night there. The charge is about £3/$5 for room and board, and your stay there is the only business these guys will see for a long time. They are fantastic – you eat with the family and sleep on the floor. Visit as many as you can if just for tea or a meal. Do not let them disappear!

Safety

There may be some disputes and conflicts in Central Asia, but the whole thing is so overblown by the media. Central Asia is safe. The American Embassy in Baku warned me several times that it was unwise to enter Azerbaijan because the country was in the state of civil war. Nothing could have been further from the truth. You will see more army movements in Turkey and even Western Europe than you'll see in Azerbaijan and Georgia provided, of course, that you stay on the main roads.

Naturally your safety should be your main concern, but that's the case anywhere. Even covered in dirt, you seem like a walking bank to some aspiring yuppies in the big cities who desperately want to have a bike like yours or your Western leather jacket. Your bike's safety at night is your primary concern whenever you're staying the night in a big city.

Checkpoints

There are many police checkpoints, remnants of the Soviet days of total control. The guards may be armed but I never saw any weapons. You will get stopped only because these guys are bored to death and fascinated with bikes which have electric starters.

Tashkent to Samara

I was about to complain about the £10/$16 the crafty Kazakhstani woman had charged me for a bowl of soup and the dirt floor I'd shared with three Tajik drivers. But when I walked outside and saw that my bike was covered in frost, I thought I should be grateful.

Her small teahouse sat lonely by the side of the road in the vastness of the barren landscape of the Kyzylkum desert. The Tajiks complained loudly about

CENTRAL ASIA TRIP NOTES

Borders

Uzbekistan to Kazakhstan via Chimkent is the strictest border crossing, and occasionally closed to vehicles if Uz and Kaz are in a strop. I couldn't get a Kazakh visa in Tashkent when it was closed, but when it re-opened drove through with no visa and no checks on the Kazakh side at all (theoretically no visa is needed for a three-day transit).

There are long queues on the Uzbek side of the border, and you get an exit stamp, but any Uzbek and Kyrgyz border in the Ferghana region is very lax. It's all done the old way and can be hard to get stamps or find anyone who knows what a carnet is.

South of Ferghana the Bishkek-Osh road passes through Uzbekistan several times. If you tell them you're just in transit the Uzbeks don't mess with your single-entry Uzbek visa. On the Kyrgyz or Kazakh side of any border you just drive through, they rarely even bother to enter you in a ledger. On the Kazakh–Kyrgyz border coming from Chimkent to Bishkek the officials on both sides didn't attempt to stop us.

Police registration

Within three days of arrival in Kyrgyzstan, you must register with the OVIR (department of internal affairs). It's best to do this in Bishkek, though it's allegedly possible in Osh. You get a slip of paper from your hotel, go to a bank, pay about 60 sum for a 'registratsya OVIR' and find your local police station (not the main OVIR offices in town). They stamp your passport and that's it – no need to register anywhere else in Kyrgyzia.

In Uzbekistan, relic of the Soviet Union, you need a piece of paper from every hotel for every night. In practice, if you're missing a few due to camping or staying at someone's home, it shouldn't matter, but keep all those bits of paper as they are often checked at the border. The hotel paper means you've been automatically registered with OVIR for that night so unless you're staying in a private home you don't need to visit an OVIR office.

Also keep any Customs form (*declaratsya*) you get at the border on entry. You have to list your foreign currency, weapons (don't forget the ammo), narcotics as well as lethal musical instruments on it and hand it in at the end.

Currency

The Uzbek official rate is 120 sum per dollar. Officially you need to have some currency exchange stamped on the Customs declaration form that you get on arrival, but in practice no one checks if you leave overland. The black market rate is 440-500 sum per dollar, but unless you like jail food try and get a local to do it for you.

In Kyrgyzstan you get 40 sum per dollar. There are lots of legal money exchange offices in major towns, which give slightly better rates than the bank so there is no black market.

Police checkpoints

In Uzbekistan there are police posts every few kilometres, each with a 'Stop' sign. You have to stop at the sign, even if there seems to be no one there, wait to be ignored, then drive on. If you don't wait to be ignored, someone will appear from nowhere and pull you over. The same applies, for some reason, to stop signs by disused railway crossings: everyone stops, despite the fact that the line may run into a newly-built concrete wall.

Uzbek police are generally not the friendliest. If you get stopped, the standard bribe is 500 sum, about a dollar. It's worth keeping that amount in your document wallet as foreigners are likely to be asked for

the price too as they criticised her hospitality in what I perceived as a harsh tone of voice. Warning me about bad road conditions ahead and the lack of gas stations, they gave me a 20-litre jerrican and said: 'Bad people those Kazakhs. All they want is money, money, money. Don't go up that road. Come with us to Tajikistan!'

With the jerrican strapped to the BM's saddle, I hit the road as the sun crawled out and melted the frost away. It was my second day on the Taskent-Samara Highway, a road stretching for 2400km through the middle of nowhere to the Volga River and Russia proper. Kazakhstan itself is a country four times the size of Texas, with only three or four towns of any decent size

CENTRAL ASIA TRIP NOTES (continued)

more and it's bad form to rummage in that moneybelt full of $100 bills.

Kyrgyzstan also has regular police checks, but at these ones you just slow right down; it's the same deal in Kazakhstan. Where you must stop is at posts on the approach to Lake Issy Kul. There is a $25 'ecology tax' to pay, and you're constantly asked for this paper.

The Kyrgyz police are quite friendly, however. Once they've got their money they'll help you with any questions or directions. In Uzbekistan they just take the cash and tell you to piss off!

Petrol

Uzbekistan   12 cents/litre
Kyrgyzstan   30 cents/litre
Kazakhstan   20 cents/litre

There is a more expensive, higher quality petrol available too, but generally the quality is variable so it's always best to fill up in bigger towns.

Petrol is usually sold in multiples of five litres. You pay in advance at the kiosk, then take a chit of paper to the attendant. Sometimes you fill up yourself: the cashier switches on the pump for the paid-up number of litres.

In Uzbekistan you're not allowed to fill jerricans at filling stations (it's a way of limiting the smuggling of cheap Uzbek petrol). If you have to fill up, drive just outside the station, siphon into your jerries in full view of the attendants, then drive back in and refill. Calibration of pumps is not always what it should be so check you are getting the right amount!!

Also, in Uzbekistan, petrol stations in towns are well hidden so fill up when you can, and try to avoid weekend mornings when there are mile-long queues. The Ferghana region of Uzbekistan occasionally runs out of petrol when too much has been smuggled to Kyrgyzia. In remote areas of Kyrgyzia fuel is again hard to find. You'll often see small hand-written signs at farms or at truck stops advertising 'benzin', the price is slightly higher, and the quality is worse than British Rail tea.

Incidental discovery

When buying my Ural in Tashkent, I found out that if you buy or sell anything expensive enough to warrant a lawyer's official letter, your spouse has to go with you to the office and sign his/her approval of the transaction. I imagine this is to stop drunken husbands selling the family Lada from under the wife's nose!

Parking, road rules and helmets

No one seems to leave their vehicle on the street overnight and there's always a manned 'stayanka' (parking) nearby, for a small fee. A locking petrol cap is a good idea as the stayankachniks in Uzbekistan constantly supplemented their income from my tank!

Road rules are give way to things joining roundabouts. Elsewhere radar guns are a popular wage-supplementing device.

Despite the famously hard-drinking habits of the population, nobody drink drives in Uzbekistan. The penalties are brutal, and even money does not work. Helmets are obligatory in Central Asia for rider and passenger. In Kyrgyzia this is often ignored, in Uzbekistan less so, but never in cities.

Cultural tip: Never throw away bread in Central Asia. You can crumble it for the birds, you can leave your stale crusts on a ledge, but to dump it is the ultimate sin.

'Bread is life, chucking it feeds the devil' or something like that.

Nicki McCormick

for its entire length. The straight road shot out to the horizon.

With no one around and under the enormous desert skies, I was overwhelmed by an incredible feeling of freedom. Strong warm winds blew from the south, driving a mist of sand over the road and threatening to topple the bike. I was making good progress but the potholes, stretches of dirt road, and the sand, made me worry. I kept thinking: 'It's bound to get better. It has to. After all Russia's answer to 'Cape Canaveral is along this road'.

That hope lasted about an hour. A Russian driver passed me in his Lada and asked me to pull over. He looked at my BMW K100RS in total disbelief. 'Where are you headed on this machine?' he said. 'Samara', I responded with confidence. 'It is a thousand kilometres of dirt road ahead. It is Paris-Dakar, Paris-Dakar, I tell you!!' he yelped, gripping his imaginary handlebars and bouncing up and down to show me what I was up against.

Seeing that I had no intention of turning back, he shook his head and continued on his way. I gave it a thought. The sun was high in the sky and it was getting hot. But no, I wasn't going back. Whatever lay ahead, I was going to deal with it whenever I got there. The second night found me at another teahouse. This time I was the only guest so I had the whole floor to myself. And this time I was smart enough to ask the price in advance and was told three bucks! The promised Paris-Dakar experience did not materialise that day. Was that guy pulling my leg? I was ready for adventure. At that point, I was almost asking for it.

Well, it came. About sixty miles north of Aralsk, the road dived into the ground to be replaced by foot-deep ruts of dried mud. Like the Russian guy promised, the bouncing began and progress slowed with my saddlebags occasionally scraping against the mud ruts.

Just 8 miles into it and both the bike and I started to get hot. I used those rest stops to jot a few quick words in my diary: '11:51am Advanced 8 miles in 45 mins. Will I stay on the bike without falling? 12:30pm. Another 9 miles. It has begun to look like the surface of the Moon. 1:07pm. Nearly 8 miles. Thirty wild horses just crossed the road. Clouds are moving in and the wind is picking up'.

I was moving at an average speed of about 10mph. Six hundred miles!? That's five full days! Five days of this! I began to have serious doubts that the bike and I would make it out in one piece. Another hour and another 13 miles into it, I began to feel as if I was the only living creature on the planet. I pushed on. Two hours later, the dirt road ended and I hit hard top which felt like paradise. 'No, this can't be true. This has got to be just a short good stretch. The guy said six hundred.' I looked at the odometer – the bad stretch was 58 miles long. 'Did he mean sixty? Or was it my Russian?' At the next teahouse I inquired about road conditions ahead.

'Oh, the road is fine', the owner said. 'All asphalt. Plenty of potholes, big and small. But the road is fine' he assured me as he helped me fill up my tank from the jerry. The news about the road was so good, I decided to stay and celebrate with him. His teenage son offered to go to the nearest village to buy a bottle of vodka. I gave him the money, he got on his horse and two hours later I was raising a toast to friendship with the owner. He had not seen vodka, he said, in a long time and drank with gusto. I let him finish the bottle by himself. Two glasses was enough for me – it had been a hard day.

SOUTH-EAST ASIA
Based on original material by Colette Smith and Steve Coleman

Motorcycles are allowed into **Thailand** for up to six months with a carnet or a cash deposit. Shipping worldwide from Bangkok to major ports is straightforward but 'Indian' driving standards are the norm here. At around 25p/40 cents a litre, fuel is readily available with petrol stations on major roads or hand pumps at roadside stalls in villages.

SOUTH-EAST ASIA ~ TRIUMPH TIGER

Name	Ian Foster
Year of birth	1963
Occupation	Architect/City designer
Nationality	British
Previous travels	Europe, N America, Colombia
Bike travels	Europe, USA, China

This trip	SE Asia (9 countries)
Trip duration	3 months
Departure date	April 1997
Number in group	1
Distance covered	10,000 miles (16,000km)
Sponsorship	Perrier, Shell, Crown (for charity)

Best day	New mountain road in Chiang Mai
Worst day	Borneo jungles with road tyres!
Favourite place	Deserted beaches north of Phuket
Biggest headache	Progress through the Philippines...
Biggest mistake	Trying Indonesia. Corruption rules!
Pleasant surprise	Singapore has nightlife
Any illness	No
Cost of trip	£2500
Other trips planned	Anchorage to Tierra del Fuego'93

Bike model	Triumph Tiger 900
Age, mileage	4 years, 8000 miles
Modifications	Higher screen
Wish you'd done...	Scott oiler
Tyres used	Metzlers
Punctures	1 in Manila right at the end
Type of baggage	Givi (it was completely crap)

Bike's weak point	Chain, high centre of gravity
Strong point	Speed, pose-value with the girlies
Bike problems	None
Accidents	None
Same bike again	No, Triumph pissed me off. BM-GS
Any advice	Keep it between the hedges!

The best riding is in the Chiang Mai region in the north where with a good map there is plenty of scope for off-roading in the Mae Hong Son region along the Burmese border. For more information check out David Unkovich's website: The Golden Triangle Riders (see AM Website links).

Malaysia

Malaysia is often used as a through road to the more exotic destinations of Thailand and Indochina. Whilst there is little of architectural interest, the natural beauty is stunning. Eastern beaches are quiet and relaxing and accommodation from just £4/$6.50 with breakfast is very clean. The roads are excellent and distances short although there aren't many possibilities for off-roading apart from logging tracks through plantations.

Check with truck drivers on conditions after heavy rain as the monsoon can flood roads very quickly. Malaysia is tuned into motorbikers and you'll find basic wooden shelters for bikers built along all major roads and diversions around tolls. There are plenty of petrol stations with good quality fuel at around 30p/50 cents per litre.

After India and Thailand, riding is a dream. The only road hazards are boy racers on smelly strokers and reptiles. Motorcycle dealers in Kuala Lumpur and Penang stock parts and accessories for foreign bikes.

SHIPPING FROM SOUTH-EAST ASIA TO AUSTRALIA OR INDIA

With the reputed bureaucratic complications of importing a bike into **Indonesia**, you need to make a big leap to get over to Australia from Malaysia or Singapore.

Luckily, as shipping goes, this is a relatively straightforward procedure and **Kuala Lumpur** and **Singapore** are both major ports with worldwide links. Most ships from Malaysia go via Singapore, but Kuala Lumpur makes for a cheaper and more pleasant alternative to spending time in Singapore.

Expect to pay around £300/$500 from Singapore to Sydney all in, based on a two-cubic-metre crate. There'll be another £140/$225 handling and quarantine charges in Sydney.

Reader's recommendation #1

The Singapore agent for **VB Perkins** is:
Jesselton Shipping Pte Ltd
9, Tai Seng Drive, #02-01
Singapore 535227
☎ (65) 2883456
🖳 jspl@jesselton.com

Mrs Jane (ext 36) was most helpful with all my enquiries. Not only did she gave me a breakdown of the overall cost, she even took the trouble to explain all the shipping terms and gave me some discounts here and there.

Recommendation #2

I managed to get a quote of $360 from a local shipping company in Singapore for shipping my Djebel 250 to Calcutta. This quote included the ocean freight, transportation, port charges, all documentations and hire of an Indian agent to process the documents/Customs clearance in Calcutta ($150).

The crating charge was rather expensive at $64 per cubic metre but I managed to get hold of an empty crate from a local bike shop free of charge. The freight charge is $25 per cubic metre but it varies from port to port. Air freight costs almost twice as much.

I was told they could arrange for Calcutta to Bangkok seafreight as well.
RIL Shipping Services Pte Ltd
☎ 65 2788577; 🖹 65 2782009

(Opposite) Top: Time for breakfast in Wadi Rum, Jordan. © Chris Bright.
Bottom: Giant termite mounds in Queensland, Australia. © Rob van Driesum.
(Following pages): Under a sickle moon in Africa. © Peter Kik.

Heading south from Thailand to Singapore the most direct route is to cross the border at Sadao on the west coast. Pick up Highway 1 down to Butterworth and continue south to Kuala Lumpur, straight down to Johor Bahru and the Singapore border. This could be done in one long day. All other border crossings are straightforward on the Malay side and not subject to the nightmarish bureaucracy and scrutiny of western Asia.

Singapore

The cross-roads on the Asia to Australia overland route is anachronistically fast-paced, clean and modern and can be a shock to the system if you've ridden from the west. Bemused motorcyclists can often be found haunting the offices of shipping agents so it's a good place for swapping information. Johor Bahru is the road route in from Malaysia and entry is smooth and efficient.

Singapore is a major port shipping to most worldwide destinations. There are numerous agents – shop around for the best deals. VB Perkins Shipping ply the route between Singapore and Darwin (ten days – address in box opposite). The advantage of using Perkins is that crating is not necessary (crating alone can cost £65/$100 in Singapore). The bike can be wheeled straight into the container. The cost to Darwin is a flat rate of around £150/$240. Unless you're in a hurry or the season is wrong, head for Darwin and not straight down to Sydney. There's plenty of good riding to be done between the two cities; it's the best part of Australia (see p.176).

Compared to the rest of Asia, Singapore is expensive and waiting around for shipping can add up. Peony Mansions on Bencoolen Street has cheap accommodation and plenty of parking around the back. Cheap eats can be found in the food halls of shopping malls. Singapore is also a good place to stock up on bike parts and accessories. One shop that's recommended is:

Mah Motorcycles
19, Jalan Besar, Singapore 0820
☎ 294 4048 or 293 3841; 🖹 295 0767
It's across from the Sim Lim Tower which everyone knows.

INDOCHINA

Very few riders cross Asia from Europe and head down into Indochina: Laos, Cambodia and Vietnam. Until recently this used to be for sound reasons of self-preservation but while there are still real dangers and difficulties here, the Thai borders with Laos and Cambodia are opening up to overland travellers. Vietnam, it seems, has taken bureaucracy lessons from India, so riding your own machine into this country will take some perseverance. By far the more common solution is to rent or buy locally. Check out the Minsk Club of Hanoi at AMW Links. Assuming you're in Thailand, the Bangkok embassies of the three Indochinese countries would be the place to check on entry formalities. Visas can be issued in a couple of days. If you're intent on exploring this area for some time, **November to February** are the coolest and driest months.

(Opposite) Camping in Cape York, Australia (see p.183-6). © Rob van Driesum.

VIETNAM ~ MINSK 125

Name	Erik J. Schelzig
Year of birth	1975
Occupation	Student
Nationality	American
Previous travels	West Africa, Europe, USA, SE Asia
Bike travels	None

This trip	Hanoi to Saigon
Trip duration	1 month
Departure date	June 1996
Number in group	2
Distance covered	1500 miles (2400km)
Sponsorship	Khong (as they say out here)

Best day	Sharing spit wine with mountain folk
Worst day	Shredded tyre in a three-hut village
Favourite place	Hué City
Biggest headache	Endless hassles with authorities
Biggest mistake	Should have taken a slower pace
Pleasant surprise	Being American wasn't a problem
Any illness	Nothing major
Cost of trip	US$1000
Other trips planned	Anywhere and everywhere

Bike model	Minsk 125
Age, mileage	6 years, mileage anyone's guess
Modifications	Tyres, shocks, clutch, seat padding
Wish you'd done...	For $200 I did all I could, really
Tyres used	Crappy Soviet and Chinese brands
Punctures	1
Type of baggage	Backpack held on with inner tube

Bike's weak point	It broke down a lot
Strong point	It was easy to fix
Bike problems	Not very reliable
Accidents	Cut up by woman on bike + jellyfish
Same bike again	Only in Vietnam
Any advice	Enjoy

BANGKOK TO ANGKOR WAT ~ KDX200

Name	Pierre Mugnier
Year of birth	1973
Occupation	None
Nationality	French
Previous travels	S Africa, S America, Australia
Bike travels	None

This trip	Bangkok to Angkor Wat and back
Trip duration	5 weeks
Departure date	March 2000
Number in group	1
Distance covered	12,000 km (7500 miles)
Sponsorship	No

Best day	Day 1 Cambodia: Siem Reap
Worst day	Last day on the very same road
Favourite place	Between Sisophon and Siem Reap
Biggest headache	Finding a reliable mechanic
Biggest mistake	Not renewing my chainset
Pleasant surprise	No hassle outside tourist places
Any illness	Minor digestion disorders
Cost of trip	US$350
Other trips planned	Southern Africa, ideally with a bike

Bike model	Kawasaki KDX200
Age, mileage	4 years, who knows
Modifications	None
Wish you'd done...	Better lights
Tyres used	Dunlop
Punctures	4
Type of baggage	Backpack and elastic

Bike's weak point	None really
Strong point	Light, cheap, flexible, any gas will do
Bike problems	None
Accidents	None
Same bike again	Definitely
Any advice	A good wheelie works wonders

Laos and Cambodia

After the Americans had finished with it, Laos gained the unfortunate record of being the most bombed country in the history of warfare. To this day large areas of the country are littered with what's become known as 'UXO' (Unexploded Ordnance) which includes mines as well as shells. The worst areas are in the southern arm of Laos because the Viet Cong's 'Ho Chi Minh' supply route once wove it way through here. The further from Vietnam you get the lesser the menace.

As if that isn't enough, **banditry** is also a problem along certain well-known routes, with buses and bikes getting highjacked and robbed, and victims sometimes even killed. The *Rough Guide to Laos* has fuller details on mined areas and bandit-prone routes as well as some positive reasons for visiting this country. The **hills of the north-west** ought to provide an environment matching Thailand's well known Chiang Mai district, but without the ingrained tourism. So if you're not put off and fancy doing something different, the easiest way to get into Laos is from **Nong Khai** in Thailand across the Friendship Bridge just south of the Laotian capital, **Vientiane**. At the border you'll get a visa issued on the spot.

Cambodia too has a reputation for mines, although in fact it's not anywhere near as bad as Laos. Instead you can expect some of the worst roads in Asia. Banditry here is of the semi-official kind with roadblocks manned by disbanded Khmer Rouge activists extracting tolls from passing travellers. The main entry point from Thailand is at **Aranyaprathet** to **Poi Pet** in Cambodia where again it's said you can obtain a visa on the spot, but check in Bangkok about bringing a bike in. If the temple complex of Angkor Wat near Siem Reap is your destination, it's about a six-hour ride.

Central and South America

Like Africa, Central and South America conjure up their fair share of negative images: seasonal governments, cruel or corrupt regimes, the risk of kidnapping by terrorists and audacious banditry. As usual the reality is far more benign and the experience immeasurably rewarding. As you'll see from Ken McLean's tale on p.243, Colombia, a place where you'd expect to get mown down in the crossfire of battling cartels, is often cited as a favourite South American country with heart-warming hospitality.

If you're intent on a tip-to-tail run along the Americas, the sign at Tierra del Fuego in southern Chile advises it's 17,848km (around 11,100 miles) from there to Alaska. For such a trip allow three months at the very least.

As you'd expect, the **US dollar** is the most useful hard currency to carry and some knowledge of **Spanish** will transform your trip and may even help rid you of the 'gringo' epithet. In addition the following items should not to overlooked when travelling in Central and South America:
● Yellow Fever certificate – mandatory in countries where the disease is endemic
● a Libreta de Pasos por Aduana (see box on p.168)

POINTS OF ENTRY

If you're not starting your travels through Central and South America from the US, the following are points and methods of entry worth investigating. These connections also apply if you're leaving South America for other continents.

For riders coming from Europe, **Venezuela's** strong shipping links make this the chosen country to freight a bike. The need for a *libreta* (full story on p.168), only available here, also makes Venezuela a good place to start.

Coming from Australia or New Zealand, you may find it cheaper to fly your bike to **Santiago** in Chile rather than ship it. The same goes if you're crossing the South Atlantic: fly your bike from Cape Town to **Buenos Aires** in Argentina and save a whole lot of shipping hassles and time.

South America includes many Westernised countries which are as **expensive** as their former European colonial homelands. Brazil, Uruguay, Argentina and Chile top the list. These countries enjoy a high standard of living and relative political stability, making border crossings and travel off the beaten track straightforward and safe.

At the other end of the scale are the 'Andean' countries of Ecuador, Peru and Bolivia (the latter is the least expensive) which have rougher edges but by their very difference make a more memorable trip.

MEXICO

Mexico is to North American riders what Morocco is for Europeans: a simple border crossing into a substantial cultural change which sharpens both senses and anxieties simultaneously. The 625-mile/1000km-long Baja Peninsula is a dirt bikers' paradise, bereft of US environmental restrictions and brimming with cactus-lined tracks, ranges of low hills and the Sea of Cortez or the Pacific never far away. On the mainland, **Copper Canyon** also presents opportunities to get off the highways, but in this country you have to actively seek out interesting trails. Mexico's true highlights are the spectacular Mayan ruins in the provinces south of the capital, Mexico City, and the fact that it's emphatically not Northern America.

Clement Salvadori's *Baja* book features 20 route guides as well as a colourful background on the peninsula.

THE WEATHER

Stretching from above the equator to just 625 miles/1000km from the Antarctic mainland, and with several Andean summits peaking over 21,000ft/6500m within sight of the Pacific, the weather in this region is difficult to summarise.

Technically, the tropics stretch from the southern tip of the Baja to Rio de Janeiro. In lowland areas closer to the equator you can expect temperatures in the low 30°C year-round, with seriously heavy rains from April to July when overland travel comes to a standstill. In coastal regions near the equator, dry seasons last just a couple of months. Southern Panama is such a place, which is one of the reasons why crossing the Darien Gap remains so difficult.

If you're heading for Cape Horn from North America, try and hit the northern countries of Latin America in the early part of the year and plan to arrive in Patagonia for the southern spring when temperatures begin to warm up, but before the summer winds reach their full force.

A comprehensive tour around South America will demand a full range of clothing. Some rare days may see you sweltering along jungle track to end the day shivering over a 15,000ft/5000m pass. The only answer is to be prepared for everything.

CENTRAL AMERICA ~ YAMAHA SR250

Name	Ron Grant
Year of birth	1946
Occupation	Semi-retired teacher
Nationality	Canadian, Oz resident 10 years
Previous travels	All over
Bike travels	Ditto

This trip	Florida to San Jose, Costa Rica
Trip duration	2 months
Departure date	November 1997
Number in group	Uno
Distance covered	8000 miles (5000km)
Sponsorship	Nada

Best day	Christmas Eve in San Salvador
Worst day	Rain rain rain in that dump, Trujillo
Favourite place	Any cigar factory in Nicaragua
Biggest headache	That damn jumping drive chain
Biggest mistake	Giving a Nicaraguan cop my license
Pleasant surprise	How great an SR is in Central America
Any illness	Nada
Cost of trip	$1900
Other trips planned	Always. South Africa and USA next

Bike model	Yamaha SR 250
Age, mileage	1981, 30,000km
Modifications	Top box for my Bushtucker Man hat
Wish you'd done...	Fixed fork seals before leaving
Tyres used	2 new ones in Corpus Christi, TX
Punctures	Nada
Type of baggage	Soft throwovers, tank bag (no tent)

Bike's weak point	Heavy to lift onto the Ometepe ferry
Strong point	A musclebike on selling in Costa R
Bike problems	Chain and sprocket wear
Accidents	Nada
Same bike again	Or an even smaller two-stroke
Any advice	Buy/sell there. Shipping is for fools

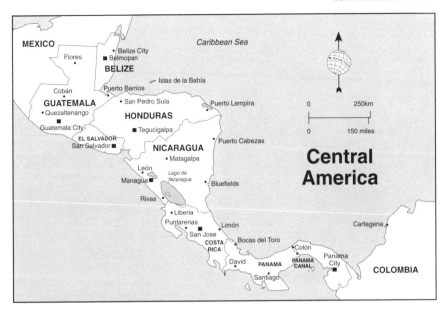

CENTRAL AMERICA

This compact isthmus of seven small countries, many of which can be crossed in a day or two, takes the southbound rider another stage further away from the familiar trappings of Western culture. Traffic 'irregulations' and border crossings start to become challenging and with a long way to go, some riders press on with a scowl, not bothering to give each country a chance.

Guatemala and Costa Rica cause few problems, while Honduras and Nicaragua seem the worst for undefined border formalities including the impo-

---

THE DARIEN GAP

Once you've got to Panama it's the end of the road unless you want to join the adventurous elite of *Darienistas* who've ridden across the jungles, swamps, muddy ravines and torrents of the Darien Gap.

At only 75 miles/120km wide, this tropical impasse spanning the borders of Panama and Colombia has become infiltrated by Colombian guerrillas and while revisiting the area in early 1997, Helge Pedersen heard that two European backpackers had recently been murdered. In view of these current and real dangers, the information below is not to be considered a recommendation to attempt the crossing.

Despite periodic announcements, no road will ever be cut through this region for various ecological and political reasons. For greater detail you'll learn much about the crossing by reading Ed Culberson's *Obsessions Die Hard* (see p.270).

Part of the reason the crossing has always been so hard with a vehicle is that it rarely stops raining here; the dry season months of February and March offer the best climatic window. It took Helge Pedersen nearly three weeks to be the first to reverse Culberson's achievement by crossing from Colombia to Yaviza in Panama, an average of around 6-10 miles/10-15km per day...

In the unlikely event of the security situation improving, remember there's a lot of dragging, winching, falling off and loading on boats or *piraguas* (dug-out canoes). Using a lightweight bike with little luggage makes the endeavour a whole lot easier.

DO YOU NEED A LIBRETA?

If you're thinking of visiting just South America (rather than incorporating it into a broader world trip), you can do without a Carnet de Passages (as described on p.19).

Instead, a **Libreta de Pasos por Aduana** (aka *triptico*) is a much cheaper option and fulfils the same purpose. Libretas are available in Caracas or San Cristobal from:

Touring y Automovíl Club de Venezuela
☎ 794 1032, 781 7491, 793 5865
Torre Phelps
Piso 15, Officinas A & C
Plaza Venezuela
Caracas, Venezuela

Touring y Automovíl Club de Venezuela
☎ 442 542, 442 664, 442 675

Avenida Libertador C and Avenida Principal Las Lomas
Edificio Olga, San Cristobal, Venezuela

Several riders have, however, reported that they have managed to ride through nearly all the countries in South America without either a carnet or *libreta* and with little or no penalty for not having one. As it says earlier on, if you can get by without one, do so.

Avoid the whole business of registration and deposits, and deal with each border individually. As elsewhere in the world, you may find your motorcycle details stamped into your passport; a simple way of ensuring that you leave the country with the same machine with which you entered.

---

sition of arbitrary fees (to search your baggage, for example!). As they rarely amount to more than $5-10, it's best not to be bullheaded and to pay up, though you should certainly contest anything over 10 or 20 dollars. Asking for an official receipt is a good way of reducing or eliminating excessive demands. Remember, don't take it personally and try to remain good humoured.

SOUTH AMERICA

Wherever you arrive in South America, you should be prepared to negotiate an extreme range of terrains. Humid jungles, hyper-arid deserts, the barren altiplano and the snowbound passes across the Andes tempt you in all directions. Be sure your planned tour also takes into account the equally diverse climates of this continent.

South America is a relatively stable place that, border-wise, is easier to get around than some Central American countries. Only the so-called Guyanas, the three small states of Guyana, Surinam and French Guyana sitting on top of Brazil, seem to present insoluble accessibility problems to overland travel (or at least the need for three more visas). And the border crossing between Ecuador and Peru can be protracted and prone to corruption.

The biggest dangers are street crime in larger cities and ports and, as ever, other traffic, both in urban and rural areas, but especially on steep Andean roads. Here more than ever the line between 'your' and 'their' side of the road is academic. Might has the right of way so ride alert and don't ride at all in conditions of poor visibility, heavy rain or ice or of, course, at night.

Along the Pan-American Highway

Having arrived in Colombia, you need to decide which side of the Andes to ride down. Squeezed along the extreme west coast is the so-called Pan-American or Interamerican Highway, a network of sealed routes linking Alaska with southern Argentina. Much of the continent's road freight travels along the Pan-Am, which is a good reason to avoid it. On a trail bike it's useful only as a speedy link to get to the interesting dirt track regions.

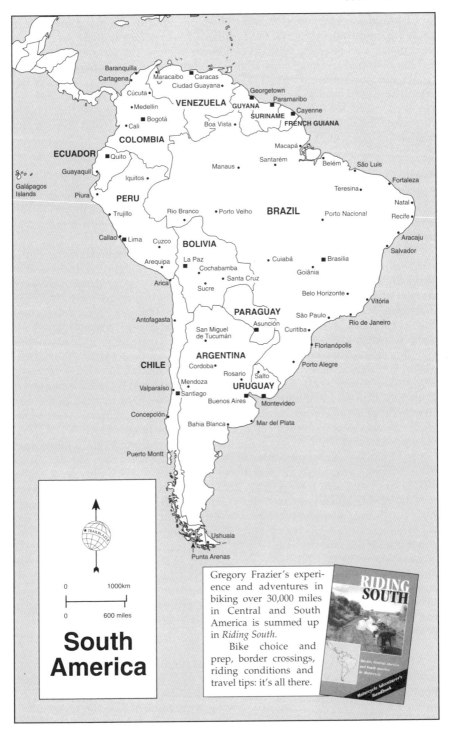

South America

Gregory Frazier's experience and adventures in biking over 30,000 miles in Central and South America is summed up in *Riding South.*

Bike choice and prep, border crossings, riding conditions and travel tips: it's all there.

RIDING SOUTH

Through Colombia and Ecuador the roads tend to run along the valleys dividing the parallel ridges of the cordillera. Make sure you fill up with petrol in Ecuador: fuel is nearly twice as expensive in Peru. The standard of driving is famously insane along these highways, until you reach orderly and sanitised Chile. In southern Peru you'll pass through the northern expanses of the Atacama Desert which leads to the even starker Chilean sections with no water or shade, let alone fuel, for up to 190 miles/300km at a stretch. This is the world's driest region, just a few hundred kilometres from some of its wettest jungles. When exploring off the main highway be sure to carry adequate provisions and be ready for extreme weather.

Trans-Amazon

East of the Andes, the Amazon and its hundreds of tributaries, along with what rainforest remains, create a barrier to normal overland travel. Roads might boldly be carved, but one good wet season and the passing of a few heavy trucks turns them into an unnavigable mire.

The only reliable road from the north of the Amazon basin starts in southern Venezuela and crosses into Brazil and the gold-smuggling outpost of Boa Vista. From here a partly-sealed road takes you south via Caracarai over a succession of rickety plank bridges to Manaus. Allow two full days to cover the 625 miles/1000km from the Venezuelan border to Manaus in the dry season: July to February. At other times it will take at least a week, if you can make it at all. Consider taking a boat down the Rio Branco instead.

This trans-Amazonian road link continues south of Manaus to Porto Velho. Wet season or dry, the remains of the 560 mile/900km track to Porto Velho should only be attempted if you're prepared for sub-Darien conditions. Collapsed bridges have been left unrepaired, forcing you to cross numerous rivers whose depth cannot be predicted. Like the east–west Trans-Amazonian Highway, this road has now been abandoned to the jungle.

Instead use the river boat up the Rio Madiera to Porto Velho, a journey of around four days. Fares for bikes are good value at around £30/$50 and about the same for a passenger. Once at Porto Velho, a dry-season-only road heads 125 miles/200km south-west to the Bolivian border at Abuna and there south to Guajara–Mirim or west past the town of Rio Branco and Assis. The road from Rio Branco north-west to Cruzeiro du Sol is usually impassable, so fill up the tank, let down the tyres a bit and get stuck in!

If you're determined to get off the beaten track in this region, fit a couple of pontoons and a propeller to your bike: river boats are the best and often the only way of getting around. Otherwise most of your time will be spent battling along muddy logging tracks or transporting your bike along rivers in anything from cranky-engined tramp steamers to dug-out canoes. This in itself can be a very agreeable form of travel and is ultimately adventurous, but progress will be very slow and utterly dependent on the season and the reliability of the vessel.

To the west of Brazil there's no coast road running between Venezuela and Argentina, but once you're in southern or western Brazil the network of sealed highways broadens greatly and progress becomes easier. All you have to worry about now is the demented driving; truly the worst on the continent.

LA TO LIMA ~ KLR650S AND TRIUMPH

Name	Scott and Steve Griffith
Year of birth	1972
Occupation	Students
Nationality	USA
Previous travels	Stephen PCV-ed in Africa
Bike travels	Mexico, US, Africa and Europe

This trip	Los Angeles to Lima
Trip duration	6 weeks
Departure date	August 1998
Number in group	4 people, 3 motorcycles
Distance covered	6000 miles (9600km)
Sponsorship	No

Best day	Crossing Panama Canal
Worst day	Separated just north of Lima
Favourite place	Jaco Beach, Costa Rica
Biggest headache	Faulty water pump gasket on KLR
Biggest mistake	Not bringing a spare
Pleasant surprise	Half the police were nice
Any illness	Three cases of food poisoning
Cost of trip	$1500 each
Other trips planned	North America, Australia

Bike model	2 '91 KLRs and a '95 Tiger
Age, mileage	KLRs: 6 years, 7000 miles
Modifications	Tiger: Givi cases and crash bars
Wish you'd done...	Reinforce subframe behind battery
Tyres used	Metzler T66
Punctures	0
Type of baggage	Givi

Bike's weak point	Subframe can't take heavy loads
Strong point	FUN FUN FUN Triple motor hum!
Bike problems	None
Accidents	Zero
Same bike again	Hope so
Any advice	Keep the wind in your face

SOUTH OF THE BORDER ~ BMW GS P-D

Name	Jon Saltzman
Year of birth	1946
Occupation	Bike dealer, farmer, pilot, film maker
Nationality	American
Previous travels	Japan, Canada, Europe
Bike travels	Canada and USA

This trip	Mexico, Central and South America
Trip duration	Over 2 years
Departure date	1993
Number in group	1
Distance covered	105,000km (65,000 miles)
Sponsorship	WP, Aerostich, Bill Saltzman M/cs

Best day	There are too many best days!
Worst day	Attacked in Brazil, lots of blood lost!
Favourite place	Too many – see my videos
Biggest headache	Police and military checkpoints
Biggest mistake	Marrying a girl I met on the trip!
Pleasant surprise	Anaconda killed a dog next to me!
Any illness	Machinegun diarrhoea, snake bite
Cost of trip	Still counting
Other trips planned	Definitely yes

Bike model	BMW R100GSPD
Age, mileage	This trip used up two bikes
Modifications	BMW #2 had many flaws corrected
Wish you'd done...	Nothing
Tyres used	20: if the shoe fits wear it
Punctures	Who keeps count in the jungle?
Type of baggage	Own ally box & rack, Aerostich bags

Bike's weak point	Alt', frame, driveshaft, shock, seals...
Strong point	That motor keeps hammering along
Bike problems	Plenty; see AMW Report #17
Accidents	Nothing major
Same bike again	Undecided, depends on the route
Any advice	Be self-sufficient and able to prove it

CHILE & PATAGONIA ~ R100GS

Name	Marco Bellini
Year of birth	1964
Occupation	R&D Software Designer
Nationality	Italian
Previous travels	Europe, Asia
Bike travels	All over Europe

This trip	Valparaiso–Ushuaia – Ruta 40
Trip duration	December 1997
Departure date	2
Number in group	1 month
Distance covered	10,200km (6400 miles) – 75% off-road
Sponsorship	No

Best day	Opening crate & found bikes inside
Worst day	Shipping agent missing back in Val
Favourite place	Ruta 40; everywhere in the wild!
Biggest headache	The winds in Patagonia
Biggest mistake	Nothing really
Pleasant surprise	Friendly people everywhere
Any illness	No
Cost of trip	About US$4500
Other trips planned	Peru and Bolivia

Bike model	R100 GS 1991
Age, mileage	New
Modifications	Driveshaft/U-joints, Ohlins, etc, etc
Wish you'd done...	All the above! (see AMW 105)
Tyres used	Michelin T63 (tube type)
Punctures	None
Type of baggage	Hepco & Becker boxes

Bike's weak point	After radical modifications, none
Strong point	Engine torque and reliability
Bike problems	Rack cracked, easily bodged
Accidents	None
Same bike again	My lightest BMW GS (140kg)
Any advice	Use a simple bike you know well

CAPE HORN UPWARDS ~ TWO DOMINATORS

Name	Dan Moore and Charles Capel
Year of birth	Both 1972
Occupation	Engineer, Manager
Nationality	Mancunian, English
Previous travels	Went to London once, didn't like it
Bike travels	Cat and Fiddle

This trip	Tierra del Fuego northwards
Trip duration	CC: 6 months; me: rest of natural
Departure date	January 1998
Number in group	2 + space for a couple of chicas!
Distance covered	10,000km (6250 miles) so far
Sponsorship	American Express

Best day	Finding the bikes at Punta Arenas
Worst day	Charles wiping out in Argentina
Favourite place	Gobernador Greg Hospital, Ward B
Biggest headache	Gobernador Greg Hospital, Ward B
Biggest mistake	CRASH!! at the onset of dark
Pleasant surprise	Charlie's memory coming back
Any illness	German word 'Durchfall' sums it up
Cost of trip	Shit loads
Other trips planned	Return

Bike model	Honda NX650 Dominator
Age, mileage	New
Modifications	Rapidly in Patagonia one night...
Wish you'd done...	Stabilisers
Tyres used	Trailmax; now Pirelli knobblies
Punctures	Egos: 1 Tyres: 0
Type of baggage	Emotional: I fucking hate Givi racks

Bike's weak point	Choice of rider
Strong point	Dead solid
Bike problems	Reaching the ground
Accidents	Charlie: 1 (2 drops), Dan: 1 (37)
Same bike again	Yes, probably another 37
Any advice	Small bike, light pack, speed kills

Bolivia

Landlocked between the mountains and the jungle, Bolivia is well worth exploring by bike. It's also one of the less expensive South American countries to travel in and one in which half the population remains indigenous Indian. And despite having grown into a major cocaine producer, Bolivia manages to get on with this illicit trade without the political or civil discord for which Colombia is famed. In Bolivia, the lesser routes across the desolate altiplano into Chile and Peru provide some great biking and spectacular scenery, but remember that this is a remote and rugged region with changeable weather. See Sarah Crofts' tale about riding across the Salar salt pans on p.230.

Coming from Peru or Arica in northern Chile you cross borders at 15,000ft/4500m passes where *ripio* dirt roads lead to La Paz. Having caught your breath (unacclimatised people frequently pass-out on arriving at La Paz airport), an even more dramatic ascent continues across the 4700m La Cumbre Pass to be followed by a 3500m drop into Bolivia's humid Yungas region.

This is a ride to remember not least because the altitude can play havoc with your carburation (fuel-injected bikes will be immune). The thin air creates an over-rich fuel mixture with power and fuel consumption diving just when you need them most – and Bolivia's single-figure octane fuel doesn't help. As in the Karakoram in northern Pakistan, the easiest solution is either to take it easy and not strain the motor or fit a smaller main jet in the carb to bring the air/fuel mix back in line. This may be something worth doing if you're staying above 2000m for a while.

Southern Andes and Patagonia

South of Bolivia, it's either Chile or Argentina for the road south. After Bolivia, you'll find these Europeanised countries very expensive. In southern Chile, around Puerto Montt, the Pan-Am hits the fjord and lake district and so crosses over into Argentina and windy Patagonia.

The Andean section of both countries gets more spectacular here, particularly the Torres del Paine National Park, no better place to dump the bike and stretch your legs for a few days. On the other side in Patagonia (many crossings require ferry connections across glacial lakes) the unmade *ripio* tracks of dirt and rock comprising Routes 40, 17 and 258 can make riding pretty hard. It's not the place for worn trail tyres, not least because you'll need all the grip you can get to face the famously **high winds** which sweep across Patagonia, at their absolute worst in December when they exceed 100mph (160kph). Riding up Ruta 40 is a classic challenge of South American biking and one that you won't forget in a hurry.

At the end of the road, crossing the Magellan Straits onto the island of Tierra del Fuego brings you to Ushuaia: the Last Town. In the last few years Ushuaia has become a venue for an impromptu get-together of travelling bikers convening from all around the continent.

The town is horrendously expensive of course, it's often raining and always cold. From this point it's twice as far to the Argentine capital of Buenos Aires as it is to Antarctica, but you've reached one of the world's handful of continental extremes.

Congratulations! Unless you're a penguin the way home is north.

Australia

While on its fringes Australia may be a familiarly Western country, its barely inhabited core, the Outback, provides as vast a wilderness as you'll find anywhere. The world's most arid continent, you can ride for thousands of kilometres across Australia without giving a thought to all the administrative and political hassles which typify travel in Third World countries.

This lack of aggravation (which you might miss if you've travelled in Africa and Asia) added to the sometimes monotonous terrain can undermine the possibilities for the adventure-hungry biker. The country can be circumnavigated on tarmac in a fortnight, but it is away from the bitumen where you'll discover the true flavour of the Outback: dust, heat, eccentricity born of isolation (aided by a few tinnies), and a dispersed selection of beauty spots.

The outline of downunder dirt biking offered here focuses on three particularly scenic regions of the Outback: Cape York, the Central Deserts and the Kimberley. Here you can get stuck into some challenging off-road routes and visiting all three (linked by as little tarmac as possible) would provide just about the best 6250-mile/10,000km off-road tour the country could offer.

Major Outback tracks

Several former droving or prospecting trails have developed into corrugated cross-country 'dirt motorways' that converge on the centre of Australia. None of them offer exciting or challenging riding if you're on a well-equipped trail bike (unless it rains…), but they all add up to agreeable short cuts between key areas.

Don't forget though, the riding may be relatively easy if you keep under 60mph/100kph but distances between fuel points can be up to 250 miles/400km and summer temperatures will require up to ten litres of drink-

---

THE WEATHER IN AUSTRALIA

For the recommended areas of exploration, the summer months from December to March are the ones to avoid. Unfortunately this lines up with many Europeans' visits downunder during the northern winter – the worst time to travel in remote corners of the Outback. In the Central Deserts most days will reach 40°C or more, with an aridity that will devour your water supplies and your energy. Even if accessible, these areas are little visited at this time and stranded without water, you'll pass out in a couple of days.

At the same time the north, more or less above the latitude linking Derby WA with Cairns QLD, experiences its wet season. Dirt roads become impassable and even the sealed highways can get inundated for days at a time. Cyclones usually occur at either end of the Wet – follow local radio/roadhouse weather reports closely and get off the road when the storm hits. Rain can fall at any time in the Central Deserts too, but while patterns are erratic it's usually in the form of a brief torrential downpour.

Don't be fooled by the 'winter' in the far north – it's better described as the dry season with temperatures reliably over 30°C every day. In the arid interior you might get the odd freezing night around July.

Make the most of Australia's excellent weather service. If you're travelling in remote areas, a small radio may be useful.

OUTBACK & CAPE YORK ~ DR650

Name	Mike Saunders
Year of birth	1969
Occupation	IT
Nationality	English
Previous travels	USA, Europe Africa, India, Thailand
Bike travels	UK only

This trip	Outback Australia
Trip duration	2 months
Departure date	July 98
Number in group	1
Distance covered	14,000km (8750 miles)
Sponsorship	None really

Best day	Telegraph Track, Cape York (QLD)
Worst day	Ood' to Coober Pedy after storms
Favourite place	Hells Gate, QLD, very friendly spot
Biggest headache	Stuck in roadhouse waiting for tyre
Biggest mistake	Left thermal lining (Vic was freezing)
Pleasant surprise	Rescued by a lady on a XT600
Any illness	None
Cost of trip	£1500
Other trips planned	North Africa

Bike model	Suzuki DR650
Age, mileage	7 years, 55,000km
Modifications	Gearsack rally guards, bashplate
Wish you'd done...	Zip-tied spare levers to the frame
Tyres used	Pirelli MT21
Punctures	1, caused by heat (take a pump)
Type of baggage	Gearsack (v good), throwovers

Bike's weak point	Thirsty over 90kph (12kpl...)
Strong point	Handled really well on dirt
Bike problems	Frame cracked, electrics died
Accidents	Lots of little drops in sand
Same bike again	No, I'll probably take an XT600
Any advice	Wear good motocross boots

OUTBACK CENTRAL ~ DOMINATOR

Name	David Nicholas
Year of birth	1964
Occupation	Police Officer
Nationality	Australian
Previous travels	Numerous places in Australia
Bike travels	Cape York

This trip	Plenty, Ood' & Birdsville tracks
Trip duration	10 days
Departure date	April 1999
Number in group	Me, Chris and Darin
Distance covered	5000km (3100 miles) – 70% dirt
Sponsorship	Not bloody likely

Best day	Along the old Ghan rail line, NT
Worst day	Broke down in Mount Isa
Favourite place	Anywhere but Oodnadatta
Biggest headache	Electrical problems
Biggest mistake	None
Pleasant surprise	Very friendly people in the Outback
Any illness	Just headache and sore arse
Cost of trip	Approx A$1000
Other trips planned	Lots in my head

Bike model	1996 Honda NX650 Dominator
Age, mileage	New
Modifications	24-litre tank. Clock on fairing
Wish you'd done...	None
Tyres used	Pirelli MT21 front, Mich Desert rear
Punctures	1 on rear
Type of baggage	Backpack & large bag on rack

Bike's weak point	Poor wind protection
Strong point	Moderate off-road ability
Bike problems	Mysterious electrical problem
Accidents	1 fall over in the Finke
Same bike again	Yes, or Yamaha XTZ660
Any advice	Travel light

ing water per day. Don't take any chances – both experienced locals and urban, all-terrain thrill seekers die every year on these tracks.

Birdsville Track ~ Birdsville QLD to Marree SA ~ 520km (325 miles)

Australia's best known track is a much-tamed version of the once ill-defined stock route which cost many lives. All you'll get is dust storms, bleak, flat monotony and the Mungeranie Hotel (fuel) halfway along.

Oodnadatta Track ~ Marree to Marla SA ~ 645km (400 miles)

Historically and scenically much more interesting, this track follows explorer John Stuart's 1860 route to the north coast and the telegraph line, railway and old Alice–Adelaide road which followed. The pick of the tracks in this area, it's also a good way of getting between Alice and Adelaide without resorting to the bitumen.

Strzelecki Track ~ Lyndhurst to Innamincka SA ~ 460km (290 miles)

A little-used and unexceptional track through very arid land that runs east of the Birdsville to Innamincka, a historic middle of nowhere close to Coopers Creek where doomed national heroes Burke and Wills met their end.

Sandover Highway ~ North of Alice to NT/QLD border ~ 550km (345 miles)

A remote, little used but straightforward short cut between Mount Isa and Alice Springs with a 400km fuel stage between the Aboriginal communities of Arlparra and Alpurrurulam close to the Queensland border.

Plenty Highway ~ North of Alice to Boulia QLD ~ 740km (465 miles)

Southern version of the above; a good way of getting to Alice from Birdsville

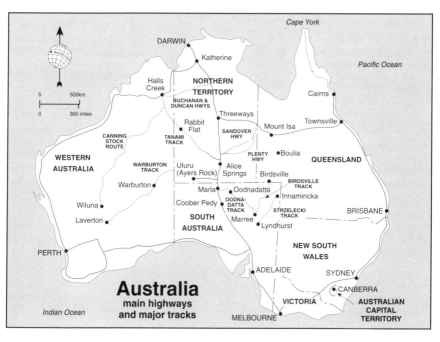

in the east if you don't want to cross the Simpson 'against the dunes', and marginally enlivened as it passes the Harts Range near Alice.

Tanami Track ~ North of Alice NT to Halls Creek WA ~ 1060km (660 miles)
Very handy shortcut to the north-west from Alice, the Tanami is a long flat 'dirtbahn' up to the WA border and a little rougher and sandier after that. Note the limited opening (Friday to Monday only) at the Rabbit Flat roadhouse.

Buchanan and Duncan Highways ~ Dunmarra Roadhouse NT to Halls Creek WA ~ 750 km (470 miles)
A particularly desolate link if heading cross country from Queensland to Western Australia without the detour north to Katherine and the Victoria Highway. If you want to spice up your north-west-bound Tanami crossing take the 360km Lajamanu Road, 45km after Rabbit Flat to Kalkaringi and explore the rough tracks of barely-visited Gregory National Park.

RECOMMENDED BOOKS AND MAPS

There are several books on survival and motor travel around the Outback, but one which puts it all together in a neat package is Lonely Planet's *Outback Australia*. Although inevitably biased towards 4WD, it's still an excellent guide to all the tracks described below and more besides. If you're from overseas, back it up with a conventional travel guide like the *Rough Guide to Australia* (Chris Scott wrote the NT and WA chapters so you can be sure he's looking after your off-highway needs!).

Other books and maps
Cape York, an Adventurer's Guide by Moon and *Cape York a 4WD Experience* by Lynn and Yvonne Fraser both offer detailed practical information.

Without a doubt the most detailed and practical book on the CSR is *The Canning Stock Route* by Gard. There are a number of excellent maps on the CSR. The RAA of WA produces an excellent strip map of the CSR. Others include Hema Maps, Australian Geographic and Westprint (see below).
Royal Automobile Association of WA
228 Adelaide Terrace, Perth, WA 6839
☎ 1800 807 011 (within Australia)
🖳 www.rac.com.au/travel/index.htm

Australian Geographic publishes a good series of guide books which include *The Red Centre*, *Corner Country* (includes Birdsville and Oodnadatta Tracks plus Simpson Desert), the *Nullabor*, *CSR*, *Cape York and the Kimberley*. Each contains a detailed map of the area, beautiful pictures but are short on practical information.
Australian Geographic
PO Box 321 Terrey Hills, NSW 2084
☎ 1800 555 509 (within Australia)
🖳 www.australiangeographic.com/ausgeo/index.htm

For the outback west of Alice, Hema Maps have produced *Great Desert Tracks of Australia*: four maps covering CSR, Tanami Track, Gunbarrel Highway, Connie Sue Highway, Sandy Blight Junction Road, Kidson Track and more.
HEMA Maps
PO Box 2660, Logan City DC, QLD 4114
☎ 07 3290 0322
🖳 www.hemamaps.com.au/

Westprint specialises in strip maps of much of the Outback. These include Alice Springs-Ayers Rock, CSR, Gunbarrel Highway, Plenty Highway, Alice Springs-Oodnadatta, Dalhousie and Simpson Desert, Flinders Ranges, MacDonnell Ranges, South West Queensland, Tanami Track, Anne Beadell Hwy, Birdsville and Strzelecki Track, Gulf Country, Innamincka and Coongie Lake, Oodnadatta Track and Cape York.
Westprint
6 Park St, Nhill, VIC 3418
☎ 03 5391 1466
🖳 www.westprint.com.au

Geoff Kingsmill

EAST & CENTRAL ~ BMW F650

Name	Bruce Clarke
Year of birth	1966
Occupation	Computer geek
Nationality	Canadian
Previous travels	NZ, Costa Rica, Mexico, AK, India
Bike travels	As above

This trip	Australia, eastern loop
Trip duration	12 months
Departure date	September 1996
Number in group	1
Distance covered	6000 miles (19,600km)
Sponsorship	Are you kidding?

Best day	All of 'em
Worst day	Any day of riding is a good day
Favourite place	All of the Red Centre, Coober Pedy
Biggest headache	Finding ATMs that worked
Biggest mistake	Didn't drink enough water at first
Pleasant surprise	Wildlife: roos, camels, birds
Any illness	Dehydration first night outback
Cost of trip	$1000 + flight + bike rental
Other trips planned	Anywhere I can afford to go

Bike model	BMW F650 (rented)
Age, mileage	1 year, 6000 miles
Modifications	Givi panniers (very nice)
Wish you'd done...	None
Tyres used	Avon & Bridgestone rears
Punctures	None but Avon lasted only 4000 miles
Type of baggage	Givi, much better than BMW's own

Bike's weak point	Slow in winds, poor cold starting
Strong point	Reliable and economical (60+mpg)
Bike problems	None
Accidents	A couple of roos came close
Same bike again	Yes
Any advice	Pack light, stash travellers' cheques

Warburton Track ~ Yulara NT to Laverton WA ~ 1140km (710 miles)
Often confused with the now obsolete Gunbarrel Highway, this is a very useful link between southern Western Australia and the Centre that's recently become free of the need for permits. Longest fuel stage 320km.

Canning Stock Route ~ Wiluna to Halls Creek WA ~ 1860km (1160 miles)
Almost two thousand kilometres, much of it on sandy 'twin-ruts', this off-road trek across the Gibson and Great Sandy Deserts of WA is in a league of its own. Fuel can be dumped in 200-litre drums at Well 23 by the Capricorn Roadhouse in Newman, but this needs arranging months in advance and still leaves nearly 1100km to Halls Creek – that's 15 UK gallons or 70 litres at the absolute minimum. Tours exist with 4WD support; some supply bikes.

Life on the Outback road
Apart from the risk of drunk or tired drivers, suicidal marsupials and dehydration, Australia is a very safe country to travel in. You'll find surprisingly little evidence of rural redneck bigotry – in the north and west at least, and while common sense should never be abandoned, the desolate highway paranoia customary in the US is rare. The danger of **hazardous wildlife:** sharks, crocs, jellyfish and particularly spiders and snakes are all much exaggerated by yarn-spinning locals. Other road users and the heat are the real killers.

Fuel gets expensive in remote regions but comes surprisingly cheap at far northern ports such as Wyndham, WA, where it comes ashore. Elsewhere, like the Rabbit Flat roadhouse in the Tanami, Mt Dare in the Simpson or Kalumburu up on the Kimberley coast, expect to pay up to double southern city prices. Many of these places don't accept credit cards, so carry cash.

One thing you'll have to get used to if you're cruising the Outback's highways is roadhouse food. If camped on the coast you're bound to meet recreational fishermen who'll have a fish or two to spare: gut it, wrap it in foil and stick it on some embers. On the other hand Outback pubs – often called 'hotels' and offering grungy if inexpensive rooms – will provide many memorable encounters as well accommodation. Friday nights are especially lively...

This brings us around to the dangers of highway driving. Single vehicle rollovers (SVOs) are among the most common causes of death for young men in the Northern Territory, and Australia has a bad record for highway fatalities

although nothing compared to Brazil or India. For the motorcyclist the chief dangers are in other road users, drunk or otherwise, and more significantly animals, most especially marsupials of various varieties which hop across the road, especially between dusk and dawn. A kangaroo is one tough animal to hit and you'll always come away worse. For this reason alone, it's not worth risking **riding at night**, even on tarmac. It's the instinctive swerving to avoid these beasts (along with losing concentration or dropping off to sleep) that accounts for all those SVOs.

Many guides recommend HF radios for travel in the Outback but these are impractical on a bike, while ordinary mobile phones are well out of range. Vodafone now produces a GSM/satellite phone with Australian-wide coverage (🖳 www. vodafone.com.au) but before you shell out, recognise that HF radios or sat phones are not required unless you're travelling alone in very remote areas.

Nevertheless, don't let the fact that 'it's only Australia' lull you into a false sense of security, take all the precautions and preparation outlined in earlier chapters seriously. GPS is a gadget beloved of urban-based four-wheel drivers, but unnecessary on the tracks described here as long as you pay attention to conventional navigational practice.

CAPE YORK

The ride up from Cairns to the tip of Cape York, just 10 degrees below the equator, may not all be the gladed rainforest run many imagine, but still involves enough off-road action to make it special. The Cape's remoteness adds the necessary excitement, while occasional access to the sea adds an element of fun you won't find on the harsh desert routes across the interior.

Cairns to Cape York ~ 1100km (690 miles)
Garry Whittle

Heading north from Cairns, it's 76km on bitumen to Mossman along the Captain Cook Highway. The Highway follows the coast and has some great views of the coastline as it winds and dips its way from the coast into sugarcane country.

From Mossman it's another 25km to the turn-off for the Daintree River ferry crossing. From here you can continue straight onto Daintree township and from there head north towards the CREB (Cairns Regional Electricity Board) Track which winds through the rainforest and whose gravely surface is a real favourite with dirt bikers. Check on track conditions from bike shops in Cairns or the local police as the track is sometimes closed.

If the CREB is closed, don't be too disappointed because by simply crossing the Daintree River on the ferry and using the coast road, you get a fantastic ride up through Cape Tribulation National Park. A few kilometres after the ferry, the bitumen ends and the road turns back into a dirt track which takes you through beautiful rainforest and past various tourist resorts onto Cape Trib itself.

Heading north again, the track cuts back through more rainforest that meets the ocean and rolls over mountain ranges. The trail can get quite steep in places and when damp gets extra slippery. On the way it crosses a few rocky-bottomed creeks, some of which are best walked through first.

The road eventually crosses the Bloomfield River where a left turn after the crossing takes you to the lovely Bloomfield Falls for a well-earned dip.

Turning right leads to Wujul Wujul Aboriginal Mission and Cooktown passing the Lions Den Hotel, Queensland's oldest pub, on the way.

CSR ~ BMW 1100GS

Name	Peter Moltmann
Year of birth	1962
Occupation	Technician
Nationality	Australian living in Amsterdam
Previous travels	Australia, Asia and Europe
Bike travels	Australia and Europe

This trip	Canning Stock Route
Trip duration	3 weeks
Departure date	1995
Number in group	12
Distance covered	5000km (3125 miles)
Sponsorship	Two 4WD backup vehicles

Best day	Fast on sand without crashing
Worst day	Breaking footpeg on termite hill
Favourite place	Durbah Springs
Biggest headache	Adapting gear lever to rear footpeg
Biggest mistake	Hitting termites nest
Pleasant surprise	The BM was faster than most XR6's
Any illness	None
Cost of trip	A$2500
Other trips planned	Africa

Bike model	R1100GS
Age, mileage	New
Modifications	Guards for cooler, heads, lights etc
Wish you'd done...	Harder front suspension
Tyres used	Sand knobbies
Punctures	0
Type of baggage	4WD

Bike's weak point	Heavy compared with Enduro bikes
Strong point	Powerful in sand bogs
Bike problems	None
Accidents	5 (sand falls, nothing serious)
Same bike again	Why not?
Any advice	Accelerate in sand; don't back off

Leaving Cooktown, follow Battlecamp Road which turns back to dirt after a few kilometres. As with all roads and tracks in the Cape York region, its condition can change rapidly, so be ready for wash-outs, rocks, changing road surfaces and fallen trees. The 100km to Old Laura Homestead varies from gravel to sand with some river crossings, and is altogether fairly typical of Cape York's trails. There are a few gates along this stretch: leave gates as you find them (open or shut); station owners know what they're doing.

Once at Old Laura Homestead you enter Lakefield National Park with some good waterholes off the main road, though always be aware of crocodiles. After Kalpower, 59km north-west of Old Laura, track conditions deteriorate for the next 40km, with the main feature being single vehicle tracks, sand and bulldust. For those who haven't yet experienced bulldust, it's a fine talcum powder-like dust which settles in holes and hides anything from tree roots to potholes and must be approached with extreme caution or avoided altogether. It's usually a lighter colour than the surrounding dirt. Be warned, a lot of riders have come to grief in bulldust. From here it's a fairly easy ride west into Musgrave, a good place to acquire information about road conditions and river crossings further north.

The road north of Musgrave is a well-maintained dirt highway. You'll have learned by now that many of tracks in the Cape have 'DIP' warning signs which can be anything from a slight decline and incline to a steep drop into a creek bed. Approach them with great care.

A hundred kilometres up the road, Coen is a small town with stores and an extensive workshop where repairs can be carried out. The next stop is the Archer River Roadhouse, the last chance for fuel and supplies until Bamaga, 315km to the north, just below the tip of the Cape.

You're now on the Telegraph Road where the next obstacle is the Wenlock River, usually impassable till June. At this time you'll usually find travellers camping on the south bank waiting for the river to recede, so unless you like watching water levels drop or have another plan, leave your trip till later in the dry season when most rivers can be crossed easily. After the Wenlock, the Telegraph Road becomes quite rough in places; washouts, rocks and fallen trees being the main obstacles soon after dry season access is re-established.

About 40km after the Wenlock, the track forks. The Telegraph Track continues straight (left), while to the right the Southern Bypass Road has a branch to Captain Billy Landing on the Cape's east coast. If you use the Telegraph Road get ready for a memorable and challenging ride! There are a few creek crossings – if some are too deep there'll be another way across somewhere else. The most famous crossing in the Cape region is Gunshot Creek with steep banks on either side making crossing in a 4WD difficult; bikes usually have no problem.

In places along this section there are a number of tracks, but they all eventually converge on the main route. They're usually formed by vehicles detouring around bog holes just after the wet season. Riding along the Telegraph, you'll eventually meet up with the Southern Bypass Road coming in from the east. The track improves until 9km later when it forks again. The left track is the Northern Bypass Road which takes you straight to the Jardine River Ferry crossing, 52km away. The ferry costs about A$80, and although the crocs resent it, it's the approved way of crossing the Jardine. The track to the right is the

Telegraph Track which leads to a Jardine crossing that is not for the faint-hearted, as it rarely gets shallower than one metre and is 100–150m wide. The riverbed is very sandy, and with many stories of crocodile attacks on the Jardine, the ferry is the way to go.

A good place to make your mind up which way to go at the Northern Bypass/Telegraph Road fork is Fruitbat and Elliott Falls a couple of kms to the north-east. Elliott Falls is a great swimming and camping spot, with clear water and beautiful scenery. Elliott Falls is considered a must-see on the Cape.

After crossing the Jardine, the road to Bamaga is straightforward enough. Bamaga is the town at the top. Here you'll find a supermarket, hotel, petrol station and all the services you would expect in a lively little country town. Most people either stay at Seisia, Punsand Bay, Somerset or Pajinka camping grounds. Seisia and Punsand Bay are the least basic, offering a wide variety of facilities including licenced restaurants and tour bookings, if required.

To get to the very top of the Cape walk about 1km from Pajinka campgrounds car park, following a boardwalk through some coastal forest then over a large rocky headland until you eventually reach a sign that indicates you are at the northernmost tip of Australia.

THE CENTRAL DESERTS

This area, which principally covers the Northern Territory below Alice Springs and northern South Australia, offers perhaps the greatest encounter with the truly arid Outback. Other states like subtropical Queensland can be monotonously flat and boring, while the interior of Western Australia is a largely inaccessible carpet of spinifex grass away from the main tracks.

Some good routes from Alice Springs

Alice is a busy tourist town set amid the ridges of the West MacDonnell Ranges and ideally placed to explore its hinterland of dirt tracks and waterholes. In town you'll find a couple of bike shops and second-hand/camping stores plus half a dozen good backpackers hostels for somewhere cheap and fun to stay.

Finke River Gorge and Mereenie Loop Track ~ 900km (560 miles; 60% dirt)

This is one of the best short tours from Alice, taking in the waterholes of the West Macs, Palm Valley and the tricky run along the Finke River Gorge and west to Kings Canyon. From here the corrugated Mereenie Loop Track brings you back to the Palm Valley area and a straight run back east to Alice.

The first 40km along the usually dry Finke riverbed just south of Hermansburg will involve some demanding conditions as you ride through one or two sandy or pebbly ruts created by passing 4WDs – letting your tyres down and standing on the footrests will make the ride much easier. Towards the end of the Finke Gorge route there are some low dunes and the sandy Palmer River crossing which again will need to be tackled assertively. Route finding is easy with a good map and the longest fuel range is the 200km of the Mereenie Loop Track between Kings Canyon and Hermansburg.

Note that the route travels through Aboriginal-owned lands which require cheap permits and include various restrictions – chiefly on overnight camping. Unofficially, as long as you're discrete and don't leave any traces of your camp, no one's going to come after you.

The Finke and Old Andado Tracks ~ 670km (420 miles; 98% dirt!)

This is a loop which begins right near Alice Springs' airport south of town. Taken anti-clockwise you head down the Old South Road (the original route from Adelaide via Oodnadatta), past Maryvale (fuel), where there's a turn-off to the historic butte of Chambers Pillar (some dune crossings).

From Maryvale the riding's pretty easy over corrugated sand, a robust 2WD car could manage it until you get to Finke community (fuel). Here you head east to Old Andado Homestead, before turning north along this less used track to Santa Teresa community, where the surface improves, soon bringing you back to Alice. The longest fuel range is a pretty hefty 410km between New Crown Station (just after Finke) and Alice.

Simpson Desert crossing ~ 550km (345 miles; 45% soft sand)

This is a serious desert crossing without fuel or fresh water for 550km along the most direct route: the French Line. The next shortest alternative to the south is 200km longer.

Purists will head down from Alice along the Finke Track (described above) and from there continue south another 100km to Mt Dare Homestead. Here you fill up every last container for the run east over the desert to Birdsville in Queensland. Around 160km from Mt Dare, having passed the warm springs at Dalhousie, you reach a junction and the beginning of the low dunes; there are several hundred between yourself and Birdsville.

These are not the huge barchans of the Sahara, at most they're 10-15m high, but nevertheless the 4WD ruts and the soft sand will demand full concentration. In the cool months of July and August be very careful of oncoming 4WDs cresting the dunes. Traffic tends to travel west-east along the French Line, so that descents are down the steeper east-facing slopes, though most cars wanting some desert fun avoid the repetitive up-and-downing of the tedious French Line. In fact the Simpson is nothing special to look at, it's more the challenge which inspires people to cross it.

At the tiny settlement of Birdsville there's a pub, fuel, and a long, dull ride back to anywhere interesting: Alice is over 1000km away via the Plenty and Port Augusta is a little further via the Birdsville Track.

THE KIMBERLEY

About the size of Ireland, the Kimberley is a flood- and fire-ravaged region in Australia's far north-west. Few Australians from the populated east coast get to this barely-developed frontier land and, as it is, the whole region is washed-out from December to April when even the local station owners fly out and let the monsoon run its course.

It's a land of rugged ranges, deeply-carved river gorges, remote Aboriginal communities and a virtually inaccessible coastline fissured with tide-swept inlets and saltwater crocodiles. Only the mission settlement at Kalumburu gives you access to the coast.

There are just two main tracks that access the Kimberley, the 710km Gibb River Road linking the old ports of Wyndham and Derby, and the 270km Kalumburu Road which leaves the Gibb River halfway along and heads up to Kalumburu.

NORTH AMERICA ~ BMW R80 GS

Name	Bradford Duval
Year of birth	1973
Occupation	Stockbroker (but I quit!!!)
Nationality	American
Previous travels	Honduras, Mexico
Bike travels	South-west US

This trip	North America
Trip duration	3 months
Departure date	July 1998
Number in group	1
Distance covered	15,000 miles (24,000km)
Sponsorship	Me

Best day	Arctic Circle
Worst day	Crashing at the Circle at 60mph
Favourite place	Arctic Circle!!!
Biggest headache	Puncture, snowstorm, frozen glue
Biggest mistake	Crashing 300 miles from nowhere!
Pleasant surprise	Bike and me OK after the crash
Any illness	Flu
Cost of trip	$6500
Other trips planned	Africa

Bike model	BMW R80 GS
Age, mileage	1981, 6000 miles
Modifications	Shock
Wish you'd done...	None
Tyres used	Bridgestone and Avon
Punctures	2
Type of baggage	Stock BMW bags

Bike's weak point	None
Strong point	Durable, serviceable, low C of G
Bike problems	None
Accidents	1, quite fun actually!
Same bike again	Without question
Any advice	Lid & armoured suit saved my ass

The Gibb River Road ~ 710km (445 miles)
What makes the Gibb River's corrugations tolerable, especially in its western half, are the many gorges decorated with year-round waterfalls or pools. Seeing as 'winter' temperatures are only a degree or two lower than the summer, they make a pleasant string of breaks between Derby and Wyndham. Bell Creek Gorge is probably the pick of the crop. Fuel and even accommodation is not the problem you might think up here as many near-bankrupt cattle stations have turned towards serving adventuresome tourists visiting the area.

The Kalumburu Road ~ 270km (170 miles)
A bit more than halfway up, a turn-off leads up along a very corrugated track through a forest of palms to the Mitchell Plateau with another turn-off to its falls. Ironically, watch out for traffic in the cooler months as this is a popular destination with intrepid four-wheel drivers. Before the turn-off to the falls, a very rough track leads down to the coast at Port Warrender, a tiny settlement in about as remote a corner of Australia as you're likely to find.

Up at Kalumburu there's ultra-expensive fuel, a store and a couple of ultra-basic camp-sites by pretty bays about 25km north of town.

North America

For overseas visitors to the US and Canada, North America offers a host of images made familiar through TV and cinema. Among the most enduring of of these is the great wilderness of the west stretching from the cactus-riddled desert along the Mexican border up the spine of the Rockies to the cabin-crazed fur trappers of the far north in the Yukon and untamed Alaska.

North America offers a chance to star in your own Western or road movie, one of the highlights of adventure motorcycling anywhere in the world. Sure, like Australia, it won't challenge you like heading south of the US border or Africa and Asia, but culturally it offers a rich experience.

Tours
Perhaps more than any other place in the world, there are plenty of opportunities for renting bikes or joining a tour. Just about the whole range of motorcycle touring is offered: from hogging along Route 66 to dirt-biking across the high plains of Nevada. Have a look at the listings at ▱ www.mcguide.com.

This section focuses on just two areas: South-west USA and the north and west of Canada. For more information, Falcon Guides' *Scenic Byways* and *Historic Trail Guides* series and the various *Motorcycle Journeys Through...* from Whitehorse Press, will come up with many more ideas.

SOUTH-WEST USA
Allen Naille

The south-west of the United States offers some outstanding opportunities for two-wheeled adventures, when few would believe anything remote still exists. Much of Nevada reminds me of Patagonia, while Death Valley resembles the descent into the Skeleton Coast of Namibia. And all over the Four Corners (Arizona, Utah, Colorado, New Mexico) are petroglyphs similar to ones found in Argentina, Africa and Australia.

The difference is, of course, that much of the US is developed: five million visitors a year seek out the Grand Canyon. Yet it's not so hard to remove oneself from the throng and explore some of the region's scenic wonders by a different path.

Even a standard vacation of just two weeks is enough to visit many of the south-west's natural wonders, although if you want to have a more relaxed trip, do some hiking and take in some museums, you can do that too – it need not be throttle-based action all the time.

Seasons can play a major role in timing your visit. Avoid the summer in the Mojave Desert, where Death Valley temperatures reach 50°C (120°F). At the other extreme, winter brings snow to the Four Corners and it can snow anytime in the high country of Arizona and Colorado while summer rain can turn dusty dry trails into slippery clay. Spring and fall are the ideal times – early fall (September) is one of my favourite times in the Four Corners. The possibilities here are as endless as your imagination, of course, but I've concentrated on two trips. The USA is very large, so too is the South-west. There are many choices, so just take off and enjoy.

A Four Corners adventure

The following trip takes about 10 to 14 days and visits more than 30 national parks, monuments, forests, state and tribal parks en route. The whole thing is rideable from late April to mid-October. Outside these times rain and snow will turn Utah's clay into a nightmare and Colorado's high passes (12,000ft +/3600m) are out.

Try to spend an extra day on the Million Dollar Highway loop out of Durango, and an extra day in Santa Fe's museums or art galleries (and while there, eat only the south-west's cuisine – at its best in the west). Ninety per cent of this trip is on the AAA *Guide to Indian Country*, a fantastic map just to look at. This description follows it closely.

Arizona

If you start in Phoenix head out to Carefree north-east of the city and take FS (Forest Service) 24 to Camp Creek and Cave Creel (camping). Continue north to the junction with FS269, and turn west onto the Bloody Basin Road which can get a bit rough compared to the preceding section.

Once back on US17, go north to Flagstaff and pick up FS417, the beginning of the Old Moqui Stage (Coach) Route, just north of Flagstaff on US89. Stay with the route to Cedar Ranch, where you follow the wooden markers of the Arizona Trail (a hiking trail that overlays the local ranch roads). Go around Tubs Ranch and through Rockwood Canyon, picking up FS301 to the Moqui Stage Historic Marker. The road ends near Grand View Point on the Grand Canyon South Rim.

From the Canyon, you can attempt Navajo Reservation roads to Blue Moon Bench overlooking the Colorado River, but you can really get lost out here! It's easier to continue back on US89 to cross the Colorado River at Marble

TEXAS TO PRUDHOE BAY ~ BMW GS/PD

Name	Michael Slaughter
Year of birth	1974
Occupation	Entrepreneur
Nationality	USA
Previous travels	Hitchhiking southern Africa
Bike travels	Dallas to Ushuaia

This trip	Dallas–Prudhoe Bay, Alaska
Trip duration	4 months
Departure date	April 1998
Number in group	1
Distance covered	17,000 miles (27,000km)
Sponsorship	None

Best day	Watching grizzlies trash my camp
Worst day	Watching grizzlies trash my camp
Favourite place	Wrangle – St Elias National Park
Biggest headache	Getting parts in Alaska
Biggest mistake	Having a defined return date
Pleasant surprise	AK, Yukon, NWT were amazing
Any illness	None
Cost of trip	$2000
Other trips planned	Nordkaap to Cape Town

Bike model	BMW R100 GS/PD
Age, mileage	5 years, 11,000 miles
Modifications	None
Wish you'd done...	None
Tyres used	Metz' Enduro 3 – not the best tyres
Punctures	Dozens
Type of baggage	BMW hard cases, kayaking duffle

Bike's weak point	Very heavy off-road
Strong point	Huge tank, steady, a real workhorse
Bike problems	None
Accidents	Small wrecks in the Arctic snow
Same bike again	Absolutely
Any advice	Dress warmly if going to the Arctic

BAJA ~ KLR650

Name	Taber DeHart
Year of birth	1959
Occupation	Geologist
Nationality	USA
Previous travels	US, Canada, Central America
Bike travels	US, Canada, Mexico

This trip	Baja, Mexico
Trip duration	3 weeks
Departure date	September 1997
Number in group	1
Distance covered	3500 miles (5600km)
Sponsorship	A skinny piggy bank

Best day	Cruising a dirt road to a great beach
Worst day	Searched at gun point (same day)
Favourite place	Sea of Cortez – all of it
Biggest headache	Finding gas
Biggest mistake	Timing – it was HOT
Pleasant surprise	Wonderful locals and expatriates
Any illness	Montazuma on the way home
Cost of trip	$500
Other trips planned	Same place

Bike model	KLR650
Age, mileage	Used, 700 miles
Modifications	Milk crate tied on for storage
Wish you'd done...	Better seat
Tyres used	Dunlops
Punctures	0
Type of baggage	Soft bags, canvas Boy Scout pack

Bike's weak point	Seat
Strong point	Reliability
Bike problems	Head loosened (several times)
Accidents	Fell over while checking the view
Same bike again	Yes
Any advice	Ride a lot, it gets easier

THE GREAT WESTERN TRAIL

The Great Western Trail, a multi-use route, is a 4x4 trail lending itself to adventure motorcycles. It traverses mostly public lands, from Canada to Mexico, for 2400 miles/3800km through Idaho, Utah and Arizona, with some side roads into Montana and Wyoming. Still in the planning stages, it's already marked and mapped in Utah and parts of Arizona.

Current maps show the trail winding its way from Nogales up the middle of Arizona and Utah and along the eastern border of Idaho to the tip of the Panhandle.

It's designed to follow existing National Forest (NF) and similar scenic roads and will not be a single trail but a 'corridor' offering various routes for different recreational users such as hikers, equestrians and mountain bikers. And while 'out there', it passes near or has side routes to communities for gas, food and lodging.

When complete it will be the first of its kind in scope and is presently under consideration by the US Congress to be designated a National Trail, which assures its protection.

The GWT corridor intersects with the east/west American Discovery Trail near the town of Escalante UT, where the Golden Spike was driven in linking railroads from the west and east coasts.

Other nationally designated trails with which the GWT intersects include the Pony Express National Historic Trail, the Mormon Pioneer National Historic Trail, the California National Historic Trail, the Oregon National Historic Trail, the Continental Divide National Scenic Trail, the Lewis & Clark National Historic Trail, and the Nez Perce National Historic Trail.

Further information
Join the Great Western Trail Association, PO Box 41, Kayesville, Utah 84037 USA.

GWT
http://gwt.org/

Arizona
http://www.azgwt.org

Utah
www.gorp.com/gorp/resource/us_trail/ut_great.htm

Allen Naille

Canyon and carry on around to Buffalo Ranch Road (FS/BLM8910), East Side Road (220) and FS213 to the Canyon's North Rim, and a different viewpoint.

Heading back up AZ67, take FS22 west from Kaibab Lodge all the way to Fredonia via Big Springs. A recommended side trip of 250–300 miles southwest into the Arizona Strip (the area north of the Canyon and below the Utah border) leads from Fredonia via Toroweap Point and the Mt Trumbell schoolhouse, Main Street Valley, and Navajo Trail, cutting up to Colorado City on AZ389, just below the Utah border.

Utah
Alternatively get on the Smithsonian Butte Byway from Fredonia to Zion National Park, visiting the ghost town of Grafton (UT) where *Butch Cassidy and the Sundance Kid* was filmed (and was most likely visited by the real duo too).

After exploring the wonders of Zion (ideally on foot), turn north from Virgin past the Kolob Reservoir and on towards Cedar City. Coming off Cedar Mountain you'll get a phenomenal view to the north-west over the city to the Black Mountains beyond.

Suitably inspired, turn west for Cedar Breaks National Monument, up to Panguitch and down to Bryce Canyon National Park, another one of southern Utah's wonders. A dual sporting alternative would see you arrive at Bryce

(Previous page) Taking the high road in Baja, Mexico. © Clement Salvadori.
(Opposite) Top: At the summit of Klappan Pass, BC, Canada (see p.206). © Tom Grenon.
Bottom: Cutting through the creeks on the Canol Road, Yukon, Canada (see p.202). © Tom Grenon.

© Allen Naille

along the Great Western Trail (GWT, see box p.193) from near the North Rim.

From Bryce Canyon many options open up: north to Widstoe Jct and south-east to Escalante, picking up Hell's Backbone BLM byway to Boulder (UT12 over a ridgeback is also very nice); or from Canonville down Cottonwood Creek Road, a lovely dirt ride with the odd sandy patch to Big Water on UT89, then back into the hills along the Smoky Mountain Road to Escalante, all in the recently-created Grand Staircase –Escalante National Monument. As you climb above Big Water, turn back to take in Lake Powell National Recreation Area. Just east of Escalante another side trip leads to Hole in the Rock, (about 110 miles round trip). In the late 1800s a group of Mormons lowered their wagons, oxen and personnel down through a rock opening to cross the Colorado River – a monumental task.

If you end up in Boulder, follow the Burr Trail, a paved portion starts at the village's southern end and wanders west to Capitol Reef National Park where you can either head north-west to cross the Henry Mountains or south to Bullfrog (full resort services). From here you can take the ferry across Lake Powell and UT276 west to Natural Bridges National Monument.

Then, on the way south to Mexican Hat and just after the radical Moki Dugway descent (which will give your brakes some exercise), take a spin through the Valley of the Gods Loop. From Mexican Hat, it's a short ride south to Monument Valley on the Arizona border, where a beautiful 20-mile dirt loop takes you through the park, right past those famous buttes.

Colorado

The Anasazi cliff dwellings of Mesa Verde National Park are next on the agenda. Head down to Kayenta and east along AZ160 into Colorado. Plan for an overnight in Durango, a fun tourist town which offers everything including a couple of motorcycle shops.

From Durango you can do the Silverton Loop: north to Ouray and Telluride, south-east Cortez and back to Durango. This is the Million Dollar Highway, so named after the gold mined in the 1800s which supposedly made its way into the road bed. I like to think of it for the million dollar views.

From late July to mid-September, you can climb from Silverton over Cinnamon Pass and the Continental Divide to Lake City (a difficult task, two-up on a big bike). From Lake City, head straight south to Creede, Pagosa Springs, Chama, Taos and Santa Fe.

New Mexico and back to Arizona

Numerous routes depart from Santa Fe, but I'd recommend a freeway as the

SF TO ARCTIC ~ KTM ADVENTURE

Name	Michael Lieberman
Year of birth	1960
Occupation	Attorney
Nationality	USA
Previous travels	All over
Bike travels	All over North America and Mexico

This trip	San Francisco to Inuvik, NWT
Trip duration	2 weeks
Departure date	July 1999
Number in group	1
Distance covered	4200 miles (6720km)
Sponsorship	Nope

Best day	Camping on the Mackenzie River
Worst day	Day before leaving: overloaded
Favourite place	Desolate stretch Dawson–Inuvik
Biggest headache	Keeping the bike up when stopped
Biggest mistake	Overpacking
Pleasant surprise	Kindness and interest of the locals
Any illness	Nope
Cost of trip	Less than $1000
Other trips planned	Arctic again, South America

Bike model	1997 KTM Adventure
Age, mileage	New
Modifications	GPS, heated vest and grips
Wish you'd done...	Centre stand; upgraded pipes
Tyres used	Metzeler Saharas
Punctures	0
Type of baggage	Touratech aluminium panniers

Bike's weak point	Unsteady stand, mirrors that snap
Strong point	Conversation starter, big tank, light
Bike problems	After 2000 miles both exhausts broken
Accidents	0 (with me on the bike)
Same bike again	Yes
Any advice	Talk to people

Nova Scotia ~Transalp

Name	Kevin Daniels
Year of birth	1971
Occupation	Naval officer, submariner
Nationality	American
Previous travels	All over the map
Bike travels	Various east-coast trips

This trip	Connecticut to Nova Scotia
Trip duration	9 days
Departure date	September 1999
Number in group	Me and Jay Stevens
Distance covered	3300 miles (5280km)
Sponsorship	Nope

Best day	Cabot Trail-Cape Breton, N. Scotia
Worst day	#1: 5hrs trying to 'get outta Dodge'
Favourite place	Many: lonely road to Murdochville
Biggest headache	Hmm...
Biggest mistake	Not enough time for Newfoundland
Pleasant surprise	Food is really cheap in Canada
Any illness	Seasick on stormy ferries
Cost of trip	US$400
Other trips planned	Alaska and Mexico

Bike model	'89 XL600V Transalp
Age, mileage	9 months, 5500 miles
Modifications	Higher gearing, Pro fork springs
Wish you'd done...	Throttle lock
Tyres used	Dunlop D604
Punctures	Zero
Type of baggage	Aerostich dry bags

Bike's weak point	It's heavy
Strong point	Reliable and versatile
Bike problems	It's dirtier now
Accidents	Wet myself climbing Mt Washington
Same bike again	Yes, if I were to go to Newfoundland
Any advice	Know your plate number at the border

objective is Acoma Sky City (near Grants, NM), the oldest continually inhabited community in the USA. The pueblo offers walking tours, Indian fry bread, and beautiful pottery. From Grants, head south to Quemado via El Malpais National Monument, Lava Beds, Apache Creek and Glenwood on the Arizona border. Carry on to Clifton (AZ) via Mule Creek and then get ready for no less than 525 curves and a 7000-ft climb all packed into the 120-odd miles north to Alpine.

Should your side knobs be getting a bit cooked along this lateral roller-coaster, take FS24 near Hannagan Meadows north to Big Lake, then FS113 and FS87 to Greer. From Greer it's west by north-west along AZ260 to Show Low (named after a long-gone poker hand) and head 2.5 miles south on US60. Watch out for the FS300 heading west, the Mogollon Rim Road or the General George Crook Trail, an old military wagon road named after the famous Indian fighter, which follows the southern edge of the Colorado Plateau. It crosses the AZ260 a couple of times before emptying out south of Clint's Well, where you can descend to Phoenix via the Young, AZ288 and AZ88 (The Apache Trail) alongside Roosevelt Lake.

The Mojave Desert Road (California/Arizona)

The Mojave Road or Trail follows 150 miles/240km of an old military wagon road that supplied former outposts and protected travellers from Indian attacks in the late 1800s. It runs from Needles on the 'three corners' of

---

MAPS AND INFORMATION

South-west

Bureau of Land Management
18th and C Streets, NW
MIB 5600
Washington DC 20240
For BLM Byway information

Arizona Strip Interpretive Association
345 East Riverside Drive
St George, UT 84790
Maps and books of national forest areas including the AAA Guide to Indian Country.

Delorme
2 Delorme Drive
PO Box 298
Yarmouth, ME 04096
Large-format atlas for each state and CDs for all of the USA in topo-like series

National Park Service
Rocky Mountain Regional Office
PO Box 25287
Denver, CO 80225-0287
Information on parks from Wyoming to Arizona

National Forest Service
USDA Forest Service Information Desk
Union Station

25th Street and Wall Avenue
Ogden, UT 84401
Utah Forests-Dixie NF

USDA Forest Service
Public Affairs Office
517 Gold Avenue SW
Albuqerque, NM 87102
*AZ: Coconino, Kaibab, Tonto, Apache-Sitgreaves
NM; NV: Carson, Santa Fe, Gila*

Rocky Mountain Region Forest Service USDA
11177 West 8th Avenue
Box 25127
Lake Wood, CO 80225

Mojave

Friends of the Mojave Road
Goffs Schoolhouse
37198 Lanfair Road
PO Box 7
Essex, CA 92332-007
Guidebooks for the Bradshaw and Mojave trails

California Desert Information BLM
831 Barstow Road
Barstow, CA 92311
Maps for the Mojave and Bradshaw Trails.

California, Arizona and Nevada, south of old Route 66 to Barstow (CA).

On the way back take the 100-mile **Bradshaw Trail** (see below) from the Salton Sea west of Blythe CA to La Paz AZ. Both routes are maintained as 4x4 scenic trails by the Friends of the Mojave Road (see box p.197) who produce excellent guide books packed with natural and historic information.

A good starting point would be at the Avi Resort Casino and Avi Park north of Needles on the River Road. The Mojave Road starts a few miles further up the track and is marked by rock cairns. This trip to Barstow will take the entire day as you traverse rocks, deep sandy stretches, dry lake beds and several mountain ranges.

A side trip can extend into a couple of extra days to Death Valley National Park. Leaving the Mojave Road, head north beyond Baker about 30 miles and pick up the road entering Death Valley's southern boundary. Go towards Ashford Mill Historic Site and on to West Side Road to Furnace Creek Resort (full services). A loop goes around the Panamint Mountains to Indian Ranch Road and Ballarat (a ghost town). Take Goler Wash to West Side Road again (Goler washes out with every storm). A further excursion picks up the Saline Valley Road about 15 miles west of Panamint Springs Resort (limited services). Continue to Big Pine or loop to Scotty's Castle and back to Furnace Creek.

From Death Valley return to Baker and the Mojave Trail to Barstow. Once you get to Barstow you can continue onto Lucerne Valley Pioneer Town and Joshua Tree National Park to overnight in the Palm Springs-Indio area.

The Bradshaw Trail

Just south-west of Indio, the Bradshaw Trail starts at Northshore on the Salton Sea and continues north-east to Blythe. There are numerous little side canyons and roads to explore, but keep in mind there's a gunnery range south of the trail. Once in Blythe, the more scenic route follows AZ95 through Parker and Lake Havasu. Give some consideration to following old Route 66 from Topoc through Oatman. It continues to Seligman (AZ), or through Amboy, and on towards Los Angeles.

Bear in mind that although these two trails are fun, scenic, 4x4 routes offering beauty, history, and challenges, they can also be dangerous due to the scarcity of traffic and extremely high summer temperatures.

NORTH-WESTERN CANADA
Tom Grenon

Luckily, living on Vancouver Island, I can take my KLR out into the bush most weekends. If time is short I'll head out to explore the coastal mountains of south-west British Colombia (BC), a comparatively civilised region of logging and mining tracks leading into the Rockies which themselves offer some of the most spectacular vistas this side of the Hindu Kush.

If I've a bit more time, I'll head up into the true wilderness in northern BC, Yukon and the North-west Territories (NWT) which stretch across to Greenland. These are the barely inhabited homelands of big rivers, early snows, grizzlies, moose and caribou. Up here adventure motorcycling is as serious a business as in any desert, with an even smaller climatic window of opportunity and for the two-wheeled explorer, the same limitations of payload versus range.

THE TRANS-AMERICA TRAIL

Travelling on a motorcycle is fun. No doubt about it. Travelling on a motorcycle, off pavement is even more fun. Travelling on a motorcycle, off pavement from virtually one side of the United States to the other is an adventure that would have Lewis and Clarke signing up at reincarnation.com.

Following nearly eight long years of gruelling research, a dozen sets of tyres and more nights in downbeat motels than I care to remember, I've put together the ultimate long-distance trail: a route across almost the entire USA that is **98% free of any paved surface.**

For your riding pleasure I've hooked up a network of gravel roads, dirt roads, old creek beds, forest roads, jeep trails, some single tracks; in fact anything I could link together that is suitable for a dual-sport motorcycle and won't put the rider at the wrong end of an irate farmer's shotgun.

The Trans-America Trail crosses the USA from west to east, with the trailhead just south-east of **Nashville, Tennessee**. From there, the intrepid rider crosses Mississippi, Arkansas, Oklahoma, New Mexico, Colorado, Utah, Nevada, California and ends up at **Port Oregon** on the coast of the Pacific Ocean. On the way he or she will experience just about every dirt road surface that man and nature could come up with, and probably every type of weather too. Each day the rider will be rewarded with subtle changes in the people, the food, the culture and, of course, the horizon.

The Trail covers **4400 miles/7000km** and can be done in about three weeks at a push, though in the summer of 2000 a British guy called Russell Fisher attempted the whole trail in one go on an XR650L, adding a start in Florida (see 🖥 www.adventure-motor cycling.com/transam/) Most riders tick off a section or a state on weekend rides.

Navigating the Trans Am

I've created 105 detailed maps of the entire route which get updated annually as certain sections of the Trail get sealed. With scales down to 1/100th of a mile the maps are designed to be used in a roll chart holder in conjunction with your bike's odometer. On each map, the trail is high-lighted in colour and includes both the turn-to-turn and the accumulative mileage. Each hand-made map costs around $5, depending on the state.

Tempted? Then contact me via my website: 🖥 www.transamtrail.com. I'll be glad to help in any way that I can. See you on the Trail.

Sam Correro

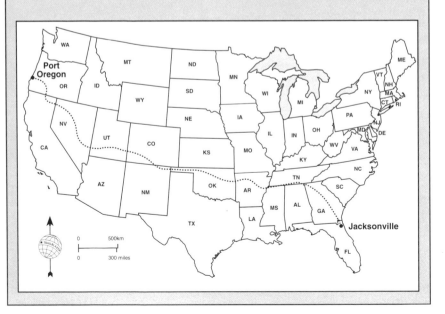

LABRADOR ~ KLR650

Name	Riley Harlton
Year of birth	1965
Occupation	Video editor
Nationality	Canadian
Previous travels	Touring America by Goldwing
Bike travels	This was my first trip off-roading

This trip	Quebec, Labrador, Newfoundland
Trip duration	2 weeks
Departure date	June 1999
Number in group	1
Distance covered	6500km (4000 miles)
Sponsorship	None

Best day	Riding the cliffs at dusk in Newfld
Worst day	Freezing Quebec-Labrador border
Favourite place	Gros Morne Park – one of many
Biggest headache	Not having proper off-road boots
Biggest mistake	Luggage position too high
Pleasant surprise	Seeing icebergs
Any illness	None
Cost of trip	Less than US$1000
Other trips planned	North-west Territories

Bike model	KLR650
Age, mileage	New
Modifications	Ally hand guards, engine guard
Wish you'd done...	C' stand, hard cases, lower gearing
Tyres used	Stock
Punctures	0
Type of baggage	Pelican case, soft bags, tank bag

Bike's weak point	Tyres and rear suspension
Strong point	Great seat: 400km+ range
Bike problems	Lost a couple of bolts, none critical
Accidents	1, not serious
Same bike again	Yes
Any advice	Good maps + GPS make life easier

DANGEROUS WILDLIFE

Rule number one in the remote corners of the north-west is that you are *not* at the top of the food chain. Once this fact is appreciated everything else becomes elementary.

It's like a jungle out there...

All wild animals instinctively avoid man and if an animal sees or smells a human it will flee. For once it helps to smell like a stinking outlaw biker as bears especially have an extremely acute sense of smell. Many incidents arise when the aroma of a cooked meal lingers around your camp-site after you have retired into the tent. A bear approaches, you react in panic and the bear is alarmed to suddenly encounter a competitor to his food and will try to defend it.

Camp behaviour

The last edition of *AMH* ran a story by Gregory Frazier, whose camp and edible parts of his BMW were ransacked by a bear, while he was stranded without fuel on the Dalton Highway in Alaska.

Keep your camp-site clean of food scraps. Suspend food in a bag 10m high between two trees and 100m downwind from your camp-site. Cook 50m downwind from the tent. When preparing a meal clean utensils properly, *not on a sleeve or pant leg*. Burn all packaging materials thoroughly, tin cans should be packed out after burning clean. If catching fish, clean the fish as far away from the camp-site as possible, and wash up afterwards.

When buying food for an upcoming trip into an area with a heavy bear population, get non-fatty type foods: avoid bacon, butter or margarine and canned fish. Beef jerky should be consumed immediately and containers incinerated in a good hot fire. This is especially important in the Barrens areas of the Yukon and NWT were there are no trees to hang up a food cache.

Other odours that will attract wildlife come from soap, deodorant, toothpaste and scented moisture creams. Have these sealed in zip bags, in with the food bag, which should be a roll-top dry bag.

It is easy to detect areas frequented by bears as they tend to defecate on roads and tracks. A pile twice the size of a dog would be a timid black bear, but anything the size of horse droppings would be the more aggressive grizzly. On the North Canol the grizzly

bear is dominant and once in the NWT, where grizzlies are protected, their numbers increase greatly.

When traversing isolated back-country trails you might come across a strong smell of rotting: a very good chance you're close to a bear kill. A bear will feed on a large kill for many days so keep moving. Garbage dumps (every settlement has one) will attract bears that travel to and from the dump daily, so both the dump and the surrounding area are bad places to be on a motorcycle. Give a dump a 10km no-stop zone, and don't camp within at least twice that distance.

On the road

The risk of hitting animals on the roadways can be lessened by reducing speed. This is especially important at **dawn and dusk** when wildlife is most active. I've observed that even on roadways with lots of traffic wildlife feeding alongside won't give a car or truck a second glance, but when an unfamiliar motorcycle approaches they're liable to do anything, including jumping out in front of you.

Avoid camping on game trails and in the back country where old roads and minor tracks should be considered game trails. Just like you, wildlife would much rather travel from one feeding spot to another along a clear trail than beating through the bush. After a time, if a road is rarely used by humans it becomes a game trail.

Protection and precautions

Pepper spray (CS gas, Mace) is the best protection against an attacking bear: spray directly into the bear's eyes and nose (not all over yourself as one Japanese tourist once did!). Have several spare emergency flares, as these can be used to ward off an undecided attacker from a distance.

Making plenty of noise while going through the bush – especially into the wind – will alert bears and other large wildlife. Moose, elk and caribou can also become aggressive if surprised and cut off from their escape route or young.

Keep a bear whistle in your jacket pocket for those occasions away from the bike. If your bike is quiet, there are times on a twisty, overgrown track when it would be wise to sound the horn if you're solo or the first in a group of riders. **Tom Grenon**

I've chosen a couple of routes that'll give you an idea what north-western Canada has to offer. You'll find more on my website, linked off AMW.

The Canol Road – 1120km (700 miles) return

The Canol (Canadian Oil) Road was built along with a telegraph line by the US military between 1942 and 1943. The idea was to move oil by pipeline from Norman Wells on the Mackenzie River in the NWT to the Alaska Highway near Whitehorse, for the defence of Alaska. It was used for only two years before being abandoned due to the annual break up of the pipeline and the repeated collapse of bridges over frozen rivers and streams.

Route description

This route heads north-west from Johnson's Crossing, into the Mackenzie Mountains and up to Caribou Pass, 280km short of Norman Wells. Unless your bike has stilts, a very high air intake, or you time it just right, continuation all the way to Norman Wells is not possible at present.

THE WEATHER

The 3700km (2300 miles) between the Canadian–US border and Inuvik in the Yukon Territory just 20° from the North Pole offers a hugely diverse climate range.

Starting with the southern BC coast, the weather is mild enough to ride year-round. But this mild weather is limited to the *western side* of the coastal mountain range, anywhere to the east it will be a frozen winter wonderland that won't yield good riding conditions until somewhere around mid-April, when trips at lower elevations can be enjoyed in the southern interior of BC.

In the spring (April–June), BC, Washington and Oregon have the north-west's equivalent of the monsoon rolling off the Pacific Ocean. This rain coupled with the melting snow creates flooding; not normally a problem on paved highways but restricting off-road exploration especially at higher elevations where the ground is saturated.

In the far north the situation evolves very rapidly from winter into spring (June) and is much drier. At this time daylight lasts nearly 24 hours north of Whitehorse.

As July rolls around most of the snow has melted along the routes but water levels in the streams and rivers peak from the run-off. Meanwhile by this time water levels are low in southern BC.

Another weather-related factor is the famous man-eating **mosquitoes and flies** of the north. I'm sorry to tell you that the horror stories are all true: I've seen a full-grown bull elk carried off by a swarm of well-equipped mozzies. The intensity will vary

with the topography, but as a rule of thumb flat wetlands are major bug activity centres, sloping mountain sides less so.

The intensity also varies through the summer: up to early June the buggers haven't warmed up enough to hatch, but as soon as there's a five-day period of warm weather the infernal multiplication begins!

By the beginning of August areas of wetland produce clouds of blood-sucking bugs, that will magically disappear with the first frosty nights in the last weeks of August. Not all areas in the north are like this but generally it's the norm. So the ideal time to explore north of Whitehorse is mid-August to mid-September, when the water levels are at their lowest, bugs are bearable and the fall colours will make you wonder what exactly *were* those mushrooms you just ate!

From mid-September backroad exploration becomes a gamble against early snowfalls. Being caught out far from a maintained road will make things a little more challenging than bargained for.

The fall (Sept–Oct) still offers great riding conditions throughout BC though: water levels are low, the weather is drier and there are fewer tourists clogging up the highways. Some of the small service centers – the Ma and Pa operations – may shut down after September, so plan to gas up in main towns when travelling off season.

And to turn it all upside down, snow can fall on any day in the Rockies, while Inuvik in the far north can get 30°C for days on end. Expect the unexpected.   **Tom Grenon**

The first 225km section from Johnson's Crossing to Ross River is an easy ride on a well-maintained gravel road. However, it's well worth making allowance for an added 100-150km on top of this to take in some great riding on mining exploration roads that head off east near Lapie Lake (75km from Ross River). Ross River is the last settlement along the Canol Road (gas, food and beer). Fuel up here as to Caribou Pass

Cabin at Caribou Pass. © Tom Grenon

and back requires a fuel range of 660km (410 miles).

Once you get to the Macmillan Pass (3800ft/1170m) and cross the Selwyn range of the Mackenzie Mountains there are plenty of other enticing mining tracks that would add to that distance. Should you try to push beyond Caribou Pass to the Godlin Lakes (see below), expect to add another 70km plus another day or two to the trip (as well as a lot of wet clothing!).

The road from Ross River to the Yukon-NWT border at Macmillan Pass is composed of lightly maintained dirt, so in wet conditions considerable concentration and a tyre with an aggressive tread pattern are needed to remain upright. Other than that, the undulating twisty track becomes increasingly scenic as you approach the Pass, which crosses the Mackenzie range from Yukon into the Territories.

Once at Macmillan Pass there's a game check station; it's a good idea to let them know when you expect to return from Caribou Pass. You can also get the latest word on what to expect for water levels in the creeks and rivers to the north-east. Plus you can find out if there's anyone else out on the road, which could be handy in an emergency.

From Macmillan Pass the road has not had any maintenance since the War, so it's best to go when the water levels are at their lowest – usually the last two weeks in August and first two weeks of September. This timing is a bit like threading a needle, sometimes you're successful sometimes not. The trick is to avoid too much meltwater or get caught in early snow.

About 70km from Macmillan Pass you come to Old Squaw Lodge, a top dollar fly-in eco-resort. If they're open it would be possible to use their radio to get emergency help or order expensive fuel. (In 1996 I ordered gas but by 1999 the ownership had changed and it was closed.)

Some 15km further on the Intga River must be crossed and this one may turn you back if you're unlucky. The water is fast, deep and about 30m wide, so at the best of times it needs extensive scouting before an attempt is made. The rest of the way to Caribou Pass is made up of large muddy potholes, dozens of minor water crossings and some surprisingly good two track for short stretches. By the time you get to Caribou Pass (about 330km from Ross River) the land-

FLA TO AK ~KLR 650

Name	Stuart Heaslet
Year of birth	1953
Occupation	Consultant
Nationality	USA
Previous travels	Latin America, Pacific
Bike travels	USA only

This trip	South Florida to Prudhoe Bay, AK
Trip duration	7 weeks
Departure date	May 1999
Number in group	1
Distance covered	12,300 miles (19,700km)
Sponsorship	None

Best day	Dalton and Top of the World Hwys
Worst day	Snowstorm in Bowman, ND
Favourite place	Yukon, Kenai and northern Alaska
Biggest headache	Electrical grounding problem
Biggest mistake	Took too much stuff, rode too fast
Pleasant surprise	Beautiful women (forgive me, honey)
Any illness	None
Cost of trip	US$2300
Other trips planned	Mexico and British Columbia

Bike model	KLR650
Age, mileage	1998, new
Modifications	Russell seat, Works shock, stand
Wish you'd done...	None
Tyres used	Avon Gripsters and MT 21s
Punctures	None
Type of baggage	Jesse panniers

Bike's weak point	Electrical system is not heavy duty
Strong point	Simple and easy to maintain
Bike problems	Earthing problem (my fault)
Accidents	None
Same bike again	Probably, or import an Africa Twin
Any advice	If you can, buy time not equipment

scape is barren and treeless but the views stretch to infinity in all directions.

The limit of my current explorations of the Canol Road is about 20km beyond Caribou Pass thanks to a mean little river called the Ekwi. Twice I've had to turn back here. The water is very fast and about a metre and a half deep, but frustratingly it's only about 10m wide. One of these days the situation will be right – if not for myself then for some other intrepid biker who'll get across and continue to Godlin Lakes another 35km down the track where I hear there are some cabins and great fishing. It would possibly be the first time a motorcycle travelled through to that point on the road.

The Nahanni Range Road – 750km (470 miles) return
The road was constructed in 1963 to service what was one of the world's richest mines and the adjacent town of Tungsten. In 1986 the mine was closed and Tungsten's population of 500 packed up and left.

Route description
This route takes you north and east from Watson Lake, just over the BC border in Yukon, and into the Mackenzies to the abandoned town on the NWT side of the ranges.

Leave Watson Lake with a fuel range of 700km if returning to Watson Lake, or up to 900km if continuing on to Ross River. There are no services along the way. The first 15km north from Watson Lake on the Campbell Highway (#4) are paved and the rest of the 110km to Tuchitua at the junction of the Nahanni Range Road (#10) is good high speed gravel. From the junction to the Frances River (20km) keep moving until you're over the bridge; there's a garbage dump over the first hill from the junction, and so plenty of bears.

From here the road is mostly good two track that gets graded maybe once a year. At about 135km from Tuchitua Junction the track is no longer maintained and the last 75km to Tungsten includes several water crossings that require some care. At this point the road starts climbing up onto the southern slopes of the Mackenzie ranges.

In 1987 the ghost mining town of Tungsten was boarded up and put in mothballs. Except for a caretaker there's nobody living there, but in 1999 it was decided to dismantle the refinery and sell off the town's buildings (swimming pool, bowling alley, library, shops and houses, any reasonable offer accepted) so it's hard to say what to expect in the future. However, in addition to the spectacle of the Mackenzies, there are two large hot springs to soak in at the trail's end. You'll appreciate the rest – it's a long hard ride back.

Maps
Yukon Territory International Travel Maps
345 West Broadway, Vancouver, BC V5Y 1P8
☎ 604-687-3320; 🖷 604-687-5925
National Topographic Maps: 1/250,000 – 105-O, 105P for the NWT section and 105F for the Lapie Lake section.

Abandoned BC railway – 350km (220 miles) return
In 1971 they came up with a plan to run a rail line up to the Yukon and Alaska from the existing line at Prince George. Then some influential politician was

found in a bar dressed as a moose and the whole project was abandoned. The area is so rugged and remote it was said the cost to just lay the bed in was Can$1 million per kilometre! Based on the research I've done, the gap between the southernmost extent of the northern railbed (described below) and the point where the railbed begins again is 75–90km. The track connecting the north and south sections could be done with the right preparations and luck. If you decide to go for it, the total distance from Tatogga Lake to Fort St James is about 650km.

Route description
The turn-off for the access road to the railway grade is 2km north of the Tatogga Lake Resort (gas, food and lodging) on Hwy #37. The first 30km is a poorly-maintained and corrugated gravel track. Once on the rail grade there are 40km of solid corrugations, after which it becomes a fairly smooth two track through to Klappan Pass. At the pass (4300ft/1315m) you're in an alpine area that has mining exploration tracks pushing out in all directions from the railbed.

One side track worth exploring is at the KM Post 111 (111km from where exactly I'm not sure). This well-built haul road will bring you to the summit of Mt Klappan with views that would rival any African plain – something that's all the more satisfying when you realise you're the only human for over 100km. There are other small exploration tracks heading out from this summit area that looked passable to me, and there are plenty of good camping spots nearby to set yourself up and explore on an unloaded bike.

After Klappan Pass the railbed gets much worse with some long sections of mud and water-filled ruts. At 154km from Tatogga there's a parking area for white water adventurers that paddle down the Spatsizi River. Beyond the parking area the track becomes a goat path. When I went through in August 1999 the rain turned the track into a muddy strip through the wilderness; the one thing that made it passable was the fact that it was built for railway use so there were no steep grades. Around here you'll notice most tracks in the mud are not vehicular but large bear, wolf, moose and elk.

Muddy conditions continue for another 20km, then 175km from Tatogga Lake the railbed stops and the track continues through the cleared right of way, following the lay of the land rather than shallow grades. With the terrain so waterlogged I stopped here, but in drier conditions the possibility of pushing through to Fort St James would be a great adventure. Let me know how it goes!

From information I've received from a guy who worked on the survey back in 1970 and still goes hunting here, it's possible to get another 50km south until a big river blocks access to Fort St James. He guessed if this river could be crossed it would be clear sailing the rest of the way...

Maps
British Columbia Recreational Atlas
🖳 www.recreationalatlas.com
National Topographic Maps 1: 250,000: 104H, 104A, 94D, 93M
(🖳 http://Maps.NRCan.gc.ca/main_e.html)
☎ 1-800-435-6277; 🖹 1-613-947-7948

The Kettle Valley Railway – 650km (405 miles)

The last spike was driven into the Kettle Valley Railway (KVR) in 1916 and was pulled out to permanently close the line in 1962. The short life of this line was partially due to high maintenance and the danger of derailments across the very rough terrain. You know you're in for quite a ride when you realise that the 61-km section between Hope and Coquihalla Summit originally had no less than 43 bridges, 12 tunnels and 15 snowsheds.

Route description

The remaining railbed, following the removal of the rails and ties, starts at Hope, some 150km west of Vancouver. The first 30km of the actual rail line isn't worth following; so many bridges are missing that it's best to just ride along Hwy #5 west to Portia – Exit 202. From there the KVR has a good gravel surface for the next 30km.

At Coquihalla Summit you can take a diversion and loop north on the railbed to Brookmere (at times the track is obliterated by the highway) and then double back south to Tulameen. Or you can take a fine gravel road that splits east on the Tulameen–Britton Creek Road and hooks up with the Lawless Creek Road to put you back onto the railbed at Tulameen (food, gas, beer).

From here it's a short 8km hop to Coalmont (more G, F & B) but thereafter the railbed has quite a few wash outs, so it's a great little ride on pavement for the 25km into Princeton. At Princeton go north on Hwy #40 for 8km then turn left where the railbed crosses the road. For the next 40km the KVR breezes through open range on good two track. Once past Milford Lake, a further 10–12km, it's just as well to get back on Hwy #40 and scoot along the last 50km of twisty pavement into Penticton to sample the regional wines.

As the railbed is heavily used as a bicycle path within the city limits, run north out of Penticton about 10km on Naramata Road and turn right up any one of a dozen farm roads to intersect with the KVR again. Once out of town the railbed climbs up over Okanagan Lake on a great two track surface. Courtesy should be given to other trail users in this area. As long as the mountain bikers and horsemen yield to each other through the next 70km the KVR will remain open to all, including tough-as-nails *Adventure Motorcycling Handbook* readers.

In the Myra Canyon section there are eighteen trestles in about 10km. To stop MTBers falling to their deaths, all now have plank decks and railings. Once past the camp-site at Hydraulic Lake (about 90km from Penticton) the recreational traffic drops off and it should be an undisturbed ride for 110km to Rock Creek (G, F & B).

From Rock Creek it's once again a good idea to jump on Hwy #3 as the KVR shadows

Riding the trestles through Myra Canyon on the KVR. © Tom Grenon

the highway for about 47km through the towns of Midway and Greenwood (great food at Cooper Eagle Café), until you reach a small dirt road that connects to the KVR at Eholt. The ensuing 25km into Grande Forks includes a couple of tunnels along the railbed which elsewhere is just a ledge cut into the side of the steep mountain with a long drop down the low side. Stay alert!

From Grande Forks to about 27km beyond Christina Lake it's best to ride on Hwy #3 again while about 25km north from Christina Lake Hwy #3 goes high over the KVR situated down in a canyon 125 metres below. About 2km beyond the bridge watch for a turn-off left to Paulson Station; this will bring you back down to the railbed.

The last 50km stretch to Castlegar heads off into the wilderness and includes five tunnels (one almost 1km long) plus a couple of trestles and several short slide areas to negotiate high above Lower Arrow Lake, before dropping down into town.

Maps
Backroad Mapbook volume 3 & 4; Mussio Ventures Ltd
(🖳 www.backroadsmap books.com)

SUB-ARCTIC ATTIRE

Some may think you have to be some kinda adventure motorcycling masochist to head into the far north. Not true. I hate discomfort with a passion but with proper preparation there should be very few occasions when you will be anything more than just disappointed with the weather.

The foundation for this comfort starts with stoking the internal fires. If the day looks cold get a hearty breakfast inside you and remember to eat throughout the day. A great way of maintaining body heat without messing around with stoves or fires at midday is to **fill a thermos flask** in the morning with whatever you like. A good metal item will keep a beverage hot all day and last many years of being knocked about.

Suitably fed, the first layer must be a material such as **polypropylene**: it wicks moisture away from the body so producing an insulating layer of *dry* air between you and the second layer, which in extreme conditions could be a wool shirt. Then pull on one of the most venerated garments known to northern motorcycledom: the windstop fleece pullover or jacket, featuring a layer of Gore-Tex between two layers of thin fleece.

All the aforementioned articles of clothing also have one more important quality: they dry quickly.

Whatever you do **avoid cotton** inner garments (including socks) in wet and cold conditions. Wet cotton draws away body heat, accelerating the possible onset of hypothermia and takes ages to dry.

Over all this you want a nice **loose fitting** riding jacket (see p.66) so you won't feel like a stuffed sausage. Call me old fashioned but the **waxed cotton jacket** is rugged and fool-proof, if it leaks re-wax it. Simple.

The added protection from waterproof overmittens from Outdoor Research and lightweight zip-up overboots from Tour Master also go a long way to making a wet day's riding almost enjoyable.

If you lived on the motorcycle 24 hours a day, never broke down, and never had to walk anywhere, MX boots would be perfect. But you don't so in my opinion the best of two worlds is Viberg's dual sport boot. They offer as much protection as an MX boot but if the bike croaks 100km from nowhere you can comfortably walk out with no blisters or slipping up slopes. **Tom Grenon**

Slow Boat from Panama

With the vital ferry link between Central and South America suspended and in no mood to take on the Darien Gap, **Michael Slaughter** *and his partner resort to smuggling their bikes into Colombia.*

'If you're looking for the *Crucero Express* it's gone!' came a voice over my shoulder. I turned round to see a giant Honda with the words Thunder Rider glued to the fairing. Straddling the machine was a sprightly man of just over five foot, one foot on the saddle and the other braced on the ground. Our US license plates and stacks were a dead give-away. There is no reason for two Americans to be in Colón on motorbikes if they're not looking for a passage to South America.

'It's not safe for you to stop here, follow me.'

Thinking that I probably shouldn't, but not wanting to be where I was, I did as I was told. My partner Mark and I tailed Thunder Rider to a nearby petrol station and dismounted to chat about the *Crucero Express*.

'What! You didn't hear? It's been closed for over a month, I can't believe that you didn't know,' he asserted. No, we hadn't heard.

'You guys are never gonna get to Colombia without the *Crucero*, but if you want you can check out the wharf. In the meantime don't go to Colón, it's not safe. I know, I live there.' We thanked Thunder Rider for his help and he disappeared again, a bundle of energy atop 200 kilos of steel.

The *Crucero Express* had operated between the ports of Colón and Cartagena, Colombia. We'd planned to take the ferry since not so much as a goat track yet connects North America with South, and without the *Crucero* the crossing was going to be a challenge.

Mark and I graduated from college in May '96. We worked multiple jobs, he in Boston, me in Dallas, and eventually scraped together enough cash to buy our first bikes. By November we were ready to travel to Tierra del Fuego and left the States in high spirits, leaving responsibilities behind.

So far the journey was delivering all we'd hoped for, but after an exhilarating, harmonious and heartwarming journey through Central America, Colón felt like a bucket of cold water. The streets were filled with trash, buildings were falling down and the aggressive atmosphere made me feel far from home. Hundreds of people mulled about in the streets as laundry hung from the steel bars on the high-rise tenements. The whole city appeared to be low-income housing with only a few cheap hotels and Chinese restaurants to mark the city centre.

The Panamanian government had tried to curb the economic collapse when the United States military vacated the area by establishing a tariff-free trading zone. The project was touted by the government as a job-creating, local economy-boosting solution to the region's problems. Unfortunately, the multi-national companies, which trade at Colón, have no allegiance to Panama or its people and the trade zone has done little to revive the city's economy. Thousands migrated from rural areas in search of work, sending unemployment levels in the city as high as seventy-five per cent.

As night fell, we locked the bikes up at a sleazy hotel, checked in, and paid the armed guard at the entrance a small fee to ensure the bikes would be there when we returned. For dinner, the waiter at a Chinese restaurant served us 10oz bottles of Guinness with our egg drop soup. Mark made friends with Orlando, a Colombian, who had been in Colón for two weeks waiting for his car to be released by Customs. Orlando sympathised with our situation and agreed to help us with our Customs and Immigration clearance in the morning.

Finding a cargo ship to Colombia was not too difficult. Few captains were willing to deal with motorbikes, but despite early morning rains it was not long before I found one who was. As we negotiated the price of the passage, I watched a knife fight between two sailors out of the corner of my eye. No one else seemed especially interested and after a few minutes a nifty escape by the younger of the two brought the sideshow to a bloodless conclusion.

The Customs office in Colón only deals with new vehicles, so after some confusion, Mark and I made the 45-minute trip to Panama with a calm and cool Orlando along for the ride. Without Orlando we'd have been stuck in the country for weeks. He oiled a few key palms and dished out some kind, if not quite sincere words and before long we were through. The bureaucratic labyrinth of departments and regulations in Central America never ceases to amaze me.

We got to work loading the bikes on board the ship, removing brake levers and mirrors, locking valuables and securing the bikes under tarps to protect them from rain and sea water. Waiting for the *Santa Lucia* to leave as the sun set, Mark and I found a small restaurant at the dock to devour our first meal of the day.

The restaurant was just a corrugated iron roof covering a few tables and served fried chicken and fries. Here we met some other travellers trying to get to Colombia. One was a guy from New York who kept talking about how bad the roads had been and how after digging his Chevy Blazer out of the mud four times, he'd finally decided to try shipping the truck instead of driving. Everyone in the restaurant stared at him in awe. He had driven more than three thousand miles from NYC with a hang glider strapped to his roof and no one had told him the Darien Gap was impassable to automobiles and just about any other form of wheeled transport!

The *Santa Lucia* cast off shortly after midnight. It was a wonderful feeling to be aboard a ship where control of time and destination vanish and the mind is left to wander. After the ominous broodiness of Colón, the ship was a safe haven where I could lay awake under the stars and feel the rocking of the boat and the laughter of the crew. It was bliss. Of the 15 of us on the boat, ten rode atop the blue tarp, which protected the cargo. We shared the boat with Panamanian and Colombian sailors, but there were other travellers on board including a surly, over-travelled Scotsman, a Uruguayan and a German woman.

Mysterious lights passed in the night but as dawn broke they dimmed and human shapes appeared on the small islands. People could be seen fishing and going about their daily life and I dearly wished we could have had a chance to explore the islands. That afternoon the *Santa Lucia* docked and the second night was spent alongside a concrete pier.

As we set off next morning for what I imagined would be the last leg of our voyage, I began to inquire about what lay beneath the blue tarp.

'*Contrabando*', came the reply.

'*Drogas?*' I asked as coolly as I could muster.

'*No, contrabando para vender en Colombia.*'

As the conversation progressed I came to realise that the *Santa Lucia* was part of a large fleet of smuggling ships which transport goods from the Tariff Free Zone in Colón to Colombia. I also discovered that we were going to be waiting in the islands of the Kuna Yala for a while because the coastguard was looking for boats such as ours to stop the flow of untaxed goods into the country for the Christmas shopping season. As the conversation expired we pulled up to the island of Tup Bak.

We were never told how long we would be at Tup Bak, so Mark and I

I asked the captain what would happen to us if the coast guard caught us... *'La carcel'*, he said. Jail.

stayed within shouting distance of the boat. Every couple of hours we received a scouting report from some radio operator on the islands who was spying on the movements of the coastguard ships. We had to be ready to leave at a moment's notice. Had I known we'd be there for a week I'd have taken advantage of the time to see the whole island. Nervous about our immediate future, I asked the captain what would happen if we were caught. He grabbed his right wrist with his left hand, then his left wrist with his right hand.

'*La carcel*', he said. Jail.

Since the Kuna islanders speak their own language there were not many on the island with whom I could communicate besides the others on the boat. Mark did make friends with one of the islanders, a Spanish teacher from another island. He was home for the holidays and invited us in for coffee and let us use his dugout to go fishing, sending his nephew David along as a guide. The canoe was barely wider than my hips and rocking in the waves allowed water in.

Nevertheless, we enjoyed it so much that we made it a daily affair and the fish helped to supplement the rice diet we were fed on the boat. Looking out from the dugout I could see the mainland and the dense forests of the mysterious Darien Gap. I imagined the muddy trails and deep rivers, a vast roadless land controlled by the politically-autonomous Kuna.

The sun dropped over the tree-covered ridges, thin clouds hung low shrouding the detail I tried to discern. As I lost myself in the sublime beauty, David caught a big fish and since we were using hand lines, finesse was needed to bring the catch aboard. David was so excited that he followed the fish from the front of the canoe to the back as it struggled to free itself. He moved with an agility of one born in a dugout, stepping on my knees, shoulder, head and down my back, sprinting over Mark in a similar fashion and back again. Mark and I clung desperately to the canoe to keep it from sinking but the fish got away.

We returned to the island to prepare the day's catch for the pan. As we sat in the grass with our hands covered in scales and fish parts, Ray the Scotsman came by with two freshly-scrounged coconuts. The San Blas Islands' coconuts are the main source of income for the Kuna people and each islander has his own plot on which he can grow coconuts. On a hike around to the back of the island, Ray had poached coconuts and the tribal elders were not happy. A screaming match ensued and Ray, unpleasant and insensitive at the best of times, told them to go to hell and take their coconuts with them. As the dust settled, Mark and I worked to repair relations. We made sure that the islanders knew that we were not with Ray and that he was not a typical traveller. The night ended with m a n y

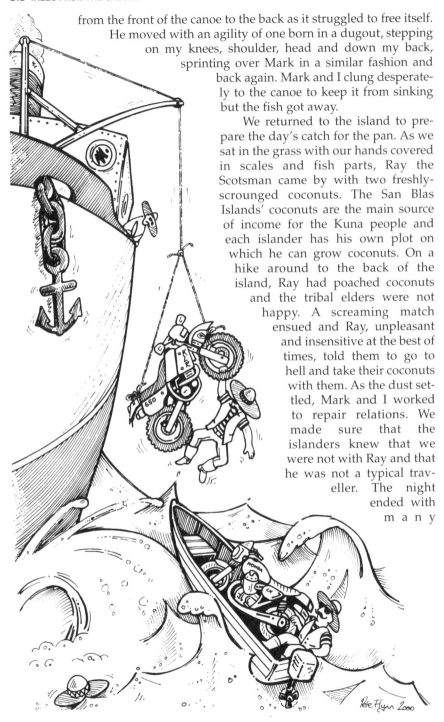

new friends and many jokes about the miserly, miserable Scotsman. Travel does not always broaden the mind; five years on the road had burned out any humanity Ray may once have had.

The call came early in the morning on Christmas Eve; the coast was clear to continue our run to Colombia. To save time, we diverged from our original course that followed the mainland and headed directly for the Colombian coastline. Out on the swells of the open seas, the normally steady *Santa Lucia* pitched about violently. I tangled myself in the ropes off the starboard side with my head hanging over the edge and fed the fishes. The waves were so high that when I lifted my head they towered over me like tall buildings in a city. My head spun and my stomach churned while the crew sat back and enjoyed the sight of a landlubber *gringo* on the high seas.

After the sun went down, the distant lights of the mainland came into view and we dropped anchor a hundred metres off shore. I was told that the bikes would be the last to be unloaded and so I hitched a ride in a small wooden kayak. One of the passengers gave me a beer and a hearty '*Bienvenidos a Colombia*'. I felt so relieved. I returned later to the boat to join Mark who had not yet disembarked and watched the men unload the cargo of refrigerators, beer and whiskey into a small wooden boat fondly referred to as a *chalupa*.

My mind tried in vain to think of a way to get our bikes into that boat under these conditions until at 5am the moment of truth was upon us. All that remained on board were Mark, myself, my KLR and his CX500. Eventually the *chalupa* returned with thirty men. We were told that the work of getting the bikes to shore could be done, but for a price. One hundred dollars came the first bid; $5 came the counter bid. In the end we paid twenty bucks and after seeing the work it took to get the bikes ashore, we would have gotten a good deal had we paid $100!

At one point all that was visible was a dozen arms protruding from the waves clutching a CX500.

Ten men stood in the canoe and held it close to the *Santa Lucia* as the waves tried to toss the two boats apart. As they worked to heave the CX over the edge I busied myself with the KLR. Suddenly I heard screaming and yelling followed by a loud splash. The whole boat became silent and the blood rushed to my feet. The next few seconds crawled by as I pictured the Honda settling gently on the seabed, terminating Mark's trip.

I turned round to see the red CX high and dry and the men laughing. One guy had fallen in as he tried to grab a non-existent brake lever to stop the CX rolling off the side. Finding it missing he panicked and bravely dived in front of the machine. Twenty bucks worth, to be sure!

The bike was carefully lowered into the boat and mine soon followed. We boarded the *chalupa* and exchanged congratulations with each other for a job well done. The canoe could only get to within ten metres of the shore so again a group held the boat steady while others lifted the bikes as waves crashed over their bodies. At one point all that was visible was a dozen arms protruding from the waves clutching a CX500. Once on the beach we fired the engines and the men began to clap, sing and dance. We showed off with a couple of high speed passes for the appreciative and jovial crowd.

As the sun came up that morning I found a secluded area on the beach where I sat on some driftwood with my shadow stretching out before me and gazed out at the ocean as it slowly rocked the *Santa Lucia*. It had been ten days since we left Coco Solo Wharf and I was exhausted from the voyage. I began to think about my family back home. I should call them soon, they'd appreciate a call. After all, it was Christmas morning and I was in Colombia.

Africa on 400cc a day

Alex Marr describes a few days hard riding on his XR400 in Ethiopia and the badlands of northern Kenya, followed by the anticlimactic ride down to the Cape.

Entering Ethiopia, I had images of searing heat, desert and drought based on press coverage from the 1980s. However, as I crossed the north Kenyan border, I soon realised I'd got it wrong. Most of Ethiopia is high, regularly over 3000m, and some days reminded me of an English winter. Driving rain and near freezing temperatures sent me almost delirious, pining for heated grips, waterproof clothes and steamy windowed roadside cafés.

The plus side of this mountainous terrain is that Ethiopia is by far the most beautiful country I've ever visited. The scenery is nothing short of breathtaking. Almost every corner you turn reveals another awesome landscape, usually rugged mountains or rolling hills.

But it is also a very tough place to travel, partly because the roads are pretty terrible but mainly because of the people. Wherever *faranji* (foreigners) go, they are subjected to inordinate amounts of jeering and abuse. In almost every town they shout and whistle to an extent I had never experienced anywhere in the world.

One theory is that the men prefer their women to be ugly to lessen the chances of them being unfaithful... Personally I'd rather my wife was an absolute babe and take the risk!

'Hey, you, you, you' ... *'hey faranji, fuck off'*... Occasionally they throw sticks and stones. Charming.

Actually most of the people aren't bad, it seemed to be mainly older boys and young men presumably trying to prove their manliness by taunting us foreigners. Anyway, it's fairly harmless – half of them don't know what they're saying and there are hardly ever any serious incidents, but even so it's so unrelenting – all day, every day – it starts to give you a headache. I had a visa for 30 days and this was plenty – any more would have driven me right round the bend.

In a few parts of the country it really was like the old TV pictures – intense heat and naked screaming kids with clusters of flies fixed to the snot pouring out of their noses. Enough to put you off your lunch – mind you, lunch was never that nice anyway.

You don't see a lot of tourists in Ethiopia, but I did bump into the archetypal loony German biker on an old DR650. We ended up on a four-day trek together in the gobsmackingly scenic Simien Mountains.

When it came to money this guy was as tight as a gnat's chuff and we nearly had a fight when he started haggling over the price of a bundle of firewood with a six-year old girl who was so cold and weak she could hardly walk. Hardly appropriate I thought but 'you must bargain with zese people' he insisted.

As I headed into south-western Ethiopia on my way back into Kenya, I made a detour to try to see the Mursi tribe, famous for the large plates inserted in the women's lower lips. The size of the plates is increased as they grow up and some of the adult women's lips grow around plates up to six inches in diameter. One theory is that the men prefer their women to be grotesquely ugly to lessen the chances of them being unfaithful. This seems like rather strange logic to me – personally I'd rather my wife was an absolute babe and take the risk!

Getting to the Mursi village is something of an ordeal. It's about 70km from the small town of Jinka, itself a pretty remote spot three days from Addis Ababa. The day before I left Jinka for the Mursi village it had been raining and the muddy tracks through the bush had become very difficult.

About 20km from the village I had to cross a river where the bridge had collapsed. I rode straight in, confident that the forty or so metres would be quite shallow. Wrong again. It soon became much too deep and my attempts to blast through saw the bike keel over on its side with the engine running. Almost completely submerged, there was absolutely no way I could even pick it up, never mind push it out of the river.

As I stood there, waist-high in water wondering what crocodiles ate for lunch around here, two naked men with Kalashnikovs slung round their shoulders appeared on the bank. After I'd smiled and admired their gleaming weapons I suggested they might like to help me out. They put down their guns, waded over and having mentioned the word 'birr' (the local currency) a number of times, helped me get the waterlogged bike out of the river.

Never one to miss a photo opportunity, I managed to get them to let me take a picture (more birr) as they pushed it through the water. Back on the bank, they sat around and watched me tinker with the few tools I had as I tried to review the bike. But soon my worst fears were confirmed – there was water in the cylinder and the crankcase – the XR may be as clean as a whistle but was going nowhere.

I sat around hoping that three Israeli guys who'd been behind me would turn up at some stage but after a few hours I assumed they'd got bogged in the deep mud or gone back to Jinka. Then after another few hours a large, empty truck on its way to Jinka came crashing through the river, an amazing piece of luck. I later found out only two trucks a week pass through – I could have been there for three days. For a substantial amount of good old birr, I was allowed to put my bike on the back. An hour or so later we came across the Israelis, who had been completely bogged in the mud most of the day, and towed them free. It was very disappointing not to make it to the Mursi village but a relief nonetheless to get myself and the bike back to Jinka.

The next day I got to work on the bike. There was no spark even after cleaning and drying all the connections so I thought that one of the electrical components must have failed. The idea of being in Ethiopia and needing a new CDI unit was not that appealing.

But luck was still seemingly on my side and leaving the bike in the hot sun for a day sorted out the short. The other problem was the oil – the Shell Ultra had become a banana milkshake and after a couple of changes the new oil was still looking far from normal, so I poured petrol everywhere – in the oil filler hole, the spark-plug hole, the valve covers – and kept kicking over the engine till it came out more-or-less clear. There are probably all sorts of reasons I shouldn't have done this but I was in a rush – my visa was expiring the next day and the Ethiopians are rumoured to be very strict on tourists overstaying their welcome (ie prison).

I filled the XR with oil and after about fifty energy-sapping lunges on the kickstarter and extreme overuse of the command 'start, you bastard' it finally showed some sign of life.

The next morning I headed towards the Kenya border but things were not looking good. I wasn't sure if any damage had been done watering the engine, I was overloaded with the extra fuel and, worst of all, the border I wanted to cross was not an official crossing point at all. However, I'd heard such amazing things about this seldom-trodden route down the east coast of Lake Turkana, I just had to give it a go.

The Israelis, who had come up that way, had given me instructions of how to avoid the last police post in Ethiopia but it wasn't where they said it was and I rode straight into it. This was bad news. I took a risk and admitted I was going to Kenya but pretended I didn't know this was illegal. They told me I would have to go to the proper border crossing over

500km to the east. With the visa fading fast this was not an option and I knew I'd have to try and convince them to let me in through the sheer force of my charismatic personality. I was expecting to have to part with a big load of cash too, but after two hours of banter I was allowed to proceed minus my Matsui shortwave radio. This I didn't mind too much as it had never worked that well since the Champion's League final – I dropped it when Solskjaer scored in the 91st minute.

As I stood there in waist-high water wondering what crocodiles ate for lunch around here, two naked men with AK47s slung round their shoulders appeared on the bank.

Now in Kenya, there were no real tracks so I just headed south across sandy scrub land and reached the first Kenyan village before dark. It was such a relief to be out of Ethiopia – so many things could have gone wrong at this stage of the trip and I just hoped that if they did it was in Kenya and not Ethiopia.

I was still a long way from civilisation however, the Lake Turkana region being one of the most remote places in East Africa. It's a really hostile area, dry and very hot with the lake a stunning opaque greeny blue surrounded by mountains on all sides.

The tracks weren't much better, I had a choice of deep sand littered with thorn trees or sharp rocks. The riding was technically as tough as it had been on

the whole trip. I'd find myself riding up and down steep slopes on large pieces of jagged rubble for hours on end – incredibly tiring. One saving grace was that I never got any punctures, how I'll never know. I saw nobody for a whole day until I got close to Loyangalani, the first settlement on the lakeshore.

Two days later I was back to the comforts of Nairobi and after sleeping for a couple more days, I continued south into Uganda to see the endangered wild mountain gorillas near the Rwandan border. Since a group of tourists got mutilated here in '99 it has been easy to get a permit – previously you could end up waiting for weeks.

We walked for three hours through dense forest with rangers and armed guards until we found them: seven cuddly gorillas who, I could tell by the way they looked at us, were thinking 'oh God not more ogling tourists'. It was all very nice but I could never quite understand some people's reactions. The visitors' book at Park HQ was full of over-the-top comments (nearly always by females, nearly always American). Things like 'It was so beautiful, I cried' and 'This experience has changed my life forever' ...errr, why?

East and Southern Africa are so different from West and Central – and as I moved through Tanzania, Malawi, Zimbabwe and into South Africa, I was well and truly on the tourist trail. Game reserves, great beaches and a decent tourist infrastructure mean it's a standard backpacker route.

It was rapidly becoming clear that this part of Africa did not have the appeal of the places I'd spent the previous eight months travelling through. I suppose the challenge had gone – long hours riding on perfect tarmac roads shared with coach loads of tourists was hardly as alluring as crossing the Ténéré desert in Niger.

And so Southern Africa was pretty uneventful – my only worrying time being when one of the rear wheel bearings gave up in Tanzania. I rode over 1000km before I could find replacements with terrifying clanking and crunching noises coming from the rear whenever I braked.

When I took off the dust seal and was greeted with a hubful of square-shaped balls and mangled metal, I realised it could all have been a bit nasty. I arrived in Cape Town in October, almost a year to the day after first arriving in Africa, excited by the fact that there are supposedly six single females for every male. This unlikely demographic quirk has done absolutely nothing for me and it would appear that something is not quite right – either with me or the statistics.

> **I arrived in Cape Town... excited by the fact that there are six single females for every male. It would appear, however, that something is not quite right – either with me or the statistics.**

Another interesting statistic – true this time – is that in 37,000km I had no punctures. Amazing what heavy duty tubes and a lot of luck can do. Finding decent tyres in Africa was a continual problem but usually determined scouting got a result. In Addis Ababa, for example, I was in desperate need of a new rear when a brand-new MT21 was finished after only 4000km of Ethiopian roads. I spent a whole day going round every bike shop in the city and didn't find anything that looked like it wouldn't melt if you went over 30mph.

Someone suggested I try an old man round the corner – I explained my predicament, he went into his back shed and came back with a new Bridgestone M22 motocross tyre – absolutely perfect for the terrible terrain that was coming up. (And incidentally it lasted about twice as long as the MT21 ...)

More unlikely stats – in crossing 19 countries I was never attacked, had nothing stolen and paid no bribes (well, I did pay one but got a full refund). Ninety-five per cent of Africans I met were good honest people, nearly always willing to help. Unfortunately in some situations, like asking for directions, the quality of information never matched their enthusiasm.

The main problem is if they don't know the way, they don't admit it – they make something up. Ask three different people the same question and you're almost guaranteed to get three different answers. But you soon develop the knack of working out who was likely to be selling you a load of baloney: if they point 'that way' in response to the question 'can you please tell me the way to Ulan Bator?' the chances are it's time to speak to someone else.

Another thing was that the vast majority of rural Africans have absolutely no understanding of how fast you can go on a bike. They assume that because it's large and makes a lot of noise and shows 160kph on the speedo that is how fast you go. It doesn't matter what the terrain is, deep sand, mud, rocks, you should be 160km away in an hour.

I soon gave up trying to explain why that wasn't possible. I'm often asked if I would use the same bike again and the answer is a definite 'yes'. By the time I got to South Africa the XR was feeling tired and loose and using loads of oil but it still worked OK. With a total of nearly 60,000 hard kilometres on the clock, it just kept chugging away. The thing with XRs is they are so well built, so robust, so resilient to being chucked around and battered to death on horrible terrain. Before this trip it had done muddy enduros, desert rallies, been ridden on the road – it's not really the perfect tool for any of those things but it can competently turn its hand to all of them

With this confidence in the XR and a maturing taste for travel, I decided to keep going. All I had to decide was which way; back up north, east to India or west to the Americas.

The Road to Samarkand

Taking an excursion from Frankfurt to London (via Tashkent) **Kyril Dambuleff** *describes the ride on his K-series BMW from Turkey across the Caspian Sea and the Karakum Desert to Samarkand in the heart of Central Asia.*

The further east I rode in Turkey, the worse the roads became, and what had been pleasant and smooth riding on good tarmac soon turned into a tiring slalom between potholes. Emerging from a long, dark tunnel, I sighed with relief at again having survived unscathed – a feeling which did not last long as a huge pothole opened directly in front of me. Instinctively but foolishly I braked hard, which of course took out most of the front suspension's free play. Bang! The front wheel dropped in and the forks solidified. I gripped the handlebars with all my strength, knuckles stretching the leather gloves to the point of bursting.

The rear wheel crashed in and then again bang! on the way out. I realised I was moving and upright but for some reason the bike was leaning heavily to the right. As someone who fears a mechanical problem just slightly less than a Romanian border crossing, I refused to acknowledge that the bike's frame was now a banana and rode on. Then as my adrenaline overload slowly subsided and good sense returned, I stopped to check things out.

Ready for the worst, and much as I disliked the idea of turning back, I convinced myself that if the bike needed repair it would be wiser to ride the 700 miles back to Ankara than to press on. The next BMW dealer in my direction was Hong Kong!

I pulled over expecting a broken rim or bent forks, but a close examination revealed that the bike was just fine. But where was my left saddlebag? Cold sweat erupted from every single pore. All my money was in that saddlebag! A beautiful and very comforting wad of crisp $50 bills neatly tucked into a special pouch hiding inside the lining of the first-aid kit.

I'd put it there only a few hours earlier in preparation for the heavy search I was expecting from the Russian soldiers at the Georgian border 20 miles down the road. In blind panic and nursing very little hope, I spun a one-eighty and raced back down the road. The traffic was very light; hopefully nobody would get to it before I did.

A big truck flashed his high beams and in frantic sign language the driver indicated that I should pull over behind him and wait. I took out four cigarettes and lit up. Was this the end of the trip? I couldn't believe it. The first serious pothole took me out! I hated myself. The humiliation. The laughter at the local bar back home. I could hear it now.

Five seconds felt like an hour. Then, a white van pulled up right in front of me. The side door slid open and from the darkness inside someone handed me my saddlebag. Before I could say thank you, the door slammed shut and the van took off. The truck driver smiled, patted me on the shoulder and shook hands my hand. I stupidly offered money.

'*Yok, yok, effendi. Olmaz, Olmaz! Turkye guezell*' I said, which means 'Turkey is beautiful'. Inappropriate as it may have been it was just about the only thing I could say in Turkish.

'*Chok guezell, chok guezell*', he laughed and with the roar of his engine, disappeared in a cloud of gritty black smoke.

As I neared the Georgian border the asphalt ended and I was soon bouncing on a dirt track which seemed to pass through a construction site. After a sharp turn it appeared that the road led into a half-dug tunnel. It was already late in the day; I had a border to cross and a ride to the nearest town to find a place to put down for the night. I could not afford to get lost.

Wearied by my near-miss and the unrelenting track, for the first time I began to have doubts about my plan to ride across Asia. Are all the roads going to be like this? I'd had such a wonderful time in Turkey that the idea of plunging myself into the war-torn regions of Georgia and Azerbaijan seemed daunting. Fighting a bad road and a strong desire to turn back, I pressed on. Another sharp turn and there it was – the border post.

The formalities took forever of course, especially on the Georgian side where I was given several forms to fill out and was asked repeatedly if I carried any guns or narcotics.

I often wonder what the point is in asking anybody if they carry any drugs. Do they really think that a cunning drug smuggler would just say 'Oh, yes, officer, I have a bag of cocaine in that suitcase. You don't mind do you?'. I had no Georgian visa, but my Azerbaijani visa was good for five days in Georgia. After two hours the barrier lifted and I was waved through.

Politely declining requests for bribes from what seemed to be plainclothes Immigration officials, I soon found myself surrounded by a big mob. A police officer came to disperse the crowd but as soon as he saw the bike became as fascinated as everybody else. It wasn't until I let him press the electric start button several times and twist the throttle that he eventually ordered everybody to clear the way.

The next day I found myself crawling up a steep mountain on bad roads and 73-octane gasoline. The engine rattled like a jar full of nails. A miserable drizzle enveloped everything and water-filled potholes of unknown depth broke any rhythm I tried to maintain.

After an hour of zigzagging, my eyes would get so tired that I'd have to stop and unwind for a few minutes. As the road ascended, ever more frequent abandoned vehicles emerged from the gloom. The whole scene looked like something out of *Saving Private Ryan*. The rain intensified and chilled with each successive hairpin and at the summit I entered a long and dark tunnel with a big sigh and a feeling of trepidation.

Inside it seemed as if water was dripping from all directions. Potholes lay scattered like land mines and a big truck bore down
a few feet from my back end.

'If I can just make it out of this tunnel alive', I con-
soled my-
s e l f ,

thinking fondly of my wife and three children back home. The tunnel ended, revealing a gloomy sodden landscape with several small shacks by the road side. Trails of white smoke drifted from the chimneys, hinting at a warm interior and cooking. Though sweating, I felt very cold. Trembling, I took off my gloves – my hands were completely black.

... the camera rolled, a guy shouted 'Action!' and I barely remember the rest... the party rolled on until three in the morning.

Hot tea was needed and that's exactly what I was given as soon as I stepped into a roadhouse. Before long I found myself invited to a house in the village. I gladly accepted as the thought of riding 150 miles to Tbilisi did not appeal at all. Ten minutes later I was in my host's house and before I could even park the bike and take my boots off, the table was laid, the family had gotten together and the wine was poured!

The *tamada* (the guy who proposes toasts) sat at the head of the table and the drinking began. There were toasts to friendship, to Georgia's independence, to the successful rebuilding of the Georgian economy, democracy, Ogurek's new donkey, you name it! Two hours later a Georgian TV crew showed up and asked me for an interview. By then I was in no fit state to appear on national TV so I declined. But after another glass of wine I thought to myself 'These guys have come all the way from Tbilisi in the rain – this is not the way to respond to Georgian hospitality'.

'Oh, what the hell! Let's do it!' I said.

The lights came on, the camera rolled, a guy shouted 'Action!' and I barely remember the rest. The interview took about ten minutes after which the crew joined in and the party rolled on until three in the morning. A Georgian guy played a 12-string guitar and sang beautiful songs filled with sadness which only caused everybody to drink even more wine. I found myself deeply moved and sang and danced with the rest. I seriously contemplated calling my wife in California and telling her 'Honey, pack your bags, we're moving to Georgia'. As far as I was concerned, I had found what I had come to Asia for.

Crossing into Azerbaijan felt like going through a war zone. There were several military posts where the guards painstakingly inscribed my name and the bike's license plate into thick old ledgers. At the last one, a soldier asked me if I could give him a ride to the next town. 'Sure', I said, thinking an armed escort might not be a bad idea.

Off we went and soon he started to sing at the top of his lungs. I cranked up with a smile on my face, realising that this ride was as close to sheer bliss as he'd known for a long time. He sang all the way and at the end shook my hand for several minutes but refused to have his picture taken. I don't think I have ever seen a happier man in my life.

Having arrived in Baku, my only option of continuing east was the Caspian Sea ferry. Going south via Iran on an American passport was at this time an experiment I did not wish to try, and north via Chechnya wasn't such a hot idea either. So I went to the port and hunted down the ticket agency.

'When does the next boat sail?' I asked.

'Whenever there is cargo,' came the answer in a tone which I interpreted as 'what is wrong with this guy?'

'Can I buy a ticket?' I asked.

'Come back tomorrow morning.'

Seven am sharp I was there, hoping to secure my place on the ferry. The office was shut, as it was at 10 o'clock, and at noon. Finally, at 3pm the hatch opened.

'Hello my friend, come back at seven,' I was told, 'the cargo is not yet.'

I milled around, wondering if that ship would ever sail. Thinking that the ticket master would just go home at five, I got there early. After many cups of tea, we agreed on a cost of $149, of course, baksheesh playing a major role in the negotiations.

'So, when does the ship sail?' I ventured yet again.

'Be at the harbour at midnight,' was the answer. Midnight came and went and I ended up playing backgammon with the Customs officers.

'Cargo here yet?' I asked but they only shook their heads.

At about three in the morning, a slow-moving train passed right by the window, its wheels squeaking on the rails. The Custom officers looked at me and with a nod said 'Cargo.' What?! The train was the cargo?! 'Oh, yes,' they said, '48 wagons filled with grain.'

By dawn the loading was done. Other than my bike, the only other vehicles were two cars. Assuming a 120-mile crossing should take about five or six hours and figuring we'd be in Turkmenistan around noon, I thought I'd take a nap in my cabin. A first-class cabin especially reserved for foreigners. But when I saw it, I laughed. The cabin looked like a prison cell measuring about 6ft by 8 with gray everything and a bare double mattress.

'Five dollar for the sheet and blanket,' barked the old Russian lady who was escorting me.

'Oh, and the horse you rode in on!' I said. I think she took pity on me because she soon appeared with clean bedding and even made my bed at no charge. I dropped down in my clothes and dozed off only to be woken shortly after by the loudest buzzer I had ever heard. I jumped to my feet, bounced off the ceiling and promptly fell to the floor. Dazed, I slowly stood up. The ship was listing! ' Oh, shit! We're sinking!'

I opened the door and ran down the hallway. There was nobody around. At the end of the hallway I nearly knocked down the cabin lady.

'What are you doing?' she asked as I stared at her gasping for breath. 'The alarm,' I said, 'Why the alarm?' 'Oh, that's just regulations, testing the system in case we sink.'

> I jumped to my feet, bounced off the ceiling and promptly fell to the floor. Dazed, I slowly stood up. The ship was listing! ' Oh, shit! We're sinking!'

Determined to find out why the ship was listing, I went to see the captain, a nice man and very happy to have a foreign passenger. When the ship was built in 1984, he explained, it had a computerised stabilizing system which ensured the ship would remained level even if the cargo shifted. Unfortunately that system failed shortly after the ship went into operation and has been broken ever since.

'Pay no attention,' he advised, 'the cargo always shifts slightly, but we should be perfectly safe.' I then visited the engine room. A packet of cigarettes secured my relationship with the mechanics. When I asked how long it was going to take to do the crossing they said about nineteen hours. Nineteen hours to travel 120 miles!

'Only one of the three engines is running. We use the other two for parts.'

In Turkmenistan, Customs clearance took hours and after having been slapped with $69 fuel tax, (the government's way of compensating themselves for the low fuel prices), I was finally allowed out. On a chilly morning, the sun rose over the Karakum desert to reveal a spectacular view of the road that stretched over the barren landscape clear to the horizon, while hundreds of camels grazed by the roadside.

After the day on the listing ship, I enjoyed the sensation of the desert wind and the smell of dust. Wherever I stopped, the local people came to say 'hello' and everybody offered me *chai*. Men led me to gas stations, filled my tank with 'unobtainable' 96-octane which somehow magically appeared from carefully disguised plastic jerry cans and then firmly refused payment.

In a small village I stopped at a food stand in the hope that I could finally spend some of my money to buy a bottle of Coke, sparkling water, whatever.

'No, no,' said the merchant, 'come to my house and we'll have some tea instead.' We sat on the floor, drank the tea, the time just ticked away.

'It is a Moslem tradition,' he said, 'that we offer the traveller the best we can. And we never ask for his name or his business so as not to offend him.'

A neighbour showed up in the doorway, his hand covered in blood. He had just slaughtered a lamb, would I like to have something to eat. We ate the lamb and drank the tea in silence. At the end of the meal, they both cupped their hands, muttered a few words, then presented them to their faces with the palms running down their cheeks as if they we washing. Whatever it meant, I did the same.

And so it was that wherever I went, the local people always invited me into their homes. They shared everything they had with me including the floor on which everybody slept. I ate *plov* and drank *chall* – a drink made from a slightly-fermented camel's milk, which tasted divine – the best thirst quencher I've ever come across. On certain occasions, vodka appeared and then the younger generation initiated fiery political debates, which the older and wiser men dismissed as *yourondah*: 'It's a waste of time.'

After crossing the swollen Amurdarya River on a military pontoon bridge, I found myself in Uzbekistan. For the first time I was asked to show my immunisation certificate. I don't know if they suspected that I might be bringing some incurable diseases into their country, but after every single border guard tried on my helmet, I felt I should be the one worrying about diseases.

A couple of packs of cigarettes and a deck of playing cards helped speed up the stamping procedure and finally I was inside Uzbekistan. That night I reached legendary Samarkand just as the call to prayer was announced across the ancient city.

The Red Plateau

Chris Scott decided to take a leaf out of his own handbook and head for Libya on an F650. As usual, things turned sour.

Go to most embassies and at least you'll find a few pamphlets and a poster of a couple from the 1960s frolicking by a fountain. No such noncing about at what was then the Libyan Interests Section in London. Down in the grubby basement mean-looking guys ground another cigarette butt into a Brit passport and ignored you purposefully. Tourist literature is limited to a defiant newsletter commemorating the 'drawing of the line of death' against imperial aggressors. Charming. Just the spot to enjoy a spring biking break.

'Visa?' I asked meekly. 'Hello, visa?'

It had taken me months to get just to this point. The previous November with the third edition of *AMH* completed, I decided it was time to practise what I preached. Libya sounded interesting and BMW's Funduro trailie would make a nice change from another Yamaha Ténéré.

Buying a '94 F650 was easy, getting a visa involved countless dead-end faxing to various Libyan tourist agencies for the required invitation. Eventually a mysterious Internet connection provided an invite at a price and my permit was telexed from Tripoli in early April. A week later I was walking down Harley Street with the requisite stamp. There was no going back now.

I may have been nervous about my destination but at least I was sure of the bike. I'd always fancied the Fs: a trusty combination of Rotax engine and BMW build quality. No one had anything bad to say about them other than being a bit heavy for off-roading. I found the revvy engine took a bit of getting used to after grunty XTs, but I was sure the 650 was up for some serious Libyan piste-bashing.

Modifications were kept to a minimum. A fat Michelin Desert squeezed on the back after a bit of sawing at the outer knobs and removing that back bumper thing (EU Directive: Motorcycle Safety Appendage #35-8). The front end took a 'rear' 19" Pirelli MT21 with considerably more knob-chopping and a VT500 mudguard. Road riding on these tyres was initially hairier than a gorilla with a perm, especially the 'marbles-on-glass' MT, but I eventually got used to it. The bike had come with a new o-ring chain, some brand I'd never heard of, but I figured it would last the trip. A 27-litre Acerbis tank looked barely bigger than the original unit and promised a 450-mile range – nearly enough for my planned route. To help work out distances, I got a metric speedo which saved possible errors in converting from miles to kilometres. Lastly, I bunged on an in-line fuel filter, a cigarette-lighter power take off for the GPS, fork gaiters and a high screen. Time to head south.

> **Road riding on these tyres was initially hairier than a gorilla with a perm.**

To save my knobs (and because I'm a bit of a pansy) I caught the overnight Motorail service from Paris to Marseille and then stowed away on a tramp steamer to Tunis where ensued five hours of mind-numbing form filling from one counter to another. If this was Tunisian Immigration what would Libya be like?

And another thing troubled me: had I left it too late? By now temperatures were climbing steeply right across the Sahara and with it expected water consumption and a host of other problems.

Earlier that year a meeting with a guy who'd worked in Libya actually put me off the whole idea. Besides the grief he'd got as a reluctantly-tolerated expat worker, he warned me about the enervating *ghibli* winds which blew in April and melted strong men's brains. This story of a guy who'd driven out into the storm sounded especially grim:

'About a month after the guy'd gone missing a nomad came into the camp and asked if we wanted to know where our Toyota was. We said yes and it cost us. Then he asked did we want our body back – it cost us some more. Turns out the guy had just parked up with the engine running and walked out into the sandstorm.'

With a weather eye out for the *ghibli* and my air-con Arai on 'boost', by the next afternoon I was close to the Libyan border, a wodge of illicitly-bought Libyan currency stuffed down my crotch. At the border I was resigned to hours shuffling from one hanger to the next, filling out forms and getting stamps. But by pure chance one of the Libyan travel agents I'd given up on weeks ago recognised me and whisked me through the formalities in just twenty minutes (and 150 bucks!). Stunned at my good fortune, I set off towards Tripoli in the fading light and soon pulled over to fill up for just a dollar! That's right one greenback for a big tankful.

With dozens of roadside wrecks, traffic along Libya's main coast road is a lethal mixture of grand prix craziness and farmyard jalopies so, after a night in the bushes, I was relieved to turn south next morning towards the border town of Ghadames, 550km away.

As I rode into the desert on smooth and empty highways I wondered when the real heat would begin. I didn't have long to wait. By mid-afternoon the temperature had risen to the high thirties and out of the blue the bike started spluttering. Surely I haven't got through the tank already, I thought? Undoing the cap revealed plenty of juice. The bike started up but a few miles later cut out again. I got off and soon guessed at a cause. A combination of half-empty tank, minimal throttle at cruising speed and the 35°C-heat saw the trickling petrol evaporate in the accessory fuel filter to cause a vapour lock – cutting off the fuel supply. Stopping cooled things down and got the fuel flowing again and pouring cooling water over the hot filter body saw the petrol level rise instantly.

... he warned me about the enervating *ghibli* winds which blew in April and melted strong men's brains.

Knowing the problem was as good as solving it, so I filled up at the first chance and carried on to Ghadames, arriving zonked out at the empty campsite as the sun set. Slumped out on the sand, I had a good think. If it was reaching nearly 40°C this far north, how hot would it be further south? The vapour ock was easily fixed with a cardboard heat shield, but I was keen to get the BM on the dirt. Was I taking too great a risk riding alone? From here my plan was to ride across the Hammada el Hamra plateau and then cut around the edge of the Ubari Sand Sea down to the Acacus Mountains near the Algeria/Niger border, altogether about a week's riding.

My French guidebook claimed the route across the plateau was a straightforward 300-mile gravel track with a crucial well halfway. Just about within my range, though in these temperatures water consumption was another matter. I checked over the bike, wrote myself a road book to stick on the tank and planned to leave early next morning.

That night at 2.10am a rising gale woke me and I dozed fitfully as the tent wobbled and palms flapped overhead. Dawn revealed an ochre sky and a thick dusty haze. Was this the *ghibli* I'd been warned of? I postponed my departure, hoping it would die down, but at noon set off back to the village of Derj where the plateau track began and where I'd reassess the situation.

Filling up at Derj and on the verge of heading back north to Tunisia, my indecision was solved when a German 4WD pulled in. A brief chat revealed that Rainer and Katja were also heading across the plateau and would be happy to have another vehicle along for safety.

The Hammada el Hamra is aptly named the Red Plateau, a barren, undulating prairie of rust-coloured gravel cut by dry water courses. Rising to 2000ft, it's a pitiless void that is either freezing or baking and criss-crossed with enough tracks to confuse even the wily nomads.

> 'No, that is on the direct route, we are taking the southern route.'
> 'The *southern* route? I said with a gulp.

But, enjoying the security of another vehicle, it felt great to be back on the dirt. The BM handled the 30mph pace well and it was fun concentrating on the riding instead of sitting on the boring blacktop. As expected I was a lot quicker than Rainer's ex-trans African Isuzu, but I didn't mind stopping, their very presence made this whole excursion much less tense. But there was one thing which bothered me…

'Rainer, shouldn't we be at Bir Gazell (a landmark) by now?' According to my speedo the landmark should have been close.

'Bir Gazell? No, that is on the direct route, we are taking the southern route.'

'The *southern* route?' I said with a gulp.

'Here, look, it goes down to the Ubari Sand Sea, turns east and follows the dunes' edge to Idri. My guide book says it's much more scenic than the direct route.'

'How far is it?' I asked, not really wanting to know the answer.

'Oh, about 400 miles or so.'

'I doubt I've got enough fuel to go that far, especially if the piste gets sandy.' We paused for a moment to consider the implications.

'Well, I have some spare petrol, about six litres' said Rainer, whose Isuzu was diesel.

Topping up the bike's tank we decided to take a gamble and press on. But by late afternoon we'd got ourselves lost. The next GPS waypoint was

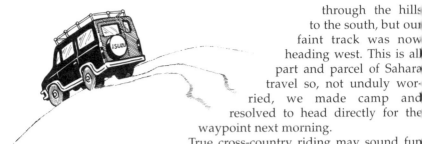

through the hills to the south, but our faint track was now heading west. This is all part and parcel of Sahara travel so, not unduly worried, we made camp and resolved to head directly for the waypoint next morning.

True cross-country riding may sound fun on a dual sport, but in fact it's incredibly slow. Once you ride off tracks, however bad they are, you find yourself walking the bike down rocky slopes, blundering up dead-end valleys or edging towards drops. Even with an early start and the bike reconnoitring a way through the hills, it still took us till noon the next day to cover the 10 miles to the waypoint and rejoin the route.

Having lost altitude coming off the plateau, the day now began to cook and, as I feared, the plateau's firm gravel turned into plains of sand. As all you beach racers know, soft sand has to be attacked standing on the pegs with a nailed throttle and eyes firmly fixed on the ground ahead. There is no easy option: lose speed and you're off – go too fast and you risk crashing. I finished the day shagged senseless by more types and shades of soft sand than the Painted Desert.

By now I was already cutting into Rainer and Katja's water reserves, so we needed to find a well. Their German guidebook identified a source 25 miles away. Having located what seemed the right place, we ploughed into the sands where the Trooper soon mired. While they shovelled I headed over the dunes, riding the sandy banks in all directions just to keep from getting stuck. After a while I found the well – bone dry and full of sand. This little excursion had cost us two hours, a heap of energy and still more water. We flopped out under some meagre shade. No one said anything.

After a while we moved on, at one point encountering the vile surface-crusted powder known as *feche-feche* (flour-like dust). Spotting it too late, the 650 broke through and sank in, engine screaming in first as a 20-ft roost spurted vertically from the back wheel. By paddling madly I just about regained firmer ground to grab yet another slug of water.

By now every minor exertion demanded a drink and the exhausting conditions went on for hours. In this sort of terrain, the Funduro was just plain Duro. While the engine was amazingly zippy on the highway, it lacked the low down pull needed to chug through soft sand at low speeds without breaking traction. And as I've found before, the super stiff Desert tyre might do the trick on a heavy Dakar racer, but at even just 10psi, with the tyre creeping round the rim, it didn't flatten out enough to give sufficient traction. Result: lots of wheelspin and wasted fuel for not much forward motion.

By dusk we'd located a good well and filled up with camels mobbing us for a hand out. Fit only to cook up some grub, we crashed out for the third night running. We all knew we'd bitten off a bit more than we could chew, but the end was surely in sight.

By nine the next morning the bike was halfway down a dune and out of gas. We'd seen no other vehicles for days so there was nothing for it but to lug 20 litres of precious water from the car for me and then watch the Isuzu chug off over the sands. With a bit of luck they'd be back tomorrow, maybe the day after.

Knowing that lying still in the shade was the best way to save water, I crawled under a make shift lean-to and forced myself to concentrate on a book.

The burning sun inched across the sky and the wind peppered me with sand.

...there was nothing for it but to watch the Isuzu chug off over the sands. With a bit of luck they'd be back tomorrow, maybe the day after.

Then, just as I began thinking the unthinkable 'What if...' a toot-tooting heralded the return of the Isuzu. After just three hours they'd chanced across a date plantation where a guy had tapped off a jerrican's-worth from his pick-up's oil drum.

Energised by this amazing stroke of luck we got on the move again but now the riding became *really* hard as the track squeezed between dunes and rocky outcrops. Again we found ourselves hunting wind-erased tracks and taking repeated blasts up boulder-strewn slopes that even the nimble bike could barely manage. Having covered just 25 miles, the Isuzu got stuck on a dune and we'd all had enough so called it a day. Hopefully an early start would finally get us to Idri.

With a 6am start and another four hours driving we finally rolled into the village of Idri, caked in dust and absolutely shattered. I felt as if I'd done a four-day enduro on a heavily-loaded bike in 120-degree temperatures. Two weeks later I was still aching.

At Idri I bade farewell to the tough German couple and headed north, butt-, leg-, arm-, hand- and back-sore after the 400-mile pummelling. Heavy winds prolonged my retreat and at one point I had the distinctly novel sensation of leaning *out* round a bend against a 50mph crosswind. By the Tunisian border that Z-brand chain was on the way out – and when o-rings go they go fast. Back across Tunisia, back across the Med, another Motorail to save the chain and a quick coffee with a mate in Paris who looked at the sprocket and said 'yeah, you'll make it'.

Well, he was wrong. I made it to the Channel, but just 25 miles from London the ultra-tight chain slipped at the slightest acceleration. The sprocket was history. There was nothing for it but to scoot to a phone, hire a van and drive the dusty F home.

Salt Pans Drifter

*On her way round the world on a Honda Dominator, **Sarah Crofts** headed out across the Bolivian altiplano on the way to Chile and a plane to Sydney.*

Having done all that I wanted in Potosi, the world's highest city, I headed for my last stop in Bolivia, the town of Uyuni and the Salar de Uyuni to the west, a 2000-square-kilometre plain of unbroken salt and transient lakes trapped between two longitudinal ridges of the Andes.

The ride down from Potosi was brilliant: a pretty good road and ever-changing terrain. After the initial mountain greenness, the land transformed into parched desert with many dried-up riverbeds. The sun shone bright and harsh and it became difficult to spot changes in the road conditions. I hit a couple of huge potholes and occasionally ploughed into deep soft sand. maintaining a steady 70kph. Despite one extremely hairy tank slapper, I arrived intact.

Uyuni is the strangest gringo town I've ever come across; the last immigration point before Chile, 400km away. On the edge of the Salar, it's the starting point for jeep tours through the salt desert to the Chilean border. As a consequence it's full of *gringos* but, windswept and dusty, Uyuni remains barely more inhabited than a ghost town. As I pulled in I had to stop and ask someone just to be sure I'd arrived in the right place.

It would have been fantastic to ride across the Salar but I knew at this time of year there was still a lot of water. I'd also heard a couple of horror stories of tours getting lost or stuck for days at a time. There was even talk of five tourists who had died after getting stuck.

So the original plan was to follow a tour but I decided against this when I realised just how tough conditions were. Although I couldn't ride right through the Salar, I certainly wanted to check it out but it was a hard job finding anyone to take a one-day tour as most gringos head on to the Chilean border. Eventually Oren (a guy I'd met) and I managed to blag our way onto a jeep after a couple of people dropped out.

And it was worth it as the Salar is just amazing, it's like driving across a sea of salt. Without a cloud in the sky, the expanse of white and blue seems to stretch to infinity. We spent a brilliant day speeding across in a convoy of jeeps swapping stories with a couple of cool Ozzie girls. When we returned the jeeps that had been so clean that morning were crusted with white salt. I was relieved not have taken the Dommie through – God knows what all that salt would've done to the engine.

The following morning Oren and I prepared for the ride to Laguna Colorada – in the middle of the desert halfway to Chile. We'd arranged to meet another traveller, Rino, to continue celebrating his birthday which was turning into a three-day affair. He promised there would a warm welcome and a bottle of rum waiting for us.

I'd heard more than I wanted to about this route through the desert. We asked all the drivers and guides we could find for information and most were astonished when they discovered we were without maps or GPS. We were given the names of a few villages and told to take a slightly different route to the jeep tours which would join the main route about 70km north of Laguna. The most consistent piece of information we were given was follow the most used track at all times. After loading up ten litres of spare gas and visiting Immigration and Customs we set off.

We'd been told it was 250km to Laguna Colorada, so we felt sure we'd be there by nightfall. The first 50km were pretty good but, you guessed it, the road soon deteriorated. Finally I was riding in a deep sand-filled rut with another rut filled with rubble running alongside. One spare fuel can ruptured and I was amazed to find I'd already used four litres of fuel. We rode separately as usual, mainly because Oren was faster, but also because of the huge dust clouds on these kinds of roads.

After a particularly deep river crossing I met an overland truck coming towards me. Grateful for an opportunity to rest my jarred body, I stopped and asked for a few directions. Basic instructions were to follow the biggest track until a small airfield, then turn left. Alas, I forgot to ask how far it was to this vital landmark.

Eventually I came to the airfield – a strange sight indeed in the middle of this mountainous desert. Preparing to turn left as instructed, I was surprised to spot Oren approaching from behind. He'd taken a wrong turn and arrived at an impassable river so had turned back. It was lucky the river was so deep otherwise he would've carried on regardless to God knows where. Our only pointers were to keep heading west and stay on the most used track.

I sat down and lit up a ciggie whilst wondering how I was going to get out of this one. Oren was miles ahead by now A siren wailed on the ridge behind me and a squadron of hungry vultures was mobilised.

After making the left turn once again, Oren sped off. The track was becoming more and more sandy and now, to make matters worse, hilly too. As I rounded a right-hander going downhill I glanced up to see a beautiful lagoon ahead. The front tyre twisted in a sand-filled rut barely wider than the tyre itself and I set off on another trip over the bars. Hadn't done that for a while. As the bike went over my second fuel reserve split, though I managed to save about three precious litres. Then I set about picking the Dommie up but just couldn't do it. It was jammed into the grass verge and I didn't have the strength to heave it out.

So I sat down and lit up a ciggie whilst wondering how I was going to get out of this one. Oren was miles ahead by now and I'd seen no-one for quite a while. I'd lost my water bottle, too, and the sun was beating down fiercely. A siren wailed on the ridge behind me and a squadron of vultures was mobilised.

After my nicotine hit, I felt a little better and set about unloading the bike. I didn't exactly turn into the Incredible Hulk but eventually managed to get it up and set off again. After passing the lagoon with barely a glance at the flamingos, I noticed a tiny sign indicating a right turn for Alota, the village where we were hoping to get gas. I also knew that this is where Oren would wait for me. Taking the turn meant leaving the track altogether and driving straight across the empty desert.

By now I was on the altiplano and could see for miles, and as far as I could see there was no evidence of human life ever having been here, never mind a town. After a moment's panic I decided to go straight on. I kept riding for what seemed like hours, having somehow persuaded myself that Alota was only about 30 clicks away, but the further I went the more worried I got.

Eventually I saw a guy pushing a bicycle towards me and almost in tears of relief I came to a stop alongside him.

'Hola señor, Villagio Alota por favor?'.

'Si. Diez minuto, es por alli,' he pointed.

And he told me he'd seen Oren at the town too. Half an hour later the town suddenly appeared before me and I was never so grateful to see a place or a person as the gas 'house' with Oren waiting there. After paying a fortune for five litres and exchanging stories of how scared we'd been, we decided to stay the night here. It had taken six hours to get this far and now we were being told Laguna Colorada was another 150km. We knew Rino would be worried about us but decided it was better to be safe than sorry.

We set the alarm clock for a time I never even knew existed and huddled under blankets for a very cold night in a tiny *hospedaje* after spending the afternoon playing football with the local kids. Well, Oren played whilst I spectated, as we were at around 4000m and I was in no mood to go running up and down the street after a ball!

Six am the following day found us astride two frozen bikes as the sun crawled out of bed like a hungover student. We wheeled them into the warming rays and waited for the bikes to defrost a little. Eventually the Dommie cranked up but Oren's XT needed a push.

There were two roads we could take, unfortunately the most travelled route involved a very deep river crossing and, as we'd left our snorkels and flippers in Mexico, we opted for the more obscure route. Once again we were faced with multiple tracks as well as deep sand, huge rocks and lots of twisty hills to aid our concentration. In a couple of places Oren left arrows in the sand where he had chosen one track over another but most of the time we just followed the instructions the villagers had given us: head west, keep the snow-capped mountain on your right and bear left at the lagoon. Pretty simple instructions and four hours later we arrived at the super highway that was the main jeep route.

Across the altiplano scores of tracks lay before us. We were finally able to get some speed up and I even managed to keep Oren in sight most of the time. We passed through yet more mind-blowing scenery and had lots of photo opps which conveniently doubled up as ciggie stops for me.

As we sped towards Laguna Colorada the sand got deep in places but I was doing pretty OK until I caught sight of the lake. A slight wobble on the front end saw me re-enact my practised endo routine. Dusting myself down I dutifully followed it with the unloading, heaving up and reloading routine and finally arrived at the refuge beside the lake where the tour group had spent the previous night.

I'd been counting on getting gas here but as usual had been mis-informed. With no gas to be had there was no choice but to continue and keep my fingers crossed for a tailwind and a returning jeep.

I wasn't disappointed and managed to buy ten litres from a bunch of tourists coming up from Chile. For once on my travels, I found someone who wasn't too pleased to be paid in dollars though he sold me what I needed however grudgingly. Back on the road we passed geysers and hot springs but resisted the urge to soothe our tired bones. Pressing on, the road actually got a lot better and by 4pm we were at Laguna Verde just seven clicks from Chile.

Arriving at the frontier we stopped to make sure all our documents were in order. The guard was surprised to see us and slapped us on the back a few times. When I asked him how far to San Pedro, our destination that night, he smiled and told us 45 minutes. Well, we knew it was about 45km not minutes and he must have seen the doubt on my face. His smile got even wider as he told us it was tarmac all the way. We were overjoyed and started dancing around hugging each other and him. Lovely liquorice-smooth tarmac, the stuff of dreams!

I brought the full force of my confused dirty blonde routine into play and feigned complete confusion with a well-practised stupid but pretty smile!

A few clicks later we found our tarmac and jumped off the bikes to dance around a bit more. The road was good, straight and downhill all the way dropping from 4500m to 2000m in a freewheeling frenzy of cooking brakes. Good job too because once I was up at speed again the bike stalled. I coasted along for five minutes before hitting the ignition. Nothing. *Nada*. So I coasted all the way down at 110kph before finally grinding to a halt on the flat. I switched everything, including the gas, off and back on again and all was well. Electrics are, and will remain, a mystery to me.

On the outskirts of San Pedro we encountered Chilean Customs – quite probably the nastiest bunch I'd met on the whole trip. Immigration demanded proof of funds and Customs made me unpack all my boxes. Eventually they let us through after a few pointed remarks about Pinochet. I brought the full force of my confused dirty blonde into play and feigned complete confusion with a well-practised stupid but pretty smile!

Finally arriving at the village square we set about finding our pre-arranged *hostal* – you'd think it would be easy in a place that small but we gave up after half an hour. We eventually found a place that looked OK and pulled in, only to have Rino come running out of the shower with a big wet welcome hug. I was exhausted and on a complete high after having made it and we ended up in a bar sitting around a campfire (inside the bar!) getting pleasantly drunk, he having already seen off some of 'our' rum from the night before.

The following day was spent in the sun and preparing to say goodbye to Oren who was heading back into Bolivia (via a proper road) to sell the XT. Rino and I were both heading for Santiago, however what would take him 24 hours by bus was going to take me four days. Waving Oren off was tough. The three of us had really had some great times in South America and riding with Oren had been so easy. But, as usual, we knew it was coming and in true form we said 'see ya later' with a laugh and a smile.

Afghanistan 1973

US motorcycle journalist **Clement Salvadori** *looks back at one of his earliest two-wheel adventures in Afghanistan, when CV carbs and disc brakes were cutting edge but the challenges and rewards of adventure motorcycling were still the same as today.*

'Why do you come to Afghanistan?' the sweaty-faced, middle-aged Immigration official asked. He stared at me over the top of his glasses, sucking purposefully at his cigarette.

Why does one come to Afghanistan? It was on the way to somewhere else. I was taking the Great Hippie Highway, stretching for some 4000 miles between Istanbul and Kathmandu. The late Sixties and early Seventies were the heyday of this Asian 'Route 66', with the long-haired youth of Europe and North America going to the East to find – whatever.

'I'm on my way to Pakistan,' I said, 'merely passing through.'

'Good! Enjoy your visit.' He slammed a stamp down on my passport.

That morning I had come from the Iranian city of Meshad, crossing the high, dry and very cold desert to the frontier, to spend the requisite several hours at the border. This artificial line of national demarcation had been arbitrarily drawn in the sand some hundred years before, and gradually a sentry box had grown into a town. Bureaucrats and police and soldiers provided a semi-transient, financially stabilizing population, but the bedrock was the merchants who sold food and clothing, and the smugglers who exist along any international frontier. The price of camels, oranges, auto parts and a thousand other items varied from one side of the border to the other, and good businessmen were quick to take advantage of these economic vagaries. As were officials who were willing to turn their heads ... in order to line their pockets.

There were also the shysters who preyed on the unwary. At one time the country bumpkins had been ignorant Iranis and Afghanis, but of late the Western innocents had provided extraordinarily good pickings. Many excuses could be found to delay the traveller a few days, even weeks, all of which meant profits for the hoteliers, the restaurateurs and moneychangers.

The key to minimising unpleasantness at a border crossing is to know what is expected. I had my paper ducks all in a row: passport, visa, vaccination certificate, proof of ownership of my BMW R75/5, international driver's license, and a wad of travellers' cheques. The only thing I lacked was Afghani insurance, and for $10 the office next to Immigration sold me a two-week policy, a very minor shakedown in the larger scheme of things.

Border towns often have their own particular fascination, but not this one. I left in mid-afternoon and crossed the hundred sun-blasted miles to the oasis city of Herat. It had blossomed in the 15th century and decayed in the 17th.

To one side was the Old Town, where things had not changed much in fifteen or twenty generations. Narrow alleys led into the warren, each occupation an open door: cobblers, butchers, gunsmiths, greengrocers, cloth merchants, tobacconists, saddlemakers. Every one was lord of his little domain, with a retinue of small boys to do his bidding, to sweep the shop, carry messages, fetch tea. The only real indication of the 20th century were the electric light bulbs and the lengths of wire running overhead.

But city planners had been at work a century ago, and I was headed into the New Town along a broad, tree-lined avenue, backed by a number of buildings which served as the local hotels. The two-storeyed versions were high-rises, exceeded in height only by a dozen minarets scattered around the city.

The long-haired, low-budget tourists had created a considerable economic stir in the place. It was the first town along the Hippie Highway in which one could buy and ingest as much hashish and marijuana as one wished without much fear of government (in the form of police) reprisals. A lot of stoned freaks got this far and no further. Anyone who had $400 could stay happily zonked for a year, room and board included.

...he reached down and brought forth a crunched-up piece of newspaper, spread it out, and showed me a large chunk of hashish.

My hotel, the New Super Behzar Garden Hotel, had an enclosed courtyard where the motorcycle could sit unmolested, the youthful concierge cheerfully indicating that I should ride across the shiny tiles of the lobby. At $1 a night for a room it was one of the higher-priced hostelries in town. That meant it had more of a transient crowd, as the low-bucks rip-heads were mostly at the $3 a week dives. The place was clean, always a consideration in this milieu, with the floor swept and the sheets reasonably white, if a little ragged. A pond was shaded by a large tree, and several European travellers were sitting in chairs industriously writing in their journals. A journal was as essential as a passport on this route, although I must admit I failed miserably in my effort.

Journal writing is a discipline which does not seem to lend itself to my travelling. I've met camel-riders on safari, trekkers in the Andes, libertines in Thailand, all with a carefully-kept journal in the bag. Myself, I end up with a thick notebook with a long entry at the start, a short one or two afterwards, and then page after page of brief notes, names and addresses, recommendations of places to stay and to see, phrases heard or read, the little bits and pieces which serve to open the correct filing drawers of the mind.

However, this shorthand works for me, which is why I can recall the name of the hotel. The main street was partially paved, and the local transport of choice were pony-powered carts and a few bicycles. On the nearest corner was a curio shop, obviously established to cater to the Euro-trade.

In the window were hand-wrought saddles, marvellously ornamented bits of harness, knives, swords, muzzle-loaders, hammered tin lanterns, ceramic dishes, artifacts of a different era.

The gentleman behind the counter, a suitably hook-nosed, rascally-looking devil, was acquiring the abandoned pieces of common culture as his countrymen moved into the age of internal-combustion engines, automatic rifles, and plastic utensils. I poked about, and the proprietor leaned on a glass case, smoking Marlboros, sizing up his customer.

As I moved closer, admiring the aged prayer rugs hanging from the wall, he reached down and brought forth a crunched-up piece of newspaper, spread it out, and showed me a large chunk of hashish. 'No thanks', I said. He scrunched the paper back up and stuffed it under the counter, then beckoned me to come into the back room. A small armoury was hanging from the walls, leaning in the corners, lying on boxes. British Enfield 303s, American Garands, Belgian FNs, shotguns, and the ubiquitous Soviet-design AK-47 assault rifle, Webley revolvers, US Army issue .45 caliber automatics, and pistols I had never seen before.

'You want?' he asked. 'No,' I said, picking up a Sten gun, compliments of some British arsenal.

'Cheap,' he said, noting what I had in my hand. True, I thought, wondering who would want a weapon whose accuracy was limited to some 12 feet. It probably got a good deal of use in later years.

My Swiss Army knife would have to do if ever I needed to defend myself or my possessions. Another motorcyclist was at the hotel, Kenny from Detroit. He had fled his hometown two steps ahead of some irate business competitors, gotten on a flight to Germany and bought himself a BMW. His vague appreciation of geography, remembering the two-dimensional maps in his school textbook, was that if he headed east long enough, eventually he would get home. For a while we rode together.

> **He'd fled Detroit two steps ahead of some irate business competitors, and bought himself a BMW in Germany ...and if he headed east long enough, eventually he'd get home.**

He was a marvellous travelling companion, never harried, always patient, willing to overcome any problem. He never despaired, never lost his temper. In many respects he was an innocent abroad, but as an innocent who had been raised in Murder City, USA, nobody ever put anything over on him.

We went to Pardees Restaurant for dinner, not quite what one would expect to find recommended in a Michelin guide, but the local hot spot. The dining-room was thickly carpeted and the tables were arranged around the edge, everybody sitting against the wall. Mutton stew poured over rice was the popular dish, but a variety of vaguely Western dishes were also available. The distaff side of a French couple was earning room and board by working in the kitchen, turning out omelettes and steaks and anything else the local market could provide the makings for. Her boyfriend slumped in the corner by the tape recorder, alternating The Grateful Dead with Edith Piaf. Kenny and I plotted our next move.

Three roads fanned out from Herat, one dirt stretch went 400 miles northeast to Mazar i Sharif; it was considered to be of tactical importance and permission to travel it had to be granted by the authorities. A second, rougher road went east to the lakes of Band-i-Amir and the Buddhist temples at Bamian; a Land Rover couple staying at the hotel said we'd have to carry enough gas to cover at least 250 miles. Plus the road was a real sump-buster, where more ground clearance than we had was highly advisable. Scratch that one; neither of us were interested in roughing it. The third route went along good concrete highway south-east to Kandahar, then up to Kabul.

We decided we would try for the Mazar i Sharif road. I wanted to visit Balkh on the way and Kenny had no preference. In the morning we presented our reasonably well-groomed selves at the police station, where the chap in charge was quite cheerful and talkative. Of course he dreamed of owning a motorcycle like ours and sadly showed us the decrepit Russian two-stroke he had to put up with. He would very much like to give us permission to travel this road, but first he would have to ask Kabul and that might take a week. Or possibly two. And there was no guarantee that permission would be granted. Perhaps it would be better to go ourselves to Kabul to seek permission and then come back.

The Kandahar option looked best. But first we wanted to go and have a look-see at this forbidden road. We rode out of town to the roadblock where the soldier in charge was happy to let us through if we left our passports with him. There were four of us on this afternoon spin. My passenger was a Carolina woman on her way to seek spiritual truth in India, and Kenny had a hitch-hiking Australian who was staying at the Super Bezhar.

Afghani landscape tends to the austere. The well-graded road travelled along a broad alluvial stretch, then began to climb into the mountains. After we motored along for a while, my passenger pointed off to the east. Look, a village! More than a mile from the road was a collection of roofs, practically invisible against the hilly backdrop except for t h e

unnatural right angles of the buildings. We had no destination other than to see something slightly different and this perhaps was a fitting goal. No road led that way, but with the motorcycles we felt we could find a way. It wasn't easy, but in half an hour we had arrived close to these brown mud walls. No broad avenue, no street, not even a lane led into the village, the bumpy trail sliding in between two houses.

Shy heads were poking over the rooftops, catching quick glances of us, then retreating. A faint cry could be heard, obviously alerting people further along. There was nobody on our little alley, only brown walls and small closed doors. Push on. We arrived in what amounted to the village common, a small square with one small leafy tree. No store, no café, no movie theatre. We stopped, parked the bikes and got off. It was hot; we doffed our helmets and jackets. We were a colourful foursome; I had a beard, Kenny a long blonde ponytail, the Aussie a bright red Fu Manchu mustache, and bare-faced Cass an obvious bosom. Within minutes the little square was filled with people, while others looked down from the rooftops. Old people and young children were on the ground; women of a sexual age, enclosed as tightly as in a bank vault, peered through veils from above. The working men were obviously off somewhere, working. Nobody spoke any language any of us could communicate in. A white-haired man took over the task of moderating this meeting.

We indicated thirst. Orders were given. Four bottles of warm, orange-coloured pop appeared on a tray, a young boy presenting them to us. It was an interesting stand-off. I was accustomed to children fingering the motorcycle. Here they only stared and more at us than at the machines. The line was clearly drawn, with four of us and two motorcycles on one side, several hundred villagers on the other, not only surrounding us, but looking down on us. We tried to come to some sort of understanding. The map meant nothing to them. After several tries at different pronunciations, the white-haired man understood Herat, and proceeded to inform the

crowd that that was where we were from. A conge-nial sigh

of recognition came from the audience. But no open arms, no sign of fraternity, no welcoming us into the life of the village. I felt the opposite was true.

Nobody wanted us around; obviously the idea was to get us out of there before the men-folk came home from the fields and the herds. Here were not only four strangers, but one was a woman who wore tight jeans and had obviously never read the Koran. Our presence was more than a tad disturbing to the local honchos and life proceeded better without such interruptions.

We took the hint. With empty soda bottle in hand I approached the boy with the tray and proffered what I thought (by Herat standards) to be a suitable amount for the four sodas. He looked at the old white-beard beside him, who nodded, and he took the money. Obviously such flatlanders as ourselves were not to be privy to the fabled Moslem hospitality. And I was just as glad. This was not a remote town, we were not in need, and we were leaving. Pay up and get out.

Afghanis lead a rough life, even before the Russians prompted the long war. If you were strong, you were okay; if you were weak, somebody smacked you and took what you had. No possible good could come of these strangers being in town. We shook hands quite formally with the patriarch and loaded up. The white-beard directed us, not down the alley we had come, but one at right angles to it. It was slightly wider, but we still poked along in first gear. The rooftops as we left were lined with people, god knows how many. And behind us the narrow lane had absolutely filled with children, trotting along behind, having as much excitement as they had probably had in six months or more. The children were yelling, the roof-toppers were crying out. I felt rather like the British Expeditionary Force attempting to flee Afghanistan in 1842.

Two days later Kenny and Cass and I left for Kabul, via the Desert of Death, Kandahar, and Ghazni. At Kabul we checked into the Friends' Hotel, well known among the travelling set. It was a converted mansion surrounded by ill-kept gardens, where rooms went for a dollar a night. Its greatest attraction was the shower room with a wood-fired water heater, so it was toasty warm and had as much hot water as you cared to heat. The restaurant served hamburgers and apple pie.

I spent a miserable night falling through space, desperately reaching out to passing stars to stop myself. It was a #1 bad trip.

Kenny disappeared into the kitchen one day. He liked the local hashish, but found that smoking it in the short, fat pipes called chillums, as was the local habit, was tearing his throat up. The way around that was to ingest it in food, and what could be better than a chocolate cake. The two fat lady cooks were absolutely entranced by watching this ponytailed foreigner whipping together his ingredients, pouring it into a pan and popping it in the oven. I licked the bowl which seemed to be a good idea at the time. So good that I followed it up with a large slice of cake when it was baked. Bad idea. I was eating a hamburger when the drug took full hold of me, and my last memory of the hamburger was clutching it in my hand and being entirely incapable of taking a bite. After half an hour of watching me hold this hamburger immobile in front of my face, my friends decided I'd had it and led me off to bed. I spent a miserable night falling through space, desperately reaching out to passing stars to stop myself. It was a #1 bad trip.

In the morning Ken and I left some gear behind and headed north to visit the ancient city of Balkh. Ken had never heard of the place but was happy for any excuse for a ride, while I still had the visions my history teacher had instilled of this legendary political and commercial centre.

Leaving Kabul and rolling northwards we went through some of the more fertile land in the country, planted with apricot orchards and millet. A few trucks were on the highway, many horses and camels off on either side. We went higher and higher, heading up for the Saleng Pass, an 11,000-foot vault to get over the Hindu Kush and onto the great Asia steppes that stretched all the way to the Arctic Circle ... though it was a good way off, some 2500 miles.

I began to appreciate what semi-sophistication in the technical world had done. Kenny had manually controlled carburettors on his 600cc BMW; twist the throttle, the slide went up, and gas and air rushed in. My 750, on the other hand, had early versions of the CV carburettor, in which my throttle controlled only a butterfly valve that allowed the air to enter, and the mixing process was up to the forces of nature, which were somewhat different at sea level and at over 10,000ft. Nature and altitude were winning, and Kenny, with a smaller, less powerful bike, was running away from me. I ended up idling over the pass, all my engine would pull.

The long ride down the northern slopes was stupendous beyond belief. I try to use these exaggerations advisedly. After switch-backing down the mountain, the road entered a broad valley and continued dead straight north. The valley narrowed, a gap appeared, the road went over a little hump and down into a slightly smaller valley. And on and on and on, each valley decreasing in size. No towns, no villages, no habitations, an occasional herdsman with a flock of sheep, only sparse grass, rocky walls and glimpses of a small river to our right. Finally we came into a valley which was no more than a hundred yards wide, steep cliffs going high on either side. No traffic, straight road, we were running about 70mph side by side, and the road was headed right into a solid wall.

I had visions of being an outlaw trying to escape a posse and running into a box canyon. We were headed for a dead end and looking at the sheer walls closing in we figured we must have screwed up somewhere and taken a wrong turn some way back down the track. Slowly the road merged with the riverbank, both heading for the blank spot ahead. The dark rocks were now looming above us, and I started looking for the brakes. Then the narrowest of cuts appeared, no more than 15ft wide, and a low overhang to our right. We went through the cut, the river ran under the overhang.

And then we were out, onto the steppes. Two thousand miles of golden grassy plain lay before us. The road veered west and a brilliant red autumn sun sat low on the horizon.

We spent the night in Mazar-i-Sharif, a commercial centre whose only real reason for existence was its proximity to what was then the USSR. Anything that was made across the Oxus River was superior to goods made in Afghanistan for the simple reason that nothing was manufactured in Afghanistan; it was the only prime market for Soviet exports. And Soviet seconds; leaky inner tubes and trousers with legs of different lengths were major items on the local market.

Balkh was a city once on a par with ancient Babylon, a Zoroastrian and Buddhist centre, but on the decline since being sacked by Genghis Khan in the 13th century and Tamerlane in the 14th. A dusty brown landscape stretched to either side, very flat. Trees appeared, and I realised that the brown in front was not just horizon, but melting mud walls, the crests worn smooth by wind and rain. On the north side an abandoned caravanserei was slowly rejoining the earth from whence its mud bricks came.

As we stopped for a closer look at the wall, an elderly man with a cane came forward, speaking a rather old-fashioned English. Would we like a guide? No, we would not, but we got one anyway. He was full of wonderful misinformation, mostly concerning Alexander the Great, who our instructor emphatically believed had indeed wintered here on his way to India in 329 BC. But I should not be critical; history books can be wrong. To prove his point, our guide reached into a baggy pocket and took out a small coin. He stated convincingly that he had it found as a young man while tilling the fields and if we wished it could be ours. It was a Bactrian Greek coin, or probably a reasonable facsimile thereof, and since the price we negotiated was about 25 cents, I felt that I, too, would believe that this had fallen out of Great Alex's pocket all those years ago.

But as for the romance that my high-school teacher had given the place, all second-hand, I might add, from books he had read, I found Balkh rather dull. The dirty 20th-century streets had no charm, nor did the inhabitants. I preferred to leave the images from Robert Byron's *Road to Oxiana* undisturbed.

We returned to Kabul. On my last night I went down to Chicken Road (where a poultry market had once existed), and settled into the cushions at Sigi's, a tea shop full of hip travellers, progressive jazz, and occasionally even members of the Afghani elite. Out in the garden was a giant chessboard, with wooden chessmen five feet high. An English-speaking Kabuli asked me if I played. I did, albeit at a rather rudimentary level. Plus I was used to plotting my strategy on a conventional board, where all players were in easy sight.

My opponent was a doctor, worked with the Afghani Olympic team, and had studied in England. He asked me what my profession was; I told him I was travelling. I called him Doctor, he addressed me as Traveller. It was easier to talk knowing we were merely strangers on a chessboard, that we would never meet again. As we roamed around the board (knight to rook three) we discussed the state of the world (pawn to bishop four), the future of Afghanistan (queen to knight three), the problems of a Westernism versus Islam (bishop to king four), and the politics of maintaining neutrality while living next to the Russian bear (rook to knight four).

'Russia would never want Afghanistan,' said the doctor, 'because there is nothing here for them. And because they would have to kill every single Afghani.' He was wrong, but he was right. Perhaps as a portent of the future, I avoided a total loss by provoking a stalemate.

Viva Colombia!

*Despite grim warnings about his life expectancy, Scotsman **Ken McLean** had himself a fiesta while riding his Triumph around Colombia.*

In some ways I felt like I was halfway there, trying to get to sleep in the Panamanian heat. I had spent the last nine months riding down from Nova Scotia with one concern at the back of my mind: how to get the bike from Panama City to South America safely, cheaply and without a carnet.

After some deliberation I'd decided to go to Colombia despite the promise of murder, kidnap and abduction by drug *cartelistas*. I was assured that if they didn't get me the terrorists or the police would – and all this from people who'd never set foot in the place. From those who had, the story was vividly different and one I much preferred. I have a favourite memory from San Salvador, the once war-torn capital of Guatemala, where they were surprised I'd scraped through Mexico in one piece! Not only can the grass be greener, but the streets more deadly on the other side of the hill (or border).

As is so often the case, challenging obstacles turn out to be walks in the park, and I could fly my Thunderbird cheaply and easily to Medellin in a couple of days. All I had to do was pay the money and deliver the bike to the cargo terminal with the tank empty. This done, I went for a beer with a few friends I'd made in Panama where I was reminded of where I'd heard of Medellin before, and my companions took a strange delight in exaggerating stories of Pablo Escobar, the FBI and a general state of lawlessness to be found there. It took a good few beers to settle my nerves and restore my courage for the flight the next day. Straight in at the deep end.

I touched down in Medellin with a throbbing head and as it was late on a Friday, would have to wait till Monday morning to get my bike. A weekend to kill (or be killed) in Medellin, I booked an upmarket hotel and a taxi straight from the airport. Everyone I'd seen so far seemed dressed in smart Italian clothes and looked very sophisticated. Obviously I was missing the true picture.

I got talking to the lads working in the hotel about the impending arrival of my motorbike (my Spanish had become quite good when it came to bikes) but by 2am sitting on the back of a DT125 spinning around the city from one salsa bar full of beautiful girls to another full of even more beautiful girls my conversational range was narrowing dramatically. I couldn't believe my first night in this country was as

A weekend to kill or be killed in Medellin...

far from my expectation as it could be! The people were so friendly, I wasn't a gringo curiosity, they were just genuinely nice people and there was a feeling of security in the small hours I had missed in many parts of Central America.

On the Monday morning at the freight carriers, I was told I had to pay what amounted to $100 additional storage and handling charges, which I refused point blank. Demanding to see the manager I said I would wait until my bike was released. Colombian women grow old with extreme grace and when the manageress asked me if I'd like a Colombian coffee whilst I waited. I said 'yes', 'That'll be $100 please' she replied, I knew I was going to have to be careful not to fall in love with this country!

My friends in Medellin had advised me where the risky areas of their country were (which of course didn't include their own backyard!) so I set off north towards Cartagena with a twitch in my saddle. After my sparkling introduction I was determined to see this country in full.

'Amigo, we are collecting money for the local hospital and ambulance which is funded by public donation would you care to...' 'HELL YEAH!!'

I knew my bike was up to the challenge, as in Guatemala and Costa Rica the T-Bird had gone head to head in a shootout with a friend on an XR600 and only come second! There was no need to stick to the mountain roads and certainly no reason to leave them! Biking heaven I thought, until I swung round a corner and there were two groups of people on either side of the road with a thick rope stretched between them. My heart shot into the red zone as I calculated my options. I decided to slow down and tried to concentrate on keeping my last meal where it should be. As the front wheel rolled up to the rope, with me ready to drop the clutch and blast my way through, one of the men approached.

'Amigo, we are collecting money for the local hospital and ambulance which is funded by public donation would you care to...'

'HELL YEAH!!' and after much shaking of hands and slapping of backs I was on my way feeling both stupid and relieved but now ready for anything!

Cartagena is described in certain guides as the most beautiful city in South America. I'm not yet qualified to dispute this but it would take something special to come close. And it's not just the girls who are beautiful, some of the old town's not so bad either! I can't remember too much about it to be perfectly honest, after being kidnapped and coerced by a Canadian fella on holiday from Lima into being his drinking buddy for a few days. A task which would be repeated in Lima on my way south!

In order to get my liver back in shape for the promised re-match in Lima, I left and headed into the Sierra Nevada and more fantastic roads, then down to Mompos, an area locked in some time warp, which included their road building programme!

In a tiny place called Santa Ana I was lucky enough to get there the week of the travelling circus; every night a different show. As I walked in the Big Top I felt like the freak as the whole place

> **...El Gonzo the Amazing Knife Thrower staggered on and requested a volunteer... the whole place yelled as one: 'Gringo!'**

stopped and turned to stare at me. But once I'd taken my seat and the amazing rubber woman (who looked remarkably like the girl I'd just paid to get in) and the miniature unicorn (a goat with a horn strapped to its head) had hit the stage, I felt I'd blended in and was ready to enjoy the show. Things went well until El Gonzo the Amazing Knife Thrower staggered on and requested a volunteer for his next demonstration of daring and skill the whole place yelled as one: 'Gringo!'

As he drunkenly turned and tried to focus on me, a young hero dived from the crowd and offered to put his life on the line for the delight of the audience. I wasn't disappointed, after all there wasn't even anyone there to take my photo! Anyway, the lad survived with his manhood intact and deserves all the medals going for this selfless act of bravery. This type of entertainment can't be found in the UK and would be sneered at as hammy, but was better than anything I've ever seen on wide-screen TV and a brilliant laugh.

If I'd known how the roads were going to be, I wouldn't have tried to take the route alongside the river to El Banco. But it always seems worse to turn back and repeat what you've just ridden through, so on I went through the first of what turned out to be four river crossings.

Pulling up at a deeper-than-Triumph river, I hadn't realised I was on the ferry (planks of wood over oil drums and a canoe with a small outboard), till the chap pulled the cord to start it! Getting off was a nightmare as there was no ramp, just a two-foot drop into mud! Luckily motorcycles were a novelty and volunteers were never far away to help this crazy gringo. The kids seemed to take great delight in out-running each other when it came to getting up to their knees in mud.

Getting back onto the asphalt to Bucaramanga was a real delight and lead to further surprises. There are rarely travellers in this part of the country and hence no Internet cafés, but the local arts and drama college had a computer I could use. Those who don't know me need to be told that I'm not exactly Brad Pitt in a ripped wet T-shirt, but *Caramba!* the place was a spider's web where all the spiders were beautiful Colombian dancers practising for a folkloric festival. I was invited to be their guest and had the unenviable task of deciding who to take on the back of my bike!

For all these years I'd wondered what it would be like to have Paul Newman looks, well my five minutes of fame let me know it must be hell for the man! The Colombian culture is as rich as it is varied and I was mesmerised by the beauty of the dance. It was hard to leave Bucaramanga, but somehow it didn't seem real and I wanted to leave before I woke up.

Back on the road and by now I was used to 'racing' DT125's and was pursued into a petrol station by some lads desperate to admire the 'Bird. The taxes levied on large engined motorcycles in Colombia puts them out of reach to all but the most wealthy.

We were all headed for Villa de Leiva, only the DT-ers were off to watch Colombia v Argentina in the Copa De America. Among us we had enough of each other's language to have a laugh, helped along by the local *aguardiente* firewater. I vaguely remember Colombia going three up and me having to sing *Flower of Scotland* at the top of my voice, much to the bar's delight. Not only was Colombia a brilliant country, but they can play football too... reminded me much of home.

Further on south the scenery quickly changed as I climbed through arid mountains towards Tunja. Cold and bleak, I was feeling miserable for the first time here when, sitting at a set of traffic lights, I heard someone shouting 'whataboutye ma man'; a fella from Belfast in the middle of the Colombian highlands! He was there as an English teacher so we had 'a crack' and I was back on my way with a new itinerary.

I arrived in Bogota, a huge but cold city (due to its altitude) despite being so close to the equator. Not surprisingly, I enjoyed the place very much, the people still friendly, and my area of town very bohemian and relaxed in character. Times are hard there at the moment, and at the weekend people just open up their houses as bars or restaurants. I hadn't realised this till I went to the bathroom of one café to find toothbrush, shampoo, razor, the lot, all around the sink! On closer inspection the furniture had just been rearranged and the stereo turned up.

Despite all this, the cold was driving me away and I'd heard that Cali was hot! hot! hot! And it was. My three days turned into three weeks, and I finally relented to the statement that Colombia is indeed a difficult country to travel around; for no reason other than the friendliness of the people.

It was here in Cali that I caught up with the latest political situation in the country. Apparently there had been an increase in counter guerrilla activity, and the army had killed a number of people over the previous weeks. I imagined my mum hearing this news and worrying even more than she normally does. I'd been quite oblivious to it all as most of the violence had taken place in the jungle, far from any roads or where any sensible traveller would go.

Undeterred, I headed south in the warmth for Tierradentro Park and its archaeological site. This area isn't considered the safest but I felt nothing there but the energy from the hills. I'm not a tree hugger but I can't deny the place was one of the most tranquil spots I've ever been. Two days on, through the rain and dirt roads cut through the jungle, I arrived in San Augustine, close to the Ecuadorian border.

I knew I would soon no longer be in Colombia. It would be a hard act to follow and I pledged to return one day. But I couldn't wait to discover what was round the next corner. I was just about to find out!

Roadside Encounters

*It's a big planet but a small world, especially if you're riding around the world on a R80GS for four years as **Peter Theuwissen** discovers.*

The best people to meet along the road are fellow travellers. And the very best are fellow bikers with whom you share so many experiences. It's amazing to discover how many people like myself left jobs, sold houses, gave up all kinds of luxury to choose life on the road. Everybody has his or her own motives to take off, but RTW bikers have so much in common that they usually become friends from the moment they meet.

I was planning to start my RTW trip alone. But it was a nice surprise to meet two fellow Dutchman willing to travel to West Africa at the same time. We took off a week before Xmas in 1996. Bart was a doctor with a Transalp, Alex was a mechanic with a BMW 650, and I was the most experienced traveller. No surprise then that Bart got sick, Alex had mechanic problems and yes, I got us lost more than once!

We met up with our first group of fellow long-distance bikers in Dahkla, Morocco. A bunch of German desert lovers with a friend in a car hauling their luggage. There was also a group of young Frenchmen on an organised tour. But the most peculiar guy was an Italian. Sometimes you meet people who run into problems all the time. Luigi was an example. Italians don't need an advance visa for Mauritania but the Moroccans refused to allow anyone without a visa to join the convoy to the border. Poor Luigi had to drive 2000km back to Rabat to apply for a visa.

A month later we met him again in a small village in Guinea. He was anxiously looking for gear oil. He told us about a night-time ride back to Dakar from the Guinea border because of a problem with Customs, and once in Guinea he hadn't managed to change money for days.

West Africa is not a easy part of the world to start a RTW-trip and I was glad to have companions to share the toughest moments. Bart flew back from

Conakry, and Alex a month later from Ouagadougou. Once alone I got sick for a week and left Burkina Faso on the last day of my visa to Ghana. There I met a very nice girl and had to decide for myself what this RTW business meant for me. I left after a week. The decision not to stay in Ghana for the rest of my life created the commitment to spur me on.

Driving on a busy highway into downtown Abidjan (Ivory Coast) I saw an overland biker coming from the other direction. Unfortunately it was not a place to stop and have a talk but the next day this guy found me. He was one of a group shipping their vehicles (two bikes and two cars) in a container to South Africa. He asked me to join them. In 1997 finding a way to cross Central Africa was very difficult so I joined the group.

Just after making the decision, Seiji and Harumi arrived on the camp-site, a very nice Japanese couple riding Honda XLR 250s. They were already three years on the road and like me were heading to South Africa then South America. They were determined to travel through Central Africa and were collecting all the necessary visas. We didn't use email at the time but decided to try to stay in contact and possibly ship together to Buenos Aires later.

In Durban the Abidjan group met again after the arrival of the container with our vehicles. A Swiss/Chilean couple and a German called Marcel were the fellow bikers. As in Ivory Coast it was a tricky affair with the Customs officers stamping our Carnet de Passages. Five different vehicles and five different nationalities. And worse still, most of the carnets were home-made! The girls at the harbour office also didn't know how to cope with the different exchange rates for charging the harbour taxes and instead of a few hundred dollars, most of us ended up paying only a few bucks.

Back at the hostel in Durban, I found a note from a German couple, Volker and Carola. We'd stayed for a week in the same hostel, but without our bikes we couldn't recognise each other as fellow world bikers. They were waiting for their bikes to arrive from Buenos Aires, having travelled through Australia and the Americas, and wanted to ride back home to Germany.

All the members of the shipping group went their own way leaving me the only one interested in going to Mozambique. Four months later I arrived at a camp-site in Nairobi on my birthday and before I even managed to park the bike Marcel said 'hello', followed by Seiji. And Carola and Volker were also camping there too!

Later on in Zimbabwe, I met Kenji Suzuki, already a few years on the road. He started his world tour in Chile and had met a nice girl there (as you do). In Japan he was famous among other bikers because he'd saved a million yen to make his RTW-trip. Unfortunately a few months after we met, he broke down in Kenya and decided to go back to Japan and marry his Chilean girlfriend.

Charlie's Honda in Cape Town is the best place in Africa to meet other overland bikers, especially when you work there on your bike to prepare it for the next leg. There was a Scottish guy, Kenny, on a very old Yamaha. He'd been through West Africa as well and told me about his difficult trip to Timbuktu. He had used fuel jerricans for drinking water: 'It tasted bad but it didn't kill me'.

But the biggest surprise was meeting a companion from my Asia trip two years before! During that time Jefim, who had ridden through Asia and Australia, went back home to make some money and decided to go to South Africa. After two weeks there he had an accident with the bike and went to Charlie's to look for parts. (Charlie's Honda was 'desperately' in the need of a guest book, so I made one. Don't forget to sign it when you are there!)

The deal with Seiji and Harumi to ship our bikes together to South America worked out well. They'd met another Japanese biker, Hiroto, who also wanted to go to Argentina. So we decided to ship our bikes in a container. Of course it would be a hassle to get our bikes out of the harbour in Buenos Aires, but we could share all the extra costs.

In Bahia Blanca (Argentina) I had electrical problems with the BM and had to spend a week at a camp-site. I pushed my bike the last few hundred metres to get it there. Because of heavy rain the owner offered me the restaurant to sleep in. He told me another biker had arrived a few days earlier, Peter from New Zealand on an KLR650. The next night he joined me in the restaurant to get out of the relentless rain.

A day later another biker arrived who Peter had met in Guatemala. Bruno was a Swiss guy who had ridden around the world through Russia, Asia, Australia and the Americas. He was the first biker I met who'd actually ridden in China. From Russia he went into Mongolia but was thrown out because of problems with Customs. From there he went by train to China. (The border officials didn't notice him bringing in a motorbike!) With only a stamp in his passport and no permit for the bike he rode around China for three months. To get out of the country was not so easy. At the border with Pakistan he had to bribe the Chinese guards. Still, he had achieved the near-impossible.

Going to Ushuaia is a 'must' for every world biker travelling in South America. In case you don't know, it's the southernmost tip of the American continent. Around Christmas it's the spot for an unofficial overland bikers' meeting. On my way south in February struggling along a tough muddy stretch, Jim from Australia suddenly appeared on a spotless Transalp. He mentioned an American couple he'd met in Ecuador, Dave and Sharon on BMWs, and was surprised to hear that I'd read about them on the Internet.

A few days later an American couple walked into the hostel I was staying in Ushuaia: the famous Dave and Sharon! They were on their honeymoon riding bikes around the world. Dave wanted to go to Africa, but Sharon told me she only was willing to go if Dave took her on his bike. Two years later Jim bought Sharon's bike and rode through Africa and shared Dave's dream.

Ishay from Israel was the next guy I met on a bike. He had ridden from New York to Ushuaia and sold his KLR650 a few months later in Buenos Aires. Fellow bikers are the most reliable source of information along the road. Ishay was at the end of his trip and gave me a lot of useful addresses.

Driving north from Ushuaia I didn't expect to see many more world bikers. But after meeting a Japanese biker on a Transalp one morning, I then met Keiji a few hours later. Both of us were rounding the same corner in opposite directions. Keiji was quick to jump off his bike, grab his video camera and circle around me asking questions: 'What's your name...'etc.

Not surprisingly we had some friends in common. In Peru he'd travelled for a while with Bruno and Ishay. He asked me about a Japanese couple he had lost contact with: Seiji and Harumi! He was very happy to hear they were still in Ushuaia. We decided to camp together. Japanese riders are famous for their cooking but all the stuff Keiji unloaded for dinner was amazing: beer, wine, fresh meat and vegetables and much more. The next morning Keiji made a phone call to the Japanese hostel in Ushuaia and spoke to his lost friends a week's ride away. Eight months later I met Keiji again in Venezuela.

Along the road I met quite a few German couples who'd shipped their bikes over to South America for a one-year trip. Detlef and Esther started on their Suzuki DR650 in Venezuela and rode through Brazil to Argentina and Chile before I met them on a camp-site in north-west Argentina. Incredibly, I was one of the first world bikers they'd met in six months and a few months later we met again in La Paz.

Frank and Ellen had shipped their bike to Buenos Aires and the cost of getting the bike out of the port was unbelievable. They took way too much gear and had no choice other than storing some of it. After a few months they decided to buy a second bike in Chile. To get the (illegal) paperwork done was a hell of a job and once on the road the driveshaft broke. To get a new one from Germany was expensive and time-consuming and other hassles made them decide to sell both bikes and continue on bicycles!

In Bolivia and Peru I travelled for three months with Martin from Munich on an R100GS. The first time we'd met was in Santiago, Chile, and after a few other encounters we were able to agree a route. Together we experienced the mud in the lowlands, the frightening Andean mountain roads and the incredible salt lake of Uyuni (see p.230)

In Cuzco, one of the most beautiful cities in South America, we went our separate ways. I changed hotels and soon met Jan from Holland on an old XT500. He's been coming back to South America every year for a five-week holiday. Every time he finds a different country to park the bike for a year. Resident in Canada, he invited me to stay on my way up to Alaska.

In Trujillo (Peru) there was Lars, a tall German student on a small Japanese bike. He was on a long trip too and had crossed Africa the year before like me. In Cape Town and then Buenos Aires he'd taken the time to fill out some missing parts of his education at the universities there. We decided to meet again in Quito around New Year.

Ecuador is the 'Malawi' of South America. Small, cheap and a country through which everybody has to pass. There was a Spanish guy, Gerardo, on a R1100GS driving from Alaska to Argentina. Every few months he went back to Madrid to see his wife and buy spare parts. The day I left Quito, I ran into two other bikers: a Swiss guy and an American named Paul. I gave them the address of the biker hostel 'Rincon the Castilla'. Lars was still there and emailed me later that he had met the Swiss guy before in the Namib desert.

On the Caribbean coast of Colombia I met some bikers who had bypassed the jungle of the Darien Gap by sea. Since the ferry went bust in 1998 most travellers have chosen to fly between Panama and Colombia and the price of taking the bike on the plane is reasonable. Without doubt it is also the fastest, safest and best way to go (see p.72) but some bikers take their chances on smuggler boats (see p.209). It's much cheaper but can be a long and risky trip. In Cartagena we heard about three Israeli bikers who had made their way down on a smuggler's boat.

At that time I was carrying a Finnish girl on the back. We were planning to drive to Bogota to take the plane to Panama City. But we ran into a American yacht owner who was looking for passengers to reach Panama by sea. We went to the yacht club to see his boat and it was a beauty. But what about taking a motorbike as well? No problem, we could tie it up against the mast. We decided to give it a try. The loading of the bike was not really difficult but securing it properly to the mast was not so easy.

The next afternoon we left the harbour but even before reaching the open sea the waves were so rough that we got sick and the only option was to head back to shore. The most scary thing was that the bike was banging against the mast with the ropes getting progressively looser. Three days later we tried again. We'd thought about cancelling the voyage and flying but how wonderful it could be to sail among Caribbean islands! My bike was not so fancy any more so I didn't worry about rust.

It turned out to be an exciting five-day trip and the night sailing was wonderful. In Colón it was impossible to arrange the correct Custom documents so there was no alternative but to put the bike ashore somewhere. It was only when trying to leave the country a few weeks later that things caught up with me.

In Central America we didn't meet a lot of world bikers. The first one was Grant, driving a Triumph Tiger and travelling on a Zimbabwean passport. He told us about the trouble he was running into every time he wanted to apply for a visa or wanted to cross a border, but when I met him in LA six months later he'd gotten American citizenship.

Another American biker was a rich guy from New York. He was driving a R1100GS packed with the most incredible stuff: laptop; diving gear (with the flippers on the side of the gas tank!), video equipment and fishing gear. In Antigua (Guatemala) we were surprised to see a look-alike of my bike on the patio of our hotel. Ed and Karen from England had bought the bike in Texas for a visit to Panama as part of their round the world trip using different kinds of transport.

On entering the States there were of course a lot of bikers but most of them had never crossed a border. Talking to them about my travels was weird, they didn't really understand what it was all about.

In Vancouver, at Jan's house, I caught up with Seiji and Harumi. After shipping our bikes to Buenos Aires we had met again (thanks to the Internet) in Santiago, La Paz, Cuzco and Bogotá. But this was the first time we were heading in the same direction. We rode together all the way to Anchorage in Alaska. Sharing riding in the rain the first few days, pitching our tents in the most beautiful spots and cooking our meals together.

Apart from another Japanese couple, we only met holiday bikers up north. In summer Alaska and western Canada are packed with bikers riding the Alaska and Dalton Highways up to Prudhoe Bay.

My original schedule was to continue to Russia after visiting Alaska but it was too late in the season so I changed my plans. However, Seiji and Harumi adopted the idea and shipped their bikes to Russia by plane. For them driving from Magadan to Vladivostok in Siberia was a perfect way to finish their five-year world tour.

In Colón it was impossible to arrange Custom documents so there was no alternative but to put the bike ashore somewhere. It was only when trying to leave the country a few weeks later that things caught up with me.

Some guys manage to get sponsors for a long trip. Nat from England was one of them. I met him on a remote road in Alaska. A week before someone on a ferry had asked me: 'Are you the guy driving from Alaska to Argentina and dedicating the journey to your father?' Nat had given an interview for a newspaper and was raising money for a health organisation his father initiated. A Honda Africa Twin with everything including roadside assistance had been supplied by sponsors.

Just after leaving Alaska I got an email from Paul, the guy I'd met just outside Quito. After driving to Ushuaia he had shipped the bike home but after getting back he set off to Alaska to complete the whole north-south route. Without seeing him, in the same week we'd managed to ride the famous and devastating Dalton Highway to Prudhoe Bay.

Back down in Oregon I met an English couple on a BMW R100GS with horror stories to tell. It took them five weeks to get all their paperwork done in Brisbane (Australia), in Malaysia a border official had stamped CANCELLED all over their carnet and they were once refused permission to board a plane because of a one-way ticket!

Anyway, after two years on the American continent I crated my bike and shipped it by freighter from LA to Sydney. During a few weeks on Pacific islands all I could do was write about the motorbikers of the world instead of meeting them. But in Australia I'm sure I'll see plenty of Japanese bikers on their small machines. They'll be useful contacts for my forthcoming visit to Japan. Eventually I plan to ride back to Holland through Siberia and eastern Europe. I'm sure I will meet a few more overland bikers wandering around. Nobody is alone for long, it's just a matter of joining the club! See you on the road.

The Village from Hell

While riding around southern Morocco, **Simon McCarthy** *took his GS on an adventurous excursion into the high passes of the Atlas.*

The Lonely Planet *Morocco* guide says that the trip through the Dades and Todra gorges is best done as part of a Land Rover safari, but they say that about a lot of trips, to stop backpackers wandering off, getting into trouble and suing LP. The road looked a bit small on the Michelin map, but studying it carefully I guessed it would be better than the desert piste I'd done a couple of days earlier.

So I rode up the Dades late that afternoon and camped at 7000ft, after meeting a postman at 6000ft on a 20-year-old Yamaha FS1E – the dream bike of every 16-year-old when I was at school. The gorge was impressive, with sheer walls that rise hundreds of metres; the setting sun picked out its contours and exposed the geology of the rolling hills above it – a bit like the Pennines with all the vegetation removed. The wind calmed down after sunset and I cooked up a horrible soya stew as I watched Orion's Belt emerge above the horizon. I made a plan for the next day: to see some nice ethnic villages, photograph some pretty scenery and get halfway to Fès. And so to bed.

The first challenge of the morning happened after just a few kilometres. I headed up and over the wrong track, only realising I'd made a mistake when the road turned to scree, then sloped sideways at 30 degrees. Hmm. Not good. Luckily, the Moroccan countryside yielded its secret weapon – an incredibly strong local man appeared out of nowhere and helped to turn the bike around, before returning to dig up some mineral or other out of the side of the road. I still suspect that he had actually destroyed my short-cut with his digging.

I concluded I'd have to go right up the Dades valley and right down the Todra, and that started the first major stress – do I have enough petrol? This sort of travelling turns you into an obsessive 'mental calculator', especially converting from miles into kilometres and back, and there are no petrol stations up here, where everything runs on either diesel, hay or kebabs. A few days before I'd been amazed that the bike was doing about 70mpg when just pottering along at 20 or 30mph, so I had a vague but unconfirmed hope that my range could be over 250 miles, rather than the usual 170 I get thrashing up and down motorways. I'd already done about 70 miles since the last fill-up, so I had between 100 and 180 miles left.

In most of lowland Morocco there are useful reminders of the French colonial era in the form of good roads with those cute little white-and-yellow kilometre markings you get in France, and name plates for each village. Out in the wilds there are none of these luxuries, so it was easy to waste time and effort as well as 20 kilometres worth of petrol following the biggest tracks along a riverbed full of water, ice and snow. The village at the top of the valley ended in a one-in-one slope and a crowd of kids. A quick chat to the only adult told me I had missed a right-turn three kms ago.

Back along the valley, onto the elusive track, and then the up and up really started. About 40km of up and up as it turned out, following the sides of steep hills. After only five kilometres I was on the point of turning back, thinking I couldn't possibly be on the right road, but up popped a local again and assured me that the village in question was only 20km away. I concluded that the missing 15km were down to the inaccurate odometer on his donkey. On and on, with only a few women gathering scrubby tumbleweed to witness the idiot Westerner. Each new horizon, higher than the previous, added an extra stab of doubt. At the top of one pass I could see that the snow in the rutted road had no tyre prints.

Then without warning, a tumble from the bike. Usually my greatest fear is falling off the bike. The pain, the cost, the inconvenience, the ignominy, the damage to 'my baby'. But after a few tumbles at low speed on dirt roads, you realise that it's not so bad and get into a routine of sorting things out. Turn off the engine, turn off the petrol, stop for breath. Take off the tank-bag (full of tools, spares and water – too heavy to lift with the bike), heave the bike up, stop for breath. Put everything back together (including a bit more tape for the broken windshield), fire up and ride on. Apologise to the bike and sing a rude song or two. Take a couple of photos to show your mum when you get home and you can convince yourself that you're some sort of hero.

Eventually the village at the head of the pass appeared, looking bleak, arid and windswept, but so welcome. Sixty miles to run down the Todra valley and possibly only enough fuel for 60 miles – better be careful. Lots of freewheeling down-valley ensued, pleasantly quiet but not very quick. I was getting very tired, but surviving on a lot of optimism, some calm thoughts, and reassurance from my compass.

Coming from the head of the valley, it's difficult to find your way through the village of Tamtattouchte as there's a huge river running through it. The local kids have worked out that if they block off all the roads with rocks and generally swarm around, they can charge tourists for guidance. Then they twist the knife by sending the hapless tourist over the high road, which is actually the other end of the 'short-cut over the tops' that I had tried to find that morning, which of course takes you back to the Dades gorge.

So an exhausting half-hour followed as I was mobbed by the kids, raced off in all sorts of wrong directions and ended up

I bluffed that I was getting some money out but pulled my knife on him instead, which gave me enough space to get away before a hail of rocks followed.

dropping the bike down a slope. Only then did I agree to be guided for the price of four cigarettes and some coconut cakes left from breakfast. The chosen kid sat on the back of the bike and took me in the wrong direction, accepted his payment (whilst complaining that he couldn't eat the cakes because of Ramadan), and then threatened me with rocks so as to get some hard cash – he even gripped my hand over the clutch so I couldn't blast away. I bluffed that I was getting some money out but pulled my knife on him instead, which gave me enough space to get away before a hail of rocks followed.

I rode on for a couple of minutes to see if the track took a turn to the south. The compass said it was wrong, my guts said it was wrong, and the distant sight of the white Land Cruiser I'd seen earlier confirmed that it was indeed the wrong direction. The little bastard had wasted valuable petrol, but I decided to return to the village and try again.

Time for a bold approach! There was a football match in progress in the village square so I rode into the middle of the pitch, turned the engine off and waited for something to happen. The oldest player, obviously fed up with tourists, the kids' antics, and now the disruption of his game of footie, obliged with some terse directions, a handshake and I was off.

Water in the spark plug caps was the next hurdle, which felt unnervingly like the dreaded empty tank I'd been expecting for hours. Trying to keep up momentum (to save fuel) I was hitting lots of deep puddles, sending waves of

water over the cylinders. The first time it happened I started to look for a place to camp, too tired to consider walking to the next town for petrol or stripping the bike to fix the problem. But luckily the bike dried out a bit, fired up again and we were off. In all I had to stop three times to let the bike dry out as I hit water-splash after water-splash in the dark.

I finally reached Tinerhir and could focus only on one thought – petrol. It turned out that I still had a couple of litres left in the tank, so my pottering calculations had been accurate; another set of numbers to obsess over. I found a street light to park under and consulted the Lonely Planet guide again to try and decide whether to stay in town or not.

If in doubt, cheer yourself up with a song... so I started belting out *Creep* by Radiohead, all about unrequited love and alienation. An urchin wandered up...

If in doubt, cheer yourself up with a song... so I started belting out *Creep* by Radiohead, all about unrequited love and alienation. An urchin wandered up and stood staring at me so I serenaded him and, just as I had delivered the words 'what the hell am I doing here, I don't belong here', a huge Berber man in a dark *djellaba* with a pointed hood walked purposefully over. Shit, this is it, he knows I pulled a knife on the kid earlier today! The man was massive, with an overpowering look of Samuel L Jackson in *Pulp Fiction*. Then, in perfect English: 'So nice to hear you singing. I'm an English teacher... not really thinking of riding on are you?... let me have a word with my friend at this hotel....there is a café over there... you can have a room in the hotel for $4... is that OK?.. he says you can bring your bike into the hotel and park it outside your room....see you later... we'll drink tea together.'

Such extremes; one minute my life is being threatened and I'm cursing every wretched metre and person of this land, and the next I'm overwhelmed by how beautiful, kind and genuine everything is.

So, for once in my life, I allowed somebody else to tell me what to do. I rode my bike, still covered in sand and mud, into the hotel (couldn't do that in the Hilton, I thought), had omelette and chips in the café, and wandered back to take mint tea with Abdullah and his mates. We swapped stories as he bought single cigarettes from a vendor wandering from bar to bar. He'd been born in a tent in the desert, was actually only half Berber, had been married to an English girl for five years but had never been to the UK. He saw a copy of the Koran in my pocket (I was trying to be culturally sensitive after the recent bombing of Iraq) and insisted on kissing the book; a nice touch, which I tried to return by later sending him a copy of the English translation.

Somehow I'd managed to pack in about a week's worth of stress, breakdowns, crashes, human interaction, up and ups, emotions and sandstone into one day, and I'd survived. Being so alive can make you feel damned tired, so I slept well that night, with the bike just outside my bedroom door. I even managed to sleep through the 4.15am call to prayers – bliss!

Sergei's Birthday

Having already tasted the pleasures of Enfielding from India to the UK, **Nicki McCormick** *decided Uraling around the Central Asian 'stans would offer a fruitful adventure.*

It was big, blue, gleaming and scary, and when it was wheeled out of Valera's garage for my inspection, I fairly swooned. At 350kg, 650cc, and US$300, with sidecar, reverse gear, and a new spare wheel neatly attached to the chair, this was to be my transport for the summer.

'Go on, have a try', encouraged Sergei, the mechanic friend who was helping me bike-shop. Nervously, and unaccustomed to machines with three wheels, I clambered aboard the Ural, found first and promptly nose-dived into a ditch.

Lesson #1 – sidecars don't behave like normal motorbikes. After retrieving bike and rider from their predicament, Sergei explained the rules: drive straight and, without sufficient heaving on the right arm, the bike pulls left. Turn right too fast, and the sidecar (on the right-hand side) lifts up at a most alarming angle. And (obvious this one, but some habits die hard) you don't have to put your feet down when stopped!

'Now, try again.'

I practised my Uraling on the streets of Tashkent. Despite independence and being in the heart of Central Asia, Tashkent is still a thoroughly Russian city, with low-rise concrete Soviet apartment blocks, wide leafy boulevards and vast plazas displaying monumental statues. Russian women with big hair and tight white miniskirts clash glaringly with the conservative Moslem population. A week later I was ready to risk the highways of Uzbekistan for a test ride to Samarkand. Lesson #2 – a Ural drives like a truck, consumes almost as much fuel, has a top speed of 100kph, and requires regular cooling-off stops in the heat of the Central Asian summer.

The highlight of Samarkand, 300km away along a dead straight highway, is undoubtedly the Registan, a collection of 15th-century theological schools. Despite brutal Soviet restoration the tilting minarets, shimmering tilework and swooping birds were magical. By way of a dramatic contrast, the Hotel Turist – thirteen crumbling floors and a dragon for a floor guardian – was less magical, but no less fascinating, with its mouldy, peeling walls, electrified plumbing, cockroaches and sixteen different types of cracked tile in each bathroom. A typical Soviet hotel then.

By this stage Sergei was turning out to be quite a find, being marvellous for my Russian, able to get local prices in bazaars and hotels, and having a wicked way with a Ural tool kit. Over vodka in Samarkand, I also discovered he had trained as a photographer, and promptly invited him along for the trip proper – a month in Kyrgyzstan.

We welded up a few brackets and drove to the bazaar to acquire some spares. Tashkent's Sunday market is like nothing I've ever seen – there's no uch thing as a bike shop in Uzbekistan, only a sea of used parts laid out on he ground. Sergei poked at some brown, leather-wrapped blobs that looked ike they'd been knocked up with an 11-year-old's home electronics set, pronounced them to be quality ignition coils, and bought two. He haggled feroriously for other unidentifiable necessities and, with a rucksack full of metal objects, we picked our way out of the bazaar through budgie-vendors, elderly refrigerators, acres of polyester clothing and a few stolen stereos. Lesson #3 – sidecars are marvellous things for messy people – there's none of that strategic packing to worry about every morning.

> **Sidecars are marvellous things for messy people – there's none of that strategic packing to worry about every morning.**

I'd rather fondly imagined leaving the inferno of Tashkent and spending my first night in flower-trewn meadows beside an idyllic Alpine lake, with snow-capped peaks in the distance – you know the scene. In actual fact we broke down twice in 30km and spent two hours at the border among Ladas queuing to get their trade goods and contraband into Kazakhstan. We spent the rest of the day racing a towering thunderstorm, hiding in bus shelters and getting soaked to the skin. The snow-streaked mountains were there all right – alternately breathaking in stormy sunlight and obscured by the seething black deluge. And, to he north, endless rolling ochre and green hills, with the road a glistening grey wiggle reaching to the horizon.

After two days in Bishkek, it was over the pass to Lake Issy-Kul. To use guidebook analogies, Kyrgyzstan is said to be the Switzerland of Central Asia, and Issy-Kul is its Lake Geneva. Nearly 200km long and sitting at 1600m it is surrounded by mountains that have yet to be climbed. From its shores, broad valleys of pinks and purples divide the ridges, with darting marmots, roaming horses and tumbling rivers. Entering the lake valley we had the first of many encounters with Kyrgyz officialdom when we failed to pay a dubious $25 fee. We were flagged down and held for nearly two hours for allegedly not stopping to pay some 'ecology tax' at a post a way back. We eventually coughed up whereupon the policeman became our best friend and took us to an incredibly bleak army camp where we got to spend the night in the General's guest quarters. Subsequent encounters with the police and their taxes' were almost always friendly, but we did get our own back one day by selling them ten litres of incredibly poor quality petrol guaranteed to kill any engine.

Our purple bucket was regularly filled with supplies of fresh bread, honey, thick cream, tomatoes and Snickers bars, and we spent our nights in run-down, rustic holiday camps – devoid of holidaymakers due to a big chemical spill the previous year which had scared them all off.

At the far end of Issy Kul is the town of Karakol which, with its deserted streets of wooden colonial houses, still feels like the Russian frontier town it was not long ago. Once a week it awakens for the Sunday market – a seething, snorting, haggling mayhem of livestock. I briefly considered trading the Ural in for something more appropriate to the terrain (vehicles in these parts are generally four-legged and we'd caused quite a stir by our arrival in several mountain hamlets), but restrained myself and set off along another interesting-looking dotted line on the map.

Much of this particular line appeared to have been, until recently, river rapids, and the stability of three wheels came in handy as we bounced our way upwards, waving to bemused horsemen dressed in traditional high white felt hats and even more traditional Chinese nylon track suits. The road tyres were less useful when the track became a steep, muddy notch along the edge of a precipice where the outfit began to feel its weight pushed by two unfit smokers at an altitude of 2500m.

In fact the slopes became impossible so we found a picture-perfect camp site on the edge of a cliff, tethered the bike to a tree just in case, and settled down to a feast of roast ham, potatoes and Black Death vodka.

With a cool engine and a mild hangover, the road seemed marginally more roadlike in the morning and led to Altyn Arashan, a stunning 3000m-high valley of sweeping, brilliant green pastures, six houses and distant glaciers. People come here for the trekking but having had sufficient exercise persuading the bike to reach this little paradise, I was more interested in the hot springs. While Sergei amused himself carrying out minor Uralisms, I found the world's most atmospheric bathroom – a bath-sized pool of bath-tempered water in a cave high above a gushing river, deep in the forest.

Reaching this point I had discovered that my human Russian was as temperamental as my mechanical one. When they're screamed at by me, knee-deep in mud wrestling six times my weight of uncooperative metal, I find it tricky to differentiate between the Russian for 'stop!' 'start!' 'left!' 'right!' and 'what the bloody hell do you think you're doing!' This can lead to problems.

Sergei's birthday started well enough: in a sanatorium creaking with elderly Kyrgyzstanis taking the waters and admiring the scenery. Over breakfast Sergei decreed that as it was his birthday he was boss today. Fair enough. The map showed a dotted black line leading west over the mountains, and from the main road it did indeed look like a decent dirt track (dotted black lines vary between jeep- and goat-ability out here). Anyway, I was enthusiastic.

The dirt track soon turned into a beautiful and only mildly terrifying riverbed running between eroded red cliffs. At the top of a rise the track forked. The only tyre tracks led left but a woman in a yurt said the way to the next village was right and that it was a good road. The woman, curse her soul, had obviously never ridden a Ural outfit.

A short distance further on, at a small encampment the track disappeared completely into a field of wild-flowers, on the banks of a small stream. I tentatively suggested turning back.

'Why reverse?' replied Sergei, 'After, good.'

He reminded me about the dotted black line on the map (he never did come to grips with the idea that the existence of a track does not necessarily mean it's Uralable) and, as he was boss for the day, we took off up the mountainside. To give him his due, the track did reappear after a few hundred metres but then came the puddle.

> **The woman, curse her soul, had obviously never ridden a Ural outfit.**

It was an innocuous sort of puddle to look at – a large but not unreasonable expanse of mud with a steep slope to the left and a field of boggy looking grass to the right. Negotiable, so it seemed, if taken at speed and lightly laden. Unfortunately this puddle bore an ancient grudge and had been lying in wait for months, bored and restless, for a vehicle to prey on. We were the sacrifice it wanted, and within seconds the outfit was firmly embedded, engine resting on the surface of the bog.

Sergei, expert in such matters, shouted down my plan and insisted on his own. The next four and a half hours were spent moving four metres forwards across an increasingly deep, sloppy-cow-shitty bog, lifting the bike with the aid of a handy log. We shoved rocks under the wheels, slithered a few centimetres, retrieving the rocks from elbow-deep slime and repeating the process hour after hour. Our destination was a bit of firm ground, below which was friendly-looking grass that wobbled when you walked on it and sucked you to the knee if you didn't leap onto the right clumps. My sideways levering method, so firmly rubbished a few hours previously, was finally used to good effect. The $500 hidden in an elastic bandage round my mud-encrusted ankle later caused some consternation at the bank, and my back took a week to recover.

During our puddle ordeal, at the risk of being abused even further, I'd expressed reservations about the state of the road further on. The valley looked to be a dead end. Sergei assured me with the confidence of one who regularly commutes along this route that it was absolutely fine. We loaded up, drove over a rise, up a bank, across a field of grass and the road ended.

A passing horseman who cantered over to investigate this strange apparition confirmed my dead-end theory and thirty minutes later, after a heart-stopping race along a bank to avoid the bog, we were back at the main road. A wasp chose this moment to sting me on the neck and I burst into tears.

The Bishkek to Osh road, one of those classic journeys like the Karakoram Highway or the Trans-Siberian Express, and our next stage, is 619km of swooping, soaring, spine-shattering roads. At 3600m the first pass is probably the most terrifying thing I have ever ridden. It climbs gradually for 20km from the south, disappears into a long dripping tunnel, then plummets 45km down a narrow road littered with landslides, road-building equipment and truck-carcasses.

This would be fine on a deserted mountainside, but this is the main north-south highway and it's a heaving mass of grinding trucks with dodgy brakes and suicidal jeeps trying to make the trip in record time with Allah's good hand to guide them around blind bends. Oh yes – and it was pouring with rain. The second pass was almost as high, not nearly as hard, but bitterly cold with sleet lashing against us. After this it was plain if bumpy sailing down into the lowlands and the return to Uzbekistan.

Kyrgyzia seems to offer a new and untouched range of perfect mountains for every day of the week – whatever the conditions, whatever the arguments, every pass reveals a new and wondrous vista guaranteed to raise the spirits. There are black, craggy evil mountains, bizarre eroded rust-coloured mountains, snow-capped Alpine mountains, mountains so immaculately mossy-smooth, with strategically-placed babbling brooks and lichened boulders that you'd swear a Japanese gardener had been working on them all night. And that's not to mention crumbling white gorges with milky-turquoise reservoirs, rolling green hills with entire valleys of purple, pink and bright yellow wild flowers – how long have you got?

One night, we had a small accommodation crisis when the river valley I'd turned up turned out to be eminently uncampable. We were just debating our options when a young man in a suit asked if we were headed for the *turbaza* (holiday camp). This sounded promising, so our new guide perched himself on the wheel-hub of the sidecar and led us 30km up into the mountains. Night fell, and as we sped through ramshackle villages, a massive thunderstorm whipped up, flashes of lightning revealing great glowering rocks ahead of us.

Night fell, and as we sped through ramshackle villages, a massive thunderstorm whipped up, flashes of lightning revealing great glowering rocks ahead of us.

The *turbaza* appeared at 10pm, just as the heavens caved in. Unlike every other one we'd visited in the previous month, this one had people in it! While our companion, who'd come to visit friends, rustled the director out of his sauna to find us a cabin, we stood under a tree in pouring rain, outside a pounding Kyrgyz open-air disco in a sort of pagoda-thingy, drinking the vodka we'd purchased earlier and giggling furiously.

Installed in a wood cabin somewhere up a dark and slippery hill, we were immediately whisked off, still dripping, to the disco, lightning providing the strobe. Dancing the night away in a leaky pagoda to weird Russian and local music, in the company of Kyrgyz youngsters on the pull, and old men and housewives on holiday, was a most bizarre experience and sent me into still more fits of giggles.

With a final burst of the *Titanic* theme the happy throng was shooed into the night. A treacherous mission through the dark muddiness of the camp following Altyn the hitchhiker provided still more bootlegged vodka, and we took another hour to find our room. I'm still not exactly sure where we were that night, but it was a crazy, strange evening and most entertaining.

Early the next afternoon we entered Uzbekistan. Two hours later we entered it again. The borders here were randomly drawn by Stalin and resemble a complicated jigsaw, with arms and islands of the various 'stans littered all over the place. Osh, the end of the highway and our final Kyrgyz destination, was to erupt with ethnic violence a month later as an ongoing consequence of this gerrymandering. But we followed the Ferghana valley of Uzbekistan – all cotton fields, silkworms and watermelons – and the next day descended our final pass back into the heat of the Tashkent plain.

Deep Water Yukon

In August 1999 **Tom Grenon** *linked up with a bike journalist and a tour operator from Whitehorse to explore the Mackenzie Mountains and Canada's remote Northwest Territories.*

Exploring the far north-west in 1996, I'd turned been back about 250km west of the NWT's Mackenzie River, low on fuel and food, but high on boot water and enthusiasm. I'd always planned to have another go at pushing deeper into this wild region and a couple of years later I got my chance with Jamie of Arctic Motorcycle Tours and Craig Hightower of *Street Bike* magazine.

We all met up in Whitehorse where I did a quick service, fitted fresh Bridgestones and bought a machete for the expected overgrowth. Then we set off east to Johnsons Crossing, Jamie choosing to be support driver in his huge Suburban 4x4 towing his KLR and carrying about a ton of food. On the way to the Crossing, Craig and I shot off onto a chunk of the abandoned Alaska Highway and ran into a squatters cabin with a fine outdoor porcelain bath tub fed by water piped from a mountain brook – very modern and all with a million-dollar view.

Once at Johnsons Crossing we headed up Route #6 – the South Canol Road – smooth, hard packed, traffic-free gravel. We blasted along pretty steadily, anticipating the more challenging riding that lay ahead in the Northwest Territories. Around 170 clicks from Johnsons we turned east near Rose Lake onto an old mining exploration track I'd partially explored last time. Climbing into the alpine valley, we stopped at a great little cabin with a wood stove, and by the time we got back to the Canol we'd crossed dozens of creeks, all without any indication of people being out here for a long, long time.

Camping at Lapie Lake that night with nearly 400km under our belts proved ideal: no bugs, the lake smooth as glass and thanks to the Sub', a superb steak dinner chased by a couple of ice-cold brewskies.

Next morning broke perfect with the sun making its way over the mountains as a family of loons quietly fished in the drifting mist over the lake. After breakie we jumped on the bikes to check out a track which according to the topo map heads up Ground Hog Creek into the St Cyr range. The first 20km was well used with a small cabin halfway, but from there on the track got pretty challenging with several water crossings and muddy sections. Winking in appreciation at my new tyres, we nevertheless decided to turn back to keep to our schedule.

Topping up with fuel at Ross River, we continued on what was now the North Canol Road. With the lack of rain in the last week the going was fast and at times loose, and approaching Shelton Lake the snow-capped peaks of the Mackenzie Ranges came into view as the track twisted up through the Ross River valley.

We set up camp at Shelton Lake just as a beaver swam by to investigate the unaccustomed activity and loons looned in the still evening air. After another huge dinner, I tried a little fishing in the fading twilight. It was past 11 before I realised I might as well pack up: it was as dark as it gets up here at this time of year.

After another huge dinner, I tried a little fishing in the fading twilight. It was past 11 before I realised I might as well pack up: it was as dark as it gets up here at this time of year.

Day three started with a trailer wheel bearing breaking up so we repacked the truck, putting Jamie's KLR in the back. Spacious wagons, these Surburbans.

Following the delay, Craig and I blast ahead to explore another old track heading into the Selwyn Mountains near Macmillan Pass. With views of the glaciers and the snow fields on the Mackenzies, we returned down the switch backs to meet up with Jamie on the Yukon/NWT border, wondering if he wanted to push on with the truck. I warned him that after the manned checkpoint the road became much rougher with no bridges and plenty of water crossings. Addicted to the Sub's comforts, Jamie decided to push on another 35km to our intended camp at Mile 208.

At the checkpoint I enquired about water levels – a little higher than normal, I was told, with a group of quads turned back at the Intga River. I asked if any motorcycles had been through this year, the answer was no, we were probably the only motorcycles to go into the Northwest Territories on the Canol Road.

From the checkpoint Craig and I stayed close to the truck in case Jamie decided to give up or sank, but amazingly he got that big-assed truck through some very scary mud holes and boulder fields. If that thing ever stuck badly in a stream, it would still be rusting there today!

Once we got onto the plateau the track deteriorated and by this time we were getting lazy about scouting each of the many mud holes; if one made it the other would follow, if not the other would find another route with varying levels of success. We made camp a few kays past the vacant Old Squaw Lodge and after dinner we all rode on to check on the state of the Intga River. It looked grim, with a one-metre drop into fast running water. Any evidence of a bridge ever being there, let alone pilings, had long been washed away. We agreed this would not be an easy crossing and planned to scout further next day.

Unfortunately it rained that night so our return to the Intga saw the level rising. I headed up river to look for a crossing point, Jamie and Craig went downstream. Almost immediately I run into a little cabin with a mountain bike outside! It turned out to be a German guy on a six-week trip heading from Whitehorse to 'as far as he could get up the Canol'. He'd been planning this trip for 15 years, slowly plotting out the logistics of pedalling some 400km without resupply. He'd holed up in the cabin the day before and had met the quads that had turned back. The cyclist was also about to call it a day.

I continued upsteam looking for a crossing point but it was no good, the river carved deep channels on the outside of each curve so I returned noting the 'least bad' point. It was here in 1996 that I had paced up and down the bank for nearly an hour, scouting, then working up enough adrenaline to blind me of the danger of making this crossing in such an isolated region. At that time I was alone – the closest human was 15km back at Old Squaw Lodge, which really didn't mean much as you'd be floating face-down halfway to the North Pole before anyone noticed you were missing.

Putting these thoughts to the back of my mind, I'd psyched myself into seeing the other side and let her go! I was going well until the front wheel hit a submerged rock at which point the chilling reality of my possible predicament flooded in: an ice-cold river running over me and my fully loaded bike... At this point the saying 'DO OR DIE' comes to mind. If you were to figure it out on a piece of paper you couldn't do it: the heavy KLR was full of gas, gearbags were filling with water, the wheels were upstream, the handlebars downstream, and the current rushing over the side. With the first heave I got the bike to where I had the side of the seat resting on the tops of my knees, at that point I rested and looked at the situation. With another desperate lurch I brought the KLR upright.

That was three years back and I was keen not to repeat the scenario this time. When the guys returned they were also scratching their heads. We looked at my choice and came to the conclusion it was just as good as any.

I was given the honour of doing the foot recce to see if there was a route back to the road from the opposite bank. I hacked myself a walking stick, put on some sandals, rolled up my pants and took a deep breath. The water was cold enough to numb the antlers off a moose but the bottom was manageable at just over half a metre for most of the width. Once on the other side it was just a matter of crawling up a one-metre bank and riding through the brush back to the road. To be on the safe side we agreed that the other two support the rider across the stream.

> **I was going well until the front wheel hit a submerged rock at which point the chilling reality of my possible predicament flooded in: an ice-cold river running over me and my fully loaded bike...**

Having managed to cross without any drama, we discovered that the Canol again dropped down the politely-accepted local definition of 'road'. Rutted and waterlogged, it trailed the Intga River up a nameless valley towards Caribou Pass. I spotted a young Grizzly so intent on his fishing that he virtually ignored me and a couple of clicks later we sight a female caribou close to the road and clearly undisturbed by human presence (although a stock KLR silencer helps here).

About 30km beyond the Intga crossing we reached Caribou Pass, where the valley opens out to a sweeping expanse of a treeless plain rimmed with jagged 2500-metre peaks. We moved into the Ekwi River watershed which drains way up into the Arctic Ocean. In the middle of the plain was a tiny cabin where we met a native hunting party on quads and a semi-amphibious thing called an Argo. This group was the third such gathering we'd come across, each on a quest to bag a moose or caribou before the snows fell, this being both tradition and a necessity for the coming winter. All were scanning the mountains with binoculars, hoping a big bull would come down low so a kill could be made and the carcass retrieved with the Argo.

This is what adventure means to me: getting out there and using all your resources and experience to overcome problems.

After sharing several hot cups of thick coffee and information about the trail ahead we pushed on, hoping to reach the Godlin Lakes pump station for our next night's camp.

About 15km beyond the hunters' cabin the valley narrowed again and eventually dropped down into a 20m-high canyon through which the turbulent Ekwi River tore.

Looking at this daunting obstruction, it was time for a reality check. Craig has come up to have a big motorcycle adventure on the Canol Road and would not return disappointed. Jamie's objective had already been resolved: the riding up here was far too rough and dangerous for organised tours.

For me the whole trip had been planned around this moment. I had stood alone on this same bank three years ago. Right then I felt the three of us could have got across the raging little river and seen some incredible new land that no motorcyclist had ever travelled through. This is what adventure means to me: getting out there and using all your resources and experience to overcome problems. But even with all this desire, I realised it would be foolish to try to convince Craig and Jamie that we should go for it.

However, I did propose we at least ford the river on foot to explore the condition of the road beyond. Wading through the ice-cold water took complete attention, each of the crossings being nearly 20 metres from shore to shore. Once on the road the going was very good. The heavy growth I'd experienced three years ago was now cleared. The three of us walked on for around ten kilometres, passing an airstrip cut into the road and so many Grizzly pies that we felt safer yelling loudly.

Drying out back at the Caribou Pass cabin we figured we'd got our money's worth. Looking out from the deck that evening, we saw three large Caribou bulls, antlers silhouetted along the distant ridge: the classic image of the untamed Far North. As the light faded, the forlorn howl of a lone wolf wrapped up the ideal moment. We turned in and set our thoughts to home.

BOOKS

Around Australia the Hard Way in 1929 ~ Jack L Bowers

After an impoverished upbringing and the completion of their apprenticeship, Jack Bowers and Frank Smith set off to ride around Australia on an old H-D outfit as an economic depression crept across the country. Modestly underplaying the extreme hardship of their record-breaking ride, the roads turned to tracks just a day out of Sydney and stayed like that for the next 15,000km. Like present-day riders, they had their share of problems with vibration-breaking luggage carriers and tanks while living exclusively off damper and whatever they could shoot.

Battling up to Darwin, the adventurous duo continued west across the remote Buchanan Track to Halls Creek and Broome. It was the toughest part of the trip, where attacks by tribal Aborigines were still considered a danger, and one which makes the best reading.

Bullet up the Great Trunk Road ~ Jonathan Gregson

For some readers this book will conjure up scenes of motorcycling the breadth of the Indian continent, whilst others will be gripped by images of the turmoil and despair that ensued after Partition in 1947. Indian-born Gregson amply satisfies both appetites in this tale which skilfully combines the legacy of partition amidst a present-day account of motorcycle adventure and exploration. Readers with no knowledge of India or motorcycling will be enthralled and captivated by the author's roadside tales, whilst those with just a little experience of either will be quietly amused at Gregson's humorous insights into what could only be India today.

Ed Shuttleworth

Desert Travels ~ Chris Scott

'There are no modern-day adventurers,' whined the young, grunge-clothed college student, looking up from his textbook. This short snippet of overheard conversation was textbook irony, as I sat nearby reading Chris Scott's *Desert Travels*, a story of his half-dozen trips into the searing heat of a vast Saharan desert… Its pages are full of the kinds of stories that keep you reading far past your normal bedtime. Damn the cliché, but I really couldn't put it down.

Gord Mounce, Motorcycle Online

Jupiter's Travels ~ Ted Simon

This twenty-year-old RTW biking classic has yet to be beaten and has probably launched more Big Trips in bikers' beer-charged imaginations than any other book. Hardcore bikers are sometimes disappointed, but JT's enduring popularity is because the book appeals to all readers inspired by adventurous travel and the call of the wild, not just motorcyclists. Ted Simon writes with a mellow, humane and adventurous approach: 'if things get dull, just run out of

TED SIMON: 'THE INTERRUPTIONS ARE THE JOURNEY'

Q. *Do you get tired of being known for something you did over twenty years ago?*

TS. No, I love it. In many ways I'm still on the same journey.

Q. *Do you think overlanding with a motorcycle is harder these days, or do possible itineraries merely shift?*

TS. They merely shift.

Q. *Do you know what happened to the Triumph?*

TS. It's in the British Transport Museum in Coventry.

Q. *Was it the best choice of machine, looking back?*

TS. I don't know about best because I'd have to have tried it on others, but it was certainly a good choice. I might even use the same bike again. At least I'd be able to get into it. And maybe this time I could get a decent air filter.

Q. *Do you own a bike now?*

TS. Yes. A broken BMW R65.

Q. *Has the book's continuing success surprised you?*

TS. Not any more, now that I have heard people talking about it, I see why it works.

Q. *Why do you think JT remains so popular?*

TS. Because it goes beyond the nuts and bolts of bikes and travel, and deals with dreams, and reasons for being alive, and the hopeful, positive aspects of being a human being on this planet. It opens doors for people, and many, to my personal knowledge, have gone through those doors. I feel very privileged.

Q. *Has it made you rich?*

TS. No. Though there was a short period when I felt rich.

Q. *Have you revisited any of the places you passed through on the trip?*

TS. Yes, South America. I went to Fortaleza, which was a surreal experience since I could hardly even find the scenes I had remembered so well. Also Rio, Curitiba, Buenos Aires, and Santiago.

Q. *Are you still in touch with anyone you met on that trip?*

TS. A few only. Generally it has been too difficult for people to maintain contact.

Q. *What are your fondest memories?*

TS. There are too many to enumerate. But they mostly have to do with relationships I formed, however brief, all over the place.

Q. *And least happy ones?*

TS. Jail in Brazil, confusion in Santiago, misery in Malaysia.

Q. *Do you get much mail from readers? What do they say?*

TS. Yes. Mostly expressing gratitude, or asking for help in planning some journey of their own.

Q. *A couple of years ago the world was circumnavigated in 21 days (also on a Triumph). Although this was a stunt, why do you think so many riders rush their trips? (How long, if at all, did it take you to 'slow down' and get with the pace?).*

TS. Fortunately I was slowed down by the war and other difficulties in North Africa, and by the terrain in Sudan and Ethiopia. But I don't think I would ever have wanted to go faster anyway. I was interested in what was going on around me, and probably a major factor in deciding the pace was my need to record and digest the events as they unfolded. There is all the difference in the world between aimless wandering and travelling with a particular end in view – in my case a book.

Q. *What have you been doing since you returned?*

TS. Writing books, farming, watching a son grow up, making mistakes, trying to understand what's going on, wondering what to do next.

Q. *Are there any other bike travelogues that you've read and enjoyed?*

TS. *One Man Caravan* by Robert Fulton is fun and I'm just reading Jim Wilson's story about crossing Africa in the thirties – *Three Wheeling Across Africa*. Those are the only two I know that I really care for.

Q. *What other books have you written?*

TS. *The Chequered Year* (in the UK) was about Formula One in 1970. *Riding Home* (which I have just re-issued over here in an edited and expanded form as *Riding High*). *The River Stops Here*, which is about a valley, the dam that got stopped, and *Chinatown*-style politics in California. And finally, *The Gypsy in Me*, published in 1997, about tramping around Russia, Poland, Ukraine and Romania (a bike, I thought, would be too quick and easy) trying to figure the place out, and find traces of my father.

Ted Simon is planning to ride around the world again, leaving in January 2001, 25 years after his original journey.

petrol' he suggests – don't try this in the Sahara. A sequel, *Riding Home* (now out of print) surfed rather lamely on the success of the original and was rewritten and published by the author as *Riding High,* relating some of the untold tales from *Jupiter's Travels.*

Mae Hong Son Loop Touring Guide ~ David Unkovich

A pocket-sized touring guide describing on- and off-road routes in the forested hills between Chiang Mai and the Burmese border in northern Thailand. Highly detailed with distances, road conditions, elevations and recommended services, plus town and schematic maps.

By the same author: *Pocket Guide to Motorcycle Touring in North Thailand* and *A Motorcycle Guide to the Golden Triangle.*

The Motorcycle Diaries ~ Ernesto Che Guevara

In 1952, long before he became the fist-clenching revolutionary icon of the sixties, Ernesto Guevara set off with his medical student chum (or *che* in Argentine Spanish) to explore South America on a 500cc hardtail Norton. With all the short-sighted optimism that young adventurers thrive on (take note!), the two scrounge their way down to Patagonia and over to Chile where the clapped-out Norton is dumped. From here their audacious freeloading loses its most glamorous accessory and the pair continue under the guise of vagrant research leprologists.

Even at 24, Che's sympathies for the browbeaten proletariat – which developed into a heroic commitment and led to his death in Bolivia in '67 – come across in this 'diary'. However, despite the duo's high jinx and the author's subsequent fame, *The Motorcycle Diaries* adds up to a shrewd publishing ploy out to lure baby boomers; a mediocre leftist travelogue which the translation, to its credit, does not disguise.

Obsessions Die Hard ~ Ed Culberson

After retiring from army life Ed devotes five years to fulfilling a lifelong obsession: travelling the Pan-American Highway, including Panama's notorious Darien Gap. It may not be what you call motorcycling – paying Cuna Indians to drag or carry your bike through the world's foremost quagmire, but you can't help admiring his calm approach and determination. He teaches us that nothing gets you through like solid advance planning (and a couple of friends in high places). A readable tale by a well-organised man. *Alan Bradshaw*

The Perfect Vehicle ~ Melissa Holbrook Pierson

Melissa Pierson recalls over ten years spent riding the roads of America and Europe in this personal account of one woman's biking life. The fearful excitement of being a new rider, the satisfaction of achieving confidence on two wheels and the humbling realisation that a biker always has more to learn are all described in satisfying detail. Ms Pierson's love of bikes and the open road shines through as she recounts stories of tours and trips, rallies and races, adventures and disasters. It's worth buying if just for the Introduction, an evocative and inspirational piece of writing that comes as close to summing up the lure of motorcycles as anything else I've read. You'll be planning that next trip before you reach the end of it!

Sally Feldt

Running with the Moon ~ **Jonny Bealby**

Claiming somewhat improbably to be the first such achievement, Jonny Bealby rides his Ténéré around Africa the hard way to help him come to terms with the tragic death of his fiancée. With his partner crashing out early, the author continues alone, crossing the central Sahara just ahead of the border closures in 1991. It's a pattern for the rest of the book as again and again Bealby slips through just ahead of civil war and other calamities.

Once over the desert he ditches the mainstream overlanders' route to ride through Congo and Angola to the Cape before returning up Africa's east side to Cairo and the hope of fulfilling a romance initiated in Tamanrasset.

Bealby's arduous trek is one of the best biking tales since *Jupiter's Travels*, packed with the reciprocating gusts of good and ill fortune which typify a trans-African journey, although at times he sought out danger for its own sake. Like many fast-paced travelogues *Running with the Moon* suffers from the 'if-it's-Tuesday-it-must-be-Malawi' syndrome. It's at its best when he's up against it: hitching on dug-outs and slogging up to his waist through the rain-forest, or racing across Ethiopia's bandit country to confront Sudan's excruciating bureaucracy at a choking 54°C. Here the pace cranks up, clichés are discarded and some laconic humour creeps in. If you've ever thought of doing something similar, this book will confirm your worst fears and your most fervent hopes.

Ten Years on Two Wheels ~ **Helge Pedersen**

In 1982 Helge Pedersen left Norway to ride his R80 G/S across Africa. Returning two years later with plenty of tales but only ten bucks in his pocket, little had changed in his former home so he decided to keep riding. He shipped to Argentina and spent three years riding and working his way around Latin America, which included crossing Panama's uncrossable Darien Gap. North America, Australia and Asia followed: 77 countries and a speedo-frying 250,000 miles until he slackened the pace with current partner Karen in Seattle in 1992 and began putting this book together.

The result is a top-quality photographic essay and a bike travel book unlike any other. Not since *Jupiter's Travels* (which Helge used to swat a pesky scorpion in Nigeria) has a writer succeeded in letting you feel part of their adventure. But there's none of that 'Next day I got up and...' here. Instead short essays with titles like 'Palm Wine', 'Sushi', and 'War' help illustrate a subject or location. Even if you don't read a single word the photography is worth the price alone.

Travellers' Health: How to Stay Healthy Abroad ~ **Richard Dawood**
Staying Healthy in Asia, Africa & Latin America ~ **Dirk Schroeder**
The Tropical Traveller ~ **John Hatt**

Any of these three books will lucidly expand on all sorts of toe-curling details of travellers' health.

Zen And The Art Of Motorcycle Maintenance ~ **Robert Pirsig**

A baffling cult classic that many bikers understandably attempt. Still popular, the gist of the book's central dissertation is 'if it works, don't fix it'. I have hereby saved you a long and impenetrable slog.

CONTRIBUTORS

Simon McCarthy Born in 1963. Riding for 20 years, but never anything with more than two cylinders and usually the right bike on the wrong terrain. Currently owns a R100GS. Used to work in computers, but now a full-time sculptor (💻 www.simonthesculptor.com). Saving for a round-the-world trip.

Bruce Clark Rides roughly 15,000 kilometres per year, mostly commuting or short day trips in the Victoria-Vancouver BC area. Once every year or so he flies somewhere and rents a motorcycle for a week to a month.

Kyril Dambuleff Thought motorcycles were just a convenient way to beat SoCal traffic. Then in 1998 he embarked on a trip from Lisbon to Hong Kong. Things didn't quite go to plan but he covered over 10,000 miles and enjoyed every minute of it. He now lives on a farm near Frenchtown, New Jersey, and whenever he gets a chance contemplates his next motorbiking adventure.

Tom Grenon Born Vancouver and started riding at 15. Worked on logging camps in BC, and from 1981 lived in Paris, Milan, Barcelona, NYC and Seattle before returning to BC to focus on motorcycle adventure touring, photography, and computer graphics.

Iris Heiremans and Trui Hanoulle Belgians. Backpacked in Africa and Asia. After Trui started biking, combining both pleasures was the next step. For their overland trip to India, Iris learned to ride and Trui took a mechanic's course. Discovered they belong to the rare breed of women motorbike travellers. Future projects include overland to Finland and to reconquer the Himalayas.

Rupert Humphrey Born in England in 1964. Stumbled upon Riga, Latvia, while travelling in early 1993, liked it so stayed. Director of own trading company. 'Pragmatic motorcycle traveller' and travelled all over Eastern Europe, France and Morocco on back roads. 💻 rupert@latnet.lv

Noah Maltz Used to keep himself out of trouble by working as a stockbroker on Wall Street and then a management consultant in London. At the tender age of 30 he abandoned this nonsense to pursue the joys of adventure motorcycling. He is currently on a round-the-world mission with his friend Trevor.

Ken McLean Born in 1966, studied mining and worked in quarrying for nine years, then threw away a promising career to travel the Americas on a Triumph, his only travelling experience apart from a fortnight's disease collecting in Nepal. Back home he looked for a job, changed his mind and is now cycling around Scotland.

Allen Naille Spent 25 years as a resort company president and lives in the mountains of northern Arizona. A former Vietnam helicopter pilot, he and his wife, Carol, have travelled throughout Europe, Africa, and South America by Ducati Elefant. He raced a KTM Rallye in the 1988 Incas Rally in Peru.

Clement Salvadori Born 'at an early age' and began riding motorcycles some 15 years later. After failing to adjust to normal life, aged 33 he got on his BMW R75/5 and spent three years riding around the world; he now ekes out a living as a freelance moto-journalist, based on the central California coast.

Michael Slaughter – SWM – 26 – Currently lives in Dallas, Texas, USA. Graduated from Colorado College in 1996 with a degree in Economics. Loves motorbikes, travel and writing. Looking for SF with similar interests.

Not all contributors to this book supplied a biography.

Fuel consumption conversion table

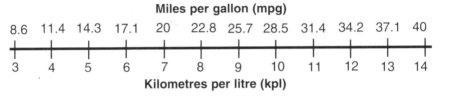

Miles per gallon (mpg)

| 8.6 | 11.4 | 14.3 | 17.1 | 20 | 22.8 | 25.7 | 28.5 | 31.4 | 34.2 | 37.1 | 40 |
| 3 | 4 | 5 | 6 | 7 | 8 | 9 | 10 | 11 | 12 | 13 | 14 |

Kilometres per litre (kpl)

Miles per gallon (mpg)

| 42.9 | 45.6 | 48.5 | 51.3 | 54.2 | 57 | 59.9 | 62.8 | 31.4 | 68.4 | 71.5 | 74.2 |
| 15 | 16 | 17 | 18 | 19 | 20 | 21 | 22 | 23 | 24 | 25 | 26 |

Kilometres per litre (kpl)

mpg x 0.35 = kpl

kpl x 2.85 = mpg

100 divided by kpl = L/100km

100 divided by L/100km = kpl

Other conversion figures
1 kilogram (kg) = 2.2lb
1 pound = 454 grams (0.45kg)

1 metre = 3 feet 3.4 inches
1 kilometre (km) = 0.62 miles
1 mile = 1.6 km

1 litre = 0.22 Imperial gallons
1 litre = 0.26 US gallons
1 US gallon = 3.78 litres
1 US gallon = 0.8 Imperial gallons
1 Imperial gallon = 4.55 litres

This section includes recently updated information correct at time of going to press. Part headings and page references to which the information relates are given.

PART 1: PRACTICALITIES

Enfields – pp32-3

If you want a reliable Enfield then the best choice is the new 350 Bullet featuring electronic ignition. In the standard garb the prices of this machine range around Rs65,000, though discounts can bring the price down by a couple of thousand rupees. The electronic ignition model also features better electrics all round, including an alternator. The Enfield Lightning 500 costs in the region of Rs80,000 and features a custom look that appeals to many, plus a high capacity oil pump. This model also seems to have come to grips with electrical niggles, mainly with the regulator and charging circuit.

But by far the biggest innovation is finally putting the **gear lever on the left** and the **foot brake on the right** while incorporating a five-speed gearbox. A popular crash scenario for many inexperienced Bulleteers accustomed to modern machinery was frantically stamping on the gear lever thinking it was the back brake, a hang over from over 40 years ago when British bikes, including the Royal Enfields, had foot brakes on the left.

Also without besmirching the character of the Karol Bagh 'bike preparers' it's definitely true that most of the parts used are 'crap Indian' and not original Enfield spares which are available only at authorised dealers.

One item which requires frequent replacement are the **cush drive rubbers** in the rear hub. Designed to reduce transmission shock, a Bullet's rear brake (the more powerful of the two), will heat up the rear drum during a long descent, bringing the rubbers to melting point! Every single time I have gone with someone on a quick recce of a downhill stage, the cush drive rubbers have melted. You have been warned.

But on the bright side, for the princely sum of about Rs5000 you can get a **Brembo disc brake** fitted to the front wheel. This necessitates the change of the front wheel rim to mag alloy and makes the bike look downright modern.

The Enfield Bullet 500 comes with **two types of exhausts** now. The longer one found on the 500s is quieter, but aficionados immediately trade it for the the noisier, smaller 350 unit. Apart from an increase in decibels, performance seems to remain the same.

The only thing to watch out for on a new bike is following the **running in period** scrupulously, avoiding sustained speeds above 90kph for the first 1000kms.

Lalli Singh and others will assist in the purchase of new bikes and promptly sell you the twin-seat modifications (tassels extra) that are popular with foreign visitors. Also available is the equally-useful luggage carrier which looks solid but will disintegrate after the first small fall!

The breakdown rate of a new Enfield as described on p.147 is not so appalling – by and large it is the badly-reconditioned examples that give trouble. **Papers** required to run a Bullet in India are:

a) Registration certificate (in anyone's name is fine. You need to carry a sale letter from the seller stating you to be the buyer. Easier than getting an endorsement on the registration book).

b) Insurance certificate (third party at least).

c) Driver's licence (any will do). It is not the rule but in practice almost every foreign rider can get by in India with their own country's driving licence as the average policeman doesn't even know what an International Driving Permit looks like. However, if entering overland across the border it would be sensible to be armed with an IDP.

Kullu and **Manali** have good Bullet mechanics. Rentals of bikes are possible in Manali at Nirvana Cafe through its owner, Manas Sircar, who also offers Japanese 125s. Prices range from Rs350 per day upwards.

Helmets are required in India, though the sight of Israeli hippies racing across the landscape with windblown hair is common. Besides the fact that it can save your life, wearing a helmet avoids tickets and the hassle of a court appearance later (in most places fines are not on the spot). Driver's licences are often confiscated to make sure you show up in court.

If Enfields aren't for you then **the Suzuki range** is the most reliable for India these days. Their newly-launched four-stroke Fiero 150cc is both economical and reliable and can put out quite a turn of speed when required. Suzuki's Shogun and Shaolin bikes are more prevalent but two-stroke.

The **Honda 125 CBZ** is also a popular bike for touring. It sports an ultra-fat rear tyre, great economy, disc brake up front and also superb styling and four-stroke sound.

For retro fans the 175 cc **Kawasaki Eliminator** is the way to go after the Bullet. Very popular but limited sales because of its price: Rs85,000. Also too low for the average foreign tourist's height. Could be unsuitable for areas requiring higher ground clearance but it's trouble-free, though.

Vijay Parmar – *Himalayan Motorsports Association*

p.36 Kawasaki KLR650, box
Having recently ridden a KLR650 in Canada, I'd agree with many of Rupert's observations and add that on the road the KLR is surprisingly **light and economical** (up to 70 mpg/25 kpl), while in deep water it's a real submarine once you've done the breather mod (see p.95 – it not only suits Yamahas). But in rough conditions, besides fitting a decent bashplate and one less tooth on the gearbox sprocket, a **fork brace** will greatly improve steering.

p.52 Hand pumps
On reflection, mini compressors aren't worth the bother, a good quality mountain bike hand pump works fine (10 pumps equals around 1psi), but go for a plastic bodied item – metal ones can get dented and so lose their seal.

p.61 Dry bags

For wet-weather riding with soft luggage (or non-waterproof hard cases) I'm now a fan of Cascade Designs SealLine dry bags. In particular, the 'Baja' version, which is a heavy PVC kit bag in various capacities. Just let the air out, roll the open end up, click the buckle and head for white water. They're best protected inside an old holdall or panniers. With the possibility of total sub-

SealLine dry bags. Down periscope...

mergence I found the end-loading SealLines had better sealing than an Ortlieb Rack Pack L with a longitudinal opening, even if the latter is easier to pack. Dry bags also make handy pillows or even buoyancy aids!

PART 2: CONTINENTAL ROUTE OUTLINES

p.118 Libya

Since the start of 2001 entry into Libya has proved difficult without securing the compulsory services of a guide. This can add $100/day to your budget and is, of course, impractical for independent travellers.

p.121 Algeria

Algeria offers none of Libya's drawbacks; updated and new GPS routes are at www.sahara-overland.com/updates/algroutes.htm.

p.128 Overland to India

As this is written, bombing of Afghanistan continues and Pakistan is looking unstable, so as things stand, you'll be lucky to get into Iran or out of India into Pakistan.

p.205 The Nahanni Range Road

With demand for tungsten resumed, in the Fall of 2001 the mine was set to reopen. The good news is that the Nahanni Range Road is now likely to remain maintained all the way to Tungsten township. The bad news is that, owing to the heavy traffic, they may try to close the road but if you do get in you're in for a treat.

Even if you're not permitted to ride through the township itself (and so to the airstrip and hot springs alongside), the track south of town eventually ends at a dilapidated riverside cabin, only another 7km beyond (N61° 54.45' W128° 12.34'). But before you get to town, a track breaks off northwards (left) from the Tungsten road and, beaver dams, wash-outs and rivers permitting, it will still be a challenging ride to the broken bridge at Fork Creek, 54km from Tungsten (N62° 16.13' W128° 49.8') where your commitment to go further will be tested (see *Call of the Wild* video, p.280).

INDEX